PARTY SYSTEMS
AND ELECTIONS
IN LATIN AMERICA

PARTY SYSTEMS AND ELECTIONS IN LATIN AMERICA

RONALD H. McDONALD

Syracuse University

MARKHAM PUBLISHING COMPANY / Chicago

MARKHAM POLITICAL SCIENCE SERIES
Aaron Wildavsky, Editor

JL
969
·A45
M3

To

Russell H. Fitzgibbon

Foreword

Since political parties are found almost everywhere in Latin America, they would seem to be a common denominator in the region's political life. Yet this is not the case. Cultural, environmental, and historical influences on party development are so varied they challenge conventional notions. Most nations hold periodic elections, but, like parties, the implications of elections differ profoundly from those we assume from our own culture. The variable meanings of party and election in Latin America and the causal factors that prompt these variations may be of marginal interest to the sophisticated observer of Latin American politics, but seem essential for the general student of comparative politics. We ask here a simple question: how do political parties and elections differ in Latin America from those of the United States, and what differences between Latin American nations are important?

Party system has been selected as the focus for the study, because more structural, functional, and developmental similarities can be found for party systems than for separate parties. We emphasize the evolution of party systems, their relation to national decision-making processes, and external factors that promote and control the evolution. We view political party systems as critical variables for three high-priority tasks in Latin American nations: (1) the integration of political communities and their diverse interests through agreement or consensus; (2) building institutions (institutionalization) out of organizations to persist beyond the career of a strong leader; and (3) the strengthening of governmental "capacity" to create and implement public policy.

Participation and negotiation of regional, racial, class, economic, and other interests common in Latin American environments is the main theme of integration. Party systems are important, if not ex-

clusive, arenas for integration through electoral or legislative participation and negotiation. Institutionalization is viewed in regard
to party structures: their capacity to persist apart from or beyond
the political fortunes of a leader who creates and dominates
them temporarily. A central issue of institutionalization is the communication and socialization of party symbols, particularly through
electoral campaigns, into the traditions of a national community, and
the entrance of a party into the national party system through legislative representation or electoral participation. Capacity is viewed
only in regard to the political relevance of party systems, although
the concept obviously has equal, if not greater, importance for other
national institutions. Central to party system capacity are the
balances assigned parties through elections, and the ability of one
or several parties to "dominate" others by (1) building a political base broad enough to encompass a significant portion of the
relevant national community; (2) imposing control over other parties
by force and government subsidization; or (3) nullifying opposition
by confining or destroying embryonic party organizations.

Historically, Latin American party systems have tended to expand their functions, their relevance to national policy-making, and
their constitutencies. This continuing expansion, which can be
viewed as part of the political development of a national community,
is erratic and uncertain, as illustrated by the success and frustrations of the Latin American nations discussed in this book. There is
no certainty that the expansion of a party system is inevitable, although once started the process seems somewhat self-amplifying.
Expansion is a common, regional experience, frustrated only with
great difficulty. These themes are broad, and the conclusions intentionally propositional.

The study draws, as feasible, upon existing research on Latin
American party politics. The research base is limited, and has necessitated some compromises. Despite pleas by Fitzgibbon (1957) and
others to direct more research toward party politics in Latin America,
relatively little research has been published. Judgments have also
been made on what to exclude from this survey, although these
standards are by no means rigid. In general, only those variables
that affect or reveal party politics are included. Governmental,
administrative, ideological, historical, cultural, and economic factors
are introduced with restraint.

Each party system is treated as an entity, generating comparisons within and between groups of nations. There is still value in
stressing the interconnections within as well as between cultures.

This book is a series of connected area studies, grouped by general traits, and integrated by the common focus of party systems.

Not all nations are treated equally in the study, and several are excluded. Emphasis given a nation depends on several factors. Most important is the significance of the party system to the overall political environment of a nation, and the utility of viewing national political forces through party activity. Several nations are excluded from the analysis, either because their party systems are undeveloped (Haiti and Guatemala), highly unstable over the past few decades (Bolivia, Peru, and the Dominican Republic), or repressed for an extended period (Cuba and Paraguay). The party systems that vacillate often from one mode of competition to another are potentially important for isolating causal factors in party system instability, but the problems raised by their analysis creates complexities beyond the purpose of this book. The few countries where my own research has been relevant I have understandably stressed somewhat more.

John Martz correctly observed recently that thirteen years intervened between the first, full-length study of a Latin American political party (1953) and the next, his own Venezuelan study of 1966. Even journal publications on party politics have been limited, although more have been appearing recently. This scarcity of research material, not to mention its variability in style, mode of analysis, and purpose, has required pragmatic decisions about what could be most usefully discussed for each nation. Lack of comparability has occasionally produced conclusions whose data base is not totally representative.

Sufficient voting studies on Latin America, even for the principal nations, do not exist to permit any general survey of the topic. In many instances data is not collected or even available. What is presented here in the way of voting analysis is tentative and only suggestive, dealing with data aggregated at the province, state, or department levels.

What emerges optimistically is a general statement on Latin American party politics, for which many gaps need to be filled. General statements need to be treated more as hypotheses than conclusions, and exposed to the stronger light of more dependable evidence. For the student of comparative politics, I hope this study will provide an exposure to how party institutions and processes evolve and operate in Latin America. The region is an exciting one for comparative analysis: it blends the developed with the developing nation context; it disperses political systems evenly along many analytic axes, providing an excellent opportunity for comparison; it offers an opportunity to make meaningful trend analyses from sustained electoral experience. It is my belief that, at least for the present, trend analyses within Latin American nations are more analytically promising than cross-national analyses, for we are more able to isolate the key variables of change in the former. For the student of Latin America, the book distills in a comparative way one of the most essential aspects of Latin American politics.

The research for most of the study was conducted over a three-year period, 1965–1968, two years of which were supported by a Foreign Area Fellowship Program postdoctoral grant. This opportunity permitted me to travel extensively throughout Latin America, observing elections and campaigns in a majority of countries, and gathering a substantial amount of data. It is my practice when interviewing to grant complete anonymity to my interviewees, for I feel what is sacrificed in footnotes is reciprocated by frankness and confidence from my respondents. Interviews were used in this study as a check upon other evidence and conclusions. rather than as a source of evidence.

Syracuse, New York   Ronald H. McDonald

Contents

CHAPTER 1

Concepts of Political Party System and Voting in Latin America

I. INTRODUCTION

Governmental and political institutions are a consequence of national organization—mechanisms through which collective behavior is expressed. Political parties are one of the most universal and elemental national institutions.[1] In the United States political parties have long been appreciated as a useful historical and behavioral focus for viewing national politics. The evolution of political parties in our own country can be traced to the emergence of fundamental national political conflicts, and party history can be viewed as a process of conflict resolution and institutional development. Political parties provide a primary channel for leadership recruitment, outlets for personal political ambitions, and mechanisms for exerting political influence. Their persistence, structure, and style are culturally and functionally rooted in North American society, and their evolution and interaction is an informative reflection of North American politics. Political parties began to emerge in Latin America about the same time as in the United States, and for similar reasons.[2] Although there have been significant cultural differences in the evolution of parties, regular party activity is a historical fact of national political development throughout the western hemisphere.[3]

Contrasts exist in the development patterns and contemporary status of political parties in Latin American states, and a generalization about their importance as political institutions relative to other political institutions in national contexts may be appropriate at the outset. Recognizing functional differences in party systems, a generalization can be made about cultural relevance of parties to overall political processes of states. Since our interest is essentially con-

1

temporary rather than historical, and since parties historically have varied in their significance relative to other political factors, the following categories make only a general comment on contemporary political cultures:

Parties normally relevant	Parties occasionally relevant	Parties infrequently relevant
Uruguay	Peru	Haiti
Argentina	Ecuador	Nicaragua
Chile	Guatemala	Panama
Colombia	Salvador	Paraguay
Costa Rica	Honduras	
Venezuela	Cuba	
Brazil	Dominican Republic	
Mexico		

Inclusion in these categories is arbitrary and impressionistic, but generally corresponds with perceptions of Latin American "experts" reported elsewhere.[4] The categorization does not imply functional or other similarities among party systems in any group. Viewed in respect to other politically relevant institutions (the presidency, the military, the church, the bureaucracy, the aristocracy, socioeconomic classes, etc.), this general approximation of political relevancy seems justified.

Parties included in the infrequently relevant category cannot be entirely dismissed. Political parties do exist in each of the four nations, and occasionally in limited ways must be taken into consideration or used by political and government leaders. All party systems go through periods of ascending or descending relevancy. Since 1959, Cuba has had no party system as such, and Argentina since 1966 and Brazil since 1964 have been ruled by military regimes unsympathetic to party politics. Periodic vacillations in party relevancy are not important to these categories.

Political parties in Uruguay, Argentina, Chile, Colombia, and Costa Rica have not only contemporary relevance but, as in the United States, strong nineteenth-century roots. Similarly, some parties in Ecuador, Honduras, and even Nicaragua and Paraguay have nineteenth-century origins. In most of the remaining nations political parties can be viewed as largely a twentieth-century development. New parties exist in all countries, but party traditions are strong and politically relevant in an impressive number.

It is perhaps wise to reject from the beginning any connection between politically relevant party systems and democracy or political competition. By our definition, party relevance does not either assume or produce democracy or political competition. There is an abiding ideological faith in the United States and elsewhere that political parties are intimately identified with political freedom and democracy. Although parties were not anticipated by our Constitution nor generally conceived as necessary by the founding fathers, many of the freedoms contained in the Bill of Rights are exemplified by political parties: freedom of association, speech, petition, assembly, and press. In the different cultural contexts of Latin America, however, no relationship between party activity and democratic government can be validly presumed. Parties are often used for personal and dictatorial ends. Likewise, parties sometimes forcibly try to eliminate other parties. To state it another way, the "rules of the game" and boundaries of party activity are broader and less restricted in parts of Latin America than in the United States.

Parties are identified by either legal or behavioral analysis. They can be perceived legally since all nations regulate their behavior, and thereby give parties a legal reality; but purely legal perceptions are often arbitrary and irrelevant to political realities. A more useful orientation to political parties can be made, and from this orientation our survey of Latin American parties and elections proceeds. Political parties have a behavioral reality.[5] A party is perceived as a product of collective or aggregate behavior by people who in limited and varied ways periodically join their number to achieve power or influence policy-makers and other persons living in the same national community. Parties so conceived become an expression of political behavior, if not a source of it. Besides their legal status, empirical expression is given to political parties by the similarities in behavior patterns of persons identifying with their symbols and participating in their structures and processes.

Most parties in a national political system perform important functions, but not all parties perform the same functions. Party functions are transferable to other political structures or institutions, but primary governmental functions may accrue to parties even when other institutions simultaneously perform them. Common party functions include: recruitment of political elites, militants, and the rank and file, especially toward positions of power and influence; participation and influence of party elites in the formation of public policy by articulation of desired goals and strategies or by challenging proposed and existing ones. Parties are also a source of political communication and socialization, a function as common and central as any to Latin American politics. The range of additional and alternative functions is wide.

Political parties participate in elections unless they choose to withdraw strategically or are restrained legally. The *meaning* of elections varies, and electoral activity may be less central for parties in some political systems than others. In Latin America the myth of popular elections is strong, and this myth helps foster a favorable context for the growth and influence of political parties. Only in Cuba and Haiti has any significant period of time elapsed (in Cuba only since 1959) without at least the ritual of national elections. Even military leaders and governments feel pressure for elections and take into consideration party activity, latent party support, or the threat of party activity. Dictatorial governments must contend with the cultural expectation of popular elections, however often it is frustrated. In such instances, political parties may not make or affect public policy or recruit leaders by representative means, but they can possess influence relative to the strength of the myth of national elections.

In summary, the Latin American political party has both a legal and a behavioral reality, exists within political cultures that partly determine its relevance and processes, and performs functions necessary to governing and long-range systemic change.

II. INSTRUMENTAL FUNCTIONS OF LATIN AMERICAN PARTIES

Latin American parties perform functions instrumental to governing, many of which are commonly observed in party systems elsewhere.[6] A distinction must be made between these *instrumental* government functions of parties, and the *systemic* functions discussed below that help reorient and reconstitute the political system. If the instrumental functions are obvious and perhaps universal, their performance style is often characteristically Latin American.

1. POLITICAL RECRUITMENT

Groups that affiliate with parties are a key to understanding Latin American political parties. The existence of these groups—

normally more broadly based in the culture—is the base of political parties. Groups defined in almost any nominal way coalesce individuals with shared goals, perspectives, and expectations.[7] In Latin America, group differentiation is great, unlike the United States where pluralistic divisions tend to superimpose one upon another. Differentiation often reinforces the autonomy of groups, a fact of considerable political significance in Latin America. The common groups are not hard to find. They are based upon some of the following foundations: class, family, race, geography, color, culture, economics, and power. It is true in Latin America as in the United States that there is a "group basis to politics." The difference is in the composition of that base: the nature of the groups, and the independence of their existence.[8]

Political parties recruit individuals into national politics. The most crucial party role is that of leadership, and problems of leadership recruitment are endemic in Latin America. Leaders are recruited as rewards are provided, but political parties in Latin America are often unable to offer adequate rewards because of the relatively greater incentives for leaders to rise through alternative institutions of the military, the clergy, and the social and economic elites. Rewards offered by parties have not always been consistent with strengthening or institutionalizing party organizations. Government patronage, graft, corruption, and economic payoff have retarded the development of independent party organizations. When party leadership elites are consciously and consistently denied any realistic prospect of competing or participating in national governmental elites, the traditional power incentives for leadership recruitment are destroyed. Lesser rewards attract less qualified or less motivated leaders, who in turn fail to strengthen party institutions or provide further rewards to more qualified or more highly motivated leaders who can challenge their positions. For these reasons Latin American parties sometimes find themselves in a spiral of weakness vis-à-vis other institutions, or alternatively become personalistic vehicles for a single leader's political ambitions.

The success of rank-and-file recruitment is a reflection of leadership.[9] The breadth and solidarity of the party's base, the large bottom strata of its hierarchical pyramid, rests squarely on leadership skills. There must be a coalescing of personal and party rewards for recruitment, and the closer the correlation the more highly motivated and activated are the rank and file. Politicization of the rank and file in Latin America as elsewhere varies at intervals. It is highest during elections when common myths are invoked to stimulate personal commitment and involvement by the rank and file, and subsides during political inaction or in the absence of party competition. Rank-and-file recruitment depends on communication and financial resources. The modern instruments of communication and the traditional craft of patronage are expensive for contemporary political parties. Financial resources accrue to parties whose leaders correlate their personal interests with those able to provide financial support, whether these be domestic plutocrats, the rank and file, external religious or lay organizations, or external governments. Nearly all Latin American nations have parties financed by these means. Considering the frustrations imposed on party activity and recruitment in Latin America, particularly the barriers to leisure imposed on the majority of party adherents, the vitality of political parties and the level of politicization of the rank and file is in many ways a remarkable phenomena in Latin American politics.

2. DECISION-MAKING

A second function performed by Latin American political parties is participation in the formation of public policy. The traditional representational model is inappropriate for Latin America, since elections rarely decide public policy. Political party elites exert influence and occasionally veto governmental decision-makers, but the process is informal and implicit. Legislatures ratify government policy, or afford party elites an arena to express their opposition and create a confrontation between government and opposition elites.

3. SPECIALIZED FUNCTIONS OF PARTIES

Beyond the traditional instrumental functions performed by parties, a number of specialized ones are periodically performed.[10] When there is no conflict between party and presidential elites and a party controls the legislature, parties may perform rule-making functions within their own organizations. The PRI in Mexico performs some rule-making functions within its own structures and processes. Another specialized function is that of administration. Strong, ruling political parties find themselves in a more effective position to administer than do bureaucracies, for party organization is often more efficient, more cohesive, and more rationally conceived than bureaucracies. Administration has a salutary feedback upon the welfare and viability of the party. It is not coincidental that in several nations the primary source of fertilizer in rural areas is the dominant party headquarters. Another function periodically performed is that of *rule-adjudicator* or *conflict-resolver*. This quasi-judicial function implies as much a political as a judicial or legal task.

Another specialized function commonly performed by Latin American political parties is public relations and propaganda. Many of the same realities that make party structures suitable vehicles for administration make them appropriate for disseminating propaganda. Government parties find it helpful to correlate party symbols with national ones, and party elites with national elites. If the assumption that parties are an elemental unit of national institutionalization has validity, then adherence to party symbols may be more fundamental and primary than adherence to national ones.

Parties also serve revolutionary functions. This is most obvious with some Communist parties in Latin America, though not all Communist parties are equally committed or engaged in revolutionary activity, and some are not revolutionary at all. Conversely, revolutionary causes are not the exclusive property of Marxist groups. Very few contemporary parties in Latin America have not historically been involved with a revolutionary cause. If the cause is victorious, parties become respectable and lose their revolutionary facade. Within the broad term *revolutionary* (those parties that seek to overthrow a government by force or violence), many non-Communist parties, such as the MNR in Bolivia, have been important politically in Latin America.

Finally, political parties function as *status elites* in some countries. As such they are organized, regularized channels of communication among the "politically relevant" leaders of the country. Often the party serves this purpose in conjunction with other institutions, and rarely creates status elites itself except in the top leadership echelons.

III. STRUCTURAL CHARACTERISTICS OF LATIN AMERICAN PARTIES

There are fundamental structural characteristics of Latin American political parties that require specification. Such a level of generalization is valuable only to differentiate Latin American political parties from those of other political cultures and provide a departure for more sophisticated thought. Some basic structural similarities in Latin American parties include their elitism, regionalism, transitionalism, personalism, factionalism, and organization.[11]

1. ELITISM

Latin American parties tend to be elitist in the control of internal decision-making processes and recruitment. There are many variations in the nature of elitism and its pervasiveness. The extinct *Partido Dominicano*, which was the official party of Rafael Trujillo's regime, was elitist in that it was nothing more than an extension of that dictator's personal control over the Dominican Republic. Nearly all power and decision-making was concentrated in the person of Trujillo. The Nicaraguan *Partido Liberal Nacionalista*, following the 1956 assassination of Anastasio Somoza, was transformed from a personal to a family vehicle as power descended from Somoza to his two sons. A small, landed aristocracy, sometimes in conjunction with the military, controls the dominant political parties in El Salvador and Panama. Both Colombia and Ecuador are known to have similar elitist party structures. In Mexico a proportionately small, natural elite of powerful Mexican leaders controls the PRI. The military controls the dominant political parties in Bolivia, Brazil, and Paraguay. In the remaining countries more broadly based parties exist. It should be remembered that even the elitist parties can achieve a degree of popular support, although the fiction of popular control and participation never becomes a reality. Likewise, highly elitist parties can compete internally or with other elite parties. Even where broadly based political parties do exist, such as the *Apristas* in Peru, the Christian Democrats in Chile, the Radical and *Peronista* parties in Argentina, the Colorados and Blancos in Uruguay, the elite structures of the parties tend to be largely self-perpetuating, despite the fact that the rank and file exert influence on the elites.

Elitism is not restricted to Latin American political parties, but is a highly characteristic and consistent feature of them. Much literature in the field of comparative parties suggests the traditionally elitist nature of party institutions. However, in Latin America where political centralization at either the national or regional level has been a dominant cultural trait, the degree of elite centralization in parties is correspondingly high.[12]

2. REGIONALISM

As with elitism, Latin American parties are influenced by regional factors. It is often suggested that regional parties are characteristic of "developing nations" where regional cultural and economic ties are stronger than national ones. Yet regionalism is characteristic of parties in modern states; traditionally, U.S. parties have had regional bases, although these bases are perhaps less rigid today than in the past.[13] Not all Latin American nations are equally regionalized, and few if any are dominantly regional in their party politics. Even Chile, whose peculiar geography promotes regional economic and cultural differences, has thoroughly national parties. Most of the "smaller" Latin American nations possess few regional traits, even when national awareness is not high. As was suggested above, regionalism often coexists with national centralization in Latin America. Political divisions provide subcenters of national power that activate only on specific issues. The two major Colombian parties offer a good illustration of centralization coexisting with regional political patterns. Both parties compete nationally in most departments, yet certain areas are traditionally Conservative or Liberal. The emergence of former Colombian dictator Rojas Pinilla's ANAPO movement demonstrates strong regional characteristics in its support and organization. Regionalism may be less characteristic of Latin American political parties than new parties in the emerging African states. A century of independence and the absence of geographically focused religious, racial, and tribal conflicts may be the differentiating factor.

3. TRANSITIONALISM

Probably it is confusing to describe Latin American politics as transitional although the term is often applied to so-called developing nations.[14] Common sense suggests that the politics of any nation is always in transition; change in political parties is a persistent trait of the institutions. Still the profound economic, cultural, and subsequently political change occurring in parts of Latin America is constantly provoking fundamental realignments in political parties. New kinds of political parties, particularly those appealing to urban proletariates, are visible throughout Latin America. Aristocratic parties, long characteristic of such family dominated countries as El Salvador, Honduras, Panama, and Peru, are gradually yielding to pressures for change.

Toward what are Latin American parties moving? Certain developmental constructs can be offered based on recent experience.[15] Latin American parties are slowly developing a broader base of affiliation, if not recruitment or participation in the decision-making processes. The emergence of "mass parties" threatens most traditional elite party systems. The basic transition is toward a collection of political parties in which one or some are more sensitive to the changing nature of political demands within the system, and the growing relevancy of previously irrelevant groups within the system. These persons, whether the remote Indian, the urban worker, or the rural *campesino,* are acquiring new political expectations on which parties are moving to breed. Marxist and other types of more broadly based parties (Christian Democrats, the *Aprista*-type parties) are increasingly successful in challenging existing parties. Consequently, not only are new parties emerging, but old ones are reconstituting themselves to meet the challenge.

Too much can be superficially read into the political transition of Latin America. Essentially the transition is not revolutionary, although it contains elements of revolutionary thought and carries the portent of fundamental change. But many political systems are subject to revolutionary or fundamental change; the transition of U.S. political parties in the past three decades has been profound, and, in some ways perhaps for the culture, more profound than contemporary transitions in Latin America. Latin American politics, correctly or not, seems to be in a period of very rapid, perhaps fundamental transition that in turn is reflected in collective political party behavior.

4. PERSONALISM

Personalism (*personalismo*) is both characteristic of Latin American political parties and distinctive from its expression in North American parties.[16] The tedious process of leadership recruitment in the United States encourages successful leaders to shape the political party they lead by the force of their personality. But when the party is subjected to new leadership, it persists and reshapes itself around the personalities of the new leaders. In Latin America parties often become extensions of political personalities, and fail to reshape themselves when the leader dies, retires, or is discredited. Although few Latin American party systems produce an overwhelming political figure like de Gaulle, whose party fits the Latin American stereotype, most possess one or more highly charismatic, personalistic parties. Perón and the *Peronistas* in Argentina are an obvious case in point. Other cases are perhaps less obvious. The *Partido Revolucionario* in Guatemala was formed about the personality of Mario Méndez Montenegro, who was succeeded following his abrupt assassination by his brother, President César Méndez Montenegro. César was politically inexperienced, but drew upon the personalism of his brother and the family name, and in less than one year rose to the presidency. Nearly all parties in Panama, except certain Marxist organizations, are highly personalistic, with the followings of Ricardo Arias Espinosa, Marco A. Robles, and Arnulfo Arias as recent examples. The *Partido Revolucionario Dominicano* under Juan Bosch, Uruguay's *Partido Colorado* under the mantle of José Batlle, Ecuador's charismatic José María Velasco Ibarra and his followers, Peru's General Manuel Odría and the *Partido Nacional Odrista* are additional examples. Even in those parties that show prospects of surviving their personalistic tutelage, *personalismo* often persists. José Figueres' influence on Costa Rica's *Partido de Liberación Nacional* is strong, as is Rómulo Betancourt's on Venezuela's *Acción Democrática,* and until 1968, Belaúnde-Terry's on his personally created *Partido de Acción Popular* in Peru. All are examples of *personalismo* persisting over successful but relatively weaker party institutions.

The explanation for the characteristic of *personalismo* is complex. Only a few tentative propositions can be offered now. Latin governmental institutions have been historically weak and subject to manipulation by *caudillos* whose skill and popular following perpetuated their power. Alternatives to *caudillos* have necessarily been other *caudillos,* whose personalities could challenge the status quo more effectively than the abstract image of a political party. Latin economics has in many areas been tied to the large *fundos,* whose *patrón* was himself the supreme arbiter of disputes and, in the absence of social, political, and economic intercourse with the remainder of the nation, an effective *caudillo.* These learned social concepts are easily displaced onto the national political scene. The centralization of the Church, its hierarchy, and its emphasis on church personalities also reinforces the other cultural factors. Mass identification with an individual has been more easily achieved by leaders than identification with party symbols, and it is not surprising that nearly all political parties, with the possible exception of some Marxist ones, have concentrated upon personalities and individual leaders often to the exclusion of institutional identities.

5. FACTIONALISM

Latin American political parties factionalize about individual personal followings. Only when a strong leader or a very strong cause has sufficient cohesive power to eliminate potential party rivals does factionalism subside. In Uruguay, factionalism is the dominant trait of the country's two-party system, and is legally institutionalized by the electoral laws. Major factions, centering about dominant political leaders, disperse followers of the two major parties among dozens of factions. Even so personalistic a party as the Argentine *Peronistas* is divided into factions based on individual leaders and issues.

The effects of intense factionalism are numerous. One effect is the frequent appearance of "new parties" that are really offshoots of existing ones. Socialist parties are particularly likely to splinter. Splinter parties that attract a small minority must make alliances to achieve any degree of political influence. Normally such alliances are "marriages of convenience" and not enduring, but occasionally they can effectively block majority party action. When splinters combine to support a presidential leader or candidate, dissension inevitably follows a successful election as factions turn on one another to extract patronage, appointments, and concessions. If alliances in power are normally unsuccessful, alliances out of power normally are successful. Hardly a Latin American nation has avoided an opposition alliance or the division of major parties into personalistically dominated factions.

Factions may also arise—as they sometimes do in the United States and Europe—on substantive axes of economic issues or interests. Urban commercial interests vie with rural agrarian interests in the traditional, oligarchic parties of Latin America. Military interests compete with traditional alignments. Rural peasant interests compete with urban proletarian ones, and occasionally with middle-class urban interests in center or center-reform type parties. Ideological splits regularly occur in leftist and revolutionary parties. In both Guatemala and Colombia three-way splits have occurred in the Communist parties with each nation having two small guerrilla groups, one aligned toward Castro and the other toward the Chinese, while a third faction of more sedate party hierarchy remains in the capital advocating Russian evolutionary concepts of communism. While the advantage of unity or coalition is obvious in a reality of factionalization, unity for Latin American parties has been historically difficult to achieve.

6. ORGANIZATION

Political parties in Latin America come alive during electoral campaigns, often the only time that parties operate at full capacity. Legislatures by and large afford little opportunity for parties to compete or engage in national dialogues. There are periods of legislative party activity in Costa Rica, Uruguay, and Chile, and occasionally in Venezuela, Brazil, Argentina, Peru, and Colombia. Parties rarely have clearly organized campaign structures, and where they do they tend to be strongest in the capital and major cities. A few parties—the Christian Democrats in Chile, the Colorados and Blancos in Uruguay, and the PRI in Mexico—are highly organized throughout their entire nation. Most Argentine parties have also been reasonably well organized.

The means of organization do not differ markedly from the United States, with one exception: historically, organization of government parties has been an adjunct of administration. Where there were local or regional *caudillos*, one also finds local or regional party organizations. This is particularly true in Uruguay, Argentina, Mexico, and Colombia. In Uruguay clubs throughout the cities organize party workers who adhere through a vast system of political patronage, not unlike the Tammany politics of earlier days in New York City. The PRI in Mexico affiliates or co-opts many external organizations to its three major sectors, and thereby employs for political purposes organizational structures of affiliated groups. The Christian Democrats in Chile attempted to create new organizations that find a governmental counterpart in the nation's local administration. These civic action groups, while presumably nonpolitical, carry tremendous political leverage for the Christian Democratic party.

Although some Latin American parties have permanent organizations, more common are ad hoc organizations improvised on a temporary basis during electoral campaigns.[17] Ad hoc organizations are clumsy and inefficient, relying on those who are ideologically inspired by the party and donate their services, and those who are in debt to the party for patronage or are available for hire. The most successful permanent party organizations rely on government jobs and contracts to build support. Few parties in power fail to make the connection between broad governmental patronage and party welfare. In competitive systems party organizations built by patronage can persist as vested interests out of power, since structures for regularized communication and recruitment stimulate party adherence from militants and the rank and file.

Revolutionary parties in Latin America organize in a characteristic way.[18] Organizational nuclei are often formed around university students, since they are particularly highly politicized, more politically aware, more "liberal" in their youth, and more seriously challenged by the lack of socioeconomic mobility that characterizes many cultures. Most national political parties participate in student elections, which are often very meaningful in campus politics, and organize student political clubs, sometimes with paid professional "students" whose sole task is party recruitment and organization. Revolutionary, and particularly Marxist parties, have been most successful on university campuses in Venezuela, Peru, Chile, Uruguay and Brazil. Revolutionary parties, unless well subsidized from outside the country, have difficulty raising funds for campaign expenses. Students furnish an inexhaustible supply of volunteer workers who are motivated by ideological rather than monetary rewards, and are useful instruments for propaganda, demonstrations, and leadership. Universities that are most restricted to the upper classes tend to be least political in campus activities, while so-called autonomous, more heterogeneous national universities tend to be most political.

Revolutionary and extremist parties are inclined to be more effectively organized in the capital areas, where they can concentrate upon proletarian dissatisfaction. They also affiliate with other proletarian organizations, particularly labor unions. It is worth remembering that not just Marxist parties affiliate with unions as a means of strengthening their party following and facilitating their organizational efforts. The *Peronistas* in Argentina relied heavily upon their control of the *Confederación de Trabajadores Nacional,* a vast federation of unions, as the MNR in Bolivia once relied upon its influence with the tin miners organized by the radical Juan Lechín. Rojas Pinilla in Colombia, emulating Perón, tried but failed to use a labor organization as a basis for his political power. The PRI recruits unions to control their demands as well as tap their reservoir of political support for furthering party goals. Christian Democratic parties have as far as possible tried to recruit lay religious organizations for political activity. In a few instances this has even included recruiting church leaders for political causes. The Church has been recruited by other political parties in power because of its influence over the masses. Nearly all governments must come to terms with the Church, and dissatisfaction of a church hierarchy often can mean trouble for the regime. A few regimes—such as the PRI in Mexico—have by contrast used anti-clericalism to rally mass support.

There are two critical qualities to party structure: scarcity and dominance. Historic institutional weakness creates a structural scarcity in Latin America relative to the functions parties perform. This in turn allows the occasional stronger party structure and other environmental or governmental groups to dominate weaker parties by absorbing their functions. Scarcity encourages many of the characteristics of Latin American party structure: elitism, personalism, regionalism, factionalization, and transient organizations. Scarcity results, as discussed below, from inadequate integration and institutionalization.

Dominance, the ability of one party structure to control another, is revealed by the mode of party competition in the system and legislative representation. Dominant parties in Latin America are usually those that have a monopoly on structure, and thereby acquire the capacity to control party functions. Changing balances and party competition indicate shifting dominance, and implicitly, growth or decay in alternative party structures. How dominance is created, classified, and changed is discussed below.

IV. TYPES OF PARTY SYSTEMS IN LATIN AMERICA

There are many ways to classify political parties in Latin America. Numerous typologies have been suggested already; the problem is that most existing ones are largely impressionistic. Some of the categories used include: personalistic parties, ideological parties, traditional parties, revolutionary parties.[19] In reality these types in Latin America often combine in one party; more genuinely distinguishing cultural, legal, and historical traits are unidentified by the categories. A communist party, or the *Peronistas* in Argentina, or the Bolivian MNR, may simultaneously be ideological, personalistic, traditional (in competition with other parties through normal electoral processes), and revolutionary.

Another type of classification involves the number of parties in the party system. The notion of a party system is valid and useful, for it defines the context or arena in which parties compete, and suggests the kind of competition that can be expected. Normally the gross distinctions are made between one-party, two-party, and multi-party systems. For many reasons this trichotomy has little utility for Latin America. The pervasive problem in using this typology is empirical. How is a decision made about the number of parties a political system has? Mexico, for all practical purposes, would appear to be a one-party system since no party other than the PRI has ever won the presidency since the 1911 Revolution, nor until recently enjoyed more than token representation in legislative bodies. Yet other parties do exist, and one (*Partido de Acción Nacional*) appears to compete seriously with the PRI in Mexico. Uruguay would appear to have a two-party system, yet one party has been in power only eight years in the twentieth century. There fore, one might be inclined to describe Uruguay as a one-party system, except that closer examination reveals a multi-party system. The same situation occurs in Colombia, the other obvious two-party system in Latin America. Since most Latin American party systems appear to be multi-party, the utility of such a category is reduced.

Another problem with conventional categories of party systems is that they often presume or suggest a moral relationship between the number of parties operating and the kind of political competition, public policy, or governmental biases which result. There is a culturally based assumption in the United States and England that multi-party systems are inferior to two-party systems, a bias that is injected into introductory courses and textbooks in comparative government. Without debating the issue at this point, it is clear that our own tradition of two-party competitive government culturally discredits alternative systems. If one were to be truly precise in describing party systems in Latin America, he would have to admit that none are exactly alike, and determining how many parties there are at any time may be practically impossible. Two environmental factors determine party systems in Latin America: one is the electoral system, essentially a legal influence; the other is the political culture.

A typology for party systems can be offered, based on the product of party competition and elections: legislative representation.[20] It is assumed that legislative representation is a meaningful reflection of real party influence in a national system, the only significant exceptions being those parties that are outlawed and denied representation, and those few instances when parties choose not to participate for strategic reasons. Legislative representation is not necessarily a reflection of party popularity, although normally voting is a factor in determining representation and therefore a partial reflection of popularity. Representation is also a reflection of the impact of an electoral system upon parties. The index of legislative representation becomes a guide to the effectiveness of the party in gaining power within a given legal context and political culture. No assumption need be made that legislative representation is by itself an indication of power, for Latin American legislatures are not normally powerful. Nevertheless, parties do compete for legislative representation, which is important to a party's relationships with other parties if not with other governmental institutions.

The categories listed below are used throughout the following analysis of elections and voting in Latin America:

Single-Party Dominant Systems. A party system in which one party wins not less than 60 percent of the seats of a legislative body, and all remaining parties win less than 40 percent of the seats. A one-party dominant system may contain (as in Mexico) other parties to the extent of allowing them representation. Control of the legislature, however, is never in doubt.

Two-Party Competitive Systems. A party system in which two parties each receive not less than 40 percent of the seats nor more than 60 percent of the total seats. It is assumed that in such a system the decisions are made by the two major parties, although others may possess up to a combined maximum of 20 percent of the seats. A party system in which any single party receives more than 60 percent of the seats in a legislative body is defined above as a one-party dominant, whether there remains one or more challenging parties.

Multi-Party Dominant. A system with three or more parties in which one party receives not less than 40 percent or more than 60 percent of the seats in a legislative body, and in which no additional party receives more than 40 percent of the seats.

Multi-Party Loose. A system in which no single party receives more than 40 percent of the seats, but in which there are three or more parties competing.

These categories are arbitrary, but do group comparable party systems and facilitate general comparisons sensitive to contextural differences. Party systems in the following chapters are categorized by their customary legislative representation or party balances since about 1950. Some shifting is understandably characteristic of multi-party systems with growing or declining dominance; the other categories are more stable.

Political parties have been defined as the product of individual political behavior within a group context, serving varied and variable functions within a national political system through structures which include elites, militants, and rank-and-file members. The principle functions of parties have been governmentally defined as leadership recruitment and participation or influence in the decision-making policy processes of government. Several general traits of Latin American party systems have been suggested, including elitism, regionalism, transitionalism, personalism, factionalism, and organizational characteristics. Party competition, voting, and internal party processes such as leadership recruitment, militant and rank-and-file recruitment, internal decision-making processes, and campaign activities constitute the basis for the following analyses which are organized according to the type of party system.

V. ELECTORAL SYSTEMS IN LATIN AMERICA

Little attention is paid to electoral and representational systems in Latin America, yet even in those political systems, where the concept of representation lacks substance, electoral systems that contribute to party behavior and expectations are politically if not governmentally important.[21] Electoral institutions determine the outlets available within the system for politically ambitious leaders, or the collective expression of political opposition and hostility. I do not wish to attribute a direct causality to electoral systems for political stability or competitive democracy. On the contrary, it can be argued that electoral systems often reinforce the control of small elites by subtle but effective means. What I do suggest is that certain types of electoral systems and modifying devices control party activity selectively by determining the political and legal context in which parties operate, and thereby effectively control party participation and competition.[22] Expectations of party leaders about access to power are relevant and inevitably conditioned by the electoral system. The critical requisite for nonviolent change in Latin American party systems is the expectation for access to political decision-making structures, and where access is clearly and consciously restrained the inclination to substitute violence for electoral processes is natural and probably inevitable.

Two major types of electoral systems are employed in Latin America: the majority system, and the proportional representation

(P.R.) system.[23] The majority system has several variations, all of which share in common the principle that a candidate or party receiving the largest number of votes receives the seat (or seats) in a district. The best known form of majority system is the *simple majority*, used in the United States congressional elections, wherein the candidate is elected who receives the largest number of votes in a single-member district. This system recently has been used in Latin America only in the Mexican Chamber of Deputies and Senate, the Brazilian and Dominican Republic Senate, and in the Haitian Congress. Another form of majority system known as the *simple recurring majority* is used in multi-member constituencies wherein the number of candidates to be elected are chosen in rank order according to the total votes each receives. This system has been used in the Bolivian Senate, the unicameral Guatemalan Congress, and until 1964 the unicameral Salvadorian Assembly.[24] In the latter, the *party* that received a majority of the vote in a multi-member district received all the seats in that district.[25]

The more common type of electoral system in Latin America is proportional representation. P.R. has many universal variations, most of which are found in Latin America in addition to several indigenous variations. All P.R. forms share in common the nominal aspiration to proportion seats in legislatures in some manner consistent with the proportion of total vote received by each party. It is usually argued that P.R. encourages minority parties and stimulates multi-party systems, whereas the majority type electoral systems restrain minority parties and encourage limited (one- or two-) party systems.[26] This generalization requires careful qualification for Latin America.

There are two basic types of P.R. systems: the single transferable vote and the party list systems. The former, not used in Latin America, allows the voter to express his preference for individual candidates (who need not have party affiliation) by assigning them consecutive numbers according to his preference. Seats are then usually distributed after tallying the preferences by a device known as the *droop quota*. The second basic type of P.R., the party list system, has several variations that are used in Latin America.

The first variations involve the type of ballot used. One is the *open list*, under which the voter expresses a preference for a candidate whose name appears among several on a list submitted by the party. Another ballot variation is the *closed list* in which the voter has no choice of candidates, but votes for the entire party list. In both instances seats are proportioned according to the total number of votes the party receives. With the open list, those candidates that receive the greatest number of votes are seated consecutively until the total number of seats assigned to the party based on its total vote are filled. With the closed list, seats are assigned to candidates according to the hierarchy established by the party in its list. The open list is less common in Latin America, having been used recently only for the Brazilian Chamber of Deputies and both houses of the Chilean Congress. In all other remaining legislative elections in Latin America using proportional representation, some variation of the closed list is used. Normally the open list affords the voter a greater range of selection, providing a primary selection with a general election. The closed list allegedly strengthens party organizations and increases party discipline and responsibility by assigning the prerogative for selecting candidates to the party organization.

Seats won by either open- or closed-list ballots can be allocated in several ways depending on the formula used. Although theoretically many formulas are possible, two general types predominate. These formulas are known as the d'Hondt and the Hare. Under the d'Hondt, a party's total vote in each constituency is divided by consecutive divisors (1, 2, 3, 4, etc.) and each party's resulting quotients are arranged in numerically descending order, with seats awarded successively to the party with the highest quotient until all seats are distributed. Under the Hare formula, the total votes cast in a constituency are divided by the *total* number of seats to be distributed, with the resulting quotient being known as a quota. Seats are then awarded to each party for every multiple of the quota in its total vote. Any seats yet undistributed when this process has concluded are normally awarded according to the largest remainder of votes for each party. Sometimes an *electoral quota* is established after using the d'Hondt formula. In Chile, for example, after the quotients are ranked in descending order, the quotient in the position corresponding to the total number of seats to be allocated becomes an electoral quota. This electoral quota is then divided into each party's total vote to ascertain—along the lines of the Hare formula—how many seats a party is to receive. The fundamental difference between the two distributive formulas, other things being equal, is that when there are many parties (more than three) distribution under the d'Hondt formula tends to prevent the smallest parties from receiving seats, while a greater probability for success electorally accrues to weak parties under the Hare formula. Both formulas, however, serve as a brake upon the natural propensity for party proliferation under P.R. The d'Hondt formula has been recently employed in Argentina for the lower chamber, and currently is used for both houses of congress in Chile, Peru, Uruguay, and Venezuela. All other legislative elections employing proportional representation, whether open or closed list, use the Hare method for distribution.

Unicameralism further modifies total congressional influence of political parties. Currently six Latin American states employ unicameral legislatures: Costa Rica, El Salvador, Guatemala, Honduras, Haiti, and Panama. All Central American republics except Nicaragua employ unicameralism, reconfirming its relevance to states with smaller populations or areas. In the federal republics of Mexico, Brazil, Venezuela, and Argentina, the upper house is elected from state constituencies as in the United States. In the remaining unitary republics the upper houses are comprised of provincial representatives or administrative departments that normally are assigned seats roughly in accordance with their population. Ordinarily minimum representation and occasionally maximum representation are specified. Colombia and Peru explicitly specify that their upper houses must be proportioned according to population, in Colombia 1:190,000 and in Peru 1:250,000. In all cases of unitary bicameralism except Bolivia and the Dominican Republic both houses employ the same type of electoral system. In Bolivia and the Dominican Republic the lower house is elected by proportional representation whereas the upper house is elected by a majority system. The conservative effects upon a system of staggered elections, in which only a fraction of the entire legislative house is elected at a given time, are uncharacteristic of Latin American electoral systems. Only Argentina and Bolivia have prescribed staggered elections for both houses of congress.[27] Brazil and Chile prescribe it for their upper houses only. Guatemala has used staggered elections for its unicameral legislature. In all other instances, members of each house are elected at the same time although (as in Mexico) length of terms may vary between upper and lower houses.

Some familiar assertions about electoral systems in Latin America seem oversimplified and misleading. The idea that proportional representation tends to encourage proliferation of parties indefinitely is not supported by the prevalence of one-party and multi-party dominant legislative representation. The number of two-party competitive and multi-party dominant systems also tends to argue against the idea that parties under P.R. can afford the luxury of "extreme and demogogic appeals" that "alienate moderates but win votes elsewhere."[28] Judging by the presence of strong single parties in all but a few states, there would seem to be reasonable rewards in representation and access to power for parties that, under P.R. as under majority systems, appeal toward a *consensus* of the electorate. It is often argued that P.R. produces an emphasis on extremism conducive to deepening political cleavages and readiness to resort to violence. However, the most stable, democratic countries in Latin America (Uruguay, Costa Rica, Chile) all employ forms of P.R. while those states most often associated with violence have employed either aberrations of P.R. (Paraguay, Nicaragua) or majority systems (Haiti, Dominican Republic, Guatemala). This does not indicate any direct correlation between P.R. and political instability or extremism. MacKenzie argues that P.R. tends to strengthen discipline in parties and "fix the number of parties at more than two."[29] Yet the open-list ballot can control party prerogatives and discipline somewhat in Brazil and Chile. Both Uruguay and Colombia (even before the National Front) have always managed to achieve essentially two-party competitive legislative chambers under adapted proportional representation. This outcome has also been attained occasionally by Honduras, Peru, and even Argentina.

Without arguing that P.R. fosters competition or stability in Latin America, it can be clearly shown that it is not necessarily inhibiting. It also can be argued that majority electoral systems in Latin America have not produced competitive, responsible party systems. This is not to assert that majority systems have been a tool for dictatorship; as in Mexico, the ingredients and prerequisites for democracy are too complex to be defined merely as party competition or representation. But the idea and reality of party competition or legislative representation in the true sense of the terms have yet to appear within revolutionary ideology, even in Mexico. While Mexico possesses many fundamental qualities of a functioning democracy, party competition is not one of these. Proportional representation by itself is no guarantee either of multi-partism or democracy, but it has not, by the same token, been necessarily inhibiting in Latin America.

It can also be seen that the proliferation of multi-party systems is less than might be assumed in legislative representation. In more than 60 percent of the legislative chambers at least one party has achieved a minimum of 40 percent of the seats. This indicates that a motivated or disciplined party need bargain for no more than a maximum of 10 percent of the total seats in the chamber for a working majority.

In no case has the majority system resulted in a two-party competitive system as in the United States or Britain, or even in a multi-party dominant system. While the number of instances is small, majority systems have tended to eliminate party competition and produced highly dominant one-party legislatures.

Electoral systems vary greatly in their capacity to control the strength of party organizations or elites. The open-list ballot gives a voter a primary within a general election. Party seats used in Venezuela and Mexico, on the other hand, give some additional rewards to party voting and party organizational activity. Quotas and subquotas for distributing seats, as well as the basic formulas of the Hare and d'Hondt type systems, retard indefinite proliferation of parties and can, by minor alterations in the formulas employed, provide greater or lesser incentives for minor parties and general party participation.

The impact of electoral systems upon political socialization of party elites remains perhaps the most intriguing question related to political stability and party representation in Latin America. It is an empirical question that one day may be answered. Clearly the assumed unstable effects of proportional representation in Latin America are seriously open to question, since the enforced stability achieved by limiting party participation may in the long run be more politically unstable.

VI. CONCEPTS OF VOTING IN LATIN AMERICA

Elections are the major outlet for party behavior in Latin America. Party recruitment and competition reach their zenith during this period. Aggregated and correlated voting data reveals patterns of individual voting behavior and party activity.

We have suggested distinctive party characteristics based on historical, cultural, social, economic, and legal factors that control and condition electoral processes. So too must we acknowledge distinctive concepts of voting in Latin America, different from what we assume to exist in the North American context. Some of the differences are obvious, and require no further conceptualization. Ballot types, distributive formulas, eligibility requirements, separate voting by sex, all are obvious differences from our own experience. More subtle and profound differences also exist, and require a re-definition of voting concepts.

Different interpretations of voting are made, even in our own culture. Elections are viewed as contests in ideology, programs, decisions, or policies to be decided by the voter. Elections are also viewed as recruitment processes in which the voter selects the most qualified candidate who in turn becomes an agent for the voter and constituency and makes decisions in their behalf. Neither interpretation is sufficient for complex North American elections, but each suggests different roles for the party representative and voter. Both recruitment and decision-making describe voting in Latin America; more accurately for some countries and epochs than others. But other interpretations are relevant and must be accommodated. The specific kinds of voting characteristic of Latin America include: affirmative voting, protest voting, identification voting, alienation (or nonvoting), and ritualistic voting.

1. Affirmative Voting

Affirmative voting acknowledges that "power begets power." This type of voting is for a regime, ruler, party, or government simply because it is in power, and represents a considerable inertia in many political systems. Affirmative voting is particularly characteristic of rural or provincial areas, and among undereducated, impoverished, or subcultured persons who lack perspective of their actions and fail to relate them to conditions beyond their parochial community.[30] Affirmative voting is also induced by regimes through intimidation, and while not limited to rural areas tends to be characteristics of them. Intimidation ranges from persuasion and bribery to deprivation of personal values, and is administered by local agents (party bosses, local mayors, police, occasionally the military) who round up voters to meet an imposed quota. Intimidation is perhaps the most common form of electoral fraud in Latin America, and can be administered less conspicuously than ballot box stuffing or miscounting.[31] It also builds behavior patterns that generate more spontaneous affirmative voting. While few political systems in Latin America are free from affirmative voting, it tends to be especially characteristic in dictatorial and authoritarian regimes.

2. Protest Voting

Protest voting is found universally in many political systems outside Latin America. On an individual level it is probably more common than existing modes of analysis can reveal. In Latin America protest voting is common enough to be seen in aggregate data, and therefore significant in interpreting national political cultures. The causes of protest voting are as numerous as the sources of frustration.

Recent (1964, 1966, 1968 and 1970) Colombian elections offer clear illustrations of protest voting. ANAPO, led by former dictator Rojas Pinilla, is an alliance, drawn from the traditional two parties, that appeals for votes from dissident sectors of the electorate.[32] Similar movements are found in many other Latin American countries, particularly those controlled by a dominant party, an oligarchy, or the military.

3. Identification Voting

Our hypothesis that political parties are an elementary form of national institutionalization suggests that voting may be a preliminary focus of individual political awareness. Party awareness can exceed national awareness, and voting becomes an identification of primary importance to the voter. A Colombian peasant may primarily identify with the Liberal or Conservative party rather than the nation-state, and vote for the party with which he identifies. He may even kill others whom he identifies with the opposition. The importance of identification voting is underscored by the fragmentation of the Colombian party system. A voter can choose between two major factions in either traditional party—one an "in," the other an "out" faction—without disavowing his traditional loyalty to a party label. Party identification has produced national violence in Colombia, particularly when elites have played upon these elementary identifications to injure the opposition.[33] Yet these allegiances can be a unifying influence when so used within a political culture, and assist the task of national integration. The bases of identification vary between calculated self-interest, regional and familial traditions, and personalitic appeals.

4. Alienation (or Nonvoting)

Voting in Latin America as elsewhere has a negative counterpart: nonvoting.[34] Nonvoting normally cannot be traced to any consistent socioeconomic factors, or to any vague cultural traditions of political competition or democracy. However, voting participation data is often misleading since it glosses over large numbers of unregistered or ineligible voters. Yet nonvoting can be revealed in aggregate data despite these obstacles. To return to the example of Colombia, it can be demonstrated that during the past decade a significant trend of political alienation has developed regionally and by class.

While much must be done to clarify the meaning of nonvoting in Latin America, it is often more meaningful than voting for it isolates weakly integrated or antagonistic areas within the national political culture. Nonvoting is a significant comment on both the political party system and the political culture.

The one instance in which political alienation is revealed is in "blank voting." "*Vote en blanco*" is a common campaign slogan in Latin America from extremist groups not allowed to participate in national elections. Blank voting is indicative because the voter is clearly motivated to vote but frustrated in not finding any alternative appropriate to express his own political identification. By voting blank he withdraws from the decision-making process for the purpose of making his dissatisfaction known. *Peronista* strategy in post-Perón Argentina has often included the technique of blank voting during periods of their illegality. In one election more than 20 percent of the votes cast were blank.[35] Other examples can be found in Colombia, and among communist and other extremist groups in many political systems. Blank voting may represent more than alienation; it may represent an active hostility to the regime while nonvoting represents—among other things—passive alienation. In any event, blank voting must be carefully evaluated where its presence is a significant factor in voting patterns.

5. RITUALISTIC VOTING

There is normally much to voting in Latin America that is not political. This aspect of voting must be termed ritualistic, for elections become a national holiday (*fiesta*), a time to celebrate with friends and family, to drink (nominally an illegal act on election days in most countries), to dance, to wave flags, get into fights, and in a rather vague sense exercise one's obligations to the national community as one might toward the family or the Church. It is—to overburden our religious analogy—a day of national obligation. The cultural pervasiveness of this notion of obligation is embodied in many Latin American statutes by a formal, legal obligation to vote complete with sanctions for those who fail to meet this obligation. Of course formal penalties are almost never imposed. National customs vary from culture to culture, and the topic deserves much further study.

The general concept of voting must for Latin America take into consideration, in addition to the more familiar functions of leadership recruitment and decision-making, a varied set of characteristic, indigenous functions. Achieving a specific concept of voting for each Latin American country, is a critical first step in coming to terms with Latin American party politics, whatever general similarities may exist. With the maze of data that can be collected on voting, it must be remembered that while aggregate voting statistics are superficially comparable the concepts of voting may not be. Crossnational voting analyses, therefore, may be more misleading than informative, since they can obscure important factors that motivate and control voting, as well as oversimplify the process itself. The danger of making gross comparisons with the United States should be equally clear.

Elections are the dynamic arena in which party institutions and individual voting behavior combine to produce an experience that reveals much of the political culture of a Latin American nation. Parties are governed by a plurality of forces: the party system or number of parties operating at the national level; the influence of party institutions relative to other forces in the national political system; the legal and institutional context in which parties compete; the historical-cultural factors in party evolution and the traditions of party activity; the motivation of leadership elites and the factors that provide rewards and incentives for recruitment; the bases of voter identification and perception of parties; and the rewards (particularly legislative representation and national communication) offered party organizations for performance in electoral contexts.

VII. SYSTEMIC CHANGE AS A PARTY FUNCTION

If Latin American party politics is conceived systematically, three difficult but important concepts of systemic change are implied: integration of political communities; institutionalization of party processes and structures; and balances or "competition" between parties that affect the party system's capacity to function.

Political integration is expressed in party systems when social, class, racial, regional, and political conflicts are sufficiently controlled to permit stable, orderly change of leadership and policy. Sources of conflict find expression in the party system. Many sources of conflict are implicit in the Latin American environment: racial and class stratification and differentiation, regional isolation and traditional subcultures, and historically uncontrolled political competition. Integration is encouraged by building national symbols for awareness and identification to bridge conflicts, and devising channels for their communication and socialization. Parties are an important adjunct to the process, and in turn are influenced by it. The object of integration is not to avoid conflict, but to control it within acceptable parameters.

Party processes become institutionalized when their structures are vital and permanent enough to transcend an individual's leadership, and are reinforced by cultural, organizational, and ideological supports. Inadequately institutionalized party processes encourage, perhaps require, personalism and violence to mobilize support for leaders and policy change. Institutionalization assigns functional meaning to party structures, and in so doing minimizes the inherently unstable controls of personalism and violence. All parties are assisted by charisma or personalism, but institutionalization provides less disruptive avenues for reaching the same objectives.

As integration and institutionalization occur through the party system, the system's capacity to perform instrumental functions effectively increases. Dominance, or lack of it, is often a reflection of the party system's overall capacity, although the more pertinent question is whether the dominance is spontaneously achieved or induced and subsidized by a regime.

When integration and institutionalization occur, particularly if accompanied by growing dominance of some party organizations over others, systemic competition can change. How party systems change from one mode of competition to another is an empirical question discussed in the following chapters. Change seems governed by long-range factors, such as communal integration and party institutionalization, that spontaneously generate demands for a revised system. Change is also affected by short-range factors, such as governmental subsidies and violence, calculatedly designed by regimes to control party competition. Some kinds of change seem more easily induced than others: in an environment where political structure is scarce, single-party dominant systems are paradoxically most easily created and maintained; Latin American two-party systems are intrinsically unstable, and for maintenance require substantial subsidization; multi-party systems most frequently change from one condition of dominance to another, often as a result of spontaneous rather than imposed supports. In the following chapters, party systems are classified by their contemporary mode of competition; those few transitional systems whose party competition is intrinsically unstable are excluded.

Voting and elections are politically significant and their consequences more varied than often assumed for Latin America. Party activity, a critical aspect of political development, fundamentally aligns political divisions within a culture and survives enormous obstacles, including overt repression. Even in more underdeveloped Latin American nations, elections and voting reveal much of national politics.

NOTES

[1] The peculiar impact of political parties on developing countries is summarized concisely in G. A. Almond and G. B. Powell, *Comparative Politics: A Developmental Approach* (Boston: Little, Brown, 1966), pp. 125ff.

[2] The notion of a common history in the Americas is controversial. H. E. Bolton's thesis in this regard is exposed to criticism in Lewis Hanke, ed., *Do the Americas Have a Common History?* (New York: Knopf, 1964).

[3] The slowness with which scholarly attention has been paid to Latin American political parties is not unprecedented. Neil A. McDonald suggests that historically parties have been studied first ". . . in countries where popular participation in the political process was greater and government more sharply differentiated from nongovernmental or private affairs." See his *Study of Political Parties* (New York: Random House, 1955), pp. 2–3.

[4] Russell H. Fitzgibbon has provided a useful series of articles on the "measurement" of political change in Latin America based on perceptions of Latin American scholars. His evidence suggests a high correlation between free elections and party organization. The categories presented here are more intuitive, based on a notion of general relevance of parties to electoral functions, decision-making, and political recruitment. See Russell H. Fitzgibbon, "Measuring Democratic Change in Latin America," *Journal of Politics* 29 (February 1967): 129–66.

[5] The implications of this orientation are discussed further in Samuel J. Eldersveld, *Political Parties: A Behavioral Analysis* (Chicago: Rand McNally, 1964), pp. 1–13.

[6] Functional specification seems to be a useful concept for comparative politics in developing areas, if hardly a new one. Charles Merriam in his *The American Party System* (1922) concludes with an extensive discussion of party functions. More recent examples include Avery Leiserson's *Parties*

and Politics (New York: Knopf, 1958), pp. 8–9, and G. A. Almond's "A Functional Approach to Comparative Politics," in Almond and Coleman, *Politics of the Developing Areas* (Princeton, N.J.: Princeton University Press, 1960), pp. 3–64.

[7] See Herbert Simon, "Comments on the Theory of Organizations," *American Political Science Review* 47 (December 1952): 1130.

[8] David Truman views parties as a "bridge" between persons in two or more institutionalized groups or subdivisions thereof. See his *The Governmental Process* (New York: Knopf, 1951), p. 40.

[9] These concepts are intentionally loose, designed to draw gross distinctions between those who possess extraordinary power and influence within a party and those who don't. *Militants* by virtue of their active involvement are upwardly mobile toward party elites, and therefore more influential than the rank and file. *Militants* correspond in their power position to what H. Lasswell and A. Kaplan discuss as "mid-elites" in *Power and Society* (New Haven, Mass.: Yale University Press, 1950), pp. 201–03. There is no empirical study of this "mid-strata" in Latin American politics, but a general statement on it for the United States can be found in Dwaine Marvick and Charles R. Nixon, "Recruitment Contrasts in Rival Campaign Groups," in Dwaine Marvick, ed.. *Political Decisionmakers: Recruitment and Performance* (New York: Free Press, 1961), pp. 138–92.

[10] The range of conceivable functions performed by parties is limitless. Those mentioned in this section have been identified as particularly relevant to Latin America. A more comprehensive discussion of political parties and political functions is found in Almond and Powell, *Comparative Politics*, pp. 114–27.

[11] This is by no means an exhaustive list. They describe for Latin America what Almond and Powell identify as the basic distinguishing traits of political structure: (1) the degree to which there is differentiation or specialization of political roles, structures, and subsystems; and (2) the autonomy or subordination of these roles, structures, or subsystems to each other. Almond and Powell, *Comparative Politics*, pp. 42–49. A general discussion of the structural characteristics of Latin American political groups is found in George I. Blanksten. "Political Groups in Latin America," *American Political Science Review* 53 (March 1959): 106–27.

[12] For a further discussion of Latin American political elites, see Robert E. Scott, "Political Elites and Political Modernization: The Crisis of Transition" in S. M. Lipset and Aldo Solari, eds.), *Elites in Latin America* (New York: Oxford University Press, 1967), pp. 117–45.

[13] Viewing political regionalism through voting patterns is illustrated by A. N. Holcombe, *The More Perfect Union* (Cambridge, Mass.: Harvard University Press, 1950), especially Chapter Five. Regionalism in Latin American politics is revealed by the excellent area study by George Blanksten, *Ecuador: Constitututions and Caudillos* (Berkeley. University of California Press, 1951), pp. 28–31. Its effects on voting are suggested for Colombia in R. McDonald, "Political Protest and Alienation in Voting: The Case of Colombia," *Inter-American Economic Affairs* 21 (Autumn 1967): 3–22.

[14] Current studies in "political development" suggest factors involved with the transition of developing nations. See Almond and Powell, *Comparative Politics*, pp. 229–332; David Apter, *The Politics of Modernization* (Chicago:

University of Chicago Press, 1965); or Lucian Pye, *Aspects of Political Development* (Boston: Little, Brown, 1966).

[15] A more extensive formulation of political change in Latin America is revealed by Tad Szulc, *The Winds of Revolution* (New York: Praeger, 1963).

[16] "Personalism" as herein used is not synonymous with Weber's concept of "charisma." Personalism suggests influence or power that is based on the wits or skills of one person, around whom a party, group, movement, regime, or ideology evolves. Charisma is a special case where the individual possesses a distinctive popular appeal on which his influence and power are based. In Latin America personalistic movements or regimes normally are not led by men "naturally endowed as leaders," as Weber defined charisma. Rather, personalism is an adjunct of the leadership role assigned men by the political culture. See H. H. Gerth and C. W. Mills, *From Max Weber: Essays in Sociology* (New York: Oxford University Press, 1946), pp. 245–50. A good statement on Latin American *personalismo* is found in Martin Needler, *Latin American Politics in Perspective* (Princeton, N.J.: Van Nostrand, 1963), pp. 106–11.

[17] The formation of ad hoc parties in Ecuador is clearly discussed by Blanksten, *Ecuador: Constitutions and Caudillos*, pp. 70–71.

[18] See Walter Washington, "The Political Activity of Latin American Students," in Robert D. Tomasek, ed., *Latin American Politics* (Garden City, N.Y.: Doubleday Anchor, 1966), pp. 115–27; also, Kenneth N. Walker, "Political Socialization in Universities," in Lipset and Solari, *Elites in Latin America,* pp. 408–30.

[19] See Needler, *Latin American Politics in Perspective,* pp. 88–111, and Russell H. Fitzgibbon, "The Party Potpourri in Latin America," *Western Political Quarterly* 10 (March 1957): 3–22.

[20] This typology is taken from R. McDonald, "Electoral Systems, Party Representation, and Political Change in Latin America," *Western Political Quarterly* 20 (September 1967): 694–708.

[21] Much of the material contained in this section was published originally in *Western Political Quarterly*. The material is reproduced herein with permission.

[22] A more comprehensive review of the impact of electoral laws in general is found in Douglas W. Rae, *The Political Consequences of Electoral Laws* (New Haven, Conn.: Yale University Press, 1968).

[23] The definitions of electoral system types used here are based on those found in *Parliaments and Electoral Systems: A World Handbook* (London: Institute of Electoral Research, 1962), pp. 5–12.

[24] A system of proportional representation was established prior to the 1964 national elections.

[25] A third significant variation of the majority system, the "absolute majority," involves a second ballot or alternative vote for either single-member or multi-member districts. It is used presently for the French Parliament and the Australian House of Representatives.

[26] Martin C. Needler essentially argues this in Latin America (Martin C. Needler, *Latin American Politics in Perspective,* pp. 115–17), although W. J. M. MacKenzie cautions against the interpretation in his more general analysis, *Free Elections* (New York: Rinehart, 1958), pp. 83–84.

[27] On July 3, 1966, both houses of the Bolivian Congress were wholly renewed.

[28] Needler, *Latin American Politics in Perspective*, p. 116. A survey of party representation by separate legislative chambers can be found in McDonald, "Electoral Systems."

[29] MacKenzie, *Free Elections*, p. 83.

[30] Affirmative and habitual voting is not necessarily irrational. For a discussion of its rational dimensions, see Anthony Downs, *An Economic Theory of Democracy* (New York: Harper and Row, 1957), pp. 84–86.

[31] A summary of electoral fraud practiced in the United States is found in V. O. Key, *Politics, Parties, and Pressure Groups*, 4th ed. (New York: Crowell, 1958), pp. 685–87.

[32] A concept of "protest voting" in Latin America is found in the R. McDonald, "Political Protest and Alienation in Voting: The Case of Colombia."

[33] Further discussion of the phenomena in Colombia can be found in R. S. Weinert, "Violence in Pre-Modern Societies: Rural Colombia," *American Political Science Review* 60 (June 1966): 340–47.

[34] Downs also sees a rational basis for abstention or nonvoting, *An Economic Theory of Democracy*, pp. 260–76. Key suggests causal bases of nonvoting in the United States, *Politics, Parties, and Pressure Groups*, pp. 622–43. The effects of alienation on voting in Boston, and a general discussion of the concept, is available in Murray B. Levin, *The Alienated Voter* (New York: Holt, Rinehart, and Winston, 1960), pp. 58–75.

[35] James W. Rowe, *The Argentine Elections of 1963* (Washington, D.C.: Institute for the Comparative Study of Political Systems, 1964).

CHAPTER 2

Multi-Party Loose Systems: Venezuela, Brazil, Panama, and Ecuador

Multi-party loose systems, those in which no party receives more than 40 percent of the legislative seats and in which more than two parties compete, are the least dominated or structured of the general types. In the twentieth century, many Latin American nations have periodically had this type of party system. Multi-party loose systems sometimes arise following the overthrow of a dictatorship as repressed political factions realign and sensitize themselves to new issues and problems. Venezuela and Brazil following World War II illustrate this phenomenon, as does Bolivia prior to the MNR revolution of 1952 and following the counterrevolution of 1963. Guatemala, Ecuador, and Panama also frequently conform to this model. Other nations, notably Chile, had multi-party loose systems, but no longer can be reasonably included in the category.

Venezuela had a multi-party loose system from 1943 to 1948, and again after 1958. Brazil had one from the resignation of Vargas in 1946 until the present military regime. Neither country previously had much of a party system or any significant nineteenth-century party activity. Party politics and party systems are new, although other national institutions are not. This characteristic is more clearly seen for Latin America when contrasted with the single-party dominant systems of many recently independent Asian and African states. These systems are produced by independence movements (parties) that reconstitute themselves following independence, so that the party actually predates the political system. Early independence zeal and alliances are transformed into legitimized structures to control the governmental institutions. Rarely in contemporary Latin America has such a unifying and cohesive force as massive revolution reformed the party system or dominated it. In Latin America, nation-states predate party systems, and patterns of political culture, interest groups, and political socialization are set in past generations. Only in Mexico since 1928, Bolivia for a decade following the 1952 revolution, and perhaps contemporary Cuba, have mass-supported political parties consolidated broadly based, modern revolutions.

In multi-party loose systems it is axiomatic that entry and exit of parties from the system is relatively easy. The ease of entry and exit is due to a combination of factors. Electoral laws are one factor that facilitate the participation of groups in elections and the formalization of political parties. Other factors are inherent in the parties themselves. Multi-partism is encouraged when party cohesion is based largely on personalities, transient issues, or cultural divisions that do not encourage permanent organizations. Elections in such contexts promote ad hoc groups that proclaim themselves "parties," but whose incomplete programs, lack of organization, or extralegal status cannot attract a regular following or stabilize channels of leadership recruitment. These groups are liable to the vagaries of a single political leader, and coalesce little more than tenuous followers.

Another characteristic of multi-party loose systems is the tendency toward coalitions. Coalitions arise out of opportunism, pragmatism, mutual self-interest, and occasionally ideology. Since by definition no party can control either the electoral politics or the legislature, there are strong, obvious pressures toward coalitions to impose dominance and control the system. Coalitions may gravitate similar parties or groups toward personalities (for example, Velasco Ibarra in Ecuador, Vargas in Brazil), mutual interests (such as the brief cooperation between *Acción Democrática,* COPEI, and the URD in Venezuela under Betancourt), or ideological affinity (as the FRAP in Chile or FIDEL in Uruguay). Coalitions may not be recognized or even permitted by their respective electoral systems, so that "gentlemen's agreements" based on class, kinship, friendship, money, or patronage must induce allegiance. Coalitions may (as in Ecuador) achieve greater indentity and allegiance than their component "party" factions, or (as in Venezuela) remain highly tenuous, fragile, and subsidiary to their component parties. Maintenance of coalitions between elections and postelection legislative conformity are exceedingly difficult, for the rewards of loyalty often disappear following the election. Except possibly in Venezuela, weak coalitional discipline is of little importance, since legislative politics in most multi-party loose systems is based on personal rather than party or coalitional bargaining, and normally is overriden by strong presidential and weak legislative traditions. Coalitions tend to dissolve once they have served their electoral ends. Coalitions are easily united by common hostility, and easily fragmented by acquired power.

Multi-party loose systems produce more personalistic and perhaps more regionalistic parties than otherwise is normal in Latin America. No measurable index of personalism exists, but voting studies reveal significant political regionalism in Brazil, Venezuela, and Ecuador. This observation is more plausible stated in the negative: nearly all Latin American parties are influenced by regionalism and personalism, but in multi-party loose systems parties are often held together by little else. The process of monopolizing a party system (concentrating political party power) requires intensive national distribution of popularly recognized party symbols. Extreme regionalism may help preserve multipartism. Regionalistic and personalistic parties are also found in more dominated party systems, but are less characteristic. Venezuela's nascent party system is possibly less regionalistic than others in the category, but it still possesses these qualities in abundance. Voting trends suggest it may become less regionalistic—if not less personalistic—in the coming decade.

Parties in multi-party loose systems are probably more elitist, their recruitment practices more constrained. The existing organizational structure is based on small groups characteristically higher in socioeconomic class or lighter in color. Blanksten observes the characteristic in Ecuador, concluding that no more than a few hundred persons actively participate in national parties. The same has been true in Guatemala, Panama, and Bolivia. Brazilian parties have a broader national base, but massive participation and recruitment are unknown. Two Venezuelan parties—AD and COPEI—have attempted to build a broad base for membership and participation from among the electorate. It could still be argued, however, that effective control of recruitment in these Venezuelan parties is very elitist despite gestures to the contrary.

The smallest or weakest parties in the multi-party loose system may be so poorly organized, so ad hoc, that they disappear entirely between elections. Why multi-party loose systems fail to produce strong organizations and vigorous leadership is a difficult question. There are many partial answers, none wholly convincing: low levels of national political awareness (Ecuador, Guatemala, Panama), strong cultural dualism (Ecuador, Bolivia, Guatemala), or poor national political consensus (Brazil) where major ideological and sociocultural divisions block national party development.

It is not possible to correlate general political instability with multi-party loose systems. If political stability is defined as orderly, constitutional change in government without violence or interference from semiautonomous groups, the nations in this category are neither the most stable nor the most unstable. Nations with extended histories of one-party rule (for example, Haiti, Paraguay, and the Dominican Republic) have been chronically the most unstable. Multi-party systems, even in the loosest form, are no more destined to be politically unstable than other types, and indeed may be more stable than one-party systems since more outlets for political anxiety, hostility, and protest exist. There is little doubt that parliamentary instability is a by-product of a multi-party loose system, however. Legislative instability coexists with strong executive domination in Guatemala, Bolivia, Panama, Ecuador, and recently Brazil. Whether such domination is caused by or produces a multi-party loose system is speculative. A minor form of instability, caused by the easy entry and exit of parties from the system, may actually retard rather than promote instability in the total political system.

Conceived functionally, it is probable that multi-party loose systems are more inclined to articulate than aggregate interests. Since party elites participate less frequently and more tangentially in governmental decision-making, parties often specialize in articulation rather than recruitment, aggregation, or policy functions performed by parties in other contexts. Considerable variation must be acknowledged from one political system to another. Ecuadorian and Panamanian parties achieve minimum functional intensity and diversity, while Venezuelan parties achieve a higher level of each.

A final word must be said regarding the definitional and empirical boundaries of this general category. This category is, like the others, illustrative rather than definitive. Some Latin American nations periodically can be placed in other categories, or may rather freely move from one to another. Venezuela, for example, changed from the multi-party dominant system of 1958 to the present category toward the end of Betancourt's administration. Guatemala under its present regime has become a multi-party dominant system as a result of the 1966 elections, the political appeal of the PR party, and a coersive electoral system. Brazil's recent party politics exist only at the will of a military supported government. While

Brazil's current politics remains unsettled, it must be viewed in the traditional perspective of a multi-party loose system until it is permitted to find its own equilibrium by freer means. For many years Chile was the archetype of multi-party loose system, but recent, profound changes in Chilean politics (including the consolidation of leftist parties, the merger of the Liberal and Conservative parties, and the dominance of the Christian Democrats) places it decisively in the multi-party dominant category where it appears likely to remain. Without claiming permanence or perfection for the examples in the category, they do illustrate a general tendency in Latin American party politics.

I. VENEZUELA: ELEMENTS OF POLITICAL INTEGRATION

1. Evolution of Modern Parties in Venezuela

Venezuela like other Latin American republics was preoccupied in the nineteenth century with questions of consolidation following independence. The nation was controlled by a conservative oligarchy when it withdrew in 1830 from Gran Colombia to begin its own political history. The nineteenth century was a long series of dictatorships for Venezuela, interrupted from 1858 to 1863 by a five-year "federal war" in which forces of Liberal proponents of a federal union won over the Conservative advocates of centralism. Seven years more bickering plagued the country until, finally, in 1870 consolidation produced a federal union of twenty states led by a Liberal advocate, the tyrannical Guzmán Blanco. Following Blanco were three dictators who ruled the nation from 1892 to 1935, when the last of them, Juan Vicente Gómez, died from natural causes. It is at that point that contemporary party history began in Venezuela.[1]

The first formally organized political party was the Communist party, founded in 1931 as a clandestine and politically impotent organization. As early as 1928, however, students opposed to the Gómez tyranny organized the *Federación de Estudiantes de Venezuela* (FEV), committed to the principles of a free university and political freedom. Gómez had closed the *Universidad Central* from 1912–1923, and barely tolerated it afterward. Among the leaders of FEV were many of Venezuela's future political leaders: Rómulo Betancourt, Raúl Leoni, Jóvito Villalba, Gonzalo Carnevali, and

Juaquín Gabaldón Márquez. An abortive demonstration in 1928 scattered the FEV's leaders around the hemisphere until after the death of Gómez in late 1935.[2]

Following the death of Gómez, many additional parties formed. Among these was the *Unión Nacional Republicana* (UNR), the *Partido Republicano Progresista* (PRP), the *Movimiento de Organización Venezolana* (ORVE), and the *Bloque Nacional Democrático* (BND). The UNR was founded as a middle-class, business oriented but enlightened opposition to the authoritarian regime, and an alternative to the more radical student-supported groups. The UNR lost support in the following years, and eventually dissolved. The PRP was the first organizational effort of the Communists to be legally tolerated, but as it began to consolidate influence it was soon suppressed. The BND was a regional group from the state of Zulia, unlike the PRP and UNR which were both founded in Caracas. The BND was led by Valmore Rodríguez, a journalist and labor leader. ORVE, formed in 1936, was the predecessor of the present *Acción Democrática* (AD); AD was formed officially on September 13, 1941. Supported by leaders from FEV and a newly organized labor union (ANDE) in Caracas, ORVE demanded electoral reform, economic development, expanded education, and revised national policy to retain greater control of the petroleum industry. Largely under the ORVE leadership, a new coalitional party known as the *Partido Democrático Nacional* (PDN) was organized to include ORVE, PRP, FEV, and BND as well as several labor organizations. After several dramatic but ineffective demands by the PDN, the government declared the party illegal and it was dissolved. Elections were held in January, 1937, for a series of municipal and congressional offices. Because of a repressive electoral system that denied women and illiterates the right to vote, the potential electorate to whom the parties made their appeals was exceedingly small. The campaign was intense and convulsive. The government arrested 47 leading politicians who had supported PDN, and this had the effect of crippling the opposition.[3]

Former PDN leaders adopted somewhat milder tactics, and in 1941 won recognition for a new party, AD. The regime of Isaías Medina Angarita, meanwhile, decided to establish its own official party, *Partido Democrático Venezolano* (PDV). AD leaders, apparently frustrated by the regime and suspicious of its actions, joined with some younger military officers to stage a *golpe* that brought them to power October 18, 1945. Now better organized, AD reformed the electoral system, and began to assemble a national policy for governing.

Opposition to AD emerged on three fronts. One front came from the *Comité de Organización Política Electoral Independiente* (COPEI), which had been formed under a different name in the mid-1930s by university students as an alternative to FEV. COPEI supported the anti-Medina revolution, but criticized the radical tendencies of AD and, less explicitly, the avowed secularism of AD and its leaders. COPEI's relationship to the Church has been an informal if close one. Led by Rafael Caldera, who served briefly in the *junta* following the 1945 revolution, COPEI was regional in strength, restricted to the southwestern Andean region around Mérida.[4]

A second source of opposition to AD came from the *Unión Republicana Democrática* (URD), a personal vehicle for Jóvito Villalba who had broken with the AD leadership to become an independent senator under the Medina regime. Following the 1945 revolution, he organized the URD and attracted many former PDV supporters of the Medina regime. The URD relied heavily upon the personality of Villalba, and was slow to develop a clear image or crystalize a program.[5]

A third front of opposition to AD came from the *Partido Comunista Venezolano* (PCV). The PCV leadership had once cooperated with the PDN leaders in opposition to Gómez, but broke with the other parties over questions of labor organization.[6] These three major groups, together with the minor, regional parties that cooperated with them, prepared to compete electorally in the elections scheduled for October 27, 1946—the first free election in Venezuelan history. The election was held to establish a constituent assembly charged with the responsibility of drafting a new constitution.

AD won the election easily, capturing nearly 79 percent of the total vote and 137 out of 160 seats. COPEI won a small 19 seat delegation, the URD only 2. The assembly produced a visionary constitution, which included liberal ideas concerning social awareness and a truly open enfranchisement that eliminated literacy as a condition for voting. New congressional elections and presidential were set for December 14, 1947, along with municipal elections for May 9, 1948. The results of these elections are seen in Table 2-1.[7]

Rómulo Gallegos, a moderate, respected intellectual, was the first candidate to run with the AD label for the presidency. He

TABLE 2-1. RESULTS OF VENEZUELAN ELECTIONS OF DECEMBER 14, 1947,
AND MAY 9, 1948

Party	CONGRESS				PRESIDENCY		MUNICIPAL	
	Total vote	Per-cent of vote	Depu-ties	Sena-tors	Total vote	Per-cent	Total vote	Per-cent
AD	838,526	70.8	83	38	871,752	74.4	491,762	70.1
COPEI	240,186	20.5	6	19	262,204	22.4	146,197	21.1
URD	51,427	4.3	4	1			27,007	3.9
PCV	43,190	3.7	3	1	36,514	3.2	23,524	3.4
Other	10,435	.7	1	0			4,664	.5

waged a largely symbolic campaign against Medina in the election
of April 28, 1941. The election, held within the congress, was obviously controlled by the Medina regime. Gallegos ran again with
AD support in 1947, winning easily over Caldera for COPEI. Betancourt, who had served as president of the *junta,* gave control of
the government to Gallegos in February, 1948. But Gallegos served
no more than nine months, when he was displaced by a military
revolution and *junta.* The new *junta* drew important support from
the Church, which was angered by AD's secularism and fearful
of its continued domination. AD was immediately repressed, and
its leaders scattered. One of the *junta* members rose to a position
of dominance, Marcos Pérez Jiménez. The regime of Pérez Jiménez
was one of cruelty, repression, violence, and ineptitude. The dictator was overthrown on January 22, 1958, and later imprisoned. The
current phase of Venezuelan politics began in 1958, little over a
decade ago, when the first popularly elected regime took and held
office in the nation.[8]

2. REPRESENTATION, VOTING, AND POLITICAL CULTURE
IN VENEZUELA

Venezuela is a nation of just under 10 million people, roughly
the size of Chile or the state of Michigan. The nation is a mixture
racially, with a characteristic, dominant Venezuelan *mestizo* found
at all levels of society. There is also a small white population, part
of it immigrant from Europe, and a small Negro and even smaller
Indian component. Caracas, the federal capital and largest city,
contains just under two million inhabitants, less than 20 percent
of the total population, but dominates the nation in all ways.

Regionalism is a distinctive characteristic of the Venezuelan political culture. John Martz in his discussion of the factor isolates five basic regions:[9]

Metropolitan Core. This region includes the federal capital of Caracas and two adjacent states, Miranda and Aragua. It is the most populous of the areas with nearly a third of the national population. It tends to support the more radical parties and factions electorally. The PCV receives most of its vote in this area.

Costal Range. This region includes six states: Falcón, Lara, Yaracuy, Carabobo, Nueva Esparta, and Sucre, and comprises about 24 percent of the total national population. The area is a mixture of rural and industrial interests, and its voting is mixed. The major cities are Barquisimeto and Valencia.

Llanos-Guayana. Eight states are included in this area, which actually represents two separable regions: one of highland prairies, alternatively rainy and arrid, the other of tropical lowlands. Largely rural, the area has 80 percent of the national land but only 22 percent of its population. The largest city is Ciudad Bolívar, which along with its region is normally strongly AD in voting.

Maracaibo Basin. This area includes only one state, Zulia, and 12 percent of the national population. It is the center of petroleum exploration and production, and contains the nation's second largest city, Maracaibo. Politically it is favorable to AD, and supported by AD sponsored labor unions.

Andean Region. The states of Táchira, Mérida, and Trujillo contain 13 percent of the population in an area with strong cultural ties with Colombia. It is from this area that the so-called Andean dictators came for more than 50 years. Recently, the region has been a stronghold for COPEI. Each region is summarized in Table 2-2.

Besides political regionalism, voting patterns in Venezuela are tied to demographic and economic factors. There was a wave of European immigration before, during, and particularly after World War II. Most immigrants were middle-class, fleeing disruptions in Spain, Italy, and Portugal. Migration from Colombia and Cuba, for economic and political reasons respectively, has also been significant. The immigrants have had a strong impact on economic life in Caracas, but less impact on the nation's politics.

Overwhelming in Venezuela's political culture are the conflicts and characteristics induced by the nation's unusual economic position. Venezuela has the highest per capita income of any Latin American nation, but with great extremes between high and

TABLE 2-2. POLITICAL REGIONALISM IN VENEZUELA

Region		Population	Percent
METROPOLITAN CORE		2,329,828	28.2
Federal District			
Miranda			
Aragua			
COSTAL		1,982,713	24.0
Falcón	Carabobo		
Lara	Nueva Esparta		
Yaracuy	Sucre		
LLANOS-GUAYANA		1,838,258	22.3
Barinas	Anzoátegui		
Apure	Monagas		
Portugesa	Bolívar		
Cojedes	D. Amacuro		
Guárico	Amazonas		
MARACAIBO		1,044,047	12.6
Zulia			
ANDES		1,060,610	12.9
Táchira			
Mérida			
Trujillo			
Total	(1964 estimate)	8,255,456	100.0

low income families. The more subtle income spread characteristic of Uruguay, Argentina, and even Chile is unknown in Venezuela. Most of the national wealth comes from a single commodity:
oil. Oil and iron generate 25 percent of the national product, but
employ less than 2 percent of the labor force. Oil also produces
92 percent of the foreign exchange, and 62 percent of the government's income. Concern is now expressed over the possible exhaus-
tion of the petroleum reserves in the next decades. A major program
of economic development has been pursued by the government
with income from oil. To replace the commodity eventually as a
key ingredient in the national economy, the government takes 50
percent of the gross profits and an additional amount in corporate
taxes. The oil industry is largely owned, as are most Venezuelan
foreign investments, by U.S. interests.[10]

Agriculture is underdeveloped, but could be expanded. Now only
small amounts of coffee and cacao are exported. Nearly one-third of
all Venezuelans employed work the land, many at a subsistence
level. The government must cope with the political problem of
trying to siphon off as much revenue as possible from petroleum
for investment without destroying the industry or imposing a
politically intolerable austerity on the nation. The balance is a

difficult one. Venezuelans live with one of the highest cost of living indexes in the world, although the currency is stable and inflation controlled. Population pressures place burdens on the economy at a rate of 3.6 percent annual increase.[11]

Economic realities produce strong pressures for greater affluence and social mobility, with consumption being the principal hallmark of each. Regional, occupational, income, and class distinctions are profound, and politically significant. In a context where party traditions are weak and relatively unstable, it is not surprising that party proliferation is common, or that most parties are nationalistic and in dogma "left of center."

Constitutionally Venezuela is a federal system, but federalism is a nineteenth-century veneer with little relevance to contemporary politics and administration. The president is elected by a simple, direct vote. Governors, theoretically elected, are actually appointed by the president and responsible to him. States possess little power, although local communities retain limited taxing authority.[12] There are twenty states, a federal district, and two territories in the nation. Two senators are elected from each state and the federal district. Deputies are proportioned by population, with the territories each receiving one. Caracas has the largest congressional delegation, with about 30 deputies.

Parties must be legally recognized through a petition presented to the National Electoral Court. The electoral system employs a closed-list system with colored lists and party symbols to permit illiterate voters to participate. Seats are awarded following the general d'Hondt quotient formula. Each party can win up to six additional deputies and four senators by a special party skew. National quotients are determined separately for the lower and upper houses equal to the total valid votes cast nationally for all party lists divided by the fixed number of seats available. The total vote for each list is then divided by the national quotient. If the difference in seats awarded by this system for each party is greater than the seats otherwise won, the party receives additional representatives. The total size of the chambers changes with each election. Additional representatives, known as party delegates, are assigned districts to which they are responsible.

3. PRINCIPAL PARTIES IN CONTEMPORARY VENEZUELA

Two strong parties dominate the contemporary Venezuelan scene: AD and COPEI. The persistent factionalization of the former has substantially strengthened the latter. A sizeable component of transient parties and fronts (coalitions) affect the whole party system.

a. *Acción Democrática (AD)*. Founded in 1941 in Caracas, AD was the traditionally strongest party in modern Venezuela until it lost the presidential election of 1968. It elected three presidents, two of whom served their full terms. AD is, as John Martz has observed, a "thoroughly modern political party" in that it is well organized, financed, sensitive to contemporary political issues, committed to governing, and reasonably pragmatic. The party is proportionately weakest in the metropolitan area, but generally strong elsewhere. It receives substantial labor support. Although some observers classify AD with the general *Aprista*-type parties in Latin America, the comparison does a disservice to AD. Unlike the Peruvian APRA party, the model for which the category is derived, AD has successfully held office and found a truly national basis for its appeals. It has not, however, found as yet a means of congealing the diverse elements—particularly in its leadership elites—that comprise its organization.[13]

Since 1960, AD has experienced several serious divisions. The first produced the *Movimiento de Izquierda Revolucionario* (MIR) in 1960. Led by Domingo Alberto Rangel, the MIR constituted radical leftists, Marxists, and—most significantly—the student movement within the party. The division was generated by both ideological and generational grievances with the older AD leadership whose roots were found in the earlier student movement of 1928. About 80 percent of the university AD movement followed the MIR out of the party.

Another division occurred in 1962. Under the leadership of Ramos Giménez and other prominent leaders of AD, a small but outspoken minority left the fold. The group, known as AD-OP (*Acción Democrática en Oposición*), held a national convention in 1962 and participated in the 1963 elections. The division crippled the AD majority in the legislature, but most dissidents were replaced in 1963 by officialists supported by the AD organization in the election.

A third division developed in 1967 on the eve of the 1968 election campaign. This time another prestigious AD leader, Luis Beltrán Prieto, withdrew to form the *Movimiento Electoral del Pueblo* (MEP). Prieto withdrew, as had Ramos Giménez, because of opposition to AD's presidential candidate. Prieto challenged AD over use of the party label, but like AD-OP, lost the struggle. The third split proved too much for the old AD organization; it was unable to muster a plurality in the 1968 election.

b. Comité de Organización Política Electoral Independiente (COPEI). COPEI, known also as the Social Christian party, was founded in 1946, although it had roots in an earlier organization that participated in 1934 in the International Congress of Catholic Youth in Rome. Rafael Caldera, who attended the Rome conference, founded a student organization to challenge the hegemony of FEV and what were later AD leaders. COPEI began as a rather conservative, Christian party, having since broadened its base and liberalized its dogma. COPEI participated in the government coalition along with the URD in 1958, but withdrew in 1964. Perhaps still the most "conservative" of the major parties, COPEI has no formal connections with the Church nor is it "conservative" in the sense that the term might be used elsewhere in Latin America. It draws support from practicing Catholics, some labor groups, and the rural population of the Andean region; its student members are activist and militant.

c. Unión Republicana Democrática (URD). URD is an outgrowth of Jóvito Villalba's ambition to be Senator under the Medina regime, and has born his imprint since. A rather complex group ideologically, the URD cooperated with AD in the 1958 coalition, but since 1960 has pursued an independent course. It was permitted by the Pérez Jiménez regime to run an opposition candidate in the mock election of 1952, and received support from the AD which was illegal at the time. Apparently, the URD won the election, because the dictator's regime suddenly silenced the press during the ballot counting, and later announced that the government party had "won" the election.

d. Partido Comunista Venezolana (PCV). The PCV, the oldest of the nation's parties, has been legal for few of its many years of existence. Briefly absorbed into ORVE, it went its own way in 1937, and under the watchful eye of Medina formed another front organization, the *Unión Popular* (UP) in 1941. It participated freely in the 1958 elections, but was outlawed in 1964. The party now often aligns itself with the MIR, and draws its strongest support from the metropolitan area. A militant arm of the PCV has engaged in guerilla activities under the name *Fuerzas Armadas de Liberación Nacional* (FALN), and has been responsible for numerous incidents of violence and terrorism since its founding in 1960. In 1968, the PCV sponsored the *Unión Para Avanzar* (UPA) to participate in the national elections.

Many minor parties have also existed in Venezuela. Illustrative are the following: the *Movimiento Electoral Nacional Independiente* (MENI), a group formed to support the candidacy of Vice Admiral Wolfgang Larrazábal in 1958. Larrazábal was the leader of the *junta* which overthrew Pérez Jiménez. The *Frente Democrática Popular* (FDP) is a "one-man" party led by Jorge Dager, once a member of AD who followed the MIR revolt, then disavowed it. In 1963, FDP supported MENI and Larrazábal. The *Frente Nacional Democrático* (FND), led by Senator Arturo Uslar Pietri, and comprised of dissident members of the AD, URD, and other parties. Uslar Pietri was a cabinet member of the Medina regime, and is a right-of-center politician, teacher, and author. Other minor parties have included the *Movimiento Socialista Nacionalista* (MSN), *Cruzada Electoral Popular Agrupación Social* (CEPAS), *Asociación Venezolano Independiente* (AVI), the *Independientes Pro-Frente Nacional* (IPFN), and many, many others.[14]

In a multi-party loose system like Venezuela's, the object of the game is to coalesce *against* the incumbents; or, if you happen to be incumbent, to seek allies with whom you can exchange patronage for political support. Hopefully, an incumbent group can find an ally with harmonious if not identical interests. Unfortunately, these conditions are hard to meet. The relative tactical advantage of the "outs" over the "ins" is significant, and the decline of AD is due in part to the normal difficulties of governing in a party system like that of Venezuela.

4. Voting and Campaigning in Elections: A Comparative Study of 1958, 1963, and 1968 Elections

The ease with which parties form and participate in elections under Venezuelan electoral law is an important factor in their multiplicity. A party can, for example, nominate a presidential candidate with only two hundred literate supporters in each of the seven districts. Filing a list of party candidates for the legislature is also a simple process. A group of five persons representing one hundred literate citizens may nominate candidates for deputy in an electoral district. With the lenient electoral laws it is surprising that more political parties don't form in Venezuela.

Voting is open and compulsory to all over 21 years, regardless of literacy. Citizens register in their place of residence. Registration lists are posted in each municipal electoral board eight days prior to an election. A system of regulatory boards, courts, and a supreme electoral council with representation from all major parties supervises the procedures and adjudicates disputes arising out of them. Ballots are different sizes, colors, and designs according to the contest and party, to avoid penalizing illiterate voters. The supreme electoral council can require one ballot for an election or several. In 1958 a single ballot was used for all contests.

Voting begins at six o'clock in the morning. Party representatives watch polling locations to guarantee impartiality. A voter's registration record is certified to indicate that he has voted, and his fingerprint entered in a municipal journal. To guard against multiple voting, the voter's finger is dipped in red indelible ink, a practice common throughout Latin America. The red, ink-stained finger becomes a symbol of civic responsibility throughout the nation. Failure to vote involves penalties. Although rarely enforced, up to 5 percent of the annual earnings of a nonvoter may be taken in fines. More commonly, citizens are required to furnish proof of voting when seeking a public job or in any way making contact with the bureaucracy, such as matriculating or graduating from a public university or entering into a contract with the government.

Violence has been known during elections, particularly in 1963 when a small group of terrorists tried to disrupt procedures. The alleged reason for the terrorist activities was the government's failure to allow the PCV to participate in the election. The nearly 13 thousand polling stations were policed by 40 thousand federal troops to insure tranquility, and despire recurrent threats few incidents marred the electoral experience.[15]

Because it is compulsory, voting participation in Venezuela is very high for Latin America, as shown in Table 2-3.[16] There is far less variation between urban and rural areas or between the core area and provincial areas than is true elsewhere in Latin America.

There have been five open elections in modern Venezuelan history: those of 1946, 1947, 1958, 1963, and 1968. The last three

TABLE 2-3. REGISTRATION AND PARTICIPATION IN ELECTIONS
OF 1958, 1963, AND 1968

	1958	1963	1968
Total population	6,042,000	8,255,456	9,933,000
Eligible voters	2,930,000	3,586,000	4,600,000
Percent registered	93	94	93
Total vote	2,725,000	3,078,910	3,470,000
Percent participation	92	91	87

are of far greater importance, but the first two are worth noting in passing. A wholly disreputable election was held in 1952 under the Pérez Jiménez dictatorship, and a second one in 1957. In 1952 AD was prohibited from participating, and the regime in effect annulled the results. The 1957 election was a yes-no referendum on whether to continue Pérez Jiménez in power; a controlled election and the results were never in doubt.

The constituent assembly election of 1946 was a resounding victory for the AD, as can be seen in the graph in Table 2-4.[17] Under the new, liberal constitution the assembly produced, the election of 1947 for congress and the presidency again proved a victory for AD, which received twice the vote of its nearest competitor, COPEI. As seen in Table 2-4, each election from 1946 on has seen a corrosion of AD voting, accompanied by a rise in party competiveness and an expansion of party activity. Gallegos' election in 1947 provided a brief nine month interim of constitutional government. A *junta* headed by Colonel Carlos Delgado Chalbaud deposed Gallegos, and upon the assassination of the Colonel, the reins of government fell to Pérez Jiménez.

The 1958 elections were a hurried affair complicated by the dispersion of many political leaders in exile since 1948. The president of the *junta* that overthrew Pérez Jiménez—Wolfgang Larrazábal— was an obvious candidate with very strong following in the federal district. A new political organization, the *Movimiento Electoral Nacional Independiente* (MENI), was created to further Larrazábal's candidacy. Under pressure and persuasion from Villaba, Larrazábal accepted the official nomination of the URD, which more or less upstaged MENI as the chief vehicle for the candidate. Rómulo Betancourt received the AD nomination, and Caldera once

TABLE 2-4. Comparison of Party Voting in Venezuela, 1946–1968 (in percent)

Party	1946	1947	1948	1958	1963	1968
AD	80	74	70	49	33	28
COPEI	13	22	21	15	21	29
URD*	3		4	27	18	22
Other	4	4	5	9	28	21

SOURCE: *Consejo Supremo Electoral*
NOTE: All elections are presidential, except 1946 (constituent) and 1948 (municipal)

* The URD did not participate in the 1947 presidential race, but received 4.3 percent in the congressional contest; in 1968 it joined the FDP and FND to form the FT, which received the percent indicated.

again ran with the COPEI label. Balloting for the candidates is seen in Table 2-5.[18]

Betancourt's victory was impressive: not only did he receive nearly a majority of the popular vote, but the AD carried almost 60 percent of the senate seats and a majority of the deputies. Venezuela began its experience in representative government with a multi-party dominant system, but the fate of AD was already in evidence. The problems of incumbency accelerated the trend in the coming months and in the next two elections.

In a gesture toward consolidation and unity, Betancourt invited the COPEI and URD to participate in the government. The two parties signed a convenant with AD, prior to the election, to accept the results whatever they might be. Cabinet ministers were appointed from URD and COPEI. Caldera was elected to preside over the Chamber of Deputies, and Raúl Leoni presided in behalf of AD over the Senate. The period of party consolidation was short lived. The URD withdrew from the coalition in 1960 over policy disagreements, including Betancourt's bellicose attitude toward Fidel Castro's new regime. Disunity also broke out within the AD. Following the desertion of the MIR, which took 17 deputies and a senator, AD and COPEI still retained a majority of 75 although AD no longer retained a majority in the lower house, having only 56 deputies or 46 percent of the total. The second desertion in 1962 of the group known as the *Aristas* left AD only 21 senators (about 42 percent) and 36 deputies (about 20 percent). With COPEI's members, the coalition could generate a slim majority in the Senate (27 to 24) but lost control of the deputies 78 to 55. The opposition, comprised of URD, MIR, ARS, and PCV, was reasonably united in their hostility to Betancourt and his party. The Chamber of Deputies elected an *Arista* president, and the URD and MIR took major administrative positions in the Senate. Without even an election, AD had lost its effective control of the legislature,

TABLE 2-5. PARTY VOTING IN PRESIDENTIAL ELECTION OF DECEMBER 7, 1958

Candidate	Party	Vote	Percent
Betancourt	AD	1,284,092	49.2
Larrazábal*	URD-MENI	885,167	33.9
Caldera	COPEI	396,293	15.2

* Larrazábal also was endorsed by the PCV, which supplied 84,451 of the presidential votes included in his total.

and the coalition had even lost control of the Chamber of Deputies. Suddenly Venezuela's multi-party dominant system dissolved into the looser form. In the 1963 election the officialist AD regained many but not all of the legislative seats it lost in the defections. The end of the dictatorship and the tremendous victory of the AD in 1958 was a heady experience, perhaps the high point in the party's development.[19]

The 1963 election was a milestone in Venezuelan political history: it was the first time that one regime voluntarily relinquished government power to another following an election. AD again won a plurality of legislative seats, although with their margin reduced over the 1958 total. One of Betancourt's closest colleagues, Raúl Leoni, received the party nomination and won the presidential election. Leoni like Betancourt was one of the generation of '28, an effective politician but lacking the distinctive charisma of his predecessor. Leoni won over several familiar candidates: Caldera again ran for COPEI; Larrazábal ran with the endorsement of MENI and a newly formed group, the *Fuerza Democrática Popular* (FDP). Villalba ran himself with the URD endorsement. Several new faces appeared in the campaign, and diluted the party vote. One of the new candidates who ran was Raúl Ramos Giménez, a founder of AD who left in 1962 with the *Aristas* to form the AD-OP (*Acción Democrática en Oposición*). Another candidate was Arturo Uslar Pietri who ran under the independent group known as *Asociación Venezolano Independiente* (AVI). The voting in the 1963 presidential election is shown in Table 2-6.[20]

The PCV, which had supported Larrazábal in 1958, was declared illegal prior to the 1963 elections, and its supporters precipitated violence in both rural and urban areas. The students at the Central University of Caracas were instrumental in the process.

The elections of 1958 and 1963 illustrate the regional voting tendencies in Venezuela. Caracas was the weakest area for the AD

TABLE 2-6. PARTY VOTING IN PRESIDENTIAL ELECTION OF
DECEMBER, 1963

Candidate	Party	Vote	Percent
Leoni	AD	957,699	32.8
Caldera	COPEI	588,372	20.1
Villalba	URD	551,120	18.8
Uslar Pietri	AVI	469,240	16.0
Larrazábal	MENI-FDP	275,304	9.4
Ramos Giménez	AD-OP	66,837	2.2
Borregales	MAN	9,324	.3

in both elections. In 1958 it voted heavily for Larrazábal, partly because of his personalistic appeal as head of the *junta* and partly because of the URD endorsement. Uslar Pietri carried Caracas as an independent candidate in 1963 with the AVI label. A comparison of party voting in Caracas for 1958 and 1963 is shown in Table 2-7.[21]

In 1963, AD scored its heaviest vote in the Llanos-Guayana region, which is not only the most remote area in the nation, but one of the areas that benefited most from AD development programs since 1958. AD did well also in the Costal and Maracaibo regions. COPEI was the strongest in the Andes in both elections, an area where the Church is also relatively influential. COPEI showed heaviest gains in 1963 over 1958 in the Costal, Llanos, and Maracaibo areas, perhaps at the expense of AD, which declined almost in like amount in the same regions. Both COPEI and AD declined in the core area, although by a small margin in both cases. The URD also lost strength heavily in the core area due to the multitude of new party groupings. URD also declined in the Costal and Maracaibo regions, while gaining slightly in the Andes and Llanos regions. The regional dimension of national voting is compared in the Table 2-8.[22]

In both elections the Metropolitan Core area was most disposed to support minor political parties, and was most receptive to party proliferation. At the other extreme, the Andes region was least receptive to minor party activity. Minor party activity increased generally in 1963 over 1958, but the increase in the Metropolitan Core area and Maracaibo was spectacular. Pietri's AVI was responsible for the Metropolitan Core vote, as was Larrazábal and MENI-FDP in Maracaibo. There is no consistent correlation between population density of states and voting disposition, nor between proximity to the core area and voting. The major parties

TABLE 2-7. COMPARISON OF PARTY VOTING IN CARACAS FOR 1958 AND 1963

	1958		1963	
	Vote	Percent	Vote	Percent
AD	59,832	14.7	65,333	13.5
COPEI	64,734	15.8	50,655	10.5
URD	252,750	62.0	62,669	13.3
PVC	29,997	7.5		
AVI			191,028	39.1
MENI-FDP			98,129	20.5
AD-OP			8,357	1.9
MAN			2,285	1.3

TABLE 2-8. REGIONAL PARTY VOTING PATTERNS IN VENEZUELA, 1958–1963 (IN PERCENT)

REGIONS	AD 1958	AD 1963	COPEI 1958	COPEI 1963	URD 1958	URD 1963	OTHER 1958	OTHER 1963
Metro./Core	20.5	16.3	15.7	13.2	57.8	13.5	6.0	57.0
Costal	61.5	39.7	9.3	18.6	26.6	24.0	2.6	17.7
Llanos	68.2	45.0	8.1	15.3	21.2	26.1	2.5	13.6
Maracaibo	58.7	37.6	9.5	16.5	28.3	17.0	2.5	28.9
Andes	46.4	27.6	45.5	50.2	7.5	8.9	.6	13.3

are reasonably competitive throughout the nation despite their areas of special strengths.

Congressional representation for parties closely parallels voting patterns due to the highly sensitive proportional representation system used. Party representation, shown in Table 2-9, does not reflect the AD-OP and MIR defections from AD that occurred following the 1958 election. They were nullified somewhat by official AD gains in the 1963 election.[23]

With an election scheduled in 1968 for a new congress and president, dissension hit the AD once again in 1967 at the highest party echelons. The old guard of the AD chose for its 1968 presidential candidate the minister of government under the Leoni administration, Gonzalo Barrios. Another of AD's principal leaders, Luis Beltrán Prieto, wanted the nomination for himself, and withdrew from the party. His withdrawal was followed by another challenge of the old guard's right to use the label AD. His challenge failed, and he formed the *Movimiento Electoral del Pueblo* (MEP) to advance his presidential candidacy. The dissension of Prieto was another serious blow to AD unity, and critically weakened its position in the legislature during the final year of the Leoni administration. AD considered a coalition with the URD, but Villalba's price was high—approval of the presidential nominee—a condition AD was unwilling to accept. In the most intense, turbulent campaign of the recent series, four major candidates emerged for the Presidency:

(1) Gonzalo Barrios, official candidate of the AD. By background, Barrios was a lawyer and writer.

(2) Luis Beltrán Prieto Figueroa, one of the founders of AD, he withdrew to form the MEP and challenge Barrios' candidacy.

(3) Miguel Angel Burelli Rivas, former AD ambassador under the Leoni regime to London and Bogotá and former minister of justice under Betancourt, he returned to Caracas to seek the presi-

TABLE 2-9. PARTY REPRESENTATION IN VENEZUELAN LEGISLATURE, 1947–1963

	SENATE						DEPUTIES							
	1948	Percent	1958	Percent	1963	Percent	1947	Percent	1948	Percent	1958	Percent	1963	Percent
AD	38	86	32	63	21	46	137	87	83	65	73	56	65	37
COPEI	6	13	6	12	9	20	19	12	38	30	19	15	40	22
URD	1	.5	11	22	7	15	2	.5	4	3	34	24	29	15
PCV	1	.5	2	3			2	.5	3	2	7	5		
FDP					4	9							16	8
AD-OP					1	2							5	3
IPFN					3	7							20	11
MENI													1	2
PSV													1	2
Total	46		51		45		160		128		133		177	

dency. He received support from a coalition known as the *Frente Tripartido* (FT), comprised of Villalba's URD, the *Frente Democrático Popular* (FDP) created in 1962 to further the candidacy of Larrazábal, and the *Frente Nacional Democrático* (FND) founded in 1964 from the numerous parties and groups which supported the 1964 presidential candidacy of Arturo Uslar Pietri.

(4) Rafael Caldera, perpetual candidate of COPEI, again sought the nation's highest office.

Two additional candidates entered the race: Alejandro Hernández as candidate of the weak *Partido Socialista* (PS), and Germán Borregales, another perpetual candidate who drew support in 1968 from the *Movimiento de Acción Nacional* (MAN), an ultrarightist group. Besides the presidential candidates and their respective party groups, five more groups nominated candidates at a national level for the congressional elections. Included among these were: *Partido Revolucionario de Integración Nacionalista* (PRIN), a combination of two previous factions (AD-OP and PRN) from AD; the *Unión para Avanzar* (UPA), an electoral front for the illegal Communist party; the *Cruzada Cívica Nacionalista* (CCN), a political movement successfully led by the former dictator Pérez Jiménez as a candidate for the Senate from Caracas; the *Movimiento Demócrato Independiente* (MDI) and *Alianza Liberal Venezolana* (ALVE) also participated. At the local and state level, even more groups presented candidates for municipal and statewide offices.

The long and intense campaign exposed the most remote areas of Venezuela to party activity. An estimated 22 million dollars were spent on the campaign by the four leading presidential candidates alone, which brought the campaign cost for a nation of 10 million people surprisingly close to the cost of a presidential campaign in the United States. The government spent another estimated 15 million dollars organizing the election. Almost 100 thousand Venezuelans participated in one way or another in campaign work. The campaign was essentially peaceful, and voting proceeded without serious incident. Appeals made by the candidates and parties were largely personalistic. International observers from the OAS supplemented the party observers to guarantee impartiality.

The election produced a significant shift in Venezuelan politics. COPEI's Caldera won the presidency by a narrow margin, upsetting AD's organization for the first time in Venezuelan history. The unofficial results of the balloting are given in Table 2-10.[24]

The lesson of the 1968 election could hardly be ignored by AD. Continuation of the historical trend of division and factional-

TABLE 2-10. PARTY VOTING IN PRESIDENTIAL ELECTION OF
DECEMBER 1, 1968

Candidate	Party	Vote	Percent
Caldera	COPEI	1,075,375	29.05
Barrios	AD	1,044,081	28.21
Burelli	FT	825,233	22.29
Prieto	MEP	716,820	19.36

ization could no longer be absorbed by the AD plurality. If the party were to win, it must first reestablish its unity and again attract some of the dissident elements that had left the party. AD has begun an intensive campaign to win the younger generation, a cause long neglected by the old guard. Meanwhile, Caldera must form a working coalition since COPEI lacks a majority in the legislature.

Party politics in Venezuela is a volatile, boisterous process, which is changing rapidly within the framework of a multi-party loose system. The likelihood of COPEI capturing a dominant position seems remote, as also does the probability that AD may again recapture its predominant position. Personalism, lenient electoral laws, and a tradition of transient political parties with little claim to historical permanence, still shape Venezuela's brief experience with representative government. Nevertheless, the changes wrought by party activity on the political culture seem irreversible. Venezuela has reached, perhaps, a political plateau where imposed government or totalitarianiam seems intolerable and unlikely. It could be argued that the political system has been experiencing a degree of modernization more characteristic of the economic system. The result is a roughly hewn, noisy, and perhaps awkward political system that lacks subtlety and grace, but works amazingly well for all its problems. With the most modest of historical credentials, Venezuela has evolved a system of modern political parties, sensitive to public demands and basic issues, and functionally significant to government decision-making.

II. BRAZIL: PARLIAMENTARY AND MILITARY POLITICS

Brazilian politics, like the nation itself, defies analogy to the rest of Latin America. Contemporary party politics is a period limited by 1946 and 1964, preceded by the 15 year civilian dictatorship of Getúlio Vargas and followed by the military imposed regimes of Marshall Humberto Castelo Branco (1964–1967) and General Artur da Costa e Silva (1967–1969). Lacking military interference, party behavior would probably continue in the 1946–1964 pattern, but today the nation is without significant party activity or elections. This analysis is based on the 1946–1964 model that I shall term the parliamentary period. It is conceivable that Brazil may again return to the politics of the parliamentary period; it is also conceivable, if less likely, that the present regime may institutionalize a political system with a minimum of electoral and party activity. It is premature to view current political institutions as anything beyond a highly transitional juncture in Brazilian history.[25]

1. POLITICAL CULTURE AND CONTEXT OF PARTY ACTIVITY

The only Portuguese speaking nation in the western hemisphere, Brazil is also the largest nation in Latin America. Its population, about 90 million, is the eighth largest in the world and its area of 3.3 million square miles makes it the fifth largest in the world. Brazil is larger than continental United States, and nearly half the area of the South American continent. Brazil's population is increasing at a rate of 3.1 percent annually, with the urban areas growing at 5.4 percent annually. The nation is racially difficult to classify. There are strong regional foci to the population mixture, but few nations in the world with such disparate racial components have achieved the relative integration and harmony of Brazil. The country is culturally dominated by two great metropolitan centers: Rio de Janeiro and São Paulo. The cities reflect different faces of Brazil. The first is one of casualness, pleasure-seeking, intolerable urban problems, and economic dependence. The other in its more salubrious climate has an air of economic aggressiveness, hard working and living, with buildings and perspectives which look toward the sky. In its own way Brazil's new federal district, Brazilia, symbolizes the "new Brazil," a myth of "westward movement" and development that most Brazilians cherish but few pursue.[26]

Economic realities are important in shaping Brazil's political culture. The export economy is dominated (52 percent) by a single crop, coffee, that in past generations was preceeded by cacao and rubber. The domestic economy is relatively well industrialized; about 72 percent of the gross national product is industrial, 28 percent agricultural. The national economy is fairly self-sufficient, although not always productively efficient. The nation has tremendous opportunities for agricultural development, but like its neighbors falls short of taking advantage of its resources. Per capita income is low ($225) and unevenly distributed among classes and regions. The growth rate is unstable, falling disastrously low in the latter period of parliamentary rule (1960–1964) to less than annual population increases. Generally the economy has been unstable, thanks to soft export commodities, intolerably high inflation, rapidly rising cost of living, and manipulation of the monetary system.

Brazil, like Mexico, had a nineteenth-century monarchy. Mexico's lasted but a few years, and was imposed by France. Brazil's lasted until 1889, almost the final decade of the nineteenth century, and was reasonably popular and successful. Following the empire, Brazil launched the First Republic with a constitution carefully modeled after the United States, but with a style that was oligarchic and regionalistic. National political parties were nonexistent. During the 41 years of the First Republic (1889–1930) control rested in the hands of state political machines and dictators who built organizations called parties to maintain their regimes. These so-called republican parties convened periodically to select federal officials. The largest states of São Paulo and Minas Gerais were most influential, and alternated the presidency between them. The state governments served the limited commercial and agrarian interests of their regions.[27]

By 1920 protests to the system were increasing from newly emerging groups: industrial and commercial elites, urban proletariates, and others whose influence was superceding the traditional agrarian oligarchies. The economic chaos of the 1930 Great Depression caught Brazil in a classic situation of rising coffee production and sharply falling markets and prices. General unrest and revolts signaled the end of the Republic after the election of 1930, when President Washington Luis from São Paulo broke tradition and tried to impose another Paulista candidate on the nation. Minas Gerais leaders formed the Liberal Alliance and supported Governor Getúlio Vargas of Rio Grande do Sul for president. Although Vargas seemed to have lost the election, his supporters rejected the outcome and revolted in October, 1930. Shortly the military intervened and placed Vargas in power. He ruled with a *junta* until 1934 when a constituent assembly formalized his presidential role for four more years. In 1937 he assumed dictatorial powers that he retained until 1946. His policies were symbolized by a proto-fascist concept of an *Estado Novo* (New State) that stressed economic development.

Vargas recruited, cajoled, or intimidated state political machines until they came into his regime, but he never bothered to build the facade of a party system to lend legitimacy to his rule.[28]

Following World War II, under foreign and domestic pressure to restore constitutionality, Vargas called elections for late 1945 and permitted parties to organize. Military and other leaders doubted Vargas' resolve to transfer power, and forced him to resign his office. Vargas' hand-picked successor, General Eurico Gaspar Dutra, was easily elected, however, and ruled for five uneventful years. The new 1946 constitution reinforced the federal system, and while paying lip service to Vargas advocated social welfare reforms.

The Social Democratic party (PSD), founded by Vargas and led by Dutra, broke with its founder after winning office and pursued a colorless, conservative line. Vargas supporters rallied under the Brazilian Labor party (PTB), while the remaining anti-Vargas elements formed the National Democratic Union (UDN). The Communist party was outlawed and the Dutra regime curtailed labor organizations. The three parties continued to dominate, if not control, party politics until the 1964 revolution, but their cohesion was always weak and their structure poorly organized.[29]

Vargas, whose popular appeal remained, ran successfully for the presidency in October, 1950, but his PTB failed to gain control of the Congress that remained in conservative hands. The end of the Korean War brought another economic recession to Brazil, and once again Vargas was faced with growing discontent and unrest, and pressure from the military to resign. Instead he chose suicide. Vice President João Café Filho assumed power for a brief 15 month interim. Vargas' second term was generally undistinguished, frustrated, and toward its close scandalized over an alleged plot to murder one of his political opponents, journalist Carlos Lacerda.[30]

With the endorsement of the PSD, Juscelino Kubitschek successfully bid for the presidency in 1955. A melodramatic period that included a "preventative" military coup preceded Kubitschek's innauguration, and cast doubt on the legitimacy of his regime. The new president pledged "50 years of progress in 5," and came impressively close to realizing it. He passed numerous Vargas-type reforms, tried to strengthen the economy, and symbolized his crusade by planning a new federal capital inland, away from the congested and exhausted capital of Rio. Kubitschek's policies were visionary but expensive, and extracted a heavy toll from the country in the form of an uncontrolled inflation. Kubitschek, who by constitutional law could not succeed himself, witnessed the election to the presidency of one of his strongest political opponents, Jânio da Silva Quadros.[31]

Quadros' election in 1960 was supported by many parties, including the strong UDN. Quadros, an enigmatic and mercurial figure, had no strong party affiliation of his own. To the surprise and dismay of the nation, Quadros resigned in August, 1961, for still unclear reasons. The vice president, the radical and opportunistic Goulart, assumed office. Opposed by Kubitschek, Lacerda, the military, and many Brazilian leaders, Goulart struggled to remain in power through the congressional elections of October, 1962. Worsening domestic and international controversies plagued the final months of Goulart's administration. To avoid being removed from office, Goulart accepted a compromise revision of the constitution imposed by his opponents and the military, which established a presidential-premier form of parliamentary government. Goulart was finally forced from office in April, 1964, by a quick military revolution that installed Marshall Castelo Branco in power.[32]

Castelo Branco was formally designated "president" by an intimidated Congress, and national elections were set for October, 1965. The new president signed a series of harsh decrees, imposing economic austerity, outlawing party activity, and disenfranchizing hundreds of well-known political leaders. The 1965 elections were postponed for a year, and the president's term extended. The government decided to create two new parties for the elections rather than permit the old ones to participate. The new official party won about two-thirds of the legislative seats, and the new Congress dutifully elected Marshall Branco's carefully selected successor, General Artur da Costa e Silva.

The new president took office in late 1966, and pledged his regime to continued strengthening of the economy and gradual easing of the harsher aspects of the regime. He was able to continue the policies of economic recovery and development, but failed to achieve a more normal political situation. Strikes, protests, and several political intrigues in 1968 brought Brazil to a crisis stage again. Civilian, militant right-wing extremists began tormenting suspected communists, apparently with the acquiescence of the military. Under considerable military pressure, the president finally dissolved the increasingly unmanageable congress, imposed a rule of decree and again placed his country in the hands of a military dictatorship.[33]

From this brief resume of recent Brazilian party politics it is fairly clear that even by Latin American standards Brazil's experience with popular government and party politics has been limited and chaotic. Political parties and elections have been a post-World War II product. The failure of the parties to congeal by natural processes the diverse, disparate national political interests has had two significant results for Brazil. First the party system has been closely tied and dependent upon strong political personalities whose influence is often clearly tied to state or regional levels. The party system has also developed a strong propensity to factionalize, and reconsolidate through transient electoral coalitions. There are many institutional and historical forces working against the consolidation of parties and the political system, but this is true for many other Latin American nations. The principal cause of the Brazilian experience is the dissipation of political interests, and the fragmentation and heterogeneity of Brazilian society and territory. The military balances these interests with its own, and has struck national political institutions repeatedly in 1930, 1945, 1954, 1955, 1961, 1964 and 1968. Military opportunism and cynicism combined with ineffective civilian leadership to bring Brazil close to civil war several times in the twentieth century.[34]

2. REPRESENTATION AND ELECTIONS

Brazil is a federal system with 22 states, 3 territories, and the Federal District of Brasilia. During the parliamentary period most governmental offices were elected. A simple plurality sufficed for the national president and vice president, the state governors, and the local mayors (prefects). Proportional representation and multimember districts elected national and state deputies, and the municipal councilmen (*vereadores*). Each state elected, at large, its national deputies, and this contributed to the personalistic inclinations of the parties. Deputies had to be well known and identified within the large state, not just at the level of a small electoral district. Local assemblies and a council were also elected at large from the municipalities.

Parties could register or nominate as many candidates as there were offices to be filled. Prior to 1962, no official, government ballot was printed. Ballots were distributed and printed by parties until 1962 when states and some local municipalities tried to print their own ballots. Candidates were assigned numbers which grouped them in categories, not unlike the system of *sub-lemas* used in Uruguay. The voter entered both the name and number of his preferred candidates. Numbering became necessary as candidates proliferated. In São Paulo, almost one thousand candidates ran for 115 positions in 1962.

Votes were tallied for all candidates of a party, and seats assigned parties by a conventional electoral quotient and highest average formula. A voter had alternatives in voting. For multi-member Senate races, he could vote for several candidates; for the Chamber of Deputies, he was allowed to vote for only one, although the districts were also multimember. He could also cast a straight party ballot for all candidates, but fewer than one percent of the voters normally did.

The defense of the Brazilian electoral system is that the voter, rather than the party, retained the prerogative of selecting which candidates would be seated. The system might be described as incorporating a primary within a general election. Inhibited party growth resulted from denying parties one of their strongest techniques for enforcing unity: the ability to determine hierarchy in the electoral list. The system encouraged candidates to run not only against opposition candidates, but also against colleagues from his own party, since election depended not just on the fate of the party but also on the relative strength of a candidate's vote vis-à-vis his colleagues. Since disqualification of a colleague would raise a candidate's chances for receiving a legislative seat, Brazilian politicians, during the parliamentary period, were as likely to challenge the election of a party colleague as they were to challenge an opposition party candidate. Candidates were in effect rewarded by the system for waging personalistic campaigns, while receiving few, if any, rewards for party cohesion. This process screened candidates, recruiting those who by nature or personality were adroit at building a strong personalistic following.

Personalism promoted wide ideological mixtures in nearly all Brazilian parties. Contrary to the familiar argument that multi-party systems promote extreme, doctrinaire political appeals, Brazil's personalistic politics produced parties with little if any ideological commitment. Urban campaigning, especially, was intensely personal as individuals curried the favor of large electorates through modern communications techniques. The personal components of the elections were so strong that rarely, if ever, could a single party capture a majority of the vote in any district, even single-member districts.[35]

Financial problems also reinforced the personal basis of party politics. Campaigns were organized and financed normally by the candidate rather than the party. Less than independently wealthy candidates had to reach compromises with financial interests to lend the necessary financial support to the campaign. Statewide campaigns were expensive, and participation was restricted to those whose personal chances of victory were sufficient to attract the necessary financial resources. While overdrawn, perhaps, there is an analogy between Brazilian campaigns during the parliamentary period and those in the nineteenth-century United States.

Representation followed the federal plan. An equal number of senators (3) were allotted to each state. Senators had eight-year terms, with one, then two, being elected alternately from each state every four years. States also received a minimum of seven deputies, the territories one. Additional deputies were awarded for each 250 thousand inhabitants. Deputies served four-year terms, and were all elected simultaneously.[36]

Some of the confusion of Brazilian elections was due to the 1945 electoral code, which was revised continually until the 1964 revolution. Originally, a candidate could run for as many offices at one time as he wished, although he could hold only one. In 1950 this was changed to require that all offices be from one state. Prior to 1958 voters did not use official ballots but could deposit any slip of paper with the candidate's name on it in the official envelope and ballot box. Accurate, not to mention efficient, tabulation was nearly impossible.

Literacy has always been required to vote in Brazil, which automatically disqualifies nearly 50 percent of those who otherwise could meet the necessary legal requirements. More significantly, it disqualified groups and interests selectively.

Political parties since 1945 have been regulated as organic entities of the state. Parties were formalized through a petition process, with signatories having to be distributed more or less evenly across the nation. Requirements, however, were nominal. Individuals had to meet age, citizenship, and language requirements to become candidates. The requirement to be Portuguese-speaking excluded many civic leaders in southern Brazil who spoke primarily their European language. Candidates had to run with endorsement of a registered party, and parties could be declared dissolved if they failed to receive a minimum vote in the preceding election.[37]

Administration of elections and resolution of electoral disputes lay in the hands of electoral courts, presided over by the national electoral tribunal. Courts were established at various levels: states, regions, and territories. Even polling places had structures designed to resolve disputes. Polling places were required to register a minimum of 50 and a maximum of 300 in urban areas, 400 in state capitals. Party observers were provided for each polling area. Voting was compulsory, fines were required of those not voting. In practice enforcement of voting was impossible. Extensive changes were made prior to the 1966 elections by the military regime, particularly designed to limit party participation and assign greater power and authority to administrative electoral courts. Many changes in electoral law were politically inspired.

3. Political Parties, Coalitions, and Groups

All major parties are new since 1945. Of the dozen or so principal ones, only three (PSD, PTB, UDN) are strong enough to be considered national. Two of these, the PSD and PTB, were inspired by Vargas. The former is more conservative, although the difference is not truly ideological. The remaining parties are regionalistic, personalistic, or limited to a single state. During the parliamentary period, parties factionalized increasingly, and were weak in structure, ideology, discipline, and allegiances.[38]

Partido Social Democrático (PSD). The PSD emerged with Vargas' support prior to his resignation in 1945 as a politician's party. It was comprised of state political machines and leaders upon whom the Vargas regime had relied. Many of its supporters were conservative, an establishment which tried to preserve rather than provoke the status quo. Political power was the principal aim of the party, and its leaders were experienced in using it. Rural and agrarian interests affiliated with the party, but urban areas remained aloof. The PSD elected General Eurico Gaspar Dutra in 1945 and Juscelino Kubitschek in 1956. Through its vast patronage, the PSD remained in power or close to power throughout the parliamentary period. A brief coalition with the other Vargas party, the PTB, proved unworkable. In later years the PSD's power was eroded considerably by the rising importance of uban interests in Brazilian life. Most state governments and governors, however, remained PSD. The eagerness of PSD leaders to reach a compromise with those who held power in order to retain their patronage, produced an unfortunate popular image of the party, and probably contributed to its gradual decline and chronic factionalization. Geographically, the party was most successful in the state of Minas Gerais, with considerable influence also in Maranhão, Bahia, Ceará, and Goiás.

It was normally weak in the critical states of São Paulo, Rio de Janeiro, Guanabara, and Pernambuco.

Partido Trabalhista Brasileiro (PTB). Vargas viewed the PTB as his personal vehicle because its support came through broadly based lower classes and could challenge the appeals of other mass parties, particularly Marxist ones. The PTB was organized originally by Vargas' minister of labor and his employees.[39] Despite its proletarian base, the PTB also drew support from many additional sectors, including influential, wealthy leaders who saw the PTB as a good long-range investment. Geographically, the PTB found its strongest support in the relatively rural state of Rio Grande do Sul, but it fought to establish a strong front in more industrialized states like São Paulo and Minas Gerais. Prior to the 1964 revolution, the PTB had made inroads in the large states of Rio de Janeiro and Guanabara, as well as Paraná, Bahia, and Pernambuco.

Like the PSD, the PTB was crippled by divisive factions and internal divisions. Many divisions were produced by personal animosities rather than ideological differences. One faction, dominated by Fernando Ferrari, a leading PTB deputy, tried to transform the PTB into a true labor movement committed to social and economic reform. Another leader, João Goulart, tried to use the PTB as a personal vehicle for his political ambitions. Following the 1964 revolution the party split, like most Brazilian parties, over whether to cooperate with the new regime.

União Democrática Nacional (UDN). The National Democratic Union was also formed in 1945, but by anti-Vargas military and civilian leaders. It participated in the effort to remove Vargas, but failed to impose its own candidate as his successor. The UDN remained in opposition until 1960, when its candidate Jânio Quadros won the presidency. Quadros, however, had not previously been associated with any party.

A party united primarily by its opposition to most contemporary trends in Brazil, it lacked personal and ideological fervor. Voting for the UDN declined even more rapidly than for the other two major parties. Regionally its strength lay in Minas Gerais, Bahia, Guanabara, Santa Catarina, and the northeastern states of Ceará, Pernambuco, and Paraíba. While political radicalism was strongest in the northeast, UDN support came from orthodox residents of the area who were not disenfranchised by literacy requirements or other devices. The party was weak in the larger, southern states. Political machines in many rural areas were controlled by

UDN sympathizers, and many middle-class urban Brazilians affiliated with it. One of its most articulate spokesmen was Carlos Lacerda, former governor of Guanabara, who was a constant government critic during the parliamentary period.

Besides the three major parties there are an additional dozen or so minor ones of some significance. Most are regionally localized. São Paulo was the most receptive of the states to minor parties; none of the three major ones were ever successful in appealing for the state's votes. Below are summarized some of the principal minor parties.[40]

Partido Social Progressista (PSP). The Social Progressive party emerged in 1946 as a vehicle for the governor of São Paulo, Adhemar de Barros. An unusual figure, known and perhaps admired for his extravagant corruption, the governor appealed to lower classes for his support. Adhemar de Barros ran for president several times, once receiving nearly two million votes, but the influence of the party was declining in the latter days of the parliamentary period.

Partido Democrata Cristão (PDC). The Christian Democrats organized in 1948, and immediately began to divide over ideological questions. While liberal in doctrine, the PDC's anticommunism has alienated many reformers and even moderate Brazilian elements viewed as crypto-communist, a term that occasionally becomes synonymous with secular. Its 1955 candidate for the presidency, General Juárez Távora, received the UDN endorsement in the campaign against Kubitschek. In return the PDC joined the UDN to endorse Quadros in 1960; Quadros had once been associated with the PDC. By 1962, prior to the military intervention, the PDC showed signs of growth, increasing its congressional vote in that year to become the nation's fourth largest party.

Partido Socialista Brasileiro (PSB). The Socialist party emerged in 1946 as a splinter of the UDN after Vargas' resignation. The party drew support from intellectuals, many refugees from the outlawed Communist party. The PSB failed to evolve a basis for a mass appeal, however, and its total strength declined perceptively prior to the 1964 revolution.

Partido Republicano (PR). The Republican party traces its origins to the nineteenth century when it organized to oppose the monarchy. It continued during the First Republic as a loose confederation of state political organizations lacking doctrine and national leadership. The little strength the party retains is localized in Bahia and Minas Gerais. Despite a brief surge in voting between 1954 and 1958, the PR's influence declined during the parliamentary period. The PR entered into alliances with the PSD and PTB, and supported Kubitschek in 1955.

Partido Liberator (PL). Like the PR the PL is an artifact of the First Republic, formed originally to demand a secret ballot and semiparliamentary system. The former was achieved in 1945, the latter in 1961, so its ideological justification evaporated. Led by Raul Pilla, the PL's support was limited to Rio Grande do Sul.

Partido de Repaesentação Popular (PRP). An extreme right-ist group, the PRP emerged from the proto-Fascist Integralist Action movement, complete with storm troops and demands for a "cultural revolution." Led by Plínio Salgado, the PRP's personal-istic appeals were limited to the states of São Paulo and Rio Grande do Sul. In a gesture of self-justification the party recently described itself as "antifascist, anticommunist, antitotalitarian, and anti-liberal." Opposition is its fundamental reason for existing.

Four additional parties won seats in the 1962 election. All tried to obtain support from the labor movement, but none truly suc-ceeded. All are also local in their appeals. The parties include *Movimiento Trabalhista Renovador* (MTR), a splinter of the PTB led by Fernando Ferrari in opposition of the Goulart control over PTB. The *Partido Trabalhista Nacional* (PTN) is from São Paulo, led originally by Emilio Carlos and following his death briefly by Jânio Quadros. The *Partido Social Trabalhista* (PST) and *Partido Republicano Trabalhista* (PRT) are also centered in São Paulo, with support also in Rio de Janeiro.

The *Partido Comunista Brasilero* (PCB) was formed in 1922, and was legally permitted to participate from 1945 to 1947. Waves of anticommunism have characterized Brazilian history, sweeping under many moderate as well as hard-core Marxist reformers. Al-though legally banned, the PCB leaders were generally free during the parliamentary period to travel, speak and engage in restricted party activity.

Even the Communist party has been highly personalistic in Brazil. One of its most famous leaders, Luis Carlos Prestes, was a popular, charismatic military leader who returned from Moscow in 1934 to assume leadership of the party. In an effort to remove Vargas, the party encouraged a revolt in 1935 that failed, and ended its brief period of legality. Prestes was imprisoned from 1935 to 1946, when he resumed leadership of the PCB. Like other com-munist parties, the PCB has vacillated and divided ideologically over the years. During the Stalinist period, it was militantly revolutionary; since it has become more evolutionary. Following the rise of Castro a group of its supporters reoriented themselves to a pro-Castro, pro-Peking form of communism, and founded the alternative *Partido Comunista do Brazil* (PCdB). The PCdB sponsored peasant leagues in the impoverished northeastern areas, urging political and paramilitary techniques to secure their demands for improved economic and social conditions. Student groups affiliated with the movement until the government took strenuous measures to crush it. Although often a vigorous movement, the Brazilian Communists have never been a threat electorally or even politically to the regime.

Coalitional Groups. More than in any Latin American nation, Brazil has truly a "group basis" for politics. One manifestation of this is the significance of electoral and legislative coalitions to endorse candidates, form election fronts, close legislative ranks, or oppose government measures. Coalitional groups are comprised of many parties and other interest groups whose leaders cooperate on normally transient, but mutual interests. A catalog of Brazilian coalitions would be extravagant, but a few illustrations can indicate the meaning of the concept in Brazil.

Party coalitional groups are formed between minor parties or with a major party to compensate for differences in regional strength. The intensity of coalitional activity varied considerably during the parliamentary period. In 1962, 39.7 percent of all votes cast were for party alliances. The level ranged from 98.4 percent of all votes cast in the territory of Amapá to practically none in the states of Santa Catarina, Amazonas, and Paraíba. Coalitional activity has been particularly common in the states of Sergipe, Rio Grande do Norte, Espírito Santo, and São Paulo. Some coalitions acquire political cohesion, but most disintegrate. Only a few survive an election, primarily at the state rather than national level.

One national coalition of importance during the parliamentary period was the *Ação Democrática Parlamentar* (ADP), composed of UDN and PSD members opposed to the influence of another alliance, the FPN, and led by a PTB deputy (Sergio Magalhães) during the Goulart administration. With the military intervention of 1964, most FPN members were purged from Congress. At that point, the ADP group merged with the adherents of the *Bloco Parlamentar Revolucionário* (BPR) to form the nucleus of the official government party, ARENA. The original ARENA group combined 48 PSD, 23 PTB, and 90 UDN deputies. Each of these party coalitions was also fragmented into smaller groups. For example, the liberal FPN was divided in part by the *Groupo Compacto* or Compact Group, mostly left-wing PTB members led by Almino Afonso of Amazonas. Coalitional division, cohesion, and realignment was a perpetual process in parliamentary Brazil.[41]

Factional coalitional groups are alliances that have been formed by party members (or factions) within the parties. Ideologies and personalities are the basis for the factions. An illustration would be the *Ala Moca*, or Young Turks movement that arose in the PSD during the Kubitschek administration. As the name implies, the members were younger, more radical than their elder counterparts in the PSD leadership. The group later became known as the *invisibles*, from 1958 to 1962. Another intraparty coalition emerged in the UDN from a progressive wing, known curiously as the *Bossa Nova*. The group supported Quadros.

Interest group coalitions have been formed by political activists who did not hold elected office. One such group was the *Aliança Electoral pela Famila* (ALEF) or Family Electoral Alliance. The ALEF was a Catholic lay organization that endorsed candidates on the basis of their position on "questions of special concern to church-minded catholics." The group supported the 1964 revolution. A similar group was the *Cruzada Feminina Democrática* (CFD) a group of "anticommunist" women in São Paulo who in March, 1964, staged a "March of the Family with God for Freedom" designed to embarrass and weaken the Goulart government, which it probably did. The Military Club, a national organization of army officers located in Rio, has a history of political meddling. Other groups include the *Comissão Permanente das Organizações Sindicais* (CPOS), a federation of politically active trade unions; the *Confederação Nacional de Comércio* (CNC), a national business organization sympathetic to the Vargas type programs; the *Confederação Ruralista Brasileira* (CRB), a broadly based landowners group of about 250 thousand, centered in São Paulo and Minas Gerais. A group known as the *Liga Cristão de Camponesas* (LCC), an association of tenant farmers, formed to counteract a more radical group led by Father Melo in the northeastern area to achieve land reform.

These are but a small sampling of some of the groups that emerged in the latter days of the parliamentary regime. Their impact on national politics varied, and many were short lived. But they reveal the complexity of Brazilian political life, and the transient qualities of its political organizations.

4. Political Parties Under the Military

Following the 1964 military intervention, political party activity was outlawed. Many political leaders lost their political rights, or were imprisoned. Prior to the national elections of 1966, two new political parties were formed, and tolerated by the regime. The new party system was decreed in October, 1965, and preparations begun for the elections.

The dominant party, known as the official or government party, is the National Renovating Alliance, or ARENA. The opposition is the Brazilian Democratic Movement, or MDB. ARENA is supported by UDN and PSD elites, the MBD by PTB and PDC adherents, although individual leaders from most parties are found in both alliances. ARENA won two-thirds of the legislative seats in 1966, and all state offices. Both new "parties" are very unstable, and really secondary to other matters. There are indications that were the government to permit free party activity, the two new parties would collapse and older organizations would reappear.

Party politics in Brazil parallels closely the stereotype of the multi-party system: constant factionalization and proliferation of parties, transitional structures, opportunistic coalitions, intense personalism, strong regionalism and localism. For all its static, Brazilian party politics has always been essentially elitist, most groups being sensitive to economic and political demands in an electoral but not policy context. A strong argument can be made that the parties reflect the fragmented nature of contemporary Brazil; it also can be argued that institutional and legal frameworks supported the cultural tendencies through the electoral system, voting procedures, and registration requirements. The current two parties are artificial and unstable, imposed and maintained by a military regime frightened by the prospect of open party competition.

5. Voting and Participation in Recent Elections

Voting and participation patterns are influenced by political regionalism in Brazil.[42] The principal regions and their components are the following:

South. This region contains over one-third of the national population, the state and city of São Paulo, as well as the states of Rio Grande do Sul, Paraná, Santa Catarina, and the cities of Pôrto Alegre, Curitiba, Santos, and Santo André. Temperate and seasonal in climate, the South racially is 87 percent white. The region produces a greater variety and quantity of goods than many Latin American nations, with 61 percent of its output industrial. The PTB is strong in the region, receiving up to one-third of the congressional delegation, with the PSD and UDN secondarily important. The state of São Paulo, as has been discussed, is subject to minor party activity.

East. The East contains 34 percent of the population, about half of the population is in urban areas. The principal states are Guanabara (essentially the city of Rio), Minas Gerais, Bahia, and Espírito Santo. While less economically productive than the South, this region is growing rapidly in heavy industry, including iron, steel, coal, petroleum, and hydroelectric power. The mountains of Minas Gerais contain over one-fourth of the world's iron deposits. Like the South, participation in politics is high. Party voting is more dissipated than in the South, with the PSD, UDN, and PTB showing greatest strength in that order. The three parties are more competitive in this region than in the South.

Center-west. With 22 percent of the national land area, this region has only 4 percent of its population and 3 percent of the national income. The region includes the states of Goiás, Mato Grosso, and the Federal District of Brazilia. Urban areas, besides the Federal District, include the rapidly growing city of Goiânia, and Campo Grande. Climatically temperate, this region is ideally suited for habitation and agriculture. The principal industries are agriculture, cattle, and some mining. Participation is lower in politics than the South and East; with the PSD virtually having dominated its politics. The UDN was a distant competitor.

North. The North contains 42 percent of the territory but only 4 percent of the national population. About 62 percent of the area is rural, with four-fifths of the population living within 20 miles of the great Amazon River and its tributaries. The component states of the region include Pará, Amazonas, Acre, and the territories of Rondônia, Amapá, and Roraima. The major cities are Belém, Manaus, and Macapá. A tropical zone, the population is a mixture of white, Indian, and *mestizo*. The economy is agricultural and extractive with little industry. Principal products are rubber, nuts, lumber. Voting is below the national mean, with many small parties competing. The PTB is particularly influential in Amazonas, the PSD in Pará.

Northeast. The Northeast contains 21 percent of the national population, 66 percent of which is rural. The population spans a coastal belt, with principal cities of Recife, Fortaleza, Natal,

Maceio, and João Pessoa. The states include Pernambuco, Ceará, Maranhão, Paraíba, Paiuí, Alagoas, Rio Grande do Norte, and the territory of Fernando de Noronha. The population is more than 50 percent Negro, Indian, and mixtures therefrom. Economically the region is depressed. The major political parties are competitive in the area, although the PCdB is also active in forming Peasant Leagues.

A resume of the regional characteristics and their correlation to voting by party is given in Table 2-11.

Participation of eligible voters is generally high in Brazil. During the parliamentary period, the high was reached (92.3 percent) in the 1958 legislative elections, the low in the 1963 plebiscite (66.2 percent). National voting participation patterns are reasonably uniform throughout the nation.[43] In the 1962 legislative elections, the voter participation mean nationally was 79.6 percent; the lowest turnout experienced was 64.2 percent in the northeastern state of Maranhão. The median participation level for the same election

TABLE 2-11. REGIONAL CHARACTERISTICS AND VOTING IN BRAZIL

Region and states	Percent pop.	Percent area	Percent income	Percent urban	Party voting in 1962 (percent)	
SOUTH						
São Paulo, Rio Grande do Sul, Paraná, Santa Catarina	36	10	50	51	PTB PSD UDN	29 21 15
EAST						
Minas Gerais, Bahia, Rio, Guanabara, Espírito Santo, Sergipe, Serra dos Aimorés	34	15	36	49	PSD UDN PTB	29 27 24
CENTER-WEST						
Goiás, Mato Grosso, Federal District	4	22	3	35	PSD UDN	48 29
NORTH						
Pará, Amazonas, Acre, 3 territories	4	42	2	38	PTB PSD	41 41
NORTH-EAST						
Pernambuco, Ceará, Maranhão, Paraíba, Piauí, Alagoas, Rio Grande do Norte, 1 territory	21	11	9	34	PSD PTB UDN	30 30 30

TABLE 2-12. NATIONAL VOTING PARTICIPATION, 1945–1963

Election	Percent population registered	Percent population voting	Percent eligible participating
1945, Presidential	16.1	13.4	83.1
1950, Presidential	22.0	15.9	72.1
1954, Legislative	26.5	17.3	65.5
1955, Presidential	26.1	15.6	59.7
1958, Legislative	22.0	20.3	92.3
1960, Presidential	21.9	17.7	81.0
1962, Legislative	24.6	19.6	79.1
1963, Plebiscite	23.9	15.8	66.2

was an impressive 75.6 percent for the states. Table 2-12 summarizes participation patterns in Brazil from 1945 to 1963.[44]

There was no clear trend for participation during the parliamentary period; fluctuation from election to election was reasonably small. Yet even at the highest level of participation, literacy requirements prevented more than 20 percent of the national population from voting. By comparison, about 36 percent of the national population participated in the 1964 presidential election in the United States, about twice the percentage as in Brazil. From these figures, taking into consideration other demographic factors, an estimated 50 percent of Brazil's adult population are disenfranchised by literacy requirements. With this exception, participation is about that of the United States. Participation at the state and regional level is given in Table 2-13. While eligibility is lower outside the South and East, lower participation is also a reflection of the political cultures in the remaining regions. Participation of eligible voters, as well as participation from the total population, is markedly lower outside the two higher regions of the South and East.

Four presidential elections were held during the parliamentary period: 1945, 1950, 1955, and 1960. Only in 1945 did the winner receive a majority of the vote. Two presidents, Dutra and Kubitschek, served their full terms; two, Vargas and Quadros, did not. In each of the elections between fifty and sixty percent of the total national vote came from four states—Guanabara, Rio Grande do Sul, São Paulo, and Minas Gerais, all in the eastern and southern regions. With no electoral college, candidates must focus campaigns to those areas where the population is most intense. Voting trends demonstrate how pivotal the four states are in electing presidents.

TABLE 2-13. STATE AND REGIONAL VOTING PARTICIPATION, 1962

Region and states	Percent Registered	Voting	Percent Population	Voting
SOUTH	83.5		22.1	
São Paulo		86.4		23.8
Rio Grande do Sul		86.7		23.6
Paraná		74.0		16.6
Santa Catarina		87.0		24.3
EAST	29.2		20.5	
Minas Gerais		80.6		19.3
Bahia		73.5		14.2
Rio de Janeiro		81.1		24.7
Guanabara		85.3		29.9
Espírito Santo		81.0		19.7
Sergipe		73.7		18.1
CENTER-WEST	69.7		17.4	
Goiás		67.4		16.1
Mato Grosso		72.1		18.7
*Federal District				
NORTH	72.3		13.0	
Pará		65.4		16.7
Amazonas		75.4		13.5
Acre		75.9		8.7
NORTHEAST	74.4		16.5	
Pernambuco		71.4		14.2
Ceará		74.4		18.3
Maranhão		72.1		18.7
Paraíba		76.4		14.9
Piauí		73.2		17.6
Alagoas		75.5		11.1
Rio Grande do Norte		77.7		20.9
NATIONAL	79.6		19.6	

* Residents of the Federal District were ineligible to vote.

Kubitschek was the only candidate to win while losing the state of São Paulo. The other three candidates carried either all four states, or enough votes to carry the four combined. The presidential voting is summarized in Table 2-14.

During the parliamentary period, two general trends affected the three major parties in legislative elections. Parties tended to become more competitive at the national level in each successive election. Major parties also successively lost votes to minor parties and coalitions. The general impact of these two trends is graphically revealed in Table 2-15. Distinct regional patterns characterize the major parties and alliances, with smaller or less populated states displaying a stronger tendency to conform to a single party. This

TABLE 2-14. SUMMARY OF PRESIDENTIAL VOTING, 1945–1960

Election	Candidate	Party	Percent national vote	Margin in 4 pivotal states
1945	Dutra	PSD	55.3	71.0
	Gomes	UDN	34.7	
	Others		9.8	
1950	Vargas	PTB	48.7	63.2
	Gomes	UDN	29.7	
	Machado	PSD	21.5	
	Other		.1	
1955	Kubitschek	PTB/PSD	35.6	20.5
	Távora	UDN/PDC	30.3	
	de Barros	PSP	25.8	
	Other		8.3	
1960	Quadros	UDN	48.3	78.2
	Lott	PTB/PSD	32.9	
	de Barros	PSP	18.8	

trait is seen in Table 2-16, which establishes a rank order for party voting by states in the 1962 election.

The Christian Democrats also had a regional focus to their appeal, with their support being drawn principally from São Paulo, where they received nine deputies, and Paraná.[45] Otherwise, the distribution of seats in the national legislature following the 1962 election paralleled closely the general regional strengths of the parties. The distribution of seats in the lower house is summarized in Table 2-17.

Since each state had an equal number of senators, the major parties had an advantage in winning Senate representation. Out of 66 senators elected in 1962, only 12 were outside the three major parties. In the lower chamber 53 percent of the representatives be-

TABLE 2-15. COMPARISON OF PARTY VOTING, 1945–1962
(IN PERCENT)

Party	1945	1950	1954	1958	1962
PSD	42	22	22	18	15
UDN	26	14	14	13	11
PTB	10	14	15	15	12
Other	21	32	44	46	47
Blank	1	18	5	8	15

NOTE: "Other" includes minor parties, local parties, and alliances.

TABLE 2-16. Rank Order of Party Voting by States, 1962 (in percent)

PSD		UDN		PTB	
1. Maranhão	64	1. Alagoas	47	1. Acre	47
2. Acre	48	2. Mato Grosso	40	2. Rio Grande do Sul	41
3. Goiás	43	3. Paraíba	35	3. Amazonas	34
4. Minas Gerais	36	4. Guanabara	26	4. Piauí	31
5. Paraíba	34	5. Bahia	25	5. Pernambuco	31

Alliances		Others	
1. Amapá	98	1. Rodonia	50
2. Rio Branco	98	2. Amazona	26
3. Espírito Santo	90	3. Maranhão	17
4. Rio Grande do Norte	89	4. Minas Gerais	8
5. Sergipe	89	5. São Paulo	7

longed to the major parties; in the Senate, 67 percent were from the same parties. Governorships, on the other hand, were often won by alliances, normally involving participation of one of the major parties. A summary of Senate representation and allocation of governorships as of 1962 is presented in Table 2-18. Alliances

TABLE 2-17. Distribution of Seats in Chamber of Deputies by Party, 1962

State	Total	PSD	UDN	PTB	PSP	PR	PST	PL	PTN	PRT	Other
Acre	7	4		3							
Alagoas	9	1	5	1	2						
Amazonas	7	2		3			2				
Bahia	31	10	9	7		3		1			1
Ceará	21	7	7	5				2			
Espírito Santo	8	2	1	2				2			
Goiás	13	7	2	2	2						
Guanabara	21	2	6	10			1				2
Maranhão	16	11	2		3						
Mato Grosso	8	3	4	1							
Minas Gerais	48	21	16	6	1	4					
Pará	10	4	2	2	2						
Paraíba	13	5	6	2							
Paraná	25	6	5	10							4
Pernambuco	24	3	7	11			1				2
Piauí	8	2	3	3							
Rio de Janeiro	21	5	3	8	2		2				1
Rio Grande-No.	7	2	2	1							2
Rio Grande-Sul	29	7	1	14				3			4
Santa Catarina	14	6	6	2							
São Paulo	59	8	7	8	9	2	2		6	3	13
Sergipe	7	1	3	2		1					
(Territories)											
Amapá	1				1						
Roraima	1			1							
Rondonia	1				1						
TOTAL	409	119	97	104	23	10	6	5	11	3	31

TABLE 2-18. DISTRIBUTION OF PARTY SENATORS AND GOVERNORS, 1962

STATE	Total	PSD	PDB	UDN	Other	GOVERNORSHIPS Party/Alliance	Percent vote
Acre	3	1	2			PTB	49
Alagoas	3		1	1	1 (PDC)	UDN	31
Amazonas	3		3			PTB/PST/PL PDC	53
Bahia	3		1		2 (PL, Ind)	PST/UDN/PTB PR	45
Ceará	3	2	1			UDN/PSD/PTN	58
Espírito Santo	3	1		1	1 (PSP)	UDN/PTB/PRP PDC/PSP	46
Goiás	3	3				PSD	50
Guanabara	3	1		1	1 (PSB)	UDN	36
Maranhão	3	3				PSD/UDN/PTN PL	58
Mato Grosso	3	1	1	1		UDN	43
Minas Gerais	3	1	1	1		UDN/PRT/PL	44
Pará	3	1		1	1 (PTN)	PSD/PDC/PTB	51
Paraíba	3	1	1	1		PSB/UDN/PL PTB	52
Paraná	3		2	1		PDC/PL	35
Pernambuco	3		3			PST	44
Piauí		1		2		PSD/UDN/PDC	49
Rio de Janeiro	3		1		2 (PSP, MTR)	PTB/PDC	29
Rio Grande do No.	3	1	1	1		PSD	54
Rio Grande do Sul	3	1		1	1 (PL)	PSD/PL/UDN PRP/PDC	37
Santa Catarina	3		2			PSD/PDC	50
São Paulo	3	1		1	1 (PTN)	PSP/PSD	38
Sergipe	3	1			2 (PR, Ind)	PSD	48

were important also in legislative elections. A summary of party disposition to enter into alliances in elections for the Chamber of Deputies and for gubernatorial elections in 1962 is shown in Table 2-19.[46]

Party inclination to participate in alliances for legislative elections is nearly directly related to the general success of the party in winning seats. Coalitional pressures may increase with electoral competiveness. The coalition is not an instrument with which minor parties challenge major ones, since major parties are more inclined to use it than minor ones. As of 1962, only eight out of 22 governors were elected by a single party: three from the PSD and UDN, and one from the PTB and PST. The remainder were elected by party coalitions. The UDN and PDC formed gubernatorial coalitions most easily, although the inclination for parties to do so was less than for legislative elections. This may be partly explained by the fact that in a gubernatorial election only one candidate can be elected, whereas in legislative elections where multi-member districts are used, several candidates can win from different parties.

As transient as coalitions are, some parties and alliances are

TABLE 2-19. ELECTORAL ALLIANCES OF PARTIES, 1962

PARTY	LOWER HOUSE		GUBERNATORIAL	
	Frequency	Index	Frequency	Index
PSD	14	.66	7	.31
UDN	13	.63	8	.33
PTB	10	.49	7	.31
PDC	9	.44	8	.33
PSP	8	.39	2	.09
PSB	8	.39	7	.31
PTN	6	.29	1	.05
PST	5	.25	2	.09
PRT	4	.20	1	.05
PR	4	.20	1	.05
PL	3	.15	6	.22
MTR	3	.15		
PRP	2	.10	2	.09

more common than others. In 1962 the PSD and UDN coalesced six times, the UDN and PTB four. In no instance did the PSD and PTB combine, despite their similar origins. When the PSD and UDN, two traditional rivals in rural areas, succeeded in cooperating, their mutual rewards were substantial since other parties found it nearly impossible to challenge them. The confusion produced by the coalitional process can reach astounding proportions. In Sergipe in 1962, the UDN/PTB/PST coalition included as one of its principal candidates a dissident PDS deputy and former PDS governor, while the opposition PSD/PR coalition was led by a dissident UDN federal deputy. In Ceará, both candidates for governor came from the UDN party, while in Piauí both were once members of the PSD.

One additional national election was held prior to the military intervention. On January 6, 1963, a plebicite was held to decide whether to retain or reject the mixed cabinet-presidential system the military had imposed on Goulart in September, 1961. Although participation was a low 66.2 percent, those voting rejected the system 77 percent to 17 percent, with 6 percent blank ballots.

After the intervention, elections were next held October 3, 1965. Eleven governors were elected, PSD candidates winning in 5 states, UDN in 5, and the PSP by a few votes won the state of Alagoas. Some interpreted the success of PSD candidates as an antigovernment vote, although the party was less than uniformly hostile to the regime. After several political crises, the government decreed a new party registration law in November, 1965, establishing ARENA and a "loyal" opposition party, MDB. The remaining 12 governors were scheduled for election in September 1966, the president in October, and the state legislatures in November.

ARENA dutifully nominated candidates acceptable to Castello Branco. Rather than risk a popular vote, the government decided to hold the presidential election in Congress. Its nominee, Costa e Silva, received 255 votes in the Chamber of Deputies, the remainder of the once 409 members either having been removed from office, or abstaining. In the legislative elections, ARENA captured 254 seats, MDB 149, leaving 4 independents and 2 vacancies. A new constitution was promulgated following the election.

6. Conclusion

The military has assumed an awesome task in Brazil: the remaking of the entire political system. The problems of the parliamentary period were obvious to nearly everyone, but the military solutions have proved no more acceptable. Politics has always been fragmented, being in sharpest focus at state, regional, and local levels. Yet Brazilians are nationally aware and politically sensitive, despite what some identify as a national indifference to politics and government. Like Venezuela, Brazil has had little effective experience with representative government; modern parties date from less than 25 years ago. Today Brazil is no closer to solving the institutional dilemmas of national integration than it was decades ago. Perhaps the failing is one of leadership rather than institutions, for the nation is no more fragmented than other Latin American nations that have at least partially resolved the problem of national unification. Voting trends during the parliamentary period revealed a tragic deterioration of even the nominal party structures, toward an increasingly looser system of transient, weak parties. Governing one of the world's largest nations from such a fragile political base is clearly impossible. In spite of the defects of the Brazilian party system from 1946 to 1964, it is probably true that the system reflected accurately the political culture in which it grew; wishing party politics were otherwise will not make it so. Perhaps the Brazilian military is learning this lesson since abolishing the final vestiges of party politics that remained in December, 1968. Brazil is passing through a transitional period that, by one means or another, must sometime produce a more highly institutionalized form of national politics.

III. PANAMA AND ECUADOR: PREINSTITUTIONALIZED MULTI-PARTY LOOSE SYSTEMS

Panama and Ecuador have the fundamental characteristics of multi-party loose systems: easy entry and exit of parties, factions, coalitional electoral organizations, personalistic politics, and no party that can sustain 40 percent of the national legislative representation. Yet their politics is significantly different from that of either Venezuela or Brazil.

Panama has a complex system of poorly institutionalized, weak parties barely able to maintain themselves between elections. Ecuador has several conventional parties, but they too are weak and subject to domination by transient coalitions. Both nations periodically experience military interference in the political system, along with extended periods of relative stability. Parties often participate in leadership recruitment, but normally formalize rather than initiate it. Their role in policy-making is minimal. For this reason, the party systems are conceived as "preinstitutionalized." Neither system appears to be significantly changing its overall patterns.

1. PANAMANIAN PARTY POLITICS

Panama has the smallest population in Latin America. Its 1.3 million inhabitants are fewer than many Latin American cities. In scope Panamanian politics compares to local or city politics, particularly since a good portion of the nation does not participate or relate to national politics. Additional factors condense the effective national political system, such as strong oligarchic and hierarchical pressures and vast differentiation in income. These factors diminish the role of the electorate and retard the growth of institutionalized party structures. Relatively high literacy, urbanization, and concentrated population mitigate these tendencies somewhat.[47]

An environmental and historical factor conditioned Panamanian politics from the outset: the utility of the Panamanian isthmus for a canal, and the involvement of the United States in building and maintaining that canal. Panama's independence derives from the canal negotiations of 1902 and U.S. "gunboat diplomacy." Prior to 1902, Panama was a department of Colombia, with whom the United States had negotiated a treaty to build the canal. When the Colombian Senate balked at ratifying the treaty, the United States encouraged the Panamanians to declare inde-

pendence and ratify a canal treaty. Immediate recognition of
Panamanian independence by the United States was followed by
war ships to protect the newly independent nation from Colombian
retaliation. Protected by U.S. government interest in the canal zone
and subsidized by extensive U.S. private investment, a small, indigenous Panamanian elite grew prosperous and powerful.[48]

Contradictory as the idea may seem, Panamanian politics is
simultaneously oligarchic, demagogic, and competitive. The
oligarchy consists of a few dozen extended families who control
most of the nation's wealth. Demagogy is a way of politics, irrespective of ideology or party. The most common political tactic is to
appeal to strong anti-American sentiment which bridges class, region, and party. Nearly all politicians use this technique, whether
oligarch or Marxist. Heavy U.S. economic penetration and "inadequate compensation" for canal rights are common issues. The tactic
works well. It stimulates sensitive nationalistic feelings among the
masses, and for the oligarchy cuts a vital issue away from opposing
political extremists. Above all, Panamanian politics is competitive,
if not particularly representative. During periods of national elections political debate between candidates and parties is lively, often
intense, and periodically violent. Elections are the most endemically
unstable periods in Panamanian politics. The "rules of the game"
for campaigning admit virtually anything. The mood of Panamanian
politics during this period can perhaps be compared to a rough
game of poker in which the players are master gamblers and the
principal tactic is to call the opponent's bluff. Such a game encourages neither compromise nor moderation, only total victory.[49]

Environmental factors exert frustrating influences on Panamanian politics. Population increase (3.4 percent annually) is high.
Most Panamanians live in the capital city where urban problems
are serious. The use of monetary policy to stimulate development
is impossible, since U.S. currency is used as national money. This
adds the stamp "made in the U.S.A." to the economy, and has
a detrimental effect on national pride. Imports exceed exports by
more than 350 percent, the remainder being contributed by canal
revenues and tourism. The Canal Zone, the sovereignty of which
is an open sore on Panamanian politics, contains nearly 50 thousand
North Americans who live affluently amidst a city known for its
poverty. Racial bigotry was once universal among Canal Zone employees, the majority of whom were recruited from the sourthern
United States, and it remains a source of resentment among Panamanians. Agriculture is being encouraged, but benefits largely the
oligarchy. The cost of living is high, the standard of living for the

majority low. U.S. preoccupation with Panama has had some side benefits for the nation, such as good public utilities and considerable public education. Panama has an otherwise unaccountably high literacy level, and its university graduates more than the economy can adsorb. Principal export industries are bananas, shrimp, some petroleum, and a few minor crops; but Panama still must import the majority of what it consumes from the United States.[50]

Besides the oligarchy, there are two principal political forces in Panama: the national guard and the students. The national guard is comparable to institutions the U.S. Marines established in other areas like Nicaragua, the Dominican Republic, Haiti, and Cuba. Reasonably professional in training and skills, the guard is a constant meddler in national politics. It serves as the only organized source of control in the nation since there are no additional military or police forces. Relatively high pay and living standards have maintained morale and hierarchy within the guard. Politics however, is a game reserved for the officers who conspire among and between themselves to influence national politics. The guard has openly assumed authority several times in recent history, and has ruled indirectly other times. Its 35 hundred members constitute a formidable threat to any civilian regime.

Students are inherently relevant in almost all Latin American political systems, but they occupy an exceptionally important position in Panama. Their influence may be partly the result of a leadership and activist vacuum. Students are well organized, concentrated in the politically sensitive capital area, almost uniformly radical in ideology, politically alienated from national policy, and possess more "leisure" for political activism than their fellow citizens. They are also strongly anti-American, an attitude shared with many national leaders. Regimes normally deal leniently if at all with student activism, apprehensive over antagonising them, and believing they can use the students for their own political objectives. Conservative students from the upper class are educated outside the country. Student discontent is not altogether irrational, for they are likely to find the social, economic, and political systems unresponsive to their demands following graduation.[51]

Under "normal" circumstances, national elections are held every four years for the presidency and the unicameral national legislature. The party system is proliferated, although it has several centers of gravity. The legislature has 42 members, allotted one for each 25 thousand inhabitants with each province receiving a minimum of two. An open-list ballot is used with proportional representation, the d'Hondt distributive formula, and an electoral quotient. The electorate comprises fewer than 450 thousand voters. Voting is easy, with polling stations amply distributed around the nation. The national guard imposes tranquility during elections, and violence is rare. Fraud, however, occurs regularly, sometimes at the government's initiation and sometimes beyond its control. Local government in the ten provinces is appointed.

During the 1964 elections, 19 political parties participated, nominating over 2,000 candidates for the 42 legislative seats and two alternatives for each seat. The majority of parties generally supported the incumbent government, and were identified with the ranks of the oligarchy. Marcos Robles, the official government candidate (that is, the one endorsed by the majority of leaders) came from the Liberal party.

The principal organized opposition to the traditional elite is a semiinstitutionalized party known as the *Panamenistas*. This group draws upon the charisma of a single leader: Dr. Arnulfo Arias. Arias' following is based on a peculiar combination of personalism, authoritarianism, demogogery, populism, nationalism, and racism—the latter directed against an East Indian immigrant commercial class in Panama City. The *Panamenistas* is the only political group with anything like a massive following.

Arias' career dates from his first campaign for the presidency in 1940, an election he clearly won. Riding the crest of a protofascist movement popular in Latin America prior to World War II, Arias imposed a protofascist constitution on the republic. He angered the United States by refusing to grant it military bases, and by allowing U.S. ships registered in Panama to arm in clear violation of the U.S. neutrality act. Arias left in 1941 to visit his oculist in Havana, and with U.S. assistance was deposed by his own cabinet. He again ran for the presidency in 1948, but was denied the office in a highly disputed election. The commander of the national guard, José Antonio Remón, put Arias in power briefly in 1949, then threw him out. Remón, whose role in Panamanian politics was increasingly dominant, ran for the presidency in 1952, and held the office until his assassination in 1955. Three peaceful presidential elections followed, placing three traditional oligarchs— Ernesto de la Guardia, Roberto Francisco Chiari, and Marco Aurelio Robles—in power. Arias ran for the presidency in 1964, and he claims he was fraudulently denied the election by Robles' supporters. There is evidence to support his accusation.

The indefatigable Arias drew together his resources and ran for the presidency again in the 1968 election. Rising rates of inflation and other national dilemmas had corroded the support for the regime, and Arias' forces optimistically believed they would easily be elected. Prior to the election, a series of bizarre political maneuvers occurred, extreme for even Panama. President Robles was tried and impeached by a hostile legislature for supporting candidate David Samudio Avila; under the Panamanian constitution, a president is barred from explicit endorsement of a candidate. Robles rejected the impeachment, the legislature named a new president, and the supreme court had to choose which was authentic. In deciding for Robles, the court heightened bitterness and hostility. The election was turbulent, amid rumors of violence and fraud. Many of the traditional leaders, smelling defeat, switched their support to Arias in the final weeks. Arias won the election, receiving about 175 thousand to Samudio's 134 thousand votes.[52] Arias let it be known that he planned to make "necessary changes" in the guard following his assumption of power to prevent further meddling; his feud with the guard had simmered for more than 25 years. Arias assumed power October 1, 1968, about four months after the May 12 election. On October 12th, the guard, under leadership of Lieut. Col. Omar Torrijos and Major Boris Martinez, staged a successful *coup*, removing Arias from office and repeating a by now familiar pattern.

Panamanian politics is an exotic game for a restricted elite, with few rules or little stability. Parties are weak, poorly institutionalized, with little to do between elections, and dependent upon strong personalities for their vitality. The single fixed point in the national politics is a nascent and often articulated anti-Americanism which is taken seriously by the electorate and lightly by most leaders. Elections provide choices and relative freedom of expression. But electoral outcomes are periodically violated by the guard, which remains the ultimate voice in the nation's politics. Voting patterns reveal little not otherwise obvious. Most votes come from the capital, and fundamental party balances hold throughout the provinces.

The multiplicity and impermanence of parties, their low level of autonomy, weak structures, and dependence on personalities, make Panamanian politics a stereotype of preinstitutionalized, multi-party loose system.

2. Ecuadorian Party Politics

The striking characteristic of Ecuadorian party politics is its exclusiveness. An exceptionally restricted portion of the national population and territory participate.

Ecuador has 5½ million inhabitants, of whom 40 to 45 percent are Indians. They exist as they have for centuries, at best in separateness, at worst in a condition of poverty and subordination. By almost universal consensus among non-Indians, Indians are excluded from the political processes. Exclusion results automatically from literacy requirements. The Indian in Guatemala, Peru, Bolivia, and Mexico may also exert little political influence, but at least in Peru, Bolivia and Mexico he has had allies in political party movements. Ecuadorian parties ignore the Ecuadorian Indian and his plight. Of the approximately three million non-Indians, under half can meet the age requirements for participation in national elections, many of whom are disqualified for illiteracy. Official estimates of eligible voters for the 1966 constituent assembly election were about one million, an electorate smaller than that found in many Latin American cities. Of the eligible voters, many do not participate. Imposed on this already rarefied group, additional oligarchic and hierarchical tendencies further restrict participation. In the final analysis no more than a few thousand Ecuadorians actively participate in any political processes.[53]

Ecuadorian politics has many contradictions. Subject to nearly perpetual political turmoil, the country nonetheless experienced an extended period (1895–1944) of one-party dominance, and a limited (1948–1960), if no less remarkable, period of peaceful party government and respected national elections. Chronic political and governmental instability has alternated with periods of constitutional regimes. Contradictions exist also in party institutions. Unlike Venezuela, Brazil, and Panama, Ecuador has nineteenth-century party traditions which still influence contemporary politics, although the parties themselves are weak and poorly institutionalized. Coexisting with traditional parties are ad hoc groups, often coalitional, that organize on personalistic bases. Recently coalitional groups, particularly those supporting the candidacy of charismatic José Velasco Ibarra, have drawn greater support than traditional parties. A final, regional contradiction exists in Ecuadorian politics. The nation is divided politically between two cities: Quito, its highland capital, and Guayaquil, its coastal commercial center. Strong cultural dichotomies and rival economic interests separate these two urban areas. Guayaquil, located in the humid, tropical lowlands of the Pacific coast, is the center of banana production and export, a vital, commercial center. Quito, located high in the Andes, is formal in its customs, colonial in its appearance, retarded in its economy, and conservative in its politics. Guayaquil has been the traditional center for the Radical-Liberal party, and more recently has found strongest support for Velasco among its student population. Ecuadorian institutions and the cultural dichotomy lend an aura of artificiality to national politics, with a majority neither participating nor even aware of party politics. The weak parties reflect the intrinsic divisions in the nation between liberal and conservative, personalistic and traditional, the two urban centers, and the inevitable church, military, and secular influence. With political activism gravitating to two disparate urban areas, politics becomes polarized geographically.[54]

The environment to which the Ecuadorian political system must respond is perhaps inhospitable to highly representative institutions; the economy alone places almost irresoluble burdens on the system. High population growth, along with high infant mortality, low per capita consumption, and a high crude death rate, oppress the economy. Exports, principally bananas, cocoa, coffee, and rice, fall below imports, and are weak commodities. Unemployment is high, urban living conditions poor, and social services inadequate. Ecuador is one of the least industrialized nations in Latin America, and prospects are poor for advancement.

Of the traditional parties, the oldest is the *Partido Conservador* (PC), which dominated national politics from the independence until the revolution of 1895 that brought the Liberals to power. Electorally and organizationally the Conservatives have been strongest in the highland or Sierra region, with close affiliations to the landowners and the Church. Now the party is divided, with its more liberal members falling into the nascent Christian Democratic movement. As recently as 1948, the PC elected one-third of the national legislators, but in the 1962 election it received less than 20 percent.

The other principal traditional party is the *Partido Liberal Radical* (PLR), which had hegemony over the political system from 1895 to 1944. Founded in 1878, the party drew its largest following in the coastal region. The PLR was never well-organized but was structurally more coalitional than organic, united by a vague anticlericalism and opposition to traditional ruling elites.

A socialist party was formed in 1925 in Ecuador, but its history has been one of disastrous divisions and mutations which perhaps exemplify Ecuadorian politics. In 1938 the party briefly came to power through a left-wing coalition. The coalition haggled for days to try to find a suitable president to elect in the legislature. Finally, unable to reach a consensus, they were forced to turn to Aurelio

Mosquera Narváez, a leader from the Liberal Radical party. The Socialists again came to power in 1944, and with their coalition drafted a new constitution and selected as president, José Velasco Ibarra. Velasco ungraciously repaid his debt to them by repressing the party for the next 18 months. The Socialist party is so diverse and divided in its organization that it has a right-wing component in its ranks. These "conservatives" are middle-class professionals who never were absorbed in the major parties, and saw the Socialists as an avenue for opposition. In 1960 the party divided, with a traditional, evolutionary faction, led by Gonzalo Oleas, breaking from the more radical Revolutionary Socialist party led by Telmo Hidalgo. Following the 1960 division, the traditional faction redivided again, with the more conservative wing forming the paradoxically titled United Socialist party. Electorally, the party has little strength, but it does have the distinction of being the first and only Ecuadorian party to acknowledge the existence of the Ecuadorian Indian and his problems. However, even in the Socialist party, Indian representatives on the party caucus were non-Indians.[55]

The heart of Ecuadorian politics is not the party institutions, but the personalities and coalitions that form about them. Perhaps most characteristic of this phenomena is the political career and movement of José Velasco Ibarra. Velasco has been a vital catalyst and often prime force in his nation's politics for nearly four decades, and his career in its essential outline brings to mind that of Arnulfo Arias in Panama. Velasco first held power for about a year in 1934; was elected in 1944 and served three years before being removed; was elected in 1951 and served a full term; was elected in 1960 and replaced within a few months by a military *junta*; and finally ran again in 1968 and assumed power a fifth time amid rumors of an impending military takeover. Now in his mid-seventies, Velasco is a commanding political figure and orator, the archetype of a charismatic demagogue who solicits support from diverse— probably contradictory—sources. Drawing support from the urban poor, the students, the alienated middle class, and numerous opportunistic regional leaders, Velasco is still unchallenged by other political leaders in his magnetic control of the electorate. As with Arias in Panama, the alternative to Velasco Ibarra seems to be the military.

Velasco is supported by a loose coalition of regional party movements and activist groups, particularly students. Students employ violence to prod the regimes periodically into permitting elections, which they realize their leader will easily win. Fraud is a possibility, but it would have to be so widespread to prohibit Velasco from winning that the exercise would seem futile.

Other coalitions also compete. One was prominent for many years after the collapse of the PLR regime in 1944. The coalition, known as the *Movimiento Cívico Democrático Nacional* (MCDN), was created in 1947 as a means of preventing the conservatives from returning to power in the vacuum left by the PLR demise. MCDN drew support from former PLR adherents as well as socialists, communists, and even some dissident conservatives. In the 1948 election, its candidate (Galo Plaza Lasso) won the presidency. Other coalitions, particularly rightist ones, have been common. Typical of the more enduring ones was the *Alianza Revolucionario Nacional Ecuadoriana* (ARNE) led by Jorge Crespo Toral and Jorge Luna Yepez. Another is the *Unión Nacional Revolucionario Ecuadoriano* (UNRE). Neither has won more than a few seats in legislative elections. The most successful left-wing coalition was the *Concentración de Fuerzas Populares* (CFP), designed as a personal vehicle in 1960 for Carlos Guevara Moreno who, with the support of some Marxist organizers, won the mayorality election in Guayaquil. Like other coalitions, within a few years it all but disappeared through the process of factionalization.[56]

A unitary republic, Ecuador is divided electorally and administratively into 18 provinces that comprise three distinct regions: the Sierra, dominated by Quito; the Coastal, dominated by Guayaquil; and the Eastern, virtually uninhabited. Voting for all legislative bodies is by proportional representation, using a closed-list ballot. Men are legally required to vote—if eligible—but no penalties are invoked. Women originally received the right to vote in 1883, long before their counterparts in the United States, but subsequently have lost and regained the right periodically. Priests and nuns are not allowed to vote, but are a significant factor in mobilizing Conservative balloting. Electoral laws are lenient in defining parties and permitting groups to participate electorally. In the 1966 elections, 75 separate party lists were filed containing 489 candidates for the 67 seat constituent assembly. Results from legislative balloting are often not announced for weeks following the election, partly because of the complexity of the system, partly because of the difficulties in communication throughout the country, and partly because it is at this juncture that most fraudulent practices occur. When the normal legislature exists, it is bicameral; the Senate in the past has contained "functional" senators chosen directly from interest groups and professions. Voting behavior is not particularly revealing of fundamental qualities in Ecuadorian politics. The total participation is a minor portion of the adult population, the party groupings are divided between the two urban areas, and the open possibilities for fraud cast doubt on the integrity of voting returns.

The overthrow of Velasco in 1960 was followed by eight years of unsettled, imposed government. The air force removed Velasco and replaced him with the vice president, Carlos Julio Arosomena, who tried to consolidate a regime and initiate some reforms consistent with the Alliance for Progress. In July, 1963, the air force removed Arosomena following a disastrous and insulting banquet to which foreign dignitaries had been invited. This time the military itself took power by means of a three-man *junta*.[57] The *junta* became the object of increasing demonstrations, and again the air force took action by appointing an interim president and calling for a constituent assembly election in 1966. After several postponements and much indecision, general elections were called for 1968. To no one's surprise, but to the general discontent of the military, Velasco Ibarra was victorious. His tenure in office is less than secure.

Despite its roots in the nineteenth century, Ecuador's party system is perhaps the least meaningful of the multi-party loose systems. It is little more than an alluvium to a highly rarefied, personalistic sport called politics. In recent years the system has shown marked signs of proliferation rather than consolidation. The more vital structures have come from ad hoc coalitions rather than traditional or formally structured parties. Parties provide a degree of political ballyhoo during elections, a time of limited warfare between unlimited, vested interests in the nation. Whatever holds parties and coalitions together in Ecuador, it is not their institutionalization.

IV. CONCLUSION

Multi-party loose systems have been divided into two categories: those that are institutionalized, of which Venezuela and Brazil are illustrative; and those that are preinstitutional, exemplified by Panama and Ecuador. The difference is perhaps as much one of degree as of type. Institutional multi-party systems contain parties that exist and participate as organizations; in the preinstitutional context, the parties have no real existence apart from the limited elites or personalities who devise them. Moreover, preinstitutional parties exist occasionally in institutionalized systems, and vice-versa.

The common characteristics of multi-party loose systems we have suggested are the following: (1) prolificacy and fluidity of the parties, (2) dependence on personality politics, (3) constant pressure toward coalitions for electoral and legislative purposes, (4) incapacity of a single party to dominate or impose an element of order upon the system for more than a limited period, (5) pressures toward party factionalization, (6) pressures toward regional party concentration.

Venezuela has achieved more consolidation than the remaining three systems, and the recent success of COPEI suggests the metamorphosis is continuing. Brazil's present regime is wholly arbitrary and imposed, and bears no resemblance to the politics of the parliamentary period. Panama's parties are very weak and dominated by personalities. Arias' following is the only indication of a mass movement, and it is personalistic rather than institutional. The position of Velasco in Ecuador is comparable, although the remnants of a traditional, rarefied party system stubbornly persist in the face of irrelevancy.

Significantly, party politics in three of the four nations is a recent phenomena with no roots in the nineteenth century. Party politics in Venezuela and Brazil date from approximately the mid-1940s. Panama did not even gain independence until the twentieth century. Excluding nearly half its population by denying participation to be Indian community, Ecuador has yet to establish a truly national political system or find a national identity. Its politics reflects this dilemma, and its institutionalization perhaps demands first a solution to this contradiction. Whether the process of institutionalization promotes or reflects increased dominance within the party system remains the most intriguing question raised by the category of multi-party loose systems.

NOTES

[1] An interpretation of late nineteenth-century politics in Venezuela is found in Donald Marquand Dozer, *Latin America: An Interpretive History* (New York: McGraw-Hill, 1962), pp. 398–400.

[2] John D. Martz, *Acción Democrática: Evolution of a Modern Political Party in Venezuela* (Princeton, N.J.: Princeton University Press, 1966), pp. 17–48.

[3] A general introduction to Venezuelan politics is contained in Edwin Lieuwen, *Venezuela* (Oxford: Oxford University Press, 1961) and Harry Bernstein, *Venezuela and Colombia* (Englewood Cliffs, N.J.: Prentice-Hall, 1964).

[4] Further background on the COPEI is available in Franklin Tugwell, "The Christian Democrats of Venezuela," *Journal of Inter-American Studies* (April 1965): 245–67. See also, Edward J. Williams, *Latin American Christian Democratic Parties* (Knoxville: University of Tennessee Press, 1967), pp. 83–88, 204–09.

[5] See Martz, *Acción Democrática*, pp. 67–68.

[6] A very brief history of the Communist party can be found in Rollie Poppino, *International Communism in Latin America: A History of the Movement 1917–1963* (New York: Free Press, 1964), pp. 87–88.

[7] Source: *Consejo Supremo Electoral.*

[8] A useful analysis of the fall of Marcos Pérez Jiménez is found in Phillip B. Taylor, *The Venezuelan Golpe de Estado of 1958* (Washington, D.C.: Institute for Comparative Study of Political Systems, 1968).

[9] I am indebted to John Martz, *The Venezuelan Elections of December 1, 1963: An Analysis* (Washington, D.C.: Institute for Comparative Study of Political Systems, 1964), pp. 3–5, for this typology of regionalism.

[10] See Edwin Lieuwen, *Petroleum in Venezuela* (Berkeley: University of California Press, 1954).

[11] A comprehensive summary of Venezuelan economic development can be found in the International Bank for Reconstruction and Development, *The Economic Development of Venezuela* (Baltimore: Johns Hopkins University Press, 1961).

[12] Leo B. Lott, "Venezuela," in Martin Needler, ed., *Political Systems in Latin America* (Princeton, N.J.: Van Nostrand, 1964), pp. 253–56.

[13] See Martz, *Acción Democrática*, pp. 183–92.

[14] Background on political parties, factions, coalitions, and leaders is provided by *Venezuela: Election Factbook* (Washington, D.C.: Institute for Comparative Study of Political Systems, 1968).

[15] The most serious threat of violence was in Caracas, inspired allegedly by leftist university students.

[16] Source: *Consejo Supremo Electoral.*

[17] *Ibid.*

[18] Source: *Venezuela Election Factbook* (Washington, D.C.: Institute for Comparative Study of Political Systems, 1963), p. 28.

[19] An account of the Betancourt era is Robert J. Alexander, *Venezuelan Democratic Revolution* (New Brunswick, N.J.: Rutgers University Press, 1964).

[20] Final election results reproduced in *The Venezuelan Elections of December 1, 1963, Part III: Final Provisional Election Returns* (Washington, D.C.: Institute for Comparative Study of Political Systems, 1964).

[21] *Ibid.*, p. 23.

[22] *Ibid.*

[23] The effect of the division is reported by Martz, *Acción Democrática*, p. 401.

[24] Source: *La Republica* (Caracas). December 9, 1968.

[25] This point is strongly made by Bradford Burns, *Nationalism in Brazil* (New York: Praeger, 1968), pp. 128–33.

[26] An excellent look into Brazilian culture is Gilberto Freyre, *New World in the Tropics* (New York: Random House, 1959).

[27] A useful history of Brazil is J. M. Bello, *A History of Modern Brazil, 1889–1964*, tr. from Portuguese by J. L. Taylor with a concluding chapter by R. E. Poppino (Stanford: Stanford University Press, 1966).

[28] An early appraisal of the Vargas regime is Karl Lowenstein, *Brazil Under Vargas* (New York: Macmillan, 1942).

[29] One of the best introductions to Brazilian politics is Phyllis Peterson, "Brazil: Institutionalized Confusion," in Martin C. Needler, ed., *Political Systems of Latin America* (Princeton, N.J.: Van Nostrand, 1964).

[30] For a complete account, see Thomas E. Skidmore, *Politics in Brazil* (New York: Oxford University Press, 1967), pp. 136–42.

[31] *Ibid.*, pp. 163–86.

[32] An account of the 1964 revolution is contained in Charles Wagley, *Brazil: Crisis and Change*, Headline Series No. 167 (New York: Foreign Policy Association, 1964), pp. 43–54.

[33] Additional background material can be found in *Brazil: Election Factbooks*, Nos. 1 and 2 (Washington. D.C.: Institute for Comparative Study of Political Systems, 1965).

[34] A particularly useful account of the Brazilian military is John J. Johnson, *The Military and Society in Latin America* (Stanford: Stanford University Press, 1964), pp. 177–243.

[35] Glaucio Ary Dillon Soares, "The Politics of Uneven Development: The Case of Brazil," in Seymour Martin Lipset and Stein Rokkan, eds., *Party Systems and Voter Alignments: Cross-National Perspectives* (New York: Free Press, 1967), p. 493.

[36] Inequalities are clearly present even under normal circumstances. See Soares, *The Politics of Uneven Development*, p. 492.

[37] *Brazil: Election Factbook*, No. 2, pp. 72–75.

[38] A very detailed analysis of the parties is found in Phyllis Peterson, *Brazilian Political Parties: Formation, Organization, Leadership 1945–1959* (PhD dissertation, University of Michigan, 1962). For the post-Goulart period, see James W. Rowe, "The 'Revolution' and the 'System': Notes on Brazilian Politics," *American Universities Field Staff Reports Service*, East Coast South America Series, XII, Nos. 3 and 4 (Brazil).

[39] The socioeconomic correlates to party affiliation in Brazil, particularly in regard to class attitudes, is analyzed by Soares, *The Politics of Uneven Development*, pp. 487–88.

[40] A listing of minor parties is included in the *Election Factbook*, pp. 45–47.

[41] *Ibid.*, pp. 37–40.

[42] The best source on Brazilian regionalism is Preston E. James, *Latin America*, 3rd ed. (New York: The Odyssey Press, 1959). pp. 383–569.

[43] Jordan M. Young, "Some Permanent Political Characteristics of Contemporary Brazil," *Journal of Inter-American Studies* 6 (July 1964): 287–301.

[44] Source: Supreme Electoral Court (Brazilia).

[45] Dissension in the Brazilian case is described by Williams, *Latin Ameri-*

can Christian Democratic Parties, pp. 245–47; also, see Thomas G. Sanders, "Brazil's Catholic Left," *America* (November 18, 1967), pp. 598–601.

[46] Source: *Dados Estatisticos,* Vol. 6, pp. 31–36.

[47] Documentation of Panamanian politics is poor, most of the useful commentary coming from one source: Professor Daniel Goldrich. See his chapter "Panama" in Needler, *Political Systems of Latin America,* pp. 131–47; "Requisites for Political Legitimacy in Panama," *Public Opinion Quarterly* 26 (Winter 1962): 664–68; "Developing Political Orientations of Panamanian Students," with Edward W. Scott, *Journal of Politics* 23 (February 1961): 84–107; and *Sons of the Establishment: Elite Youth in Panama and Costa Rica* (Chicago: Rand McNally, 1966).

[48] An excellent account is Hubert Herring, *History of Latin America,* 3rd ed. (New York: Knopf, 1968), pp. 502–03.

[49] Background material is contained in *Panama Election Factbook* (Washington, D.C.: Institute for Comparative Study of Political Systems, 1968).

[50] Harry Kantor also suggests a period of segregation was induced in Panama, now much resented, by policies in the Canal Zone. See his chapter "Panama: The Politics of the Canal," in *Patterns of Politics & Political Systems in Latin America* (Chicago: Rand McNally, 1969), pp. 235–36.

[51] See Goldrich, *Sons of Establishment,* pp. 40–76.

[52] Election results were not certified. These figures were obtained indirectly from reliable sources in the Panamanian government.

[53] Background on recent Ecuadorian politics can be found in the *Ecuador: Election Factbook* (Washington, D.C.: Institute for Comparative Study of Political Systems, 1968).

[54] This bifurcation is clearly discussed in the classic if now somewhat dated area study by George Blanksten, *Ecuador: Constitutions and Caudillos* (Berkeley: University of California Press, 1951). See also the same author's chapter on Ecuador in Needler, *Political Systems of Latin America,* pp. 269–90.

[55] *Ibid.,* p. 28.

[56] The process of division has continued much as described earlier by Blanksten, *Ecuador: Constitutions and Caudillos.*

[57] An excellent case study of the 1963 coup is contained in Martin C. Needler, *Anatomy of a Coup d'Etat: Ecuador, 1963* (Washington, D.C.: Institute for Comparative Study of Political Systems, 1964).

CHAPTER 3

Multi-Party Dominant Systems: Argentina, Chile, and Costa Rica

In a multi-party dominant system, one party receives between forty and sixty percent of the legislative representation while the remainder receive less than forty percent. The assumption is that while the party system is proliferated, one party is sufficiently strong to dominate others. There is greater fluctuation between multi-party loose and multi-party dominant systems than between other types, perhaps because the basis of change is spontaneous rather than imposed; that is, system dominance increases as a party becomes stronger relative to others, or conversely, dominance decreases when party strength becomes more equalized. It is important to remember that within the context of these categories, the number of parties participating or represented is not the critical variable; rather, what matters is the balance between the participating parties reflected in congressional representation. Movement between loose and dominant multi-party systems can be regarded as a vital indicator of political change, as systems become more or less integrated. Whereas single- and two-party dominance is easily attained by legal, electoral, and coercive means, multi-party dominance is more difficult since it is more singularly based upon political factors.

Generation of dominance within a multi-party context seems to induce or accompany the growth of characteristic qualities in the political culture and environment. Since dominance is based upon recognition and identification with at least one party, political awareness in the cultures—and those factors such as literacy, education, and communication that promote awareness—tend to be higher. As more institutionalized parties appear, almost axiomatically they tend to have greater political longevity, deeper roots in the national culture. As one party grows increasingly dominant, incentives arise for *opposition* coalitional party activity, which are based rationally in the aspiration to maximize party influence against a strong opponent. Opposition permits diverse political groups to coalesce against the dominant party far more easily than when the same groups are in power and the spoils of victory create divisive pressures. In view of the difficulties of inducing dominance in a multi-party environment, as it occurs it probably signals substantial pressures within the nation for consolidation or integration. These are the pressures that induce voters faced with multiple alternatives to select the alternative that seems not only reasonably sympathetic to their interests and identifications, but also offers a hope for consolidating the nation politically.

There may also be a tendency in the context of politically institutionalized party dominance for more formal affiiliations between socioeconomic interest groups and party organizations; in fact such alliances may be an important factor in promoting a party's dominance as it co-opts formal support from established groups in the environment. Maintenance of party dominance also suggests the necessity for organization, at least for the dominant party, at a more intense level than would otherwise be required. Therefore, organizational questions of party behavior may be more relevant for multi-party dominant systems. It is also likely that the process of consolidation requires somewhat more stable voting patterns, to permit not only growth but anticipation by party elites of strategies required to win elections. Voting consistency is an empirical question related to the development of party dominance. There is no reason to believe that increasing dominance in a multi-party system need continue to more consolidated levels of two- and single-party systems, for maintenance of such systems seems to depend especially on institutional and governmental supports lacking in the premise of a multi-party environment.

Three Latin American nations illustrate the multi-party dominant competition: Argentina, Chile, and Costa Rica. Party dominance in each case has historically vascillated between loose and more dominant expressions. Legal-institutional factors in Argentina often supported greater dominance than would otherwise spontaneously have occurred in the party system. The Argentine experience has been periodically interrupted by military intervention. Under Perón the nation was ruled by a single political party, while more recently the military governments have permitted no political parties. Chile historically had a multi-party loose system with proliferative tendencies. Since 1947, the Chilean system has undergone progressive consolidation, to the point that it has tentatively become a multi-party dominant system with fewer participating parties. Costa Rica has had a multi-party dominant system since World War II, which following the 1966 election has shown even further consolidation and competition.

Factors external to the party systems have produced varied governmental styles in the three countries. Argentina has enjoyed little political stability or representative government in the twentieth century. The nineteenth-century struggle for governmental centralization continues to exert an influence on twentieth-century Argentine politics. Apart from its federalism, which resembles that of the United States more closely than any Latin American nation, Argentina has been torn between pressures for centralization and strong regional and state interests. The ten-year trauma of Perón still convulses the nation's politics. Chile, on the other hand, has been one of the more stable and generally competitive political systems in the hemisphere. Almost in defiance of its territorial regionalism, Chile has forged a national political culture committed to nonviolent change. Since 1947, Chile has steadily consolidated its party system, producing four general political forces now competing for national power. Costa Rica in its own way is an anomaly to its subregion. Like Chile and Uruguay, Costa Rica is a stable, competitive political system. Argentina, Chile, and Costa Rica rank high in literacy, and above average to high in socioeconomic welfare.

Obviously the Argentine experience shatters the assertion that a multi-party dominant system is inherently more "stable" governmentally than a multi-party loose system, or represents a "higher level" of political institutionalization and development; nevertheless, specific political parties in Argentina, as in the other two nations, are highly institutionalized. Although different governmental systems emerged, party institutional development in Argentina and Chile was similar. Both nations had vigorous nineteenth-century party traditions, and in the early twentieth century produced Radical and Marxist party movements along the lines of the European counterparts. Evidence suggests that political awareness in all three nations is high. Yet Argentina, the most economically and socially developed of the three, has been chronically unable to solve normal political disputes through institutionalized processes. Argentine parties reflect the nation's federalism, with decentralized organizations.

Historically the most proliferated party system of the three,

Chile has a centralized government with a strong presidency, and well-organized, centralized parties that are surprisingly competitive throughout the nation. Costa Rica's parties are broadly perceived in the national culture, if somewhat elitist in leadership recruitment. Costa Rican government is also centralized, a trait reinforced by the smallness of the national territory and compactness of the population. Legislative politics in both Costa Rica and Chile is meaningful, regularly relevant to national policy-making.

Politically generated party system dominance is an elusive, perhaps frustrating quality. There is no guarantee that once achieved it can be retained. But the consolidating and proliferating tendencies in a multi-party environment are revealing indicators of fundamental political change.

I. ARGENTINA: THE PURSUIT OF POLITICAL CONSENSUS

It is a curious comment on westernization that the most economically advanced, literate, European-like nation in Latin America is also one of the most politically unstable. For all its development, Argentina is a nation without effective regional and social consensus, unable to initiate peaceful change, recruit leaders, or make national policy by institutional means. In spite of strong cultural identity and economic sophistication, Argentina has yet to solve the elementary problems of national unification that plagued it in the nineteenth century.[1] The Argentine experience is a warning to those who single-mindedly view economic welfare and prosperity as causal determinants of governmental stability.

1. CONTEXT AND CULTURE OF ARGENTINE POLITICS

Argentina is a nation of about 22 million people, with a territory of more than 1.1 million square miles, about the size of India. The nation is over 2,300 miles long, and about 800 miles wide at its widest. Most population is located in the central-eastern region, which contains both the largest city and the capital, Buenos Aires, a metropolitan area of seven million persons, and the fertile pampa region where Argentine wealth is derived. The Pampa is one of the finest agricultural plains in the world: flat, treeless, rockless, with temperate climate and normally adequate rainfall. Argentina is one of the world's largest exporters of meat products, and an increasingly significant exporter of agricultural products. The economy is industrialized, particularly in the consumer market, although the nation lacks some of the natural resources (especially steel and coal) necessary for a viable industrial economy. Argentina has one of the highest realized and realizable economic bases in Latin America, despite poor economic performance in the past decade, brought about by a decline in agricultural production, a large foreign debt, a poor balance of payments, and particularly by chronic political instability in the post-Perón period.[2]

Demographically, Argentina presents a contrast to other Latin American nations. It is secure from the severe economic and social pressures of rapid population expansion. Annual population increase is under two percent. Ethnically, Argentines are essentially a "white" race, with fewer than 3.5 percent *mestizo* and Indian. Most of the latter are in the northern provinces, particularly around the borders of Bolivia and Paraguay. Literacy is high, 87 percent, and health standards are comparable to the United States. Argentina is a highly urbanized nation, 65 percent, with more than one-third of the population in Buenos Aires.[3] The basic qualities for political integration are present.

Like the United States, Argentina is a land of immigrants. The relatively primitive indigenous Indians were either killed or absorbed into a nineteenth-century *creole-mestizo* population that, along with the relatively larger number of Negroes and mulattoes originally brought from Brazil, has disappeared into the dominant white population. Three great waves of immigration occurred in Argentina, encouraged by the Argentine government. The largest immigration began during the nineteenth century, and was followed by subsequent waves prior to World War I and following World War II. The migration was European, particularly from northern Italy and Spain.[4] By 1914 immigrants outnumbered native-born Argentines in most provinces, and three-fourths of Buenos Aires was foreign-born. Even today at least 20 percent of Buenos Aires is foreign-born. As in the United States, the great European migration injected new political attitudes and cultures into the national politics, but unlike the United States, the new population was not easily absorbed into the dominant political culture and created new tensions in an already inflexible system.[5] Argentines sometimes define Latin America as everything between the Río Grande and the Río Plata, excluding themselves and the North Americans from the region. This lack of communal identification with Latin America is an important trait of Argentine culture, and partly responsible for the history of international rivalry between it and the United States.

Cultural and social, if not racial, differentiation is profound in Argentina. One major division is between the cosmopolitan, sophisticated *porteño* (a resident of Buenos Aires) and the rural Argentine, symbolized and oversimplified by the *gaucho*.[6] Unlike sophisticated Uruguayans, the Argentines do not idealize the rural life. This conflict was a dominant political fact of the nineteenth century, and its reverberations are still felt. Cultural differentiation is also regionally based.[7] The most obvious example is the separateness of Buenos Aires, but other subcultures also exist around major cities and centers of rural life. While on a less complex scale, perhaps, differentiation in Argentine political culture more resembles that found in the United States than any Latin American nation. Political awareness is not the sole property of any subculture, but a dominant national characteristic. Different ways of life combine with obviously separate interests to reinforce the characteristic subcultures.

The forging of the Argentine federal union was an exciting and turbulent episode in Latin American history.[8] Independence was declared in Tucumán, July 9, 1816, and within two years decisively won. Attempts to consolidate the nation in 1819 and 1827 through a premature centralist constitution failed, and the many provinces of La Plata continued on their own. Juan Manuel de Rosas capitalized on civil strife which broke out in 1828 between the centralists and the autonomists, and became governor of Buenos Aires province. Under his regime, Buenos Aires, Entre Ríos, Santa Fe, and subsequently Corrientes provinces signed the Pact of the Littoral and achieved limited consolidation. Rosas' power increased along with his centralist inclinations, until his defeat in an 1851 rebellion led by the governor of Entre Ríos, Justo José de Urquiza. Civil strife continued for the next decade until Bartolomé Mitre, governor of Buenos Aires, finally established a national government with Buenos Aires as the capital. Mitre was followed by the distinguished intellectual, Domingo F. Sarmiento, under whose leadership (1868–1874) a visionary policy of mass education was begun and immigration stimulated. The modern period in Argentine history and the final stabilization of the national territory began in 1880 under the administration of Julio Roca, who consolidated the oligarchy and ruled over the increasingly rapid economic development. At this point the political course of twentieth-century Argentina were beginning clearly to emerge: the governmental dominance of the oligarchy, the continuing regional rivalries between Buenos Aires and the provinces, the rapid economic expansion and reliance upon the pampa for wealth, the mass immigration from Europe which infused a proletarian labor class in Buenos Aires and new bourgeois political ideas in Argentine life, and the programs of education which brought national awareness to a high level at a relatively early point in national development.[9] It is also from this period that major political parties took the form from which contemporary organizations emerged.[10]

The middle-class struggle against the oligarchy was a primary political force in Argentina from the end of the nineteenth century until the *Peronista* period beginning in 1943. The initiative in the struggle was taken by the "new" political parties, particularly the Radicals.[11] Their failure to renovate Argentine life generated an intensifying quarrel between middle-class and conservative interests. Symbolic of the Radical plight were the unsuccessful regimes of Hipólito Yrigoyen, 1916–1922, and 1928–1930. The second Yrigoyen administration prompted a military takeover in 1930, in response to worsening economic conditions and presidential senility. A series of intransigently conservative regimes and military adventurism contributed to the rise of Perón in 1943. The Argentine military had been professionalized early in national development through military colleges, but its leadership remained conservative, aloof, and autocratic.[12] Governments were repressive and incompetent as the Perón epoch approached; traditional leaders finally proved no match for Perón. Despite national economic wealth and opportunity, the broad middle-class stratum in Argentina had been consistently frustrated in its attempts through political parties and state institutions to acheive relief or amelioration of its economic and social immobility.

Evaluation of the Perón period is beyond the scope of this analysis, but its impact was enormous on national politics.[13] In a longer-range perspective there is little justification for viewing the Perón experiment as anything but a social, political, and economic disaster of continuing consequences for the nation. But for a while it was a heady time for disaffected Argentine lower classes. Perón's regime was in some ways similar to other strong-arm governments in Latin America and Europe during the period. He was committed to total concentration of power in himself; he appealed to latent, unrequited nationalism for popular support; he reached agreements with major institutional forces in the nation, specifically unions, the army, and the Church; and he eventually engaged in reprehensible repression, demagoguery, economic opportunism, mismanagement, and embezzlement. But there were differences in *Peronismo*. For the first time Perón mobilized support from a laboring proletariat in Buenos Aires, building a broad base for his power. Eva Duarte Perón, his wife and political aid, built a formidable empire through a national charity organization, and broke the patronizing control of the oligarchy on that aspect of Argentine life by transferring it to the State. She led and inspired workers recruited to the *Peronista* movement, and used them more than once to maintain her husband in power.[14] Perón, as Arthur Whitaker correctly observes, "walked the other side of the street," building cordial relations with the military and systematically eliminating any potential rivals for power in that institution.[15] Perón also reached a *modus operandi* with the Church and in the early years affirmed his Catholic faith. Perón devised a protofascist ideology known as *"justicialismo,"* but assiduously avoided entangling the relationships with the clearly waning prestige of the European fascists. *Justicialismo*, whatever its ideological contributions, was truly an Argentine movement, not a transplant.[16] Perón gave lip service to democratic government and even elections, while systematically rooting out all meaningful opposition and repressing political parties. He succeeded as no one before in mobilizing a popular following and maintaining a military alliance of essentially incompatible interests. Economic groups were controlled either by incentives or punitive sanctions, often gaining short-run advantages at the expense of long-run gains. Perón and his wife crusaded against the oligarchs, much to the delight and entertainment of the majority who had suffered at oligarchic hands for half a century and bitterly resented it.

Eva Perón's death in 1952 from cancer signaled a reverse for Perón. Following in quick succession came a collapse of his working arrangement with the Church and a wave of government sponsored anticlericalism rare in contemporary Latin America. Repression became commonplace, as did inflation and deteriorating economic conditions. Several military revolts were crushed, but finally one succeeded in 1955, and Perón "retired voluntarily" to Paraguay and later Spain, where he now lives comfortably on a large fortune. The leader of the revolt, General Eduardo Leonardi, was himself removed after eight weeks for too conciliatory an attitude toward the *Peronistas*, and General Pedro E. Aramburu assumed the provisionary presidency in 1955. Arturo Frondizi, leader of one of the

Radical party factions, was elected in 1958 to the presidency of a fragmented and economically depressed nation.[17] Frondizi permitted the *Peronistas* to compete in the 1962 elections, and they made impressive gains in the state legislatures. Alarmed by this, the military again stepped in and removed Frondizi. José M. Guido, president of the Senate, was installed by the military as provisional president, and ruled until the 1963 elections.[18] Arturo Illia, candidate for the other wing of the Radical party, won the 1963 elections and served with minimum success until June, 1966, when he too was removed by the military. Illia was replaced by Colonel Juan Carlos Onganía, who pledged himself to correct the worsening economic and political conditions. A drab but persistent leader, Onganía outlawed all political parties, promised nothing but austerity, and refused to consider the eventuality of national elections.

After 1955 Argentine political culture had to contend with divisive influences from the traditional parties, the military, the Church, regionalism, and the *Peronistas*. *Peronismo* continued to draw support from the unsatisfied demands for social and economic welfare, and equalization of political power. For many *Peronista* supporters the post-Perón economic problems were not equated with their leader's mismanagement, but instead reinforced their conviction that under Perón they enjoyed a favorable position in national policy for the first time. Argentina today is as governmentally unstable and politically divided as ever, and consensus seems as distant a goal for Argentina as for any Latin American nation.

2. REPRESENTATION AND ELECTIONS

An important feature of Argentine representation is its federal base.[19] The nation is divided into 22 provinces and the federal capital (Buenos Aires). These 23 electoral districts constitute four major regions, summarized in Table 3-1. Two national senators are selected for each district by provincial legislatures, except in the federal capital where senators are chosen by a special electoral college. The 192 federal deputies are elected by direct vote. Women were enfranchised in September, 1947, as the first major accomplishment of Eva Perón. At the state (province) level, only 9 of the 22 legislatures are bicameral; the remainder have only one chamber. Deputies are allocated nationally accordingly to population: one for each 85 thousand inhabitants or fraction of not less than 42,500. Each province and its capital is guaranteed a minimum of two deputies. Deputies serve four-year terms, with half the chamber

TABLE 3-1. REPRESENTATION AND REGIONALISM IN ARGENTINA

Region	Population total	Percent nat.	Percent terr.	Pres. elec.	Nat. dep.	Prov. sen.	Prov. dep.
CENTRAL EASTERN REGION	14,470,000	73	33	300	136	116	257
Buenos Aires	6,734,548			104	50	46	92
Sante Fe	1,865,537			44	20	19	50
Córdoba	1,759,997			40	18	37	36
Entre Ríos	808,505			22	9	14	28
San Luis	174,251			8	2		30
La Pampa	158,489			8	2		21
Federal Capital	2,966,816			74	35		
NORTHERN REGION	2,100,000	11	16	64	22	17	146
Corrientes	543,226			16	6	17	33
Chaco	535,443			14	5		30
Santiago del Estero	477,156			16	6		26
Misiones	391,094			10	3		32
Formosa	178,458			8	2		25
SOUTHERN REGION	400,000	2½	25	24	6		73
Río Negro	192,595			8	2		22
Chubut	142,195			8	2		27
Santa Cruz	52,853			8	2		24
ANDEAN REGION	3,000,000	14	25	88	28	90	282
Mendoza	825,535			18	7	27	36
Tucumán	780,348			18	7	20	40
Salta	412,652			10	3	23	60
San Juan	352,461			10	3		30
Jujuy	239,783			8	2		30
Catamarca	172,407			8	2	20	36
La Rioja	128,270			8	2		25
Neuquén	111,008			8	2		25

NOTE: Representation as of 1963 election. Provinces without senators indicated are unicameral.

renewed each two years. Senators serve nine-year terms, with one-third renewed every three years.[20]

The president and vice president are elected indirectly through an electoral college. Each province and the federal capital receive twice the electors as it has senators and deputies. Presidential and vice-presidential terms are normally six years, and each must receive an absolute majority of electoral college votes on the first ballot. If no candidate receives a majority, then congress decides the election by simple majority. If there is no majority in congress after the first ballot, a second ballot follows which includes only the two candidates with the highest vote on the first ballot. If there is a tie on the first or second ballot, the voting is repeated; if the tie persists, the senate president decides. A similar plan is used for provincial governors, except that in the case of a tie the decision is made by choosing lots.

Each province and the federal capital is divided into sections, which in turn are divided into circuits containing one or more polling stations. A polling station ordinarily has 250–300 voters, but not less than fifty. Men and women vote separately.[21] Voting in

1963 under proportional representation permitted considerable choice. After receiving a ballot, the voter deposits a separate party list for each office to be filled; voters may also obtain party lists directly from party organizations. Voters can scratch out names, make substitutions, or write in names on the lists. The president of the polling station certifies the ballot and indicates on the voter's identification *carnet* that he voted. Party representatives oversee the process, and supervise the opening and counting of votes; they may also accompany the ballots to the district electoral Board to guarantee against fraud.

Parties are highly regulated. Prior to the Onganía regime, parties were allowed to form and operate freely, although radical groups (communists, ultrarightists, *Peronistas*) frequently have been declared illegal. Political parties can have several legal existences: they can exist nationally, provincially, or as part of a coalition, federation, or front. National and provincial recognition requires registration with the electoral commission the party name, address, program, charter and bylaws, and officers. Continued registration requires a minimum vote in each election, or certification of a popular petition.

Historically Argentina used a modified system of proportional representation designed to limit the number of parties which could gain national representation. The system, known as the Sáenz Peña law after the president who initiated it in 1912, guaranteed representation for "the minority party" in a district. The law provided that the party winning a plurality of a district's vote would automatically receive two-thirds of the district's seats, while the "minority" party received the remaining one-third. Additional parties received no representation. The effect of the law was to overrepresent the plurality parties, and minority parties which achieved a national voting distribution. For example, under the Sáenz Peña law the *Peronistas* with less than one-third of the popular vote well distributed could have won control of the national Chamber of Deputies. The electoral college was elected by the same means, permitting minority control of that institution also. *Peronista* success under the law in 1962 prompted revision to the d'Hondt system.[22] Members of the electoral college are legally free to vote as they wish, but usually vote for party labels indicated on the ballot, if somewhat less consistently than in the United States.

There are several regressive qualities to Argentine legislative representation. Like the United States, the provinces are accorded equal representation in the national Senate. Since the electoral college is comprised of representatives equal to twice the number of deputies and senators for a province, small provinces are over-represented in the electoral college as well. The skew is more important in Argentina than the United States, since electoral college members are less bound by tradition to vote according to the popular vote in their district. The small province of Santa Cruz receives one elector for each seven thousand inhabitants, while the province of Buenos Aires receives one elector for each seventy thousand inhabitants. Overrepresentation of small provinces in the lower chamber is less significant, but still exists. James Rowe correctly observes that in 1963 under the former Sáenz Peña electoral law, Arturo Illia's 25 percent of the popular vote would have brought him 55 percent of the electoral college, enough to win, instead of the 35 percent he received under the d'Hondt system.[23]

Since political parties must qualify separately in each province, many parties are not truly national in elections, having only limited regional influence. This is particularly true of the smaller parties which support *Peronista* leaders. Even when the national *Peronista* party was declared illegal, pro-*Peronista* and neo-*Peronista* parties could achieve official registration in some provinces. Since the Senate is elected by provincial legislatures, it reflects the regional strength of small political parties including the *Peronistas*.

The d'Hondt system was used only in the 1963 and 1965 elections. The Sáenz Peña law which constrained proliferation and guaranteed a viable opposition is the same formula now used in Paraguay and Nicaragua to maintain control for a *single* dominant party. Argentine political divisions are numerous and subtle, and the system came to have a conservative if not politically disrupting influence on party politics, which ultimately worked in favor of the *Peronistas*.

3. POLITICAL PARTY CONFIGURATION IN ARGENTINA

The earliest nineteenth-century parties expressed the fundamental conflict of national unification: centralism versus provincialism. The two groupings, known as the Federalists and the Unitarians, operated largely as political organizations for opposing leaders despite the ideological facade. Political parties gained their strongest expression at the provincial level, since this was generally the focus of political power in politically unintegrated Argentina. The first attempt to bridge regional parties and focus them nationally was made by General Julio Argention Roca, who charismatically induced regional parties to coalesce. The combination brought him to the presidency twice, in 1880 and 1898. Roca's party was perhaps the first modern political "machine" assembled in Argentina.

Historically Buenos Aires was the heartland of Argentine liberalism, because of its greater political awareness and cosmopolitanism, but Buenos Aires also had a conservative tradition. From the forging of the united provinces into the Argentine Republic in 1862 until approximately 1890 the national politics reflected the schizophrenia of liberalism and conservatism in the personalities of its leaders, even though the traditional party ideological distinctions were even less a reality in Argentina than elsewhere in Latin America.

In 1890 the first of Argentina's mass parties emerged: the *Unión Cívica* (UC) or Civic Union party, in opposition to the traditional landed oligarchy as a vehicle for the growing middle class. Shortly afterward, a liberal wing of UC under the leadership of Juan B. Justo broke away and organized the *Partido Socialista* (PS) in 1894. Small and regional parties followed. The primary political parties competing prior to the Onganía coup of 1966 are summarized below.[24]

Peronista Parties. Perón's political parties date from 1943, when he organized members of the industrial working classes into a Labor party which endorsed his successful presidential campaign of 1946. Following 1946 the party name changed to *Partido Único de la Revolución* (PUR), and shortly afterward to *Partido Peronista* (PP). The PP was a personal party, with ideological symbols, doctrine, zeal, and governmental patronage. It swept the 1951 and 1954 elections, winning 52 and 63 percent of the vote. The party was tightly controlled by Perón and Eva, who had organized a Women's *Peronista* party in 1950 after feminine enfranchisement. With the 1951 economic decline, the PP became increasingly an instrument for governmental control. The *Confederación General de Trabajadores* (CGT) was a principal component for labor support in the PP, and many CTG leaders were closely identified with the party. Legal recognition was normally withheld from non-*Peronista* unions, and workers who didn't join the CTG and pay dues often could not obtain jobs or collect pensions. Membership in the PP was also obligatory for CTG members; the party grew rapidly.[25]

After 1955 the PP was declared illegal, and in the 1957–1960 elections its followers generally cast blank ballots. In 1958 Perón urged support for the Intransigent Radical party, and contributed to the UCRI victory. In the 1961 and 1962 elections, *Peronistas* formed several pro-*Peronista* parties and realized considerable electoral success before the military intervened and annulled the elections. Today the movement, like all parties, is illegal; it is also divided on regional, personal, and ideological axes. Regional leaders often do not support national leaders. A moderate wing, led nationally by Raul Matera, adopted a conciliatory policy of electoral participation, while a more militant group led by Andrés Framini refused to compromise, threatening cooperation with the Communists if necessary to achieve power. A supervisory, coordinating council to which both Matera and Framini belong tries vainly to coordinate *Peronista* activities nationally.[26]

Unión Cívica Radical Intransigente. The UCRI is one of two Radical parties formed by a 1957 split in the *Unión Cívica Radical.* The UCR had always been factionalized, almost entirely by personal rivalries. Originally the UCR carried the strong personal imprint of its leader, Hipólito Irigoyen, and a somewhat liberal ideological orientation. Marcelo de Alvear, Irigoyen's successor, drew more from conservative supporters who, during his 1924–1928 presidency, came to control him.

The UCR divided in 1957 over Arturo Frondizi's leadership. Frondizi, wanting the presidential nomination against the wishes of other UCR leaders, formed the UCRI and won the 1958 election with 45 percent of the vote; he received support also from the *Peronistas* and Communists. Without formal *Peronista* support in 1961 and 1962, the UCRI strengthened its electoral position by winning ten of the twenty-three electoral districts, including the federal capital. There was little ideological consistency in the UCRI, its nationalistic and personalistic appeals drew support from the vast middle and lower-middle-class base. The party was least regional of any Argentine parties except the *Peronistas*, and by 1962 had begun to develop strong support in industrial and urban areas. In 1963 the UCRI split, like the UCR before, over Frondizi's leadership. UCRI control went to Oscar Alende, who ran unsuccessfully for the presidency the same year. Frondizi formed the *Movimiento de Integración y Desarrollo* (MID), which received about six percent of the national vote in 1965; the same year the UCRI obtained less than five percent.

Unión Cívica Radical del Pueblo. The UCRP is the other half of the UCR formed by the 1957 division. Its founders include Miguel Zavala Ortiz, Amadeo Sabattini, Ricardo Balbín, and Francisco Rabanal. Balbín ran for the presidency in 1958 against Frondizi; in the next two national elections the party lost electoral support. By 1962 it carried a plurality in only one province, Córdoba, where it elected Arturo Illia governor. Illia gained national recognition later the same year when he resigned, charging interference from the new military government in "internal" politics of Córdoba. His resignation won him the UCRP presidential nomination in 1963 and the presidency. The UCRP was originally weaker than the UCRI, and won only 25 percent of the 1963 national vote; internal divisions prevented the UCRI from receiving more than 4.4 percent in 1965. UCRP strength lies in the provinces of Catamarca, Tucumán, Santa Fe, and Santa Cruz. Like the UCRI, the UCRP is not a stable party organization, but a series of factions united principally by their dislike of Frondizi and a moderate policy orientation. Illia, although an unknown if uncontroversial leader, led a united party for the 1963 campaign.

Partido Socialista Argentino. The PSA is the left-wing faction of a formally united Socialist party. The left-wing won the right legally to use the party label and emblem after a 1958 party division, a recent expression of the historic propensity for the party to divide ideologically and personalistically. The PSA divided again in 1960, with one wing led by David Tieffenberg committed to *Fidelismo* and another more moderate wing controlled by the "old guard." The former group became known as the Vanguard Socialist party, the latter as the Argentine Socialist party. Before the division, the PSA had received about six percent of the national vote, nearly all of which was drawn from Buenos Aires. Unlike the Chilean Socialist party, the Argentine group has steadily declined over the past decade, and is perhaps its own worst enemy. The *Peronistas* assumed control in the labor movement, and the PSA found it difficult to find another source of political support.

Partido Socialista Democrático. The PSD is the more moderate faction of the original 1958 Socialist party. It is modeled after European counterparts, and is strongly anti-Peronist and anti-Communist. While the PSA opportunistically supported Peronist candidates in 1962, the PSD remained ideologically pure if electorally weak. Most of its support, constituting no more than three percent of the national vote, comes from Buenos Aires.

Partido Demócrata Cristiano. Like most Latin American nations, Argentina has had an incipient Christian Democratic movement. The PDC polled only 4½ percent of the vote in 1963, and like other Argentine parties has divided over ideological and personal disputes since its founding in 1955.[27] The party support is distributed evenly across the nation, but its appeal was damaged by an abortive attempt to nominate a former Peronist for the 1963 presidential elections. In 1965, PDC vote fell to 2.6 percent.

Federación de los Partidos del Centro.   The FPC is a national federation of many provincial and small national parties. Included are the Democrat, Conservative, Conservative-Democrat, Liberal, and Popular Conservative parties. In spite of their names, the parties are united ideologically by a common dedication to *laissez-faire* economics, pastoral and agrarian interests, and state assistance to develop natural resources. Only the Popular Conservative party favored cooperation with the *Peronistas*. The federation polled approximately 5.5 percent of the 1963 national vote, winning the governorships of San Luis, Mendoza, and Corrientes provinces, in addition to several provincial congressional chambers. The FPC, led by the Democrat party, has had particularly strong response in the province of Mendoza.

Partido Demócrata Progresista.   The Progressive Democratic party is a small party located in the province of Santa Fe that enjoys substantial national prestige because of its enlightened leadership. In Santa Fe the PDP received, however, only 13 percent of the vote in 1961. In 1963 the PDP was a prime mover in the UDELPA coalition to support the candidacy of General Pedro Aramburu, obtaining about six percent of the national vote.

Partido Comunista Argentino.   The PCA has been periodically legal and illegal since its formation in 1918. In 1920, its supporters broke with the Socialist party to join the Third International and adopt the name Communist. Badly factionalized in its formative years, the PCA worked in the 1930s to enlist labor support; by 1943 it claimed 100 thousand members for the National Construction Federation that it established within the CGT. The party has had an uneasy relationship with the *Peronistas,* helping Perón form unions and supporting his 1951 election, only later to suffer his persecution. The party supported Frondizi in 1958, a socialist candidate in 1961, and the Peronists in 1962. The party has never received more than five percent of the national vote, almost all of it from Buenos Aires.[28] Ideologically, the party aligns itself with Moscow.

More than one hundred minor political parties were registered for the 1963 elections, 39 of them submitting lists for national presidential electors.[29] Many of the parties are localized at the provincial level.

Coalitions and Fronts.   Minor party proliferation induces electoral coalitions. Since many minor parties are *Peronista*, an ideological if not organizational basis sometimes exists. Two coalitions from the 1963 campaign illustrate the process.[30]

The *Unión del Pueblo Argentino* (UDELPA) was created by PDP leadership to support the candidacy of General Pedro Aramburu, a military leader who helped overthrow Perón and served briefly (1955–1958) as provisional president. Aramburu was first thought to be favorable to the UCRP, later to the UCRI, and still later to the *Peronistas* whom he tried to reintegrate into the national political life. Some members of the UCRP supported Aramburu's candidacy, as did many small, conservative parties.

Another 1963 coalition was the *Frente Nacional y Popular*. FNP was an abortive attempt to combine UCRI, the *Peronista* UP, and four minor parties, which broke apart a few days before the election. UCRI leaders supporting Oscar Alende had believed the FNP would nominate Alende, and deliver *Peronista* support to him. Perón, apparently trying to prevent the FNP from eroding his influence, induced FNP leaders to nominate the small Popular Conservative party leader, Vicente Solano Lima.

In spite of the many provincial and small parties, national competition in Argentina centered about three groups from 1955 to 1966: the UCRI, the UCRP, and the often illegal *Peronistas*. Each group was profoundly divided among its leaders, yet multi-party dominant representation remained. Under the Sáenz Peña law, competition was regularly multi-party dominant; but even in 1963 under proportional representation, the UCRP obtained 40 percent of the deputies and 55 percent of the senators, with only 25 percent of the popular vote.

4. VOTING AND PARTICIPATION IN ARGENTINA

Registration and voting are high in Argentina, reflecting a high level of political awareness. Voting is compulsory, but high participation is due more to cultural than legal factors. Two trends are visible from registration and participation data: participation tends to be uniformly high throughout the nation, with minimum differentiation from the capital to more remote provincial areas; and participation tends to remain high even in the face of general political alienation, confusion, frustration, and economic decline. Registration and participation trends in national elections from 1946 to 1963 are shown in Table 3-2.

Participation in the 1963 elections continued previous trends. The election was held on a cold, mid-winter day, July 7, 1963,

TABLE 3-2. VOTING REGISTRATION AND PARTICIPATION, 1946–1963

Year	Population	Registered	Percent population registered	Participation	Percent registered participating
1946	15,654,300	3,359,992	22	2,867,709	85
1948*	16,207,700	3,914,138	24	2,828,568	72
1951	17,164,400	8,764,348	51	8,764,348	87
1954	18,121,100	9,341,069	51	7,569,286	81
1957	19,052,300	9,723,863	51	8,507,024	87
1958	19,371,400	10,042,303	52	9,065,035	90
1960	20,008,945	10,113,903	51	8,916,669	87
1962	20,647,600	11,245,294	54	9,295,136	83
1963	21,200,000	11,354,026	55	9,717,657	86

* Women were first enfranchised in September, 1947, but few were officially registered for the 1948 elections.

amid an atmosphere of apprehension and confusion.[30] Urban participation reached 88–90 percent, with comparably high rates for the densely populated provinces of San Luis, Santa Fe, and Buenos Aires. Lowest turnout averaged 68–75 percent in the more remote, inaccessible provinces of Santa Cruz, Chubut, Misiones, Río Negro, and Chaco.

National party voting trends, shown for 1957–1965 in Table 3-3, indicate remarkably stable patterns with one key variable: the *Peronistas*.[31] If the blank voting is combined with the vote for small, provincial *Peronista* parties for the elections of 1957, 1960, and 1963, the *Peronista* vote is also a relatively stable 26–30 percent of the total. Greater variation occurred for the UCRI and UCRP, but evidence suggests that these groups essentially exchanged votes

TABLE 3-3. NATIONAL PARTY VOTING TRENDS, 1957–1965 (IN PERCENT)

Party	1957	1958	1960	1962	1963	1965
UCRP	23.2	25.4	23.7	19.9	25.4	28.6
UCRI	21.2	41.8	20.6	24.5	16.2	4.4
Socialists	6.1	5.7	8.4	4.5	6.5	3.8
Consevatives	5.7	3.2	8.7	6.0	5.7	5.4
Christian/Dem.	4.8	3.6	3.9	2.3	4.6	2.6
Prog.-Dem.	3.3	1.8	2.7	1.7	5.8	3.1
Peronista				31.9	7.0	34.5
Other	11.2	9.7	7.0	6.4	11.3	14.4
Blank vote	24.5	8.8	24.9	2.8	17.5	3.2

from one election to another. The stability of Argentine voting underscores party intransigence, and party failure to generate a new consensus necessary to support change. A series of public opinion polls taken in Buenos Aires by the newspaper *Correo de la Tarde* from June 6–12, 1967, following the Onganía revolution, demonstrated a profound alienation from conventional party politics and unwillingness to return to the previous system, and substantial support for the military takeover.[32] In fairness, economic frustrations as well as political ones may have prompted the support.

One possible reason why traditional Argentine parties like the Radicals failed to resolve social conflict is suggested by recently published evidence that the same upper and upper-middle classes provided leadership for all major parties. Even Socialist and Peronist national party committees were overwhelmingly drawn from these classes.[33] Yet Gino Germani has shown in an important study correlating aggregate voting data and occupational information, a strong correlation existed in the federal capital in 1946 between party voting and occupational class.[34] His data showed working class areas tended to vote *Peronista*, middle-class areas Radical, if to a lesser extent. Similar 1962 findings based on survey data for the federal capital confirm strong lower-class support for the *Peronistas*, and nearly identical middle- and upper-middle-class support for the two Radical parties.[35]

Peronista voting was normally strongest in Buenos Aires where Perón had organized labor support. The elections of 1962 and 1963 suggested a shift in *Peronista* support toward provincial centers. Combining blank and provincial *Peronista* party voting for the 1963 election reveals two regions where the party received in excess of 35 percent of the vote. One region was the northwest, including the provinces of Jujuy, Salta, Tucumán, and Chaco; the other was the southern portion of the nation, the provinces of Río Negro, Neuquén, Mendoza, La Pampa, and Santa Cruz. Most rapid *Peronista* growth (1962–63) occurred in Chaco, Santa Cruz, and Neuquén. *Peronista* voting declined in several traditional strongholds: the federal capital, and the provinces of Catamarca and Misiones.[36]

Provincial analyses of the 1962 legislative elections show several important characteristics of UCRI, UCRP, and *Peronista* competition. Voting strength for each group varies considerably from one province to another, but the UCRP and UCRI strongholds are remarkably similar. In 1962 the UCRI consistently outpolled the

UCRP in all provinces except Mendoza and Córdoba, but both did relatively best in the same provinces. The larger the province, the more competitive the three groups were, with most intense competition coming in the city of Buenos Aires, and the provinces of Córdoba and Entre Ríos. Chaco, La Rioja, and to a lesser extent Santa Fe also had close party competition. In general, the more rural and remote provinces had more idiosyncratic party affiliations.

Minor party voting tends to be strongest in the few provinces where minor parties are well organized. The PDC is the only exception, drawing its vote more evenly from all provinces. The importance of minor party voting is demonstrated by the fact that the UCRP won only one governorship in 1962, although they carried 13 out of the 23 districts in legislative voting. *Peronistas* through diverse party instruments won control of two states (Chaco and Neuquén) and the provincial legislatures in Jujuy, Mendoza, and Salta. The FNPC won control of Corrientes and San Luis, and the governorship of Mendoza. A summary of party control of provincial government in 1963 is contained in Table 3-4.[37] Minor parties and

TABLE 3-4. PARTY CONTROL OF PROVINCIAL GOVERNMENTS, 1963 ELECTION

Province	Governor	Senate dominance	Deputies dominance
Buenos Aires	UCRP	UCRP	UCRP
Catamarca	UCRP	UCRP	UCRP
Córdoba	UCRP	UCRP	UCRP
Corrientes	FNPC	FNCP-UCRI (tie)	FNPC-UCRI (tie)
Chaco	Peronist	*	Peronist
Chubut	UCRP	*	UCRP
Entre Ríos	UCRP	UCRP	UCRP
Formosa	UCRP	*	UCRP
Jujuy	UCRI	*	Peronist
La Pampa	UCRI	*	UCRI
La Rioja	UCRP	*	UCRP
Mendoza	FNPC	Peronist	Peronist
Misiones	UCRP	*	UCRP
Neuquén	Peronist	*	Peronist
Río Negro	UCRP	*	UCRP
Salta	MFD	Peronist	Peronist
San Juan	UCRB	*	UCRB
San Luis	FNPC	*	FNPC
Santa Cruz	UCRP	*	UCRP
Santa Fe	UCRP	UCRP-UCRI (tie)	UCRP
Santiago	UCRP	*	UCRP
Tucumán	UCRP	UCRI	UCRI

* These provinces have unicameral legislatures.

coalitions did relatively poorly in the national legislative voting, winning only 3.2 to 6.8 percent of the popular vote.

5. THE CAMPAIGN OF 1963: A CASE STUDY

The 1963 campaign is an interesting example of post-Perón politics. The entire slate of officers was elected on July 7, 1963, including 476 presidential electors, 192 national deputies, 1,144 gubernatorial electors, 223 provincial senators, 758 provincial deputies, and 5,572 muncipal councilmen. Besides these 8,365 positions, there were an additional 74 senatorial electors for the federal capital, 7,393 alternates for various municipal posts, and in several provinces school board members, justices of the peace, and other municipal offices, for a grand total of 21,173 positions. National senators were elected, as prescribed in the constitution, by state legislatures; the president was elected by the electoral college.[38]

In some respects the 1963 campaign began with the military overthrow of Arturo Frondizi, March 29, 1962. The reasons for Frondizi's fall were numerous and complex. With four years of his term expired, Frondizi had successfully endured several dozen crises and possible coups. The principal cause for his removal was the results of the March 18, 1962, elections to partly renew congress and the governorships. *Peronistas* under Frondizi's lenient policy had been permitted for the first time since 1955 to run candidates under their own party labels, namely *Unión Popular, Laborista,* and *Tres Banderas.* The *Peronistas* gained a plurality, receiving 2.9 million votes or about 32 percent. They received 45 deputies and 9 governorships, including Buenos Aires. Eleven days after the ballots were counted, Frondizi was imprisoned by the military.

The military acted in a generally unanimous fashion, united by a pervasive fear of the *Peronistas* and hatred of Frondizi. To maintain a thread of legality, the military officers persuaded the president of the Senate, José María Guido, to assume the presidency since there was no vice president at the time. He ruled with military support for 18 months, while the military increasingly factionalized and rumors of countercoups spread.

Electoral reforms were enacted by decree for the 1963 campaigns. Two fundamental changes, known together as the Martinze Plan, outlawed totalitarian parties, urging a broad coalition to participate in the election, and installed a system of d'Hondt proportional representation to guarantee minority party and control *Peronista* representation. *Peronistas* were allowed to participate on the condition that they act with "restraint;" this policy was subsequently changed and the national *Peronista Unión Popular* was denied the right to submit lists for presidential and gubernatorial electors.

To maintain their leverage, the *Peronistas* (UP) agreed to a broad coalition (FNP) with other parties. The arrangement was inherently unstable, and collapsed shortly afterward; the *Peronistas* then called for a blank or protest vote. Confusion was compounded during the final week of campaigning when competitive UCRI factions fought a last minute court battle for exclusive right to the party label, with supporters of Alende and Frondizi on opposing sides. Meanwhile, the PDC opportunistically nominated disaffected *Peronista* Raul Matera for the presidency, only to have him reject the party two days before the election and force it to reendorse the party's familiar candidate, Horacio Sueldo.

The potential issues of the campaign were profound, but infrequently articulated. Economically the nation was in a disastrous downward spiral. Inflation was a growing menace, unemployment was high. Many doubted the resolve of military leaders to honor the electoral results. If their positions provided no alternatives, the candidate's personalities did. The UCRP had the least difficulty finding a candidate. The party's nominal leader, Ricardo Balbín, unsuccessful opponent of Perón (1951) and Frondizi (1958) withdrew voluntarily in favor of Arturo Illia. The country doctor from Córdoba had won the governorship in 1962, and gained national prominence when he resigned charging interference in the provincial government following the coup. The UCRI candidate, Alende, was a surgeon by profession, and formerly governor (1958–1962) of Buenos Aires. Alende supported Frondizi's policy of reintegrating *Peronistas* into Argentine political life. The small but vigorous PDP combined with other groups to form UDELPA and support the candidacy of Pedro Aramburu, a retired army general who had helped overthrow Perón in 1955. The PDC adopted a radical policy position, urging nationalization of public services and major industries, and nullification of an unpopular petroleum contract with Standard Oil of California.

Four voting districts were pivotal in the election: Buenos Aires province, the federal capital, Córdoba, and Santa Fe. Together they provided nearly 70 percent of the national votes. Aramburu did relatively best in these areas; Illia was second, Alende third, and the *Peronistas* fourth. The *Peronistas* received a total blank and provincial party vote of 22.4 percent, far less than anticipated. Some

TABLE 3-5. NATIONAL PRESIDENTIAL AND LEGISLATIVE PARTY VOTING, 1963 (IN PERCENT)

Party	Presidential candidate	Per-cent	Elec. votes	Legislative votes	Per-cent	Depu-ties	Sena-tors
UCRP	Arturo Illia	25.1	169	2,419,268	24.9	72	25
UCRI	Oscar Alende	16.4	109	1,541,452	15.9	40	5
UDELPA	Pedro Aramburu	13.9	74	656,124	6.8	15	1
-PDP				555,891	5.7	12	0
FNPC	Emilio Olmos	5.2	29	538,425	5.5	12	1
PDC	Horacio Sueldo	4.5	23	436,922	4.5	7	2
PSA	A. Palacios	2.9	12	310,729	3.2	6	0
PDS	Alfredo Orgáz	2.7	10	306,648	3.2	5	0
(Other)		4.5	30	458,569	4.7	7	3
(Peronista parties)		3.6	20	628,515	6.5	16	9
Blank votes		18.8	—	1,668,482	17.2	—	—
Null votes		2.5	—	193,955	—	—	—
TOTAL		100.0	476	9,714,780	100.0	192	46

of the blank vote can be legitimately attributed to the confusion which surrounded the election. Electoral results are provided in Table 3-5.

6. SUMMARY

An analysis of contemporary Argentine politics under the present military regimes is necessarily synthetic.[39] Political parties are illegal, their resources confiscated; no elections are announced or anticipated, and the government rules by decree under warrant from the military.

Nonetheless, the post-Perón period has seen considerable political party activity and six national elections. Three groups have dominated party politics: the UCRP, UCRI, and the Peronistas; all are divided, primarily on personal lines. The Radical parties appeal to the pervasive Argentine middle class with few stable ideological differences, and neither can command a majority of the vote. The imponderable in the system is the Peronistas, whose titular leader ages in Spain, while his lieutenants quarrel at home over control of the national movement. Peronistas, like most Argentine political organizations, are factionalized and regionalized. Their division has been encouraged by Perón, who seems dedicated to denying anyone else a dominant leadership position. Minor parties are plentiful, normally localized at the state level. The Marxist movement is hopelessly divided, although the Communist party retains a popular base in the core area despite its historic illegality.

For all the apparent instability of Argentina's party system, there are forces of gravity. Beyond the *Peronistas* only the two Radical parties are serious contenders for the plurality vote, and they are both characterized by a center ideological position. Major responsibility for party functions rests with these groups, for coalitions, while rational in the political sense, have proved unworkable. Political awareness, reflected in registration and participation, is high for Latin America, and rarely equalled in the United States. Considering the economic and institutional provocations, one might have expected increased political apathy and abstention from 1957 to 1963; even with the uncertainties of the 1963 election, however, 86 percent of the eligible voters participated. It is a curious and perhaps significant comment on the Argentine federal system that national parties coexist with provincial ones, and sometimes compete with them.

Surprisingly little is known about how Argentine parties organize, recruit leaders, and finance campaign activities. What is known about Argentine party politics is paradoxical: a highly developed political system seems unable historically to resolve political conflicts, and is subject to chronic military intervention, personalistic politics, and governmental instability. But there is another, perhaps more confounding, paradox in Argentine electoral life. Despite high voter involvement in electoral processes, a military coup like that of 1966 can pass with hardly a comment from the informed electorate. None of the recent coups have stimulated widespread violence or involvement, supporting or opposing the change. Perhaps the system has failed at a critical juncture to recruit effective, committed leaders to direct the nation, or perhaps this is merely a reflection of more fundamental problems in the national culture. Whichever, Argentina is as divided and unstable as any political system in Latin America. Multi-party dominant competition has been achieved in spite of the instability, and is all the more remarkable because of it.

II. CHILE: THE POLITICS OF ORDERLY CHANGE

Nowhere in Latin America are party politics and elections more relevant to national decision-making than in Chile. The nation has experienced a sustained period of political stability and electoral processes. Rapid change has characterized the party system during the past decade. An historically proliferated party system has consolidated and become more competitive, and a Christian Democratic party came to national power for the first time in Latin America.[40]

1. THE CONTEXT AND CULTURE OF CHILEAN POLITICS

Sandwiched between the Andes to the east and the Pacific Ocean to the west, the nation extends 2,600 miles from the arid, desert wastelands of the north to the uninhabitable if spectacular fjords of the south, with never more than 120 miles from the eastern to western borders. The northernmost borders contain lands won in battle from Peru and Bolivia in the late nineteenth century. This area is some of the driest land in the world, although the temperatures are moderated by the pervasive Humbolt current off the northern coasts. The rich, temperate central valleys contain most of Chile's national population and its capital city, Santiago. The southern provinces become increasingly verdant, wet, and cold, although snow at sea level is rare even in the southernmost regions. What Indians remain in Chile are concentrated in small areas in the south, living on reservations not unlike those in the United States until they assimilate by migration to the cities.[41]

Chile today is a distinctive *mestizo* country, with strong immigrant components. Santiago, the attractive, sprawling capital, is more European than most Latin American capitals, and has a strong German and English influence. Chile is an urban country, but unlike others it has significant cities beyond the capital. Santiago Province contains about one-third of the national population, and the next largest cities (Valparaíso and the resort, Viña del Mar) are also located in the same central region. Secondary cities are distributed from north to south, so the urban/rural division is not limited to a simple capital/province dichotomy.

Most foreign exchange comes from mining, specifically copper. The industry contributes its share of political problems also, since it has been historically controlled by two North American firms, Anaconda and Kennecott, whose attitudes toward their Chilean investments have not always been enlightened. Once a food exporter, Chile now must import nearly one-third of the food it consumes. This situation creates dire consequences politically and economically, for it absorbs a large portion of the foreign exchange, and contributes to the chronic inflationary spiral. Price controls and periodic shortages are a way of life in Chile. Inflation, fundamentally caused by the unwillingness and inability of the government to raise sufficient revenue for its expenditures, has been present in Chile for more than half a century and has had a cultural impact on the nation.[42] The standard of living (about $365. per capita) is low but has been increasing. The trend is particularly critical in relation to the high level of education (literacy 80 percent) in Chile, and the natural economic expectations arising therefrom. More Chileans attend universities than in many European nations.[43] Additional economic pressures arise from the population increase of about 2.4 percent annually.

Without the attractions of gold and silver, Chile was never highly regarded by early Spanish colonialists. The area was settled by agrarian-minded soldiers migrating from the more highly prized lands of Peru. Agrarianism was the origin of the Chilean people and their nation. Large concentrations of land were family owned, and generated comfortable lives for their owners with minimum effort. The settlement patterns produced a remarkably integrated national culture, and an ineffective agricultural system which today remains the principal economic problem.[44]

Although less influential than in Argentina, migration from Europe in the late nineteenth and early twentieth centuries affected the development of Chilean political culture. Europeans came in significant numbers from Germany, England, Italy, and Spain, attracted by an alternative to the political and economic uncertainties and instability of Europe during the period. The influence of the Germans, particularly in southern Chile, and the English in central Chile is still visible.[45]

Chile's economic prosperity came not from its land, but from its minerals. Although lacking gold and silver, Chile discovered great deposits of copper and nitrates, which stimulated foreign capital and international exploitation. Prosperity grew, particularly during the European wars, and Santiago was transformed into a great city while the nation began to construct railways, ports, and limited, highly protected national industries.[46]

National political awareness developed in Chile steadily during the nineteenth century. The 1833 Constitution provided centralized government until 1925, making it one of the most enduring constitutions in Latin America.[47] Chile's military flexed its muscles against a proposed federation of Bolivia and Peru in the war of 1836–1839, and successfully imposed its will on the northern neighbors. In 1843 President Bulnes claimed all territory to the south as far as the Straits of Magellan, establishing the city of Punta Arenas in the southernmost extremity of the nation. In 1864 Chileans successfully withstood a brief challenge by the Spanish, who attempted to reestablish their hegemony over the former colonies of Peru and Chile. In 1879–1883 Chile fought the War of the Pacific against Bolivia and Peru over the rich northern nitrate fields. The newly established Chilean navy won a series of quick victories, and Chilean troops occupied Lima from 1881 to 1884.[48] The War of the Pacific remains a source of great national pride in Chile.

A new plutocracy created by nitrate and copper joined forces with the Liberal party to break control of Conservative party forces centered in Santiago, which with the Church had been historically dominant.[49] Immigrants from Europe with middle-class perspectives and unionized miners created additional challenges to the traditional regimes. In 1886 Liberal José Manuel Balmaceda embarked on a reform program, stressing public works, sanitation, education, transportation, and simultaneously encouraging anticlericalism. Faced with intransigent opposition from a Conservative Congress, Balmaceda became increasingly arbitrary and tyrannical; he was eventually deposed in 1891 after an eight-month civil war.[50]

For the next thirty years Chile shifted its political system toward a parliamentary style, with cabinet responsibility to the legislature. Parties proliferated to reflect newly relevant interests, and cabinets fell with increasing frequency as they failed to satisfy these interests.[51] The Liberals grew relatively more conservative, and often made common cause with the Conservatives. A new party, the Radicals, has been founded in 1861 from more reform oriented members of the Liberal party. After 1891 the Radical party increasingly became the spokesman for Chilean discontent. The party recruited some of the new plutocracy, which saw vested interests in Santiago and Valparaíso as the primary challenge, but eventually the party developed a middle-class orientation. While differing little on economic questions with the two traditional parties, the Radicals were anticlerical, and advocated administrative decentralization, state supervision of education, and expanded suffrage, much like European Radical party movements.[52] Further movement on the left followed in 1912 with the formation of the Socialist Labor party with a nucleus of miners and industrial workers. In 1920, a Communist party was formed. Personalistic, ad hoc, and local parties were particularly common during the parliamentary period.[53]

Widespread political dissatisfaction spread in the early twentieth century, caused by reckless economic policies, a serious inflation, administrative corruption, and political opportunism. Strikes and street violence became a serious threat, until even the arch-conservative president, Juan Luis Sanfuentes, elected in 1915, saw the prudence of granting pay increases, limited welfare measures, and pensions to the aroused workers and populace. Unemployment after World War I worsened the situation.[54]

In 1920 Chileans elected Liberal Arturo Alessandri Palma in what was to become the first of a series of unsuccessful, "bloodless" revolutions. Whatever his intentions, Alessandri's first four years in office were unproductive, his efforts blocked by an obstreperous congress. By mid-1924, under threat of expanded violence, the military forced Alessandri into exile; a countercoup, however, led by Carlos Ibáñez and other military officers, returned Alessandri to power and prompted a new constitution.[55] The 1925 constitution, still in effect, strengthened presidential powers but limited the term to one election. Congress lost its assumed power to unseat cabinets, and the Church and state were irrevocably separated.[56] Conservative opposition mounted, and the same military leaders who returned Alessandri to power forced him out again in October, 1925. For the next six years Chileans lived under a virtual dictatorship by Colonel Carlos Ibáñez del Campo. The world depressions brought new problems for Chile, and Chileans looked for a panacea. Alessandri, less aggressive than before, won another term in 1932, but did little to resolve the problems facing Chilean society and left office with few supporters.

In 1938 Chile, like some European nations, was ruled by a popular front comprised of Radical, Socialist, and Communist parties. Like other popular fronts, the Marxists found the coalition uninhabitable, and power gravitated to the Radicals. Radicals won the following presidential elections of 1942 and 1946. In the latter, Gabriel González Videla won election by courting the support of the Communists, but like his predecessors he found them uncooperative allies, and eventually forced them underground by prodding congress to declare the party illegal.[57]

Increased demand for Chilean copper during World War II relieved the pressures on the international side, but failure to implement domestic reforms left major economic problems unresolved. After World War II the demand and price for Chilean copper collapsed, and old crises returned. By 1952 Chileans were again looking for a "bloodless revolution" to resolve the problems that dated from before World War I. Paradoxically, the military man who had ruled so arbitrarily from 1925 to 1931, Carlos Ibáñez, ran for the presidency and was easily elected. Allegedly, Ibáñez received substantial financial support from his friend, Juan Perón. Ibáñez also received support from the illegal Communist party which was eager to defeat the Radicals and restore their legality. Ibáñez' regime was generally conciliatory and restrained, and the economic situation improved until mid-1957, when copper prices fell nearly forty percent.[58]

In 1958 Chileans once again sought a solution to the chronic economic problems, and thought they had found one in Jorge Alessandri. The son of Arturo had more or less the unified support of Liberals and Conservatives, although he lacked strong party identity. Marxists coalesced with the legalized Communist party, and supported a dynamic, wealthy physician, Salvador Allende, for the presidency. The third candidate was Eduardo Frei, running with the support of the Falange, a party soon to be known as Christian Democratic.[59]

Alessandri's regime was a popular one, but his efforts to resolve the economic crises were unsuccessful. He renegotiated U.S. loans for the copper industry, and solicited economic assistance for the Chilean economy. U.S. companies in Chile had failed generally to reinvest profits in capitalization to replace outdated and inefficient equipment, which was needlessly restricting vital copper output. Alessandri also obtained a moderate land reform bill, but it too was unable to resolve that chronic problem. Alessandri, like his predecessors, left office with the country measurably worse off economically than before.

To the casual observer Chile gives the impression of a middle-class nation with many poor people. It does not appear to be a nation whose economic and health indicators are no better than Mexico, or only median for Latin America. The appearance is very deceptive. Chileans, perhaps more than any other Latin Americans, are aspiringly middle class and treasure the symbols of *bourgeois* living, particularly clothes, that can mislead foreign observers into thinking people are living better than they actually are. The dominant cultural mentality is that of middle-class Europeans, who migrated to Chile and influenced cultural and social mores. The trait is reinforced by the relatively high level of education, and an educational system that penetrates many of the more provincial areas. Educational sophistication and cultural integration far exceed the general level of economic achievement, creating a gap between expectations and realizations that pressures the political system toward economic revision, income redistribution, and "radical" economic reform. Chile is a nation of frustrated consumers, laboring under an unfair and probably self-pitying comparison with wealthier Argentines across the mountains, aware of their deprivations and for half a century unable to do very much about them. Governmentally induced inflation encourages Chileans to live on a grand buying spree, for consumer and capital goods are the only protection from an inflating money supply.[60] The Chilean industrial economy, for its size, is diversified, particularly in the consumer market, but production is inefficiently low and distribution a critical cost factor. Government policy has permitted monopolies to arise, and to control the more obvious abuses of monopolistic pricing, has set prices on many items. The government is the principal importer and wholesaler of food, and political sensitivities require it to set prices at levels often below cost. Inflation, price-setting, and government subsidization are but indirect taxes on the wage-earner, and create as many political tensions as they resolve.

Chronic economic frustration and failures of the bloodless revolutions have encouraged a potentially alienated, cynical, explosive political culture. Alienation and cynicism about politics abound in Chile, but the political processes remain essentially orderly, non-violent, and structured. Parties have so far been able to maintain the hope of an alternative road; when a ruling party's fortunes decline, others have been able to offer an alternative. The remarkable quality of Chilean political culture is this integration and passivity in the face of economic, geographic, and even social fragmentation. This cultural integration is reflected in party activity, elections, and voting, and perhaps accounts for the tranquility of Chilean politics even in the face of perpetual economic crisis and frustration.[61]

2. CONTEMPORARY POLITICAL PARTIES IN CHILE

As in most multi-party systems, party registration in Chile is relatively easy. Within 240 days of an election, a prospective party must register with the board of electoral registry, filing its statutes, executive committee names, and the signatures of ten thousand voters. The party is legally recognized as long as it receives representation in Congress; otherwise, it must reregister for each election.[62] The principal trends in Chilean party politics over the past few decades have been consolidation and increasing competition; this competition and consolidation are revealed in Table 3-6.[63] In 1949, 15 parties received congressional representation; by 1969, this

TABLE 3-6. Contraction of Chilean Party System Through Coalition and Competition Revealed by Lower House Representation

Party	1945	1949	1953	1957	1961	1965	1969	1970*
PC	30	21	16	22	23	3		
							34†	34
PL	32	33	22	29	28	6		
PDC	3	3	4	14	23	82	55	55
PR	34	42	20	36	39	20	24	
PS	1	11	7	11				60††
PCCh‡	5				28**	33	37	
Other	42	37	78	35	12	3		1
TOTALS	147	147	147	147	147	147	150	150

SOURCE: Dirección del Registro Electoral y Oficina de Informaciones, and El Mercurio, March 4, 1969.

* There were no congressional elections in 1970; the figures are inserted to indicate coalitional balances following that year's presidential election.

† PC and PL combined to form the "National party" in May, 1966.

‡ PCCh illegal from 1949–1959.

** PS and PCCh coalesced to form FRAP with other small parties for the 1958 presidential election. The coalition was more important electorally than legislatively. The PS factionalized following the 1969 elections.

†† The PS, PCCh, and PR coalesced to form UP (Unidad Popular) for the 1970 presidential election.

number was reduced to six. Balances between the parties are equalizing, and two coalitions have further reduced the effective number of political alternatives in the party system. The principal parties competing in Chile are summarized below.

Partido Nacional. The National party (PN) was created in 1966 by a fusion of the former *Partido Conservador Unido* (PCU) and the *Partido Liberal* (PL) after both suffered serious declines from 1950 to 1965. Some Conservative party strength has remained in rural Chile, particularly in the central region, where autocratic landed power maintained its power. The Liberal party drew from wealthy commercial and industrial leaders, the upper middle class, and extracted votes from both rural and urban centers.[64] As late as 1965 the Liberal party drew a substantial vote from the populous Santiago Province despite its essentially conservative appeal. Conservatives ruled Chile until the Liberals came to power for thirty years in 1861. Never at odds on economic policy, the collapse of the Church/state conflict in the late nineteenth century removed the principal obstacle between the two groups; remaining differences were specific economic interests. The Conservative party received its largest post-war vote in 1950, and has steadily declined since. The Liberal party vote remained relatively stable, and actually increased in the elections prior to 1961. Both parties nominally endorsed Frei in 1964 as the "lesser of two evils," and contributed substantially to the Christian Democratic victory. After the election, they entered the ranks of the opposition, and the Christian Democrats have made no effort to coalesce with them on a permanent basis.

Partido Radical.   The Radical party (PR) formed in 1861 from Liberal party followers, the same year the PL first achieved national power. At first the party differed from the PL primarily in the militancy of its advocates, not their doctrines.[65] It tried to attract the growing middle and lower middle classes by advocating radical policies. The two faces of the PR were particularly evident in the 1937 presidential campaign during the popular front with Marxists. Radical campaign appeals during 1937 were as strong as its collaborators, but later, when in power, the party alienated its partners by its hesitancy to act. During the 14 years (1938–1952) the party was in power it recruited heavily from the ranks of the growing bureaucracy, and established a vast system of regional patronage to reward followers in more distant provinces. Until the 1965 Christian Democratic victory, the Radicals were the dominant political party. Much of its support now is in provincial regions where party organizations and rivalries with Santiago remain strong, and in Santiago among government workers and part of the middle class. The PR supported Alessandri (1958–1964), but opposed Frei and has more recently moved steadily toward the left in an effort to increase its votes. Many Chileans still regard the PR as a "center party," highly political, willing to negotiate with anyone near power for short-run gains.[66]

Partido Demócrata Cristiano.   The Christian Democratic party (PDC) is the dominant party today in Chile. It has enjoyed a majority of lower house seats for the first time in recent years, and in the 1969 elections received a plurality of seats in both houses.[67] It has occupied the presidency and won a majority of local elective offices (*regidores*). The party formed as a youth organization from the Conservative Party in the mid-1930's, committed to liberal Christian ideals expressed in the papal encyclicals, *Rerum Novarum* and *Quadragesimo Anno*. Led by university students, the group became independent in 1938 as the *Falange Nacional* (National Falange), in no way of course related to the Spanish party of Franco by the same name. Party growth was slow during the next two decades: as late as 1953, the PDC received only 2.9 percent of the vote. Growing alienation from traditional Chilean parties helped the PDC. By 1963, when it received 23 percent of the municipal election votes, it had become the strongest national party. The most characteristic quality of the PDC is its doctrinaire base. Partly because of self-identification with liberal Christian theology, the party advocates can be more radical than their Marxist opponents, whom they see as the principal rivals. The party has enacted many reform programs, including land reform, and "Chileanization" of the mining industry.[68] With national success came ideological and generational factionalization. Frei's leadership is pragmatic, an older generation that founded the party 35 years ago. The younger congressional wing has been much more radical, and precipitated a serious intraparty confrontation at the 1967 convention. The moderate wing prevailed, but some militants withdrew to form the *Movimiento de Acción Popular Unitaria* (MAPU) and support the candidacy of Jacques Chonchol for the 1970 presidential elections. The youthful PDC leader was formerly a member of Frei's administration, and built strong support among the *campesinos* whom he helped organize. Chonchol is considered by many as a potentially strong leader on the Chilean left.

Partido Socialista. The Socialist party (PS) is the result of early efforts to mobilize the noncommunist left in Chile.[69] The PS grew rapidly in the 1930's, and participated in the unsuccessful popular front government in 1938. Like many socialist parties elsewhere, the Chilean one has perpetually divided over doctrine, leadership, and affiliation with other groups. The process was particularly disastrous during the post-popular front period, when several factions became competing parties. The specific question of cooperation with the Communists has been a particularly difficult issue. In 1956 the Socialists, who had benefited from communist support during the ten year period of that party's illegality, combined with the Communists and a few small groups to form the *Frente de Acción Popular* (FRAP), supporting as 1958 presidential candidate Socialist leader Salvador Allende.[70] In 1968 FRAP divided, and the Socialist party experienced another split. Partly because of Allende's personal friendship with Fidel Castro, the PS since the Cuban Revolution became the spokesman for *Fidelismo* in Chile, and today the party is generally regarded as more militant, more radical, more youthful, and more vital than the Communist party. Voting has remained relatively stable for the PS over the past decade, with some increases in the past two elections. The candidacy of Allende in 1958, 1964, and 1970 brought the party to an important position in national politics, but organization problems made sustained growth very difficult. Voting is reasonably well distributed throughout the nation.

Partido Comunista de Chile. The Chilean Communist party (PCCh) was founded after the 1921 Third International, using as its nucleus a labor organization. The Stalin-Trotsky feud divided the party, but it has participated in elections regularly except for the ten-year period (1948–1958) of illegality.[71] The party's vote has grown very slowly, remaining essentially unchanged throughout the years. Closely aligned to the party is the Central Union of Chilean Workers, many of whose officers are Communist party leaders. Regionally the party draws its heaviest vote from the northern mining regions, the province of Aruaco in the south, and a few other isolated areas. The party has made some progress building support in rural Chile, but has had stiff PDC competition for the university community and, particularly, the poorest neighborhoods of Santiago. The PCCh has lost some of its former vitality, partly because younger intellectual leaders affiliated instead with the more dynamic PS.[72] In 1970 the PCCH, the PS, and the PR supported Salvador Allende through an electoral alliance, *Unidad Popular,* and won the presidency. The PCCh has generally remained within the mainstream of Chilean culture, working for victory through electoral rather than revolutionary means.

Minor Parties. The only minor party to enjoy national legislative representation in 1966 was the National Democratic party (PADENA). PADENA was founded in 1960 after the municipal elections, to coalesce former supporters of President Ibáñez from the non-Marxist left. It went into the 1961 elections with six senators, but all of them were defeated; it elected 12 deputies, and received about seven percent of the vote.[73] Its vote declined to five percent in the 1963 municipal elections, and to three percent in 1965 when it elected only two deputies; by 1969, PADENA lost its remaining deputies and received less than two percent of the vote. Other minor parties participate, under such names as Democratic party, Agrarian-Labor Democracy, National People's Vanguard, Popular Commandos, and National Action, but none have received representation in the congress.

Coalitions. Coalitions were once a way of political life in Chile, necessitated by the proliferated party system and the reliance upon congress for policy leadership. In 1960 formal coalitions were prohibited by refusing recognition for them on ballots; yet Chilean parties, particularly the Marxists, found a way around the prohibition to maintain the *Frente de Acción Popular* (FRAP) which they had formed in February, 1956. FRAP contained the Communist party, two factions of the Socialist party, the *Partido del Trabajo* (PT), and a splinter of the National Democratic party. Although the prohibition of coalitions, obviously designed to restrain FRAP, denied official ballot recognition for coalitions, the participating parties reached an agreement whereby each would run candidates in alternate districts where they were strongest, concentrating all potential votes for FRAP parties in one party; only where there was a good chance of winning several seats did each FRAP party participate against each other.

Independent Candidates. Chilean electoral laws permit independent candidates, who can register by presenting signed petitions: 20 thousand signatures for a presidential candidate, 5 thousand for a senator, 2 thousand for a deputy, and from 100 to 2,000 signatures for councilman depending upon the size of the district. Once there were many independent congressmen, particularly in the Senate, but these have steadily declined or affiliated with parties until only one independent remains in the 1969 Senate.

3. REPRESENTATION IN CHILE

Representation is based upon population and a unitary, bicameral legislative system. The constitution specifies that the lower chamber shall be proportioned one delegate for each 30 thousand inhabitants, allocated to the traditional provinces serving as multimember districts. No set number of deputies is specified; presently there are 150 members. The Senate is set at 50 members elected from ten groups of provinces (with 1–6 provinces in each group) roughly equal in size, each with five senators. Lower chamber districts have between 1–18 deputies, and two provinces are subdivided: Ñuble Province has two congressional districts, Santiago Province four. Municipal councilmen (*regidores*) are also elected from multi-member districts.[74] One of the more remarkable qualities of Chilean representation is the misapportionment that resulted from failure to reapportion for an extended period, combined with strong population growth and urbanization trends. The specific impact of misapportionment on Santiago Province is discussed below.

Chilean elections are staggered. The president, who holds office for six years, is elected in alternate years with the Congress. Deputies are elected to four-year terms, senators to eight-year terms; a portion of the Senate is elected in each congressional election. Councilmen, like deputies, are elected for four-year terms, but in separate elections. A presidential election must be certified by a joint session of Congress for which a majority (quorum) must be present. If a presidential candidate receives a clear majority of the popular vote, Congress is obliged to certify him. If no candidate receives a majority, Congress may choose between the highest two candidates.[75] In the past three presidential elections, the candidate with the plurality of the vote has been chosen; Frei was the first presidential candidate since 1946 to receive a clear majority of the vote.

4. ELECTIONS AND VOTING

As is common elsewhere in Latin America, a specific agency (*Dirección del Registro Electoral*) is charged with the responsibility for conducting elections, which in Chile includes printing national ballots. Each department has its own electoral board to establish polling places and select supervisors. Appeals on electoral controversies proceed through a specified appeal hierarchy which includes: the polling station officials, the department counting colleges where tabulation occurs, the provincial qualification courts, and the national qualification court—the highest appeal agency. The national qualification court is comprised of two representatives from the congress and three from the national judiciary. The provincial qualification courts include both public officials and "taxpayers."[76]

Complex legal requirements filter prospective candidates: the president must be "natural born," at least 30 years old; senators must be at least 35, deputies 21 years old. Candidates must be literate and registered for voting; criminal offenders are excluded. Party affiliation for six months is required for candidacy, unless the candidate wishes to run as an independent. Congressional candidates must file four months prior to the elections, presidential candidates 45 days prior to the election.[77]

Voters are registered on three lists: male, female, and foreigners. Women were enfranchised with the election of 1952, and foreigners who have lived in Chile for five years can qualify for registration to vote in municipal elections. Names are collected on a master list of 300, which is renewed whenever 15 or more persons either move or die. Men and women vote in separate localities, and the vote is tallied separately. The voter receives a separate ballot for each election contest, although municipal, congressional, and presidential elections do not normally overlap. Candidates are listed on the ballot by party, in an order determined by lot. Ballots are differentiated by color, and printed as an open envelope which the voter marks, folds, and seals. Unlike the closed-list type ballot, the open-list ballot permits the Chilean voter to indicate candidate preferences, although write-in candidates are not permitted and invalidate the ballot.

Campaigning is legally limited to two months for congressional and municipal races, six months for presidential contests. These limitations are effective only in controlling propaganda, posters, advertisements, and news media reports. Two days prior to the election all propaganda must cease. Poll-watchers are used from each party to help guarantee impartiality and fair procedures, much as in the United States.[78] Voting tends to be impartial and fair; fraud is no more common in Chile than in the United States or European nations. Newspapers give full election coverage and print massive amounts of electoral information, including registration and eligibility data. Other news media provide intensive coverage of elections, both analytic and descriptive; television is less important than elsewhere, since there are relatively few receivers and few channels.

The standard d'Hondt distributive formula is used to allocate seats in congress and the municipal councils. Votes are tallied for each candidate separately, and then for all candidates of a party; seats are awarded to parties according to their total vote, then seats are awarded to candidates for the party that received the largest vote. The Chilean system institutionalizes a primary within the general election, and permits considerable latitude for personalistic campaigning.

5. Political Regionalism in Chile

Any discussion of Chilean politics must evaluate the impact of the obvious geographic and cultural regionalism upon the political processes.[79] Most of Chile's provinces are "stacked" upon one another from north (Tarapacá) to south (Magallanes). Table 3-7 summarizes the principal regions and their characteristics.[80]

Great North. The northernmost region comprises two provinces, Tarapacá and Antofagasta, and three cities: Antofagasta, Calama, and Iquique. Both provinces were won by Chile in the War of the Pacific, but have since assimilated into the national culture remarkably well. Neither province receives any rainfall,

TABLE 3-7. POLITICAL REGIONALISM IN CHILE

Region and province	Percent of population	Percent of area	Percent of electorate	Percent urban
GREAT NORTH	4.6	24.7	5.0	78.7
Tarapacá				
Antofagasta				
LITTLE NORTH	5.7	15.9	5.4	42.3
Atacama				
Coquimbo				
CENTRAL URBAN	43.4	4.4	50.0	
Aconcagua				
Valparaíso				
Santiago				
NORTH CENTRAL	10.0	4.2	8.3	37.0
O'Higgins				
Colchagua				
Curicó				
Talca				
SOUTH CENTRAL	7.3	3.9	5.9	34.0
Maule				
Linares				
Ñuble				
FRONTIER	18.6	7.4	16.5	48.9
Concepción				
Bío-Bío				
Arauco				
Malleco				
Cautín				
LAKES	7.7	6.2	6.1	36.5
Valdivia				
Osorno				
Llanquihue				
CANALS	2.8	33.0	2.9	41.0
Chiloe				
Aisén				
Magallanes				

being among the driest land in the world. This climatological phenomena concentrates most of the population in the urban areas and in the mining communities. All the nitrates and about half the copper production in Chile comes from this region. The northernmost city in Chile, Arica, has also become by government decision the center of automobile assembly, and has stimulated considerable subsidiary commercial and industrial activity. Because of the high level of union activity in the region, particularly miners, the area has a large Communist Party following.

Little North. This region includes the provinces of Atacama and Coquimbo, with La Serena, Ovalle, and Coquimbo being the primary urban areas. Once a copper mining region, the mines are now nearly exhausted and being replaced by iron mining. There is some agriculture, stimulated by rivers flowing from the Andes to the sea. Politically the region gravitates around the Radical and Communist parties.

Central Urban. This region contains the provinces of Aconcaugua, Valparaíso, and Santiago, and the nation's largest cities: Santiago, Valparaíso, and Viña del Mar. Comprised of high valleys, the region is an agricultural area as well as the industrial and commercial center of Chile. Half the national population is in this region, and the parties are very competitive.

North Central. The provinces of O'Higgins, Colchagua, Curicó, and Talca are contained in this agricultural center of Chile. Poor production and inefficient land use create economic inequalities that tend to be reflected in party activity. The strongest parties are the National, Socialist, and Communist.

South Central. Maule, Linares, and Ñuble are the provinces in this cool, verdant area. Agricultural production dominates the region's economy, with the Radicals and Christian Democrats the strongest parties.

Frontier. Concepción, Arauco, Bío-Bío, Malleco, and Cautín comprise this region. The area is wet and cold, and contains one-third of Chile's arable land, considerable timberlands, coal, and the only steel mill. Economically, it is second only to Santiago in national importance. Politically, the Radical party has been traditionally strong, but other parties are growing. The University of Concepción has always been a stronghold of Communist party support.

Lakes. The provinces of Valdivia, Osorno, and Llanquihue comprise this region, along with the cities of Osorno, Valdivia, and Puerto Montt. Germans helped settle this region, and their cultural influence is strong. The economy in this wet, cold region is almost entirely agricultural, but it is very underdeveloped and poverty is widespread. Party strength is distributed among several groups.

Canals. This southernmost region includes the provinces of Chiloe, an island just south of the city of Puerto Montt, Aisén, and Magallanes. The largest city is Punta Arenas, the southernmost city in the world. The region is rainy, windy, and cold, with mountain ranges which rise from the ocean. About 25 percent of the population is in Punta Arenas. The region depends on fishing, lumbering, sheep, agriculture, and some petroleum production. The Radicals once were strong in the region, but today the Socialist party draws nearly half its vote from the area.

Regional divisions are less important politically in Chile than might be assumed. Parties are competitive in most provinces, despite traditional areas of party strength. No area is wholly secure for a party, although economic interests—such as organized miners in the north—can give a party a strong base for electoral support.

6. VOTING: PARTICIPATION AND REGISTRATION

Based on trends over the past thirty years, voter registration has steadily risen in relation to the total national population. Important in the process was the enfranchisement of women (1949), expressed in the totals for the 1953 election. There has also been a distinct trend of increasing voter registration, indicating increasing awareness of electoral processes. The trend has probably reached a demographic maximum: about 55 percent of the population is under the legal voting age. Of those eligible to vote, participation has been consistently high, averaging between 70–80 percent. Until 1970, literacy was a voting requirement, but this excluded relatively few persons given the high literacy rate. Participation is highest in presidential elections, lowest in municipal elections. Registration and participation trends since 1938 are summarized in Table 3-8.[81] Regional factors affect participation in predictable ways. Participation falls off outside metropolitan areas, although the spread from city to city is low compared to other Latin American nations. Registration is uniformly high across the nation, reflecting Chile's uniformly high national political awareness.

7. VOTING: PARTY ALIGNMENTS

The most impressive aggregate party voting trends in Chile are obvious. The Christian Democratic party consistently grew from 1953 until 1969, when its share of the national vote declined. Likewise, the "traditional" Liberal and Conservative parties have consistently declined until 1969, when as the *Partido Nacional* the traditional forces regained much lost ground. Marxist parties, particularly if Communist and Socialist factions are combined, have steadily increased their congressional vote; but the increases have

TABLE 3-8. VOTING REGISTRATION AND
PARTICIPATION IN CHILE, 1938–1970

Election*	Percent participating of those eligible	Percent population registered	Percent population participating
1938 P	88	10	9
1941 M	70	14	10
1941 C	79	11	9
1942 P	80	11	9
1944 M	65	15	9
1945 C	70	12	8
1946 P	76	12	9
1947 M	84	12	10
1949 C	80	10	8
1950 M	74	14	11
1952 P	87	18	16
1953 M	68	18	12
1953 C	72	18	13
1956 M	62	18	11
1957 C	68	19	13
1958 P	83	21	18
1960 M	70	24	17
1961 C	75	25	19
1963 M	81	33	27
1964 P	87	36	32
1965 C	85	37	27
1967 M	80	38	26
1969 C	71	39	26
1970 P	84	36	28

* P = Presidential Election; C = Congressional Election; M = Municipal Election.

been very slight. It is easily ascertained that in Chile women tend to vote more "traditionally" than men, and that the female vote was a substantial contributor to Christian Democratic successes; nevertheless, in the first election subsequent to enfranchisement of women, all traditional parties (Liberal, Conservative, and Radical) as well as the Christian Democratic party experienced marked declines in their vote, in favor of Marxist and ad hoc parties. The general congressional party voting trends from 1925 to 1969 are summarized in Table 3-9.

Coalitions have characterized Chilean politics, particularly since 1941, expressing residual *personalismo* in the system. Presidents Ibáñez and Alessandri coalesced supporters around their

TABLE 3-9. CONGRESSIONAL VOTE FOR CHILEAN PARTIES, 1925-1969
(IN PERCENT)

Year	Conservative	Liberal	Radical	Christian Democratic	Socialist	Communist
1925	19.9	32.4	21.4	—	—	—
1932	16.9	15.8	18.1	—	5.7	—
1937	21.3	20.8	18.6	—	11.2	4.2
1941	17.1	14.0	21.7	3.4	16.7	11.8
1945	23.6	18.0	20.0	2.6	12.8	10.3
1949	22.7	18.0	21.7	3.9	9.3	—†
1953	10.1	11.0	13.3	2.8	14.1	—
1957	13.8	15.4	21.5	9.4	10.7	—
1961	14.8	16.6	22.2	15.9	11.1	11.8
1965	5.3	7.5	13.7	43.6	10.6	12.8
1969	20.9		13.4	31.1	15.1*	16.6

* Includes both Socialist and Popular Socialist parties.
† Communist party illegal in elections of 1949-1957.

candidacies. Ibáñez supporters later institutionalized themselves into an unsuccessful political party; Alessandri's support came from traditional parties. Despite the organizational fragmentation of the Marxist parties, their ideological affinity to FRAP symbolized an important force and policy alternative in Chilean party politics. Likewise, the combination of the PC and PL into the new National party consolidated another important force and policy alternative. If one accepts these two combinations, along with the Radical and Christian Democratic parties, and extrapolates trends from their popular vote, several additional conclusions can be made about Chilean party politics. Table 3-10 traces these trends.[82]

Radical party decline has been gradual compared to the Liberal and Conservative parties. Likewise, Marxist gains from 1949 to 1965 were more gradual than Christian Democratic, although since then the rate of Marxist party growth has increased while the Christian Democrats have lost strength.[83] Were the Marxist parties able to coalesce effectively, which seems a remote possibility, they could have the basis for becoming the dominant Chilean political force. The 1969 congressional elections amplified the previous trends, with all groups becoming more competitive. Christian Democratic losses have benefited all groups, not just one, in making the parties more competitive. Party representation in the Chilean Congress after the 1969 elections is shown in Table 3-11.

Presidential balloting for the past twenty years shows the same consolidating trends as legislative balloting. President Frei was the

TABLE 3-10. CHILEAN PARTY VOTE FOR CURRENT
GROUPINGS, 1925–1970 (IN PERCENT)

Election	Parties			
	National	Radical	PDC	FRAP/UP
1925	53	21	—	—
1932	33	18	—	6
1937	42	19	—	15
1941	31	22	3	29
1945	42	20	3	23
1949	41	22	4	9
1953	21	13	3	14
1957	29	21	9	11
1961	32	22	16	23
1965	13	14	44	24
1969	15	17	37	29
1970	35		28	36

SOURCE: Dirección del Registro Electoral y Oficina de
Informaciones.
NOTES: National party comprised of Conservative and
Liberal parties.
FRAP until 1969 comprised of Socialist, Communist, and
other small parties. Communist party illegal from 1948–1958.
UP (Unidad Popular) formed for 1970 presidential elec-
tions, included Socialist, Communist, Radical, Social Demo-
cratic, and MAPU parties.

first candidate since 1946 to receive a clear majority of the vote:
56 percent. In 1946, four candidates competed, with three very
competitive. In 1952, the winner (Ibáñez) led the remainder by
a large margin; only one other candidate was truly competitive.
In 1958, the leading two candidates polled very closely, while the
third was separated from the leading two more than previously.
In 1964 there were only two principal candidates, Frei (PDC)
and Allende (FRAP). The Radical party candidate, Durán, received less than five percent of the vote. The consolidation and
increasing competition of presidential voting from 1946 to 1964
is shown in Table 3-12.

Regional distribution of major party voting is strikingly uniform for the entire nation. Based on the 1965 congressional voting,
the Christian Democrats carried a plurality in all regions (if not
all provinces) except the southernmost, The Canals. In no region
did the PDC receive a majority of the vote, but its heaviest vote
was in the populous central urban region (Santiago and Valparaíso)
specifically, and all central regions generally. The Radical party

**TABLE 3-11. PARTY REPRESENTATION IN CHILE FOLLOWING
ELECTION OF MARCH, 1969**

Party		Deputies	Senators
Christian Democrat	PDC	55	23
National	PN	34	5
Radical	PR	24	9
Communist	PCCh	22	6
Socialist	PS	15	5
Other		0	2
TOTALS		150	50

SOURCE: Dirección del Registro Electoral y Oficina de Informaciones.

NOTE: Some senators changed affiliation and/or organized new parties after the 1969 elections. The Socialist party also factionalized.

polled least well in the central regions, best in the southern regions. Communist party appeal was fragmented, being strongest in the northern and southern mining regions. Socialist voting paralleled Communist party strength, with special strength in Punta Arenas. The Liberal party vote was most evenly distributed of all the parties, and the Conservative party did relatively well except in the far northern provinces.[84]

Two qualifications of the regional voting patterns must be made. Not all provinces and regions are of equal strategic importance given the magnitude of the voting; the central regions are far more important since they contain the bulk of Chilean voters. If one groups parties as was done for coalitions (PN, PR, PDC, FRAP), the level of competitiveness across the nation increases, indicating a more even distribution of ideological divisions than organizational identifications. The regional bases of party voting are compared in Table 3-13.

8. URBAN VOTING AND APPORTIONMENT: A CASE STUDY OF SANTIAGO PROVINCE[85]

Santiago Province, the principal center of urban population growth in Chile, has experienced severe distortions in its national legislative representation from a failure to reapportion the National Congress for the past 38 years. Ironically, as chronic as the distortions are, careful evaluation and projection demonstrates that their correction would have little if any significant political effects on the existing power balances between Santiago and more rural provinces, between the center city and suburban communities in

TABLE 3-12. Competition Between Two Principal Presidential Candidates in Chilean Elections, 1925–1970

Percent vote	1925	1927	1931	1932	1938	1942	1946	1952	1958	1964	1970
100											
98											
96											
94											
92											
90											
88											
86											
84											
82											
80											
78											
76											
74											
72											
70											
68											
66											
64											
62											
60											
58											
56											
54											
52											
50											
48											
46											
44											
42											
40											
38											
36											
34											
32											
30											
28											
26											
24											
22											
20											
18											
16											
14											
12											
10–0											

SOURCE: Dirección del Registro Electoral y Oficina de Informaciones.

TABLE 3-13. REGIONAL DISPERSION OF PARTY VOTING FOR CONGRESS
(MARCH 7, 1965)

Region	Regional Party Vote in Percent						
	PDC	PR	PCCh	PS	PL	PC	PADENA
Great North	32	15	28	10	9	—	2
Little North	34	19	17	18	8	—	—
North Central	44	14	.5	12	8	8	8
Central Urban	48	9	14	8	6	5	2
South Central	37	11	24	10	3	2	5
Frontier	35	18	4	3	15	7	10
Lakes	38	19	3	17	11	4	—
Canals	9	37	7	30	6	10	—
NATIONAL AVERAGE	44	14	13	11	8	5	5

SOURCE: Dirección del Registro Electoral y Oficina de Informaciones.

the metropolitan Santiago area, or between the national political parties in the legislature.

Santiago, one of twenty-five provinces in the republic, is by far the largest in population. The area contains a concentration of about 38 percent of the national population, an estimated (1968) 3.2 million inhabitants. The province has a population density of over 600 per square mile, compared to the national average of only 30 per square mile. Population growth for the Province is 3.9 percent annually, well above the national average of 2.4 percent.[86] Although there are other "metropolitan areas" within Chile, peculiar institutional-electoral factors limit the representation problem to Santiago Province.[87]

As a unitary republic, Chile is divided into historically defined provinces that are subdivided into communes. Both chambers of the national legislature are nominally constituted by population. Until recently the Senate has contained 45 members elected from nine groupings of provinces, with five senators from each. The electoral districts for the Chamber of Deputies (like the Senate) are multi-member, distributed through the d'Hondt system of proportional representation. Although the Senate districts were created to balance regional and population interests, the predictable result has been gross underrepresentation in the Senate for Santiago Province, which has had only five senators (11 percent) for 38 percent of the national population. For all provinces except Ñuble and Santiago, deputies are elected from districts coterminous with the province.[88] Few problems in underrepresentation arise for urban areas outside Santiago Province since migration normally occurs to urban centers within the same province, or to Santiago. The multi-member districts represent the total urban and rural population of a province regardless of the balance between the two.

Presumably because of its size, Santiago Province was divided into four multi-member legislative districts. Presently District 1, comprising the central city (*municipalidad*) of Santiago, has 18 deputies. Each of the remaining three districts has five. Article 37 of the Chilean Constitution specifies that representation shall be at a ratio of 1/30,000 inhabitants, or fraction over 15 thousand.[89] The representational dilemma in Santiago Province has worsened at an accelerating rate since the 1930 census, which was the last time reapportionment occurred. The regular national censuses of 1940, 1952, and 1960 have all been rejected on technicalities for political reasons. Reallocating seats in Chile is less complex than in the United States because of the multi-member districts. It involves merely an addition or subtraction of deputies following the prescribed constitutional formula. Since the districts are coterminous with the provinces, no new districts need be drawn although such conceivably could be done for Santiago. The political controversies accompanying attempts to gerrymander district boundaries are thereby avoided.

Theoretically, reapportionment is to follow presidential transmission of the latest national census to the controller general. Recent presidents have deviously avoided reapportionment responsibility. Former president Gabriel González Videla (1946–1952) postponed the regular 1950 census until 1952, when his term expired, to avoid the turmoil. President Jorge Alessandri (1958–1964) circumvented the problem by instructing the census bureau not to complete the results of the census before 1964, too late to implement a reapportionment for the 1965 congressional elections. Until 1970, the problem was in the hands of President Eduardo Frei, who showed no inclination to initiate reapportionment himself by accepting the 1960 census. Chile's unique controller general could constitutionally indite the president for failing to implement the required reapportionment, but such an action would needlessly divide the nation on an apparently dispensible issue.[90]

Since the last reapportionment following the 1930 census, Chile's population has risen from 4.3 million to 8.7 million, an increase of more than 100 percent. The population of Santiago Province relative to the nation has increased from 23 percent in

TABLE 3-14. COMPARISON OF POPULATION GROWTH AND REPRESENTATION
FOR SANTIAGO PROVINCE, 1930–1968

	1930 census	Percent	Present deputies	Percent	1960 census	Percent	Legal deputies	Percent	1968 est. population	Percent	1968 est. deputies	Percent	Represen. index*
Santiago Province	938	23	33	23	2,436	33	82	33	3,280	38	110	38	−15
District 1	550	13	18	13	648	9	22	9	628	7	21	7	+ 6
District 2	135	3	5	3.3	595	8	20	8	890	10	30	10	− 7
District 3	145	4	5	3.3	893	12	31	12	1,383	16	46	16	−12
District 4	138	3	5	3.3	264	4	9	4	379	5	13	5	− 2
Other provinces	3,319	71	114	77	4,904	67	163	67	5,454	62	182	62	+29
NATIONAL TOTAL	4,287		147		7,340		245		8,734		292		

* Representation Index is percentage points difference between actual and 1968 theoretical share
of total Deputies.

1930 to 38 percent in 1968. The impact of urbanization and population growth on representation for Santiago is revealed in Table
3-14. Growth within the province has been uneven. Although the
province has grown more than 3 times its 1930 size from 968 to
3,280 thousand, District 1 has grown only about 15 percent from
550 to 628 thousand. Relative to the entire nation, District 1 (the
central city of Santiago) is actually overrepresented in the national
legislature with 13 percent instead of the 7 percent of the deputies
it deserves. District 3 has grown nearly 10 times its 1930 size from
145 to 1,383 thousand. District 2 has grown 7 times, and District
4, 2¾ times their original size.[91] The central city, like its counterparts elsewhere in the world, has remained essentially stable while
its environs have mushroomed.

Demographic, economic, and social analyses of districts 2, 3,
and 4 confirm a characteristically Latin American heterogeneity
to the suburban communities and outlying villages. More than most
Latin American cities, Santiago's metropolitan communities contain
large middle and lower-middle class populations. Communes in the
three districts are compared in the Table 3-15 by demography,
standard of living, literacy, general development, urbanization, and
population growth rate.[92] District 2 is partly suburban, partly rural,
dominated by the communes Quinta Normal and Conchalí, both
of which are mixed suburbs of the central city. District 3, the fastest
growing, is largely urban and second only to District 1 (the city
of Santiago) in its levels of socioeconomic development. Three of
its communes (Providencia, Nuñoa, and Las Condes), decidedly
upper middle class by Chilean standards, are contiguous with the
central city. Two of its communes (La Cisterna and La Granja)
have the fastest growth in the province. Both are middle to lower

TABLE 3-15. Social, Economic, and Demographic Indicators of Congressional Districts, Santiago Province

	Demographic/occupational index	Median for communes	Standard of living index	Median for communes	Literacy index in percent	Median for communes in percent	General development index	Median for communes	Urbanization index in percent	Median for communes in percent	Population growth 1952-60 mean in percent	Median for communes in percent	Homes with electricity in percent	Median for communes in percent	Population, 1960 census (Thousands)
Santiago Province	45		81		91		74		90		3.9		88		2,437,425
District 1 (Santiago)	47	35	96	60	95	76	80	59	100	60	-.4	3.6	98	74	647,513
District 2	43	46	71	81	80	87	69	71	89	95	6.5	5.8	84	80	585,607
District 3	46	27	85	39	90	76	75	50	95	95	6.4	1.7	85	65	889,679
District 4	39		59		79		68		51		2.3		75		314,626
NATIONAL TOTAL					84				68		2.4		65		7,374,115

middle class in composition. Recently both have enjoyed considerable government programs in housing, education, and public health. District 4, the smallest of the electorial districts, is mostly rural farming communities near the city, and is the least urbanized and least affluent of the districts.

Conventionally, high growth rate in Latin American cities is attributed to migration of the poor into urban slum communities. While this does occur in Santiago, it is important to note that those communes with the highest growth rate have been those relatively prosperous ones with far above normal living standards and literacy, already highly urbanized. High literacy and prosperity are not customary attributes of slum communities. The trend is not necessarily a general one, however, since the central city (District 1) has the highest indexes of social economic development while simultaneously experiencing a .4 percent annual decline in population over the past decade.

Of the possible consequences produced by the underrepresentation of Santiago Province, two can be dismissed easily. Administration of local affairs is realistically a function of the national government. The only elected legislators at a local level represent a very limited area—the commune, or a combination of several small communes. Principal decisions are made for local units by administrators, *intendentes* (intendents) for the provinces, *alfaldes* (mayors) at the municipality (commune) level, who are appointed by and responsible to the president of the republic. Although the constitution specifies provincial assemblies, they have never been created. Local legislators (*regidores*) are elected by proportional representation from multi-member districts.[93] Because of the legislator's limited responsibilities and small constituencies, reapportionment becomes politically inconsequential. At the national level, rural and urban areas in Santiago Province except for District 1 share deputies.

The political balance of Santiago to other provinces, despite its underrepresentation, is also of minimum practical significance. We in the United States are accustomed to historically insensitive, rural dominated county, state, and national legislatures obstructing the needs of the cities. Not only is the institutional context different in Chile, but so, too, are the economic, social, and cultural environments.

In a developing nation like Chile, modernization normally proceeds far more rapidly in urban than rural areas, particularly in cities like Santiago which dominate the rest of their nation. While Latin American cities often share many of the problems of their North American counterparts, they are more advanced and enjoy a higher standard of living than most other areas of the country. The metropolitan, capital area is the center of national economic, social, and political activity. Partly as a legacy of the Spanish, there is a heritage in Latin America of interest in cities. Central cities in most nations have not declined to the benefit of the suburbs. The metropolitan Santiago area is administered in fact by the national government with as much concern as though it were a local government. Programs of reform and modernization proceed at least as rapidly there as elsewhere. Since 38 percent of the national electorate is contained in the capital province, the government's concern with the area's welfare is not surprising.

To the extent that rivalry exists between Santiago and the remaining 24 provinces, it is the latter who are envious and hostile to Santiago. To further reduce their national legislative representation, even though indicated by the constitution, would only exacerbate latent hostility to Santiago.[94] National integration is a primary, often elusive goal for governments of developing nations. In Chile and perhaps elsewhere in Latin America it does not follow that underrepresentation of the dominant urban area produces less attention from the national government.

Although we can dismiss the importance of representational distortion for Santiago Province in regard to metropolitan interests and Santiago's relative position in the National Congress, the implications cannot be so quickly dismissed for the balance of national political party power. If important skews are produced in national legislative party representation by the failure to reapportion, then there is significance to Santiago's imbalance. It is also true that if any of the districts in Santiago fails to receive proper party representation when its interests are closely aligned to a particular party, then the representational distortion is even more critical. Analysis of voting behavior and party representation in Santiago Province argues against any meaningful political distortions having been produced by underrepresentation. Reapportionment would not materially alter the overall national party balances, nor, it would seem, can the interests of any single district be correlated to the fate of a specific national party since none of the districts exhibit strong single-party voting tendencies. Moreover, each district reflects the aggregate national voting patterns almost irrespective of fundamental socioeconomic characteristics of the district or its component communes.

The high degree of political integration and party competition in Chile defies its geographic and cultural regionalism. With its distinctive shape, some 2,600 miles north to south with an average width of no more than 110 miles, the country has characteristic cultural, ethnic, and geographic regions. Yet for all its natural regionalism, Chile is remarkably integrated in party voting. Santiago Province is no exception.

Major political parties compete throughout all the provinces, and while certain ones exhibit traditional provincial strengths, none of the provinces are without meaningful political opposition. For analytic purposes, four party divisions can be assumed relevant to representation: the PN, the PR, the PDC, and the parties that participated through the elections analyzed in FRAP. Meaningful distortions in party representation would have to be extrapolated from these four alternatives.

In Santiago Province the four major groups competed effectively only in District 1 (the city of Santiago), but even here the PDC received 11 delegates under the 1965 distribution (summarized in Table 3-19) to 7 for all the remaining parties.[95] In districts 2, 3, and 4, only the PDC and FRAP achieved representation with the PDC receiving a majority in each district. Table 3-16 indicates that both the PDC and FRAP would have increased their absolute representation under a 1960 census-based reapportionment, but their relative percent of the province's delegates would change little: the PDC would decline from 64 percent to 62 percent of the deputies while FRAP would rise from 27 percent to 33 percent of the delegates. Anticipating the 1970 census by using the 1968 estimated population figures, the same trend would continue: the PDC would further decline to 61 percent of the deputies, and FRAP would increase to 35 percent. Besides the PDC the principle loser would be the PR, although its absolute total is so small that the percentage loss is deceptive. All these projections of course assume the 1965 voting patterns; it is conceivable that a voting shift within the districts could amplify the party imbalance from misapportionment over the 1965 voting patterns. Based on the 1965 congressional election, however, reapportionment of Santiago Province would have virtually no effect on national legislative balances despite a small increase in the FRAP delegation.

Without proposing a cause-effect relationship to explain the negligible effects of apportionment on representation, there does

TABLE 3-16. IMPACT OF REAPPORTIONMENT ON PARTY BALANCES: NUMBER AND PERCENT OF DEPUTIES BASED ON 1965 VOTING BEHAVIOR

PARTY	CURRENT BALANCE BASED ON 1930 CENSUS								PROJECTED BALANCE BASED ON 1960 CENSUS								PROJECTED BALANCE BASED ON 1968 ESTIMATED POPULATION							
	District 1	District 2	District 3	District 4	Santiago Province	Percent	Other provinces	NATIONAL	District 1	District 2	District 3	District 4	Santiago Province	Percent	Other provinces	NATIONAL	District 1	District 2	District 3	District 4	Santiago Province	Percent	Other provinces	NATIONAL
PDC	11	3	3	4	21	64	61	82	14	12	18	8	52	62	86	138	13	18	27	10	68	61	96	164
FRAP	4	2	2	1	9	27	24	33	5	8	13	1	27	33	34	61	5	12	19	3	39	35	38	77
PR	2	0	0	0	2	6	18	20	2	0	0	0	2	3	26	28	2	0	0	0	2	3	29	31
PN	1	0	0	0	1	3	8	9	1	0	0	0	1	2	12	13	1	0	0	0	1	1	13	14
Other	0	0	0	0	0	0	3	3	0	0	0	0	0	0	5	5	0	0	0	0	0	0	6	6
TOTAL	18	5	5	5	33		114	147	22	20	31	9	82		163	245	21	30	46	13	110		182	292
PERCENT	13	3⅓	3⅓	3⅓	23		77		9	8	12	4	33		67		7	10	16	5	38		62	

seem to be an interplay between the electoral-institutional environment and voting patterns in the province. For example, the proportional representation and multi-member districts tend to remove the deputy from as direct identification with the district as is found in majority-type, single-member districts. Unlike the United States, multi-member districts dilute responsibility for a district among many representatives and several parties. Legislator roles also differ from both the United States, where there is a high identification with the district, and from Britain, where there is a high identification with the party. In Chile, deputies gravitate toward party regularity, but often vote as free agents. The Chilean legislator's role is reinforced by the open-list type ballot, where the voter can specify preference for a candidate on the party list rather than being required to accept the party's listed heirarchy of candidates.[96] The open list both removes a potent weapon for party discipline and stimulates an element of personalism in campaign and voting processes. Voting in the Chilean legislature is rarely on a regional or local basis. It is party oriented, but often in critical votes decided by maverick deputies.

Perhaps even more critical in explaining the negligible effect of underrepresentation on party balances is the behavioral factors of voting. There is no correlation in Santiago Province at the commune level between fundamental qualities of urbanization, income and affluence, political awareness (reflected by registration and participation indexes) and party voting. Table 3-17 reveals the effects at the district level of party voting in the elections of 1964, 1965, and 1967.[97] The PDC shows comparable strength in all four districts; FRAP shows somewhat greater strength in the districts 2 and 3; the Radical party vote is similar in each district. Party voting tendencies show little relation to the aggregate characteristics of the districts. If the component communes in each electoral district

TABLE 3-17. COMPARISON OF CHILEAN PARTY VOTING IN ELECTIONS OF 1964, 1965, AND 1967 (IN PERCENT)

	PDC			FRAP			RADICAL			OTHER		
	1964	1965	1967	1964	1965	1967	1964	1965	1967	1964	1965	1967
Santiago Province	61	48	38	37	19	29	3	9	12	0	24	21
District 1	61	49	39	32	19	27	4	11	15	0	21	19
District 2	57	48	38	41	26	29	2	8	11	0	18	22
District 3	61	46	37	38	26	30	2	8	11	0	20	22
District 4	58	46	36	36	15	24	6	11	12	0	28	30
NATIONAL TOTAL	56	44	36	39	23	29	5	14	16	0	19	19

are regrouped according to common social, economic, and demographic characteristics, however, the independent quality of party competition becomes even clearer. Using the congressional election of 1965 and the municipal elections of 1967 as indicators, Table 3-18 shows that there are very few differences in communal voting tendencies within the province for each of the three major parties.[98] The PDC shows slightly greater strength in less affluent, less urban, less rapidly growing communes, but the differences are slight. The FRAP, nominally an urban-proletarian coalition, shows greatest strength in the most rapidly growing, most urban, and perhaps curiously, most affluent communes of the province. The Radical party shows weak but even strength in all communes regardless of their fundamental characteristics. Other political parties, notably the Liberal and Conservative parties in 1965 and their National party coalition in 1967, show strongest voting in more middle-class, suburban, relatively stable communes where voting participation is highest. In general, Table 3-18 shows very little differentiation in party voting by the characteristics tested. Additional analysis fails to reveal other socioeconomic or demographic variables that can explain satisfying party voting tendencies in the province. With the exception of a weak tendency toward FRAP in lower socioeconomic, rapidly growing, and urban communes, it is reasonable to assume that provincial party voting is relatively independent of traditional social, economic, and demographic factors.

Chile's political parties seem to generate a culture of their own within the province so that differentiation and identification is apparently based on specific party activity, competition, leadership skills, and voter identification rather than socioeconomic and localistic influences. To the extent that there is any "party culture" in the province that can be geographically perceived, it seems to occur in contiguous communes across district lines. FRAP's voting comes from contiguous communes on an east-west axis, south of the central city. The strongest PDC communes combine the relatively prosperous areas northeast of the central city, as well as many of the more rural communes. There is no evidence from voting and representation that the severe apportionment distortions have actually produced any gerrymandered electoral districts.

One final factor can be raised in regard to the voting and representation of Santiago Province: the importance of the four districts as governing mechanisms in the electoral process. The effects of dividing Santiago Province into four multi-member districts instead of one large multi-member district are compared in

TABLE 3-18. VOTING TENDENCIES IN SANTIAGO PROVINCE BASED ON COMMUNAL CHARACTERISTICS (IN PERCENT)

PARTY		Total provincial vote	AFFLUENCE			URBANIZATION			VOTER PARTICIPATION			POPULATION GROWTH		
			High (N = 12)	Medium (N = 13)	Low (N = 13)	Urban (N = 13)	Mixed (N = 12)	Rural (N = 13)	High (N = 13)	Medium (N = 12)	Low (N = 13)	High (N = 12)	Medium (N = 13)	Low (N = 13)
PDC	1965	48	44	46	59	49	45	51	47	48	50	45	46	48
	1967	38	37	33	43	36	39	42	38	38	39	37	37	38
FRAP	1965	19	21	18	17	22	15	18	21	24	18	23	15	18
	1967	29	29	27	23	29	24	26	27	36	27	32	23	26
PR	1965	9	10	10	10	12	11	8	9	9	11	9	9	11
	1967	12	13	12	11	13	14	10	12	12	12	10	12	15
Other	1965	24	25	26	14	17	29	23	23	19	20	23	30	23
	1967	21	21	28	23	22	23	22	23	14	22	21	28	21

TABLE 3-19. EFFECTS OF DISTRICTING UPON PARTY BALANCES IN
SANTIAGO PROVINCE: NUMBER AND PERCENT OF DEPUTIES
BASED ON 1965 VOTING BEHAVIOR

PARTY	WITH DISTRICTS					WITHOUT DISTRICTS					
	1930 census		1960 census		1968 population		1930 census		1960 census		1968 population	
PDC	82	55 %	138	57 %	164	56 %	79	53 %	129	53 %	154	53 %
FRAP	33	23	61	25	77	27	32	22	55	23	64	23
PR	20	14	28	11	31	11	21	15	34	13	40	13
PN	9	6	13	5	14	4	12	8	22	9	26	9
Other	3	2	5	2	6	2	3	2	5	2	6	2
	147	100	245	100	292	100	147	100	245	100	292	100

Table 3-19.[99] The use of several multi-member districts instead of
one, even when those districts are reapportioned to reflect actual
population size, does not produce conservative political effects on
the province. Quite the opposite: both FRAP and PDC benefit
slightly in relative representation from the province under the
district plan over what they would receive in a single, multi-member
district. It would appear that the PR and PN have the most to lose
by reapportionment under the multiple district plan, whereas regular reapportionment under a single district plan would have nearly
no effect on party balances. The explanation for this lies not in the
ideological position of the parties, but their relative strength. Votes
for the PN and PR in districts 2, 3, and 4 are insufficient under
the proportional representation, multi-member, multi-district plan
to achieve representation, but when added to their relatively
stronger voting in District 1 produce a total representation larger
than the sum of its parts.

Several conclusions emerge from our analysis of urban voting
patterns in Santiago under the severely distorted apportionment.

(1) Despite severe underrepresentation of Santiago Province
caused by expanding population and urbanization, reapportionment
would have little effect on metropolitan politics in the area, the
relation of Santiago to other provinces, or national political party
balances.

(2) Voting patterns at the provincial and district levels correlate closely in Santiago to national ones, and vary independently
of the factors of urbanization, living standards, population growth,
or political awareness at the communal level.

(3) Institutional factors tend to insulate national party politics
from excessive localistic influences. These factors include proportional representation, multi-member electoral districts, open-list

ballots, legislator representation roles, and the relative economic well-being of Santiago Province vis-à-vis other regions in the country.

(4) Division of Santiago Province into four multi-member districts amplifies the strength of strong parties (for example, PDC and FRAP) and works against those with more limited or concentrated appeals. Nevertheless, the uneven growth of the districts has had few national implications that reapportionment could correct.

(5) The two major political groups (PDC, FRAP) are very competitive in the districts, with each receiving its heaviest vote in rural or urban districts which are contiguous across district boundaries.

(6) There may be a de facto agreement in Chile to ignore redistricting and avoid extraneous political conflict that might arise from reducing representation of outlying provinces which already suffer by comparison with the well-being of Santiago Province. A political balance may have been achieved by allowing the remainder of the nation to be politically overrepresented in exchange for the reality of a superior development and perhaps governmental sensitivity to the metropolitan Santiago area.

9. Chilean Politics: A Concluding Remark

Considering its relatively small size, less than $\frac{1}{25}$ of the population of Latin America, Chile occupies a position of exceptional political interest. This interest is only partly due to the profound changes that are occurring in the political system, which seem to have significant implications for the remainder of the region. Perhaps more fundamental is Chile's extended period of electoral stability, regular elections, intense and increasing participation, vital party competition throughout the nation, and, with a few interruptions in the 1930s, peaceful transfer of power from one government to another.

Within this political culture there still are economic, social, and perhaps even political problems characteristic of Latin America more generally. Significant analyses are possible using Chilean voting data, and offer an exceptional opportunity for sharpening our understanding of voting behavior in developing nations through the Chilean experience. Preliminary research suggests that Chilean political culture has highly developed political awareness and party institutionalization, and that voting proceeds from party cultures only partly—perhaps secondarily—influenced by traditional economic and environmental factors assumed generic in North American voting studies.

III. COSTA RICA: CONSOLIDATION AND REACTION IN PARTY COMPETITION

Costa Rica, like Chile, has shifted party competition during the past two decades, but unlike Chile the change has been irregular. Party competition moved from a single-party dominant system in 1953 to a multi-party dominant system through 1965, and afterward briefly to a two-party competition. Throughout the period, one party, the *Partido de Liberación Nacional* (PLN), has been dominant as opposition loosened and coalesced; it is for this reason that Costa Rican party politics, in spite of its competitive vascillations, has most of the qualities of a multi-party dominant system.[100] The Costa Rican experience underscores the rapidity with which systemic change can occur.

1. ENVIRONMENT AND POLITICAL CULTURE IN COSTA RICA

By virtue of its exports, Costa Rica is a Central American "banana-coffee" republic; eighty percent of its exports fall into these categories. Containing only 19,575 square miles, Costa Rica is the third smallest nation in Latin America. Its population, only about 1.5 million, is literate (80 percent) and largely of European immigration. Dominantly rural (66 percent) rather than urban, Costa Rica has a modest per capita income constantly threatened by the highest population increase (4.1 percent) in Latin America. A chronically difficult trade balance and relatively weak export economy encourages economic instability, yet the nation has remained politically stable and competitive most of the present century.[101]

After independence Costa Rican politics was characteristically elitist. Revolts were common, but little violence and destruction accompanied them. The first elections were not held until 1889, following the revolt against a reform president, Tomás Guardia, who seized power from the traditional oligarchy in 1882. Although no democrat himself, Guardia did break the traditional political patterns, and ended the control of existing family-dominated parties.

Competition and popular participation in politics evolved gradually over the next half century. Elections became a regular institution in Costa Rican politics, and all but two subsequent presidents came to power peacefully. Many of the elections offered little choice, and meaningful competition remained controlled at the nomination stage where entry into the national political arena was determined by family influence and connections. Yet the expectation of elections and incremental change became important qualities of Costa Rican political culture at a relatively early stage in national development.[102]

Most contemporary forces in Costa Rican politics date from about 1940, when one of the most significant and controversial national leaders was elected president: Rafael Calderón Guardia. Calderón polarized the nation on a personalistic axis. While undeniably attracting considerable popular support, Calderón was attacked from both sides of the ideological spectrum for the alleged graft and fraud in his administration, and his autocratic inclinations. Liberal and conservative opposition, represented by José Figueres and Otilio Ulate respectively, joined forces to try to defeat a *Calderonista* candidate in the 1944 presidential elections, but the president's momentum proved too strong and his candidate, Teodoro Picado, won the election.

By the 1948 elections, anti-*Calderonista* sentiment was increasing as Calderón decided to seek another term for himself. Rumors grew that Calderón supporters would not permit his opponent, Ulate, to take office should he win the election. Some leaders, including José Figueres, threatened a civil war should the results of the election not be accepted. Ulate won, but the Calderón controlled National Assembly tried to nullify the election on technicalities, plunging the nation into a two-month civil war which eventually sent Calderón and his followers into exile. Figueres formed a *junta,* and for 18 months ruled the nation by decree, pledging to restore constitutional government and permit Ulate to take office legally.[103] Fiscal reforms were initiated, a new constitution drafted, and the Communist party and army were abolished as potential threats to the state; the latter was replaced by a nonpolitical, national police force. In 1949 Figueres kept his word, turning the government over to Ulate. The nation returned to political normalcy, and enjoyed a brief economic prosperity induced by abnormally high coffee prices.[104]

With Ulate in power Figueres organized the *Partido de Liberación Nacional* (PLN). The party took its ideological cue from the *Aprista*-type movements elsewhere in Latin America, calling for economic reform, social welfare, and greater distribution of economic benefits. In 1953 Figueres campaigned for the presidency with the PLN, and received an unprecedented 65 percent of the popular vote. With this mandate Figueres pressed economic and social legislation; the cost of the legislation soon combined with decreasing coffee revenues to produce a substantial inflation.[105]

The PLN nominated Francisco Orlich in 1958, who received 43 percent of the presidential vote. The winner was Mario Echandi, candidate of the *Partido de Unión Nacional* (PUN), with 46 percent of the vote. The PLN retained control of the National Assembly, and a deadlock between the Assembly and the president followed. Worsening international trade and widespread destruction by the active volcano, Irazú, brought Costa Rica close to economic ruin in the following years.[106]

Orlich tried in 1962 for the presidency, and received a winning 50 percent of the vote and control for the PLN of the National Assembly. Ulate's PUN received only fourteen percent of the vote, but Calderón, returned from exile, obtained nearly one-third of the assembly seats for his reformed *Partido Republicano*.[107]

Orlich's administration was beset with economic difficulties, despite the favorable position enjoyed by Costa Rica in the newly created Central American Common Market. Daniel Oduber, Orlich's foreign minister, was the PLN 1966 presidential candidate. Despite ideological and personal differences, the opposition united to defeat the PLN. Former presidents Calderón, Ulate, and Echandi joined together to form a new party, *Unión Nacional* (UN), and nominate a politically unknown but uncontroversial candidate, José Joaquín Trejos Fernández. Trejos, a university professor, won by less than one percent of the national vote. The PLN retained a slim one-vote majority in the National Assembly.[108]

Figueres won a second presidential term in 1970, defeating his familiar opponent Mario Echandi by 74 thousand votes. The PLN obtained a clear majority in the Assembly, with its widest popular vote margin since Figueres' 1953 victory. An estimated 120 thousand young voters participated for the first time in 1970, giving approximately 70 thousand of their vote to the PLN and Figueres.[109]

Educational opportunity, high literacy, well-developed communication, and a relatively compact population combine in Costa Rica to produce an integrated, politically aware culture which supports the competitive, institutionalized electoral processes. Elections and legislative politics are meaningful experiences, and make representation and party politics an important part of national gov-

ernment. The Costa Rican experience is qualified by two considera-
tions: unlike its Central American neighbors, Costa Rica lacks the
demographic and cultural conflicts that make national integration
difficult; and Costa Rican parties, while competitive, are elitist at
the critical juncture of leadership recruitment. Qualities familiar
in other Latin American political cultures such as family connections and wealth are important for political success in Costa Rica.[110]

2. POLITICAL PARTIES IN COSTA RICA

Nowhere in Latin America is it any easier to form a political
party than Costa Rica. The dominance that the system has generated exists despite the easy entry into the system. Any group
of 25 registered voters may form a party when they submit the
party statutes, name, insignia, program, and ideology to the supreme electoral tribunal which makes the final certification. The
Communist party is explicitly denied the right to participate under
provisions of the constitution; it does participate, however, under
other names.

Partido de Liberación Nacional. The PLN has been the dominant party in Costa Rica since 1953. It is reformist, self-consciously
ideological, and dominated by Figueres. Like most aprista parties,
the PLN is anticommunist but nationalistic. It won the presidency
in 1953, 1962, and 1970, and has held the National Assembly consistently since 1953, if sometimes only by a few seats. So successful
has the party become that it now is often attacked as the "establishment" in campaigns.[111]

Partido Unión Nacional. The National Union party was organized by Otilio Ulate and conservative supports to oppose the
Calderón administration. Ulate's own administration, 1949–1953, was
marked by financial consolidation but no social or economic reform.
In 1953 the party supported the presidential candidate of the small
Partido Demócrata, which had supported Ulate in 1948. After the
PD/PUN defeat, the two parties merged. The PUN won the 1958
presidential election with Mario Echandi. Subsequent internal conflicts effectively removed Ulate from a position of influence.[112]

Partido Republicano. Calderón's Republican party formed
orginally in the late 1930s as the *Partido Republicano Nacional*
(PRN). With the 1948 revolution, the PRN was outlawed and its
leaders exiled. When Calderón returned to Costa Rica, his sup-

porters regrouped as the PR and won 20 percent of the legislative vote in 1958. In 1962 Calderón obtained 35 percent of the presidential vote, combining diverse and essentially incompatible followers from the Marxist left to the wealthy landowners. In 1966 the PR joined other opposition groups in the anti-PLN coalition.

Partido Unión Republicana Auténtica. The Authentic Republican Union party was formed in 1962 to support Echandi and his followers, drawing supporters largely from the PUN. The PURA joined forces with the PUN and PR to oppose the PLN in 1966, supporting Trejos; afterward, Echandi remained within the structure of the new coalition.

Partido Unión Cívica Revolucionaria. The revolutionary Civic Union party was founded by Marshall Jiménez in 1958 to support his legislative candidacy. Jiménez won his legislative seat, and the party received 3.3 percent of the vote. The PUCR did not participate in the 1962 elections, but again in 1966 it received 5.5 percent of the vote and elected one deputy—its founder. Clearly a personalistic party, the PUCR tends to be conservative when issues are debated.

Communist Parties. A Communist party was founded in 1929 by Manuel Mora Valverde, and competed with other parties in elections during the following 14 years. In 1943 the party changed its name to the *Partido Vanguardia Popular*, or Popular Vanguard party, and continued to be active until it was declared illegal in 1948 following the revolution. Since 1949 the PVP has operated through "front" organizations. In 1962, the sympathetic organization was the *Partido de Acción Democrática Popular*, which received about two percent of the legislative vote and elected one deputy, the controversial Julio Suñol Leal. The next year, followers of the party expelled their only deputy, charging he had too close ties with Mora's Popular Vanguard party. In 1969, Mora organized the *Partido Acción Socialista* to participate in the 1970 presidential elections.[113]

Unificación Nacional. The National Unification "party" was actually a coalition of several parties (PR, PUN, and PURA) and their leaders (Calderón, Ulate, and Echandi) to defeat the PLN in 1966. They succeeded with an "independent" candidate, Trejos, and carried 27 national legislative seats. The group was unstable from the beginning. None of its leaders wanted to see another gain supremacy, and little ideological sympathy existed among the followers of the organization. The UN has been dominated by Calderón supporters, who controlled 18 or 19 of the 27 legislative seats won by the group. After the election, the UN acted with less than unanimity in the national legislature. Mario Echandi decided to seek the presidency in 1970 with the UN as his vehicle.

Frente Nacional. The National Front formed to support the 1970 presidential candidacy of Virgilio Calvo Sanchez, formerly a leader in Calderón's *Partido Republicano.* Calvo drew upon dissatisfaction with the two "traditional" candidates for 1970, Figueres and Echandi, and sought to establish a third alternative for the election.

3. CAMPAIGNS AND VOTING PROCEDURES IN COSTA RICA

Broad regulatory powers over electoral matters are given to the supreme electoral tribunal (TSE), which administers provisions of the 1949 constitution and legislative acts of 1952 and 1965 concerning elections. The TSE is comprised of three magistrates, elected by a two-thirds vote of the supreme court to staggered six-year terms.[114] The body enjoys high prestige in Costa Rica, and its decisions have the force of law. The functions of the TSE are diverse: it recognizes parties and regulates their activites; it supervises campaigning; it regulates balloting procedures and officiates at the final tabulation of votes; it adjudicates disputes over balloting; and if necessary, the TSE alone has the power to enlist aid from the National Guard to guarantee free, open elections. Subsidiary election boards also exist for provinces, cantons, and individual polling stations; these include representatives from the participating parties.

Although registration of parties is relatively simple, the burdens that a registered party assumes are formidable. Organizational structures must be established at all levels: national, provincial, and cantonal, representing some 405 different party assemblies for each organization. To appear on the ballot, a party must recruit three thousand signatures nationally, or one percent of the registered voters in a province or canton. Certification must be renewed every four years by each party, regardless of the votes it received in the last election.[115]

The TSE may also initiate action to bar a party from electoral participation. Such action requires approval of two-thirds of the National Assembly. Article 98 of the 1949 constitution specifically outlaws any party that, "by their ideological programs, methods of action, or international connections, are intended to destroy the bases of the democratic organization of Costa Rica or threaten the sovereignty of the country."

Parties that receive ten percent or more of the valid votes can receive a government subsidy for campaign expenses proportionate to its percentage of votes, but not in excess of actual expenditures. About one million dollars has been provided in the past for this purpose. Costa Rica legally recognizes and regulates party coalitions. Coalitions must be approved by a majority of each party's national organization, and a formal name and program for the coalition must be filed with the TSE. Informal coalitions, such as affirmations of support, are not regulated.

Costa Rica is both a unitary and a unicameral nation. The National Assembly contains 57 members, proportioned to the provinces by the TSE according to population. There are also local, elected officials for the cantons, known as *regidores*, the number being determined by the population of a canton.

Elections are held every four years in Costa Rica. All national and local offices are elected simultaneously, from *regidores* to president. The president and two vice presidents are elected by a plurality of the vote, unless that plurality is under 40 percent; when that occurs, a runoff is held. Elections are scheduled for the first Sunday in February, with a runoff when needed the first Sunday in April. Separate ballots are used for each office, using the closed-list party ballot.

Voting was made compulsory in 1959 for all Costa Ricans; women were enfranchised in 1953, and there is no literacy requirement. To vote each person must have a *cédula* or identification card, which contains his photograph. Eligibility lists are compiled four months before an election, and posted at each district's polling places. About 200 voters are assigned to each *mesa* (table) or polling station; there are approximately 3,600 mesas in the nation. Each voter receives three ballots: presidential, legislative, and cantonal. He marks it by dipping his thumb into red indelible ink, and marking the bottom of the party list for which he is voting. Party lists are identified by name, party symbol, and color; on the presidential list a photograph of the candidate is reproduced. Votes are counted as soon as the polls close, and unofficial results forwarded directly to the TSE, which promptly announces the unofficial returns. Formal counting proceeds more slowly. Unlike other Latin American nations, Costa Rica's voters know almost immediately who has won. Seats are allocated for the legislature using the conventional d'Hondt system of proportional representation.[116]

Campaigning is carefully supervised by the TSE. Campaigning is limited to a specific period, usually beginning in August before the election; some events, such as rallies and parades, can be held only during the final two months of the campaign. Broadcast stations are required to provide free, equal time to all parties and candidates. Government employees—including the president—are forbidden to participate in election campaigns.

The various institutional and legal factors controlling entry and exit of parties from the system tend to cancel each other out, so that the number of parties functioning reflects fundamental political trends in the nation. Proportional representation, easy registration of parties, and financial assistance for campaign expenses encourage party activity and opposition growth; on the other hand, rigid structural requirements for parties, re-registration every four years for all parties, the minimum vote required for campaign subsidies—these and other factors tend to control proliferation, particularly of weakest organizations.

4. REGISTRATION, PARTICIPATION AND PARTY VOTING

Costa Rica shows the characteristics of a politically aware, culturally integrated nation, with minimum party differentiation from one province to another.[117]

Although voting is open to nearly everyone over 20 years of age, more than half the population is under the minimum age. Moreover, while voting is compulsory, each voter must initiate a registration procedure at least three months before an election. Registration and participation trends for the period 1953–1966 are compared in Table 3-20.[118]

The substantial rise in participation from 1958 to 1962 was the result of enfranchisement of women; the percentages are relatively stable, and approach the maximum realizable. Tabulation of a standard deviation for provincial participation in 1966 (5.3) showed remarkably little variation from one province to another.

Since there are only seven provinces in Costa Rica, analysis of provincial party voting trends is relatively simple. Somewhat like Chile, Costa Rica's provinces have distinctive qualities, but party competition is less differentiated than might be expected; there are areas of slight party dominance.[119]

San José. The province of San José contains the capital city and approximately one-half million inhabitants, or approximately one-third of the national population. The province is in the high-

TABLE 3-20. VOTING REGISTRATION AND PARTICIPATION IN
COSTA RICA 1953–1970

	1953	1958	1962	1966	1970
Population	898,329	1,099,962	1,302,829	1,508,000	1,700,000
Registration	294,016	354,779	483,980	537,700	675,000
Participation	197,489	229,543	391,406	441,400	537,000
Percent population registered	33	32	37	36	32
Percent registered participating	67	65	81	82	80

SOURCE: *Tribunal Supremo Electoral*

lands region, a mild climate with fertile land favorable to coffee production. The capital city of San José has been less a PLN stronghold than provincial areas, which approach the mean average. As in many nations, a lower core-area vote for the dominant party is partly a reflection of more intense political opposition and party activity; it may also reflect distress over short-run economic deprivations. The *Calderonista* forces have been historically strong in San José.

Alajuela. Alajuela Province adjoins the capital province to the north. It contains about 19 percent of the national population and the same percent of the national territory. The capital city by the same name has 25 thousand inhabitants. Climatically the province is mild in the central plateau where the capital is located, warm and humid to the north. The economy like that of San José is dominated by coffee. Provincial voting parallels the national mean for the PLN.

Cartago. Cartago Province also adjoins San José, to the east. The capital city is about 20 thousand; the province contains 12 percent of the national population and 5 percent of its land. The capital is located five thousand feet in elevation, and is climatically cool and mild; the entire province is mountainous. The province is a stronghold of PLN support.

Heredia. Heredia Province has only six percent of the national population and five percent of the land. Nearly all the population is centered in the capital city, located in the climatically mild southern region; the northern regions are hot, humid, and underpopulated. The cities of San José, Heredia, and Alajuela are all located in the same general vicinity no more than a dozen miles apart, and have more in common with each other than with the provinces for which they are capitals. Heredia reflects national PLN voting trends.

Guanacaste. Guanacaste is the northwestern province of Costa Rica, bordering Nicaragua. Liberia, the capital city, contains only seven thousand inhabitants and is hardly a city at all. The province has 21 percent of the national territory. Guanacaste is hot, for half the year very dry; it is the center of cattle production. The PLN has increased its vote in the province slightly over the years.

Puntarenas. Puntarenas and the capital city of the same name form the Pacific Coast. The capital has 20 thousand inhabitants, the province 12 percent of the population and 21 percent of the national territory. The province has an unusual shape, like a flower on a long stem with the capital city at the base of the stem. Bananas support the economy, and the province tends to vote strongly for the PLN.

Limón. Limón, the Caribbean coastal province, has only five percent of the national population but 18 percent of its territory. Tropical in climate, the province is a center for bananas and cacao. Limón has also been a center for opposition party support, particularly for the PR and more recently the PUN.

Political and demographic qualities of the provinces are summarized in Table 3-21.[120]

TABLE 3-21. DEMOGRAPHIC/POLITICAL CHARACTERISTICS OF
COSTA RICAN PROVINCES

	Est. 1967 pop. (1,000)	Percent nat. pop.	Percent nat. area	Percent nat. electorate	Percent nat. agri. workers	Percent nat. indus. workers	Percent nat. retail sales	Number of cantons	Percent population growth 1950–1964	Population of provin. capital (1,000)
San José	449	34	10	40	21	52	60	20	78	120
Alajuela	241	19	19	18	21	18	12	12	67	21
Cartago	160	12	5	12	13	11	7	8	60	20
Heredia	80	6	5	7	6	7	5	9	85	20
Guanacaste	153	12	21	9	17	5	4	9	69	7
Puntarenas	154	12	21	10	16	5	4	7	69	20
Limón	65	5	18	4	7	2	4	3	70	17
NATIONAL TOTAL	1,450	100	100	100	100	100	100	68	73	225

TABLE 3-22. PROVINCIAL AND PARTY REPRESENTATION IN COSTA RICA

PROVINCES	1966 representation	Municipal councils (number)	Regidores	Síndicos	PERCENTAGE OF VOTE FOR PLN											
					1953			1958			1962			1966		
					P*	L	M	P	L	M	P	L	M	P	L	M
San José	22	20	80	96	62	58	58	38	34	35	48	46	47	50	49	49
Alajuela	11	12	45	86	65	60	61	49	45	46	51	48	59	49	46	53
Cartago	7	8	34	38	73	67	68	39	36	38	56	54	54	51	48	49
Heredia	3	9	30	37	60	56	56	43	40	40	47	46	46	49	47	47
Guanacaste	6	9	35	31	56	47	49	44	41	42	53	49	51	52	48	50
Puntarenas	6	7	29	28	46	52	52	37	35	35	43	41	42	42	40	40
Limón	2	3	14	13	52	48	49	37	37	37	44	44	35	45	45	43
NATIONAL TOTAL	22	68	267	329	63	58	58	41	38	39	49	47	48	50	49	49

* P = Presidential Election; C = Congressional Election; M = Municipal Election.

TABLE 3-23. REPRESENTATION AND VOTING FOR COSTA RICAN LEGISLATURE

PARTY	1953		1958		1962		1966		1970	
	Seats	Percent vote	Seats	Percent vote	Seats	Percent vote	Seats	Percent vote	Seats	Percent vote
PLN	30	65	20	42	29	49	29	49	32	55
PD	11	21								
PRNI	3	7								
PUN	1	7	10	21	8	13				
PR			11	22	19	34				
PI			3	9						
PUCR			1	3			1	6		
PADP					1	3				
UN							27	43	22	41
Other				3		1		2	5	4
TOTAL	45	100	45	100	57	100	57	100	57	100

PLN voting is strong and well distributed throughout the provinces, as indicated in Table 3-22. Competition is normally greatest in legislative contests, but the PLN has retained control of the National Assembly since 1953. Local issues have encouraged additional, local parties at the municipal level, making PLN strength in such contexts even more significant. PLN victories at the municipal level seem tied to its effective organizational machinery, aided at the presidential level by charismatic appeals.

The dominant PLN position in legislative elections is shown for 1953–1966 in Table 3-23. National legislative representation reveals the transience of many opposition parties. Revision in opposition party organizations occurs with almost each election, however familiar the opposition candidates may be. A general decline in PLN voting is visible during the 1953–1966 period, but the trend is most visible for legislative contests.

Although there are stronger PLN voting tendencies in rural and provincial centers than in the capital city, paradoxically the PLN is improving gradually its capital city support while losing gradually its rural support. The long-range outlook is favorable to the PLN, since urban population growth rates far exceed rural increases. Explanations for PLN declines in rural areas are purely conjectural. They may be produced by greater opposition party activity in those areas, or perhaps by identification of rural problems with the PLN or regime and growing hostility to the regime for failing to resolve the problems.[121] The dichotomy in PLN voting trends between rural and urban areas is shown in Table 3-24.

TABLE 3-24. RURAL AND URBAN COMPONENTS OF PLN
VOTING (IN PERCENT)

	1958	1962	(Change)	1966	(Change)
Urban	45	45	(±0)	47	(+2)
Rural	57	53	(−4)	52	(−2)
National	54	50	(−4)	50	(±0)

5. SUMMARY

Costa Rica has the essential quality of a multi-party dominant system: one party that has consistently dominated others electorally. The key variable has been the opposition, which when coalesced has challenged and defeated the PLN, but when proliferated and divided has left the PLN in a clearly dominant position. Such is the situation following the 1970 national elections, with the PLN dominating the party system at least momentarily in two-party competition.

Costa Rica challenges most Latin American stereotypes. Located in tropical Central America, dependent upon an unstable coffee-banana export economy, Costa Rica has developed a well integrated, politically aware electorate with stable, institutionalized electoral practices and competitive parties. As competitive as party politics is, parties are still somewhat elitist in leadership and organization, and recent evidence suggests growing dissatisfaction with them. Like Chile, Costa Rica has maintained representative processes even during periods of economic stress. The party competition has changed, often rapidly, with PLN dominance depending more upon the party's appeals than upon governmental supports for the system. Costa Rica has had an advantage over many Latin American nations, not having to overcome profound cultural or regional divisions by political means. Consequently the nation has developed through public policy and party structures viable means for maintaining spontaneous support for governmental processes.

IV. CONCLUSIONS

Although each of the three political systems reviewed have had multi-party dominant competition, differences between the systems are significant. Radical party dominance in Argentina was maintained historically by an institutional support—the Sáenz Peña law, which discouraged party proliferation and accentuated control by the strongest party. *Peronismo* may have developed at first somewhat spontaneously, as a personalistic movement fed by genuine, widespread discontent and alienation from previous regimes; but the *Peronista* parties were heavily subsidized by the state during the Perón epoch, and other party organizations were persecuted. In the interim of electoral activity between Perón and Onganía, Argentine party politics proliferated, especially after proportional representation replaced the Sáenz Peña law. The Radical parties remained strong, reinforced by their traditions and leaders, and *Peronismo* remained strong, reinforced by unresolved social and economic inequities.

Over the past two decades Chile has seen a contraction of its party system, and recently an increasing level of competition between the remaining groups. One group, the Christian Democrats, marginally, perhaps temporarily dominated the others electorally and representationally. Costa Rica has commonly changed its mode of competition, but the PLN has dominated other national parties since 1953. The level of PLN dominance has depended particularly upon opposition consensus and fragmentation.

What all three nations share in common are qualities in their political cultures; the most important is a high level of political awareness and participation. Even in Argentina, where political uncertainties and alienation have been common since Perón, participation remains high. In each country participation tends to be uniformly high throughout the population, not just in the capital city or urban areas. Levels of participation have increased steadily in Chile, periodically in Costa Rica. Each of the three nations achieves participation comparable or higher than the United States.

Participation is probably an indicator of political awareness and the intensity of political socialization; these are conditioned by educational opportunity and quality, and communication. Each nation has high literacy and provides extensive public education in most of their territories. Awareness and political imvolvement have not necessarily brought integration. Argentina, perhaps the most culturally aware, is politically conditioned by an inflexible social system which, although dominated by a middle class, is a source of conflict. Cultural and geographic regionalism in Chile has not apparently interfered with integration of its political culture. Similarly, Costa Rica has maintained a governmentally stable, competitive party system, with an alluvium of elitism which gives political priorities to relatively few citizens. No causal relationship can be suggested between cultural awareness and party dominance, but the two are at least sympathetic: before a party organization can build enough support to bridge natural societal divisions, a relatively high level of political awareness and sophistication may be necessary. More likely, a close correlation probably does exist developmentally between cultural awareness, identification, and party institutional growth.

Since multi-party dominance relies principally upon cultural and political factors for system maintenance, it is a fragile, but meaningful indicator of fundamental trends in a multi-party political culture.

NOTES

[1] Many "introductions" to Argentina exist, but alternative ones are: James R. Scobie, *Argentina: A City and a Nation* (New York: Oxford University Press, 1964); Thomas F. McGann, *Argentina: The Divided Land* (Princeton, N.J.: Van Nostrand, 1966); and Arthur P. Whitaker, *Argentina* (Englewood Cliffs, N.J.: Prentice-Hall, 1964).

[2] Background on the Argentina economy is found in Aldo Ferrier, *The Argentine Economy*, tr. by M. M. Urquidi (Berkeley: University of California Press, 1966); see also T. R. Fillol, *Social Factors in Economic Development: The Argentine Case* (Oxford: Oxford University Press, 1961).

[3] The most useful source on Argentine population, particularly the influence of immigration on modernization, see Gino Germani, "Mass Immigration and Modernization in Argentina," in Irving Louis Horowitz, et al., eds., *Latin American Radicalism* (New York: Vintage Books, 1969), pp. 314–355.

[4] *Ibid.*, p. 319. Since 1861, Italian immigration to Argentina has outnumbered Spanish, except for 1911–1920.

[5] *Ibid.*, pp. 325–27.

[6] The impact of the *gaucho* on Argentine culture is well reviewed by Ezequiel Martinez Estrada, *Muerte y transfiguración de Martín Fierro* (Mexico: Fondo de Cultura Económica, 1948), Vol. I, especially p. 240.

[7] See C. C. Taylor, *Rural Life in Argentina* (Baton Rouge: University of Louisiana Press, 1948); also, José Luis Romero, *A History of Argentine Political Thought*, trans. by Thomas F. McGann (Stanford: Stanford University Press, 1963), pp. 167–82.

[8] Few other Latin American nations have been so well treated by historians as Argentina; among the most useful sources found for this section were: V. F. Lopez, *Historia de la Republica Argentina* 8 vols. (Buenos Aires, 1949–1950); Enrique de Gandia, *Historia de la Republica Argentina en el siglo XIX* (Buenos Aires, 1940); Ricardo Levene, *A History of Argentina*, trans. by W. S. Robertson (Chapel Hill, N.C.: University of North Carolina

166   PARTY SYSTEMS AND ELECTIONS IN LATIN AMERICA

Press, 1937); also, John W. White, *Argentina: The Life Story of a Nation* (New York, 1942).

⁹ The period is reviewed by Whitaker, *Argentina*, pp. 41–64; and Scobie, *Argentina: A City and a Nation*, pp. 189–214.

¹⁰ Argentine scholars have always been fascinated by the evolution of their political parties, and a vast literature exists on the topic. A few useful ones include: Adolfo E. Parry, *Partidos Políticos* (Buenos Aires, 1960); Antonio Castagno, *Los Partidos Políticos Argentinos* (Buenos Aires, 1959); Linares Quintana, *Los Partidos Políticos* (Buenos Aires, 1945); José S. Campobassi, et al., *Los Partidos Políticos: Estructura y Vigencia en la Argentina* (Buenos Aires, 1962).

¹¹ A more pessimistic view is taken by Rodolfo Puizzros, *Historia Crítica de los Partidos Políticos Argentinos* (Buenos Aires: Ed. Argumentos, 1956).

¹² The best source on the Argentine military is Robert A. Potash, *The Army and Politics in Argentina, 1928–1945* (Stanford: Stanford University Press, 1969), see especially pp. 1–28.

¹³ A premature and now dated survey of Perón, but still one of the most lucid is George I. Blanksten, *Perón's Argentina* (Chicago: University of Chicago Press, 1953); for more recent developments in the movement, see P. Ranis, "Peronismo without Perón: Ten years after the fall, 1955–1965," *Journal of Inter-American Studies* 8 (January 1966): 112–28.

¹⁴ Characteristic of the "devotion" given Eva during her reign is Jerónimo M. Peralta, *Semblanza Heróica de Eva Perón* (Buenos Aires: El Ateneo, 1950).

¹⁵ Whitaker, *Argentina*, p. 114.

¹⁶ See Raul A. Mende, *El Justicialismo* (Buenos Aires: ALEA, S.A., 1950), especially p. 155.

¹⁷ The 1957–1958 period was a critical one to party development. See Robert A. Potash, "Argentine Political Parties: 1957–1958," *Journal of Inter-American Studies* 1 (October 1959): 515–24.

¹⁸ See Peter G. Snow, "Parties and Politics in Argentina: The Elections of 1962–1963," *Midwest Journal of Political Science* 9 (February 1965): 1–36.

¹⁹ Argentine federalism in the governmental context is more myth than reality, but it does express important cultural, and for parties organizational, qualities. See Rosendo A. Gómez, "Argentine Federalism: Its theory and practice" (Ph.D. dissertation, University of Minnesota, 1950).

²⁰ A general, not always accuráte, survey of Argentine electoral institutions is *Argentina: Election Factbook, July 7, 1963* (Washington, D.C.: Institute for Comparative Study of Political Systems, 1693), especially pp. 27–30.

²¹ On October 13, 1948, the congress passed an amendment to the enfranchisement act for women stating that women were not required to disclose their ages, merely state that they were "over 18" and their word would be taken. See Blanksten, *Perón's Argentina* p. 99.

²² Peter G. Snow, "The Evolution of the Argentine Electoral System," *Parliamentary Affairs* 18 (Summer 1965): 330–36.

²³ James W. Rowe, *The Argentine Elections of 1963: An Analysis* (Washington, D.C.: Institute for Comparative Study of Political Systems, 1964), p. 29.

²⁴ One of the best sources on party politics is Peter G. Snow, *Argentine Radicalism* (Iowa City: University of Iowa Press, 1965).

[25] The relationship of the Argentine labor movement to political parties, especially the *Peronistas*, is reviewed by Moises Poblete Troncoso and Ben G. Burnett, *The Rise of the Latin American Labor Movement* (New Haven, Conn.: College and University Press, 1962), pp. 42–58.

[26] James W. Rowe, "Whither the Peronists?" in Robert D. Tomasek, ed., *Latin American Politics* (Garden City, N.Y.: Doubleday Anchor, 1966), pp. 429–38.

[27] More information contained in Edward J. Williams, *Latin American Christian Democratic Parties* (Knoxville: University of Tennessee Press, 1967), pp. 20–21.

[28] Rollie Poppino suggests the Argentine Communist party, in view of its following, has been especially unsuccessful; see his *International Communism in Latin America* (New York: Free Press, 1964), pp. 11–12.

[29] Voting for these parties is available in *Election Factbook*, pp. 23–24.

[30] Rowe, *Argentine Elections*, pp. 15–16.

[31] Earlier analysis is available in Eduardo Zalduendo, *Geografía electoral de la Argentina* (Buenos Aires: Ed. Amore, 1958).

[32] *Correo de la Tarde*, IX: 1824 (June 6–12, 1967), p. 9; reported in Peter G. Snow, *Argentine Political Parties and the 1966 Election* (Iowa City, Iowa: University of Iowa, Dept. of Political Science, 1968), p. 43.

[33] José Luis de Imaz, *Los que mandan* (Buenos Aires: Editorial Universitaria de Buenos Aires, 1964), p. 102; see the same author's *La clase alta de Buenos Aires* (Buenos Aires: Universidad de Buenos Aires, 1962).

[34] Gino Germani, *La estructura social de la Argentina* (Buenos Aires: Editorial Raigal, 1955), pp. 250–55.

[35] José Luis de Imaz, *Motivación Electoral* (Buenos Aires: Instituto de Desarrollo Economico y Social, 1962), p. 42.

[36] Rowe, *Argentine Elections*, p. 25.

[37] *Ibid.*, p. 6.

[38] Material for this section drawn from Rowe, *ibid.*, and Snow, "Parties and Politics."

[39] The two year period 1966–1968 is very well reported by Kenneth F. Johnson, *Argentina's Mosaic of Discord, 1966–1968* (Washington, D.C.: Institute for Comparative Study of Political Systems, 1969).

[40] A useful general introduction to Chilean politics is Federico G. Gil, *Political System of Chile* (Boston: Houghton Mifflin, 1966).

[41] See G. J. Butland, *The Human Geography of Southern Chile* (London: Royal Institute of International Affairs, 1957).

[42] See Peter Gregory, *Industrial Wages in Chile* (Ithaca, N.Y.: New York State School of Industrial and Labor Relations, Cornell University, 1967), pp. 102–07.

[43] Kalman Silvert has written convincingly on the predominant "myth" structure of Chilean society, including beliefs about their cultural attainments, about the importance of education, institutional democracy, racial homogeneity, nonviolence, and military skills; these myths are pervasive, if not always valid; see Silvert's "Coda" (Buenos Aires, American Universities Field Staff Letter, September 21, 1957).

[44] Kalman Silvert, "The State of Chilean Agriculture" (Santiago, American Universities Field Staff Letter, July 1, 1957), p. 9.

[45] Kalman Silvert, *The Conflict Society: Reaction and Revolution in Latin America* (New Orleans: Hauser Press, 1961), pp. 230–41.

[46] A classic history of Chile is D. B. Arana, *Historia general de Chile*, 16 vols. 2nd ed. (Santiago, 1930); see also Luis Galdames, *A History of Chile* (Chapel Hill: University of North Carolina Press, 1941).

[47] Fernando Campos Harriet, *Historia constitucional de Chile* (Santiago: Editorial Juridica de Chile, 1956), especially pp. 225.

[48] An interesting analysis of the importance of naval power to Chile is D. E. Worchester, *Seapower and Chilean Independence* (Gainesville: University of Florida Press, 1962); see also R. N. Burr, *By Reason or Force: Chile and the Balancing of Power in South America 1830–1905* (Berkeley: University of California Press, 1965).

[49] Gil, *Political System of Chile*, pp. 43–47.

[50] Alberto Edwards and Eduardo Frei, *Historia de los partidos politicos chilenos* (Santiago: Editorial del Pacifico, 1949), includes two separate works; Frei's covers the period 1891–1938.

[51] See: John Reese Stevenson, The Chilean Popular Front (Philadelphia: University of Pennsylvania Press, 1942); C. Ramilia Gomez and H. Llanos Mansilla, *Los gobiernos parliamentarios en Chile* (Santiago: Editorial Universitaria, 1954); and Ernest Eugene Harrill, "Origins and institutional emergence of the parliamentary system of government in Chile" (M.A. thesis, University of North Carolina, 1949).

[52] A partisan but useful account of the Radical party is Florencio Durán, *El Partido Radical* (Santiago: Ed. Noscimento, 1958).

[53] Although largely incorporated in his book, *Political System of Chile*, Gil also published a monograph, "Genesis and modernization of political parties in Chile" (Gainesville: University of Florida Press, 1962), which is useful for this period.

[54] K. H. Silvert, "A Political-Economic Sketch of Chilean History from 1879" (Santiago: American Universities Field Staff, January 27, 1947).

[55] A firsthand account of the 1924 revolution is Emilio Bello Codesido, *Recuerdos politicos* (Santiago: Ed. Nacimento, 1954), written by a participant in the coup.

[56] Campos, José Guillermo Guerra, *La constitución de 1925* (Santiago, 1929); also Mario Bernaschina, *Los constituyentes de 1925* (Santiago: Editorial Universitaria, 1945).

[57] Ernst Halperin, *Nationalism and Communism in Chile* (Cambridge, Mass.: M.I.T. Press, 1965), pp. 42–81.

[58] Donald W. Bray, "Chilean Politics during the Second Ibáñez Government" (Ph.D. dissertation, Stanford University, 1961).

[59] Gil, *Political System of Chile*, p. 223.

[60] The inflationary process is deeply rooted; see Frank W. Fetter, *La inflación monetaria en Chile* (Santiago, 1942); the current problem has been reviewed by Gregory, *Industrial Wages in Chile*, especially p. 37.

[61] A very revealing insight into Chilean intellectual culture is Ricardo Doñoso, *Las ideas politicas en Chile* (Mexico: Fondo de Cultura Economica, 1946).

[62] Chilean electoral procedures are published in *Ley General de Elecciones, No. 14.852* (Santiago: Talleres Graficos "La Nacion," 1965).

[63] All electoral information in this chapter for Chile is taken from the

official publication of the Chilean Senate: Information Office, *Boletín de Información General No. 47* (Santiago: December 31, 1968).

[64] A review of the Liberal and Conservative parties is found in Gabriel Amunategui, *Partidos politicos* (Santiago: Ed. Juridica de Chile, 1952); see also Alberto Edwards, *Organización political de Chile* (Santiago: Ed. del Pacifico, 1955); Marcial Sanfuentes Carrión, *El Partido Conservador: Doctrina y Convenciones* (Santiago, 1957); Enrique Tagle Rodrigues, *Liberales y Conservadores* (Santiago, 1917); Edgardo Garrido Merino, *Espíritu y acción del liberalismo* (Santiago, 1934); and Rene León Echaiz, *Evolución historica de los partidos politicos Chilenos* (Santiago: Prensa de la Editorial Ercilla, S.A., 1939).

[65] A revealing example of the Radical evolution is contained in Bartolome Palacios S., *El Partido Conservador y el Partido Radical: frente a frente* (Santiago, 1918); see also the excellent Chilean source, Germán Urzua Valenzuela, *Los Partidos Politicos Chilenos: Las fuerzas politicas* (Santiago; Editorial Juridica de Chile, 1968), especially pp. 53–101.

[66] Valenzuela, *Los Partidos Politicos Chilenos*, pp. 40–44.

[67] A general introduction to the Chilean Christian Democrats is contained in Williams, *Latin American Christian Democrat Parties;* an indispensable analysis of PDC organization, particularly information on party militants based on survey research, is Francis Giles Wayland-Smith, "The Christian Democratic Party in Chile: A Study of Political Organization and Activity with Primary Emphasis on the Local Level" (Ph.D. dissertation, Syracuse University, 1968), especially chapters V and VI.

[68] See Eduardo Frei, *Pensamiento y acción* (Santiago: Editorial del Pacifico, 1958) pp. 62–64; other works by Frei include *La Politica y el Espiritu* (Santiago, 1946) and *La verdad tiene su hora* (Santiago, 1955).

[69] Best sources on the PS are: Oscar Schnake, *Politica socialista* (Santiago, 1937); Luis Zuniga, *El Partido Socialista en la realidad nacional* (Santiago, Ediciones Espartaco, 1952); and Halperin, *Nationalism and Communism*, pp. 118–77.

[70] *Ibid.*, pp. 207–13.

[71] Poppino, *International Communism*, pp. 67–70. The party was also repressed from 1922–1936, particularly under Ibáñez.

[72] Halperin, *Nationalism and Communism*, pp. 42–116.

[73] See Gil, *Political System of Chile*, pp. 236, 308–309.

[74] General information is contained in *Chile: Election Factbook, September 4, 1964* (Washington, D.C.: Institute for Comparative Study of Political Systems, 1963), pp. 8–12.

[75] *Ibid.*, pp. 42–45.

[76] Gil, *Political System of Chile*, pp. 225–29.

[77] Chilean Senate: Information Office, pp. 15–25.

[78] *Ibid.*, pp. 7–12.

[79] An excellent analysis of electoral geography is Ricardo Cruz-Coke Madrid, *Geographia electoral de Chile* (Santiago: Ed. del Pacifico, 1952), which includes additional electoral information also.

[80] *Election Factbook*, pp. 4–6.

[81] Chilean Senate, pp. 7–9.

[82] *Ibid.*, pp. 12–13.

[83] Chile's elections have been reasonably well analyzed. For the election

of 1964 (presidential see Federico G. Gil and Charles J. Parrish, *The Chilean Presidential Election of September 4, 1964* (Washington, D.C.: Institute for Comparative Study of Political Systems, 1965); for the election of 1965 (congressional) see Charles J. Parrish, Arpad J. von Lazar, and Jorge Tapia Videla, *The Chilean Congressional Election of March 7, 1965: An Analysis* (Washington, D.C.: Institute for Comparative Study of Political Systems, 1967); for the election of 1967 (municipal) see Michel Francis and Eldon Lanning, "Chile's 1967 Municipal Elections," *Inter-American Economic Affairs* 21, No. 2 (Autumn 1967): 23–37.

[84] Chilean Senate, pp. 28–57.

[85] Chile's perpetual reapportionment problem was indentified even before the 1930 census by José Guillermo Guerra, *La Constitución de 1925* (Anales de la Universidad de Chile), (Santiago de Chile: Establecimientos Graficos Balcells y Cia., 1929), pp. 219–20. Portions of this section were originally published in the *Midwest Journal of Political Science* 13, No. 3 (August 1969). Reproduced with permission.

[86] Armand Mattelart, *Atlas Social de Las Comunas de Chile* (Santiago de Chile: Editorial del Pacifico, S.A., 1965), pp. 123–24.

[87] There is no standard definition of "metropolitan area" for Chile. A case could be made that the entire central region of Chile, including the city of Valparaíso and the resort of Viña del Mar could be included in such a definition, at least as easily as some of the more rural and peripheral portions of Santiago Province. But since only the Province of Santiago can be viewed as an electoral and administrative unit, we have arbitrarily chosen to limit our analysis to this single province.

[88] The Province of Ñuble, located to the South between Santiago and Conception, is dominated by Chillán, a city of only 85,000 persons. Ñuble has two electoral districts. Migration and urbanization have had a minimal effect on this province.

[89] Reprinted in Russell H. Fitzgibbon, ed., *The Constitutions of the Americas* (Chicago: University of Chicago Press, 1948), p. 146.

[90] The position of *Contraloría General* is nearly unique in the Americas. Created by constitutional amendment in 1943, the controller general has not only jurisdiction over financial matters but also has the general responsibility for protecting the "constitutionality" of executive actions. Enjoying the same tenure and general status as members of the supreme court, the controller general can in effect pass information to the legislature, or "indite" executives for violation of or failure to implement the laws. For a more complete analysis, see Gil, *Political System of Chile*, pp. 97–99.

[91] Data for 1930 and 1960 are based on official census published by *Servicio Nacional de Estadisticas y Censos*. The 1968 estimated population is based on 1960 census data projected by estimated annual growth rate for the province. Mattelart, *Atlas Social*, pp. 45–46. Representation available in *Chile: Election Factbook*, p. 9.

[92] The indexes included in Table II are taken from Mattelart, *ibid.* The "demographic-occupational" index is a weighted synthesis of rates of unemployment and employment, growth, urban population, and type of employment; "standard of living" likewise is a synthesis of several census indicators including homes with water, electricity, plumbing, and levels of health; the "general development" index is a further synthesis of the first two with level of literacy. These indexes are intended to be only suggestive, a rough compari-

son of the communes within the electoral districts of Santiago Province, and their relation to the national norms. A complete description of the components of the indexes and their statistical method is found in Mattelart, *Atlas Social*, pp. 13–18.

[93] For a further discussion of the functions and roles of local administrators and *regidores*, see Gil, *Political System of Chile*, pp. 128–33.

[94] Political regionalism in Chile is only partly a reflection, as Gil suggests (*Political System of Chile*, pp. 132–33), of traditional cultural localisms; in Chile it is also a reflection of the uneven level and rate of development between the provinces and Santiago.

[95] Projections based on official returns. translated into percent of total vote by party. See *Dirección del Registro Electoral, Elección de Diputados del 7 de marzo de 1965*.

[96] The open-list ballot is rare in Latin America; more common is the closed-list type where order of candidates seated is determined by party organization, and number seated is determined by total party vote.

[97] The elections included the presidential election of 1964, the congressional elections of 1965, and the municipal elections of 1967. Official returns are from the *Dirección del Registro Electoral*.

[98] Economic, social, and demographic indexes computed from Mattelart, *Atlas Social*, pp. 45–46. Participation indexes taken from data supplied by *Dirección del Registro Electoral*, for elections of 1965 and 1967. The "other parties" category includes primarily the Liberal and Conservative parties in 1965, their National party in 1967, the National Democratic party and various independents.

[99] Voting tendencies for the 1965 congressional election were used as a basis for this analysis. Other elections yield essentially the same result.

[100] A serious void in the literature dealing with Costa Rica was filled recently with the publication of John D. Martz, "Costa Rican Electoral Trends, 1953–1966," *Western Political Quarterly* 20, No. 4 (December 1967): 888–909. Martz' article is the most useful source presently available on Costa Rican politics.

[101] The best source on Costa Rican economics is Stacy May, Just Faaland, Albert R. Koch, Howard L. Parsons, and Clarence Senior, *Costa Rica: A Study in Economic Development* (New York: Twentieth Century Fund, 1952); see also, Oscar E. Chávez, "Land Reform in Costa Rica," *Americas* (February 1963).

[102] Costa Rican history is not well chronicled; useful is James L. Busey, "The Presidents of Costa Rica," *Americas* 18, (July 1961): 55–70; see also Hubert Herring, *A History of Latin America*, 3rd ed. (New York: Knopf, 1968), pp. 496–502.

[103] Reported in James L. Busey, *Notes on Costa Rican Democracy* (Boulder: University of Colorado Press, Series in Political Science, 1962), pp. 9–11.

[104] A highly favorable account of the Figueres *junta* is noted in Harry Kantor, "A 'New Deal' Government for Costa Rica," *World Affairs* 117 (Spring 1954): 1–13.

[105] The 1953 election is analyzed, particularly the campaign, by Harry Kantor, *The Costa Rica Election of 1953: A Case Study* (Gainesville: University of Florida Press, 1958).

[106] Martz, "Costa Rican Electoral Trends," pp. 890–91.

[107] An account of the 1966 election is contained in R. McDonald, "Stable Political Change in Central America: Three Recent Examples." *Atenea* 3, No. 4 (December 1966): 21–32.

[108] Martz, "Costa Rican Electoral Trends," pp. 892–95, is the best account, based on the personal observation and interviews with the participants.

[109] *Visión*, October 24, 1969, pp. 21–22.

[110] A most useful sociological study of Costa Rica is Charles P. Loomis, et al., Turrialba: *Social Systems and the Introduction of Change* (Glencoe, Ill.: The Free Press, 1953).

[111] Busey, *Notes*, pp. 20–23.

[112] A general source on Costa Rican parties is James L. Busey, "Foundations of political contrast: Costa Rica and Nicaragua," *Western Political Quarterly* 11 (September 1958): 627–59.

[113] The party is briefly discussed by Poppino, *International Communism, et passim;* see also Martz, "Costa Rican Electoral Trends," p. 893 regarding the 1966 elections.

[114] See *Codigo Electoral de 1952*, and *Ley Orgánica de la Registraduria Civil de 1965*, published by the Costa Rican government.

[115] Information from *Costa Rica: Election Factbook, February 6, 1966* (Washington, D.C.: Institute for Comparative Study of Political Systems, 1965), pp. 33–34.

[116] See account also in Busey, *Notes*, pp. 31–33.

[117] There is, as Daniel Goldrich implies, some differentiation in class. See his *Sons of the Establishment: Elite Youth in Panama and Costa Rica* (Chicago: Rand McNally, 1966), pp. 49–62.

[118] More complete information on the 1953, 1958, and 1962 elections is contained in *Costa Rica: Election Factbook*, p. 14.

[119] An excellent analysis of regional voting patterns is in Martz, "Costa Rican Electoral Trends," pp. 895–905.

[120] Additional information available in Costa Rica: *Election Factbook*, pp. 3–4.

[121] Further analysis in Martz, "Costa Rican Electoral Trends," pp. 903–05.

CHAPTER 4

Two-Party Competitive Systems: Colombia, Uruguay, and Honduras

Two-party competitive systems are those in which two parties receive not less than 40 nor more than 60 percent of the total seats in a legislature. Relatively few nations in Latin America have had such systems a long time. Of the three examples reviewed in this chapter, one (Honduras) is a party system only marginally relevant to national politics, while the other two (Colombia and Uruguay) resemble multi-party systems forced into two-party institutional molds. Honduras is a weakly institutionalized political system with little experience in representative government. Colombia has strong party traditions, periodically expressed within the framework of representative government, but occasionally breaking into violence, anarchy, and dictatorship. Uruguay has been institutionalized, representative, and stable for most of the twentieth century.

Recognizing the differences between the three nations, a question can be raised as to whether there are general implications for a competitive, two-party system in the Latin American context. Although the institutional analogies have few similarities with the United States' or British experience, there are common if limited structural and behavioral characteristics for the Latin American systems.[1]

One of the similarities is the relative difficulty for entry and exit into the party system. Two controls normally regulate the process: election and party registration laws, and custom or a political culture that supports existing institutions. A rigid two-party system must provide for alternation and succession in leadership to reflect new recruitment, or find some means whereby factions identified with individual leaders can be assured limited autonomy within the larger party. Recruitment to party elites in a highly

173

oligarchic system is often performed through social or familial hierarchies otherwise closed to outsiders.

A two-party context demands relatively strong penetration of party activity and party symbols throughout the national territory, although the intensity may decline outside the core areas. Profound regional influences that often produce multiple parties must somehow be accommodated by the two-party structures. Accommodation demands either a close correlation of national political divisions to political parties (for example, urban/rural, or two urban areas) or organizational and patronage mechanisms that accommodate regional pressures.

As in two-party competitive systems elsewhere, elections in the Latin American context normally organize the outs versus the ins. The confrontation carries considerable potential for instability during periods of social disorganization or economic stress, when alienated and hostile forces within the nation outnumber the sanguine. Principal loyalties and identifications are more easily focused on party than governmental institutions.

Recognizing the almost universal nineteenth-century Liberal/Conservative polarization in Latin America, it seems likely that a twentieth-century two-party system would have definite nineteenth-century roots. The persistence of earlier party traditions, socialized and defended over a century, would provide a plausible explanation for a contemporary two-party system.

As oligarchy influences politics in Latin America, it is likely to express itself as strong family identifications and traditions in a specific party, and perhaps a specialization of particular families in the function of party leadership. This functional familial specialization has strong implications for governmental leadership recruitment, for it impresses on the party context family rivalries that extend beyond the usual political conflicts.

The external cultural and contextural differences in the three nations underscore the futility of predicting solely on the basis of party system the kind of politics, environment, or "political development" that can be expected. Honduras is one of the most economically backward of the Latin American nations, Uruguay one of the most advanced, and Colombia somewhere in between. The majority of Hondurans are beyond the realm of national politics and awareness. Colombia has a history of political violence that persists today, with two political parties historically alternating periods of supremacy and persecution. Uruguay, which almost singularly has achieved a sustained period of nonviolent party competition and regular elections, emerged from a nineteenth-century experience of extended, chaotic party warfare. In spite of the stable two-party competition during the present century, one of the two parties has controlled the government for all but eight years.

I. HONDURAS: A WEAK TWO-PARTY SYSTEM

The overwhelming reality of Honduran politics is the remoteness of its parties from the majority of citizens.[2] By almost any index Honduras is one of the most backward and unintegrated of the Latin American republics. Its two million inhabitants live more or less isolated from each other and the rest of the world, spread over an inhospitable terrain. Poverty, disease, malnutrition, and illiteracy remain the primary obstacles to effective political integration and governmental control. The national economy is dominated by foreign investment, particularly the great banana plantations whose exports account for more than half of the national revenue.[3] Predominantly agricultural, Honduras is constrained by poor communication, backward technology, and inefficient subsistance farming on 80 percent of its cultivated land.

Honduran politics has been controlled historically by strongmen, political *coups*, and military influence. Despite these natural social obstacles, Honduras does lack the severe racial distinctions which have divided neighboring Guatemala. Racially most of its population is a characteristic Honduran *mestizo*. The country is so poor that even class distinctions, while profound, have wrought less havoc than might be assumed. The upper class is predictably small, but so too is the middle class. The vast majority of Hondurans acquire little material wealth or security, and do not conceive of politics as a means of improving their condition. It is perhaps coincidental to its economic, social, and political context that Honduras has produced and retained an institutionalized, two-party system.

Modern Honduran politics begins with the more or less voluntary retirement of its "last great dictator," General Tiburcio Carías Andino, in 1948. Carías came to power in 1932, but ruled through puppet presidents from 1923. Following 1932, he consolidated his personal control over national political life after a century of violent party warfare, dating from Honduran independence. His legacy was a few public works, a backward nation, and a highly personalistic *Partido Nacional* (PN), the political instrument of the conservative interests of the nation. His handpicked successor, Juan Manuel Gálvez, ruled until 1954 with decreasing reliance upon Carías' support.[4]

Gálvez did much to reconstruct the PN along more modern, less personalistic lines. He gradually loosened control over the political life of the nation, while still maintaining political order. A conservative by nature, Gálvez nevertheless recognized the overwhelming work that remained to bring his nation into the twentieth century. In 1954, he retired following the conclusion of his presidential term, and supervised impartial, national elections.

Under Honduran electoral practices, a presidential candidate cannot be elected without a clear majority of the vote. In 1954, a third party, the *Movimiento Nacional Reformista* (MNR), tried to persuade Gálvez to ignore the constitutional provision against reelection, and seek a second term. Although it failed in that purpose, the MNR did succeed in winning sufficient votes to deny a majority to either the National party candidate or that of the Liberal party (PL). Vice President Julio Lozano Díaz was subsequently elevated to the presidency as a temporary measure, and charged with the responsibility of holding new elections. Soon after Lozano assumed office it became clear he had no intention of surrendering power. Lozano fraudulently controlled the outcome of the 1956 constitutional assembly elections. Opposition leaders and outspoken opponents were arbitrarily jailed as his tyranny increased. Finally, on October 21, 1956, a revolt of junior army officers deposed Lozano and installed a three man *junta* which supervised elections the following year.[5]

The 1957 elections, perhaps the high point in Honduran electoral experience, saw Ramón Villeda Morales, a liberally inclined reformer and obstetrician from Tegucigalpa, lead the Liberal party to national power. He skillfully consolidated his personal political control, and advocated sweeping social and economic reform. Villeda was one of the first Latin American leaders to embrace enthusiastically the ideas and programs of the Alliance for Progress. His election seemed to solidify the two-party system in Honduras, producing a peaceful transfer of power from the PN to the PL through the military intermediaries. The National party leadership, however, soon reverted to a former style, making absurd accusations against Villeda and fomenting insurrections. For his part, Villeda's reforms ultimately appeared more illusion than reality. Just prior to the 1963 elections the army struck again, removing Villeda and canceling the scheduled election. Explanations for the *coup*, other than purely personal ones, are hard to find. The leader of the army *junta,* Colonel Osvaldo López Arellano, promised to call elections after a "reasonable" time.

The López regime followed a well-established formula. A new constituent assembly election was held in February, 1965, with the traditional adherents of the PN winning a comfortable majority. Colonel López was promoted to the rank of general. Fearing the possible disruptions of a popular presidential election, General López had himself "elected" president for a six-year term by the assembly, that, having drafted, another constitution converted itself into a national congress.[6]

The abortive electoral challenge in 1954 to the traditional Honduran parties by the *Movimiento Nacional Reformista* accomplished little. The MNR received enough presidential votes to prevent a candidate from the traditional parties from being elected president in 1954, and ultimately induced a military takeover. The MNR also won limited representation in the 1957 constituent assembly, but since has all but disappeared.

Party institutions in Honduras remain a very thin veneer over a highly rarefied process. National politics requires military acquiescence, while the extraordinary influence of a few leaders and the harsh realities of the electoral arena make participation difficult. Poor communication, limited political awareness, and economic stridencies restrict political life to the capital, Tegucigalpa, and the larger commercial city of San Pedro Sula. Outside these areas, politics is a matter for local bosses, colonels, government administrators, and a few landowners. The relatively free elections of 1954 and 1957 are an exception rather than a tradition in Honduran life.

The harshness of Honduran life paradoxically works against the development of radical party movements. Peasants are consumed with the immediate problems of survival, unaffected by the escalating expectations promoted by an educational system. Revolutionary guerrilla activity has been very unsuccessful in Honduras, although a few university students in the capital advocate such a course.[7] The simple reality is that a majority of Hondurans fail to conceive of politics as a means of improving their condition, a reality that contributes to the stability of the traditional, two-party system.

Honduran political parties are not modern, mass organizations, but limited groups of politically aware and motivated participants. The party system is durable and persistent because there is nothing else to challenge it except the military, which in the final analysis fails to view parties as a serious threat. In the Honduran case at least, party durability and stability are partially a function of irrelevancy.

II. COLOMBIA: A VIOLENT TWO-PARTY SYSTEM

If Honduras can be conceived as a two-party system with weak party identifications, then Colombia must be described as a two-party system with identifications so strong as to promote violent antagonisms based on little more than party affiliations. Colombian party history is striated with violence and competitiveness, acquiescence and oppression, persecution and instability.

1. CONTEXT OF COLOMBIAN PARTY POLITICS

Colombia is a nation of nearly 20 million inhabitants, growing at a rapid annual rate of over 3.4 percent. Although 55 percent rural, Colombia has many modern cities, including its capital, Bogotá, and the two thriving provincial cities of Medellín and Cali. About one-half of the population is illiterate, with public education limited and too expensive for the majority. Most education is still in the hands of the Church, but its schools also require payment.

Located in the equatorial zone, Colombia's mountainous terrain and high valleys encourage the bulk of its population to live in the more temperate climates and enjoy the advantages of fertile land and the considerable natural resources. The three mountain ranges that divide the land geographically also isolate its communities culturally, socially, and politically, and produce a significant regional dimension to national politics and a formidable barrier to economic and political integration. Disease, poverty, and malnutrition are widespread, and social and economic mobility highly restricted. Income and welfare differentiation in Colombia are classically oligarchical, with little change having occurred in the past half century. The bulk of the population is *mestizo*, with a substantial Negro influence in the coastal regions. The upper class is predominantly white European, coming principally from Spain to which immigration was once restricted. The economy, while essentially stagnant during the turbulent period of the 1950s, has more recently begun to expand at an impressive rate. Little if any of these developments have filtered down to the majority of the population in the form of increased educational or welfare facilities. The economy is reasonably well industrialized, with particularly impressive beginnings in consumer commodities and a few basic industries like steel. The export economy is precariously and perhaps needlessly tied to the vagaries of a single crop, coffee, although measures are being taken to diversify the export portion of the economy.[8]

Colombia's is a political culture explosive at its foundations, restrained today by the legacy of an extended period of violent anarchy known as *La Violencia*, by an efficient military and police establishment, and by a restrictive covenant which limits through constitutional provisions and a regressive electoral system meaningful party opposition. A few families and their extended relationships constitute a land and business oligarchy that controls a surprising amount of the national economic, social, political, and even religious life.[9]

Colombia has two principal political parties known as Liberal and Conservative. The parties are truly national in scope, although each has regional strengths and foci. Despite their names, the parties have no contemporary ideological differences. Both are products of the traditional nineteenth-century Latin American political controversies; their ideological differentiation persists in the twentieth century in name only. Historically, the Liberal party was supported by urban business interests, normally hostile to extended Church influence in secular affairs. The Conservatives, by contrast, had rural bases of support.[10] Today both parties compete in urban areas, and the countryside is a patchwork of Liberal/Conservative influence, differentiated from one village to another. Cultural ties to the parties are intense. Although real power is concentrated in the hands of a local political boss or family, most residents of an area possess party identifications. The explanation of this intense party perception is the old land system in which the *patrón* saw to it that all those under his control affiliated with the party of his choice. This strange pattern of party allegiance is responsible in part for the fury of *La Violencia* as it spread across the countryside, peasants fighting each other in the name of their party or *patrón*. Predictably, at the highest echelons of party leadership, where perceptions are most sophisticated, this irrational identification and defense of traditional party symbols is less characteristic.

The advocates of strongly differentiated, competitive two-party systems, could take a lesson from Colombia on the excesses that can be committed in the name of two political parties.

2. EVOLUTION OF MODERN POLITICAL PARTIES IN COLOMBIA

Two historical events of the past twenty years shape contemporary Colombian politics: the decade of La Violencia, and the 1957 Sitges Agreement. La Violencia evolved from regional, class, and family rivalries that had produced a fragmented, volatile political culture.[11] Climaxed by the assassination of Jorge Eliécer Gaitán, a charismatic, reform-oriented leader of the Liberal party who believed the party should attempt to bring major changes to the social and economic order, Bogotá ignited on April 9, 1948, into rioting, destruction, and increasing anarchy. The violence of the capital was echoed by a growing number of incidents in rural Colombia, where political bitterness of party adherents and local opportunism had corroded the social-political fabric of the country. Violence was committed in the name of political parties—both Liberal and Conservative—for which strong identifications existed based on historical and regional rather than ideological grounds. During the violent decade from 1948 to 1958, politically motivated slaying and banditry resulted in the death of an estimated 275 thousand persons, leaving few if any families untouched by the death and destruction of La Violencia.[12]

With the amplified social chaos and disorder, Colombian politics generally and elections specifically degenerated. The Liberal party boycotted the 1949 elections, leaving Conservative candidate Laureano Gómez unchallenged. He received, according to official reports, all but 25 of the 1,140,619 votes cast. The feuding of powerful families, compounded by Gómez' ineffective regime and his unpopular, proto-Fascist ideas, further contributed to Colombia's political deterioration and the spread of violence. Gómez was eventually evicted in a bloodless golpe, followed by an unrestrained dictatorship imposed by General Gustavo Rojas Pinilla from 1953 until his overthrow in 1957. Rojas' attempt to create a Colombian Peronismo did little to subdue open hostility or strengthen civic responsibility in the nation.[13]

Weary from ten years of political turbulence and strife, Colombia's two most influential party leaders, Conservative Laureano Gómez and Liberal Alberto Lleras Camargo, met in Spain and pledged cooperation against Rojas. They also eventually reached an agreement known as the Sitges Agreement that, after ratification by a plebicite December 1, 1957, inaugurated a transitional period during which the parties, united more or less in a *Frente de Transformación Nacional* (FTN), agreed to share equally in the powers of government. Colombia's future was to be decided neither by violence nor by elections, but by a simple rotation of the parties in the presidency (*alternación*) and by equal legislative representation (*paridad*). This kind of "gentlemen's agreement" has produced some strange and perhaps unintended results in recent Colombian politics. The Sitges Agreement has determined the course of all elections since 1958 by controlling the electoral system, and to a large extent has determined the development of Colombian politics by shaping the party system itself. *La Violencia* left an imprint on the political culture of Colombia that is best characterized as political alienation, resignation, and fear. The latter, stemming from the havoc of *La Violencia*, today counteracts most tendencies toward renewed violent expressions of political hostility without resolving their underlying causes. Hostility does find, however, periodic expression in elections.[14]

Colombia's nominal two-party system has roots in the 19th century dating from the nation's independence. Despite a vague institutional similarity with the U.S. and British models, Colombian parties have tended to be factionalized, personalistic, and unrestrained in their methods of competition.[15] Moreover, they have tended to reflect and reinforce devisive economic, class, and localistic interests within the country. Party leadership has been recruited from a rarefied economic-social elite that has used party labels as a means of furthering personal, agrarian, urban, or regionalistic interests, often unrelated to the great majority of Colombian people.

At the time of the 1958 election, the Conservative party was split between the followers of former Presidents Laureano Gómez (the *Laureanistas* or *Doctrinalistas* and Mario Ospina Pérez (*Ospinistas* or *Unionistas*). Gómez, who had formed the *Frente* with Lleras Camargo, was in control of the majority faction of the party, and Ospina, who had opposed the *Frente*, the minority faction. Following the 1960 legislative elections, the *Ospinistas* gained control of the party. As Ospina embraced the *Frente*, the *Laureanistas* disavowed it.[16]

Meanwhile, the Liberal party was experiencing its own internal division. The majority (Regular or *Llerista*) faction of the Liberal party was led by Lleras Camargo and his cousin, Carlos Lleras Restrepo. Alfonso López Michelsen, son of former president Alfonso

López (1934–1938), developed as a personal vehicle a splinter of the Liberal party which eventually became known as the *Movimiento Revolucionario Liberal* (MRL). López sought the sizable remnant of Gaitán's following by calling for reform of health, housing, and educational facilities in Colombia, and an end to the *Frente* by 1962. López polled strongly in the 1960 legislative elections, as did the other *Frente* antagonist, Ospina. The high level of voter abstention raised the ominous septre of popular alienation. From the plebicite of December 1, 1957 ratifying the *Frente* to the first presidential election of Alberto Lleras Camargo in May, 1958, popular support for the Frente, seen in Table 4-1, began to weaken. In the 1960 legislative elections with 152 deputies and 80 senators to be elected (76 and 40 respectively from each party) the MRL captured 19 deputies against the regular Liberal's 57, and the *Ospinistas* obtained a majority of the Conservative party seats. Abstention also increased over 1958.

The moderate *Ospinastas* nominated Conservative Guillermo León Valencia as their presidential choice in 1962. Of those eligible to vote, including two million who merely didn't register, no more than 41 percent of the electorate participated. Moreover, a considerable number of blank or protest ballots were deposited by those who did vote. No more than 29 percent of the electorate expressed confidence in the *Frente* by directly voting for its 1962 candidate.[17]

In the 1962 legislative elections with 184 deputies and 98 senators to be elected (92 and 49 respectively from each party) opposition to the *Frente* was expressed through the MRL, the *Laureanistas,* and a new group organized by former dictator Rojas as the *Alianza Nacional Popular* (ANAPO). The MRL siphoned off more liberal votes than in 1960, receiving 20 percent of the popular vote and 33 of the Liberal seats in the lower house. ANAPO received 6 of the Conservative's 92 seats in the lower house, the *Ospinistas* 50, and the *Laureanistas* 36. In the Senate, the MRL gained 12 seats against the regular Liberals' 37. ANAPO received 2, the *Laureanistas* 16, against 31 for the *Ospinistas* out of the

TABLE 4-1. COMPARISON OF *Frente* SUPPORT AND ABSTENTION IN COLOMBIAN ELECTIONS OF 1957, 1958, AND 1962

	Total vote	Est. percent part	Frente vote	Est. percent vote
1957 (Plebicite)	4,397,090	76	4,169,294	95
1958 (Presidential)	3,108,567	53	2,482,984	80
1962 (Presidential)	2,634,840	41	1,636,081	71

49 allowed the Conservatives. The total popular vote for the ANAPO candidates in 1962 was just under 4 percent, the vote for the pro-*Frente* factions approximately 70 percent.

Apart from alienation (abstention), Colombia's party system by 1962 provided the voter with three positive choices: an affirmative, pro-*Frente* vote (*Llerista* or *Ospinista*); a dissident vote (*Laureanista* or MRL); or a protest vote (ANAPO). Any of these three choices could be executed without encumbering the historically strong identifications of "Liberal" and "Conservative." Each choice, affirmative, dissident, and protest, had its Liberal and Conservative expressions. Even ANAPO, technically an alliance, allowed the voter to cast his ANAPO vote under either a Liberal- or Conservative-labeled ballot. An understanding of contemporary Colombian party politics starts with an appreciation of these three choices.

In the March, 1964 legislative elections the same trends continued. Abstention reached unprecedented levels with only 26 percent of the eligible voters participating. The pro-*Frente* factions of the two parties received 68 percent of the popular vote, a decline from 71 percent in 1962, while the ANAPO candidates received 18 percent of the vote compared to only 4 percent in 1962. With this election the *Frente* could command a slim two-thirds majority in the legislative chambers, which had been set under the 1957 *Frente* plebiscite as the minimum required for passage of important legislation. Although the opposition forces (*Laureanistas*, MRL, and ANAPO) could not unite effectively, Colombian legislative processes ground to a stop after 1964 and a state of siege ultimately was declared by the government. Poor administrative leadership also compounded the problem.

Political alienation can be traced from the high voter participation of 76 percent in the 1957 plebiscite through a steady decline with each subsequent election to 26 percent in 1964. Protest can be traced from a high *Frente* vote of 95 percent in 1957 through a steady decline in 1964 of 68 percent. The emergence of ANAPO by 1964 posed an organized threat to the *Frente* and indeed all four traditional party factions. ANAPO appealed for votes from both Liberals and Conservatives, although it drew its strongest support and its candidates from the Conservatives. Rojas himself had been a Conservative, but his political career can in no way be identified with this party.

The complexity of the Colombian political party system prior to the 1966 elections was apparent. Only the two traditionally labeled parties, Liberals and Conservatives, were seated under the Sitges Agreement. These two parties were divided many ways. The majority *Ospinista* faction of the Conservative party and the regular *Llerista* faction of the Liberal party supported the *Frente*. The old *Laureanista* faction, now led by Gómez' son, Álvaro Gómez Hurtado and known as the *Alvaristas*, operated within the Conservative party but opposed the *Frente*. The MRL led by López Michelsen operated within the Liberal party but opposed the *Frente*. ANAPO, an alliance of Liberal and Conservative party followers, competed for votes with both party labels although its support was heavily Conservative.[18]

Besides this fragmentation of parties, "third" parties (parties wholly outside the Conservative-Liberal labeling) exist but are of slight importance. There is an embryonic Christian-Democratic party, and a lackluster socialist party, the *Partido Popular Socialista Colombiano*. The Communist party is weak and deeply divided between those who favor violence and those who favor electoral strategies. Within the former group, there is another split between militant pro-Russian and militant pro-Chinese factions. Each is represented by separate guerrilla armies, the pro-Russian *Fuerzas Armadas Revolucionarias Colombianas* (FARC) led by Pedro Antonio Marulanda in southeastern Colombia (Tolima and Huila departments), and the pro-Chinese *Ejército de Liberación Nacional* (ELN) in the northeastern regions. Students by and large have followed the MRL, although there are many pro-Communists among their ranks. The Communists and others have found it nearly impossible to build any nucleus of support, even in the most wretched *barrios* of Bogotá, where real and imagined fear of the police and each other keep most neighborhoods immune from party organization or any kind of socio-political coordination.

3. Representation and Voting in Colombia

Presently representation in Colombia is determined both by constitutional provision and the Sitges Agreement. The two basic characteristics of the system, *alternación* and *paridad,* result from the Sitges Agreement.[19] The selection of the President is left to the party whose turn it is to occupy that office. The leaders of the majority wing of that party in theory nominate several candidates, from whom the majority wing of the opposition party selects the most acceptable. In practice, the *Lleristas* and *Ospinistas* work so closely on the question of presidential selection that agreement is reached before any formal procedures are undertaken. Legislative candidates are selected by the national party hierarchy, normally sensitive to the local nucleus of political power each prospective candidate has developed in his home district. Sometimes these nominations are bought by wealthy Colombians, particularly for the minor parties and ANAPO. Very often several members of the same extended family will represent a given district as senators and deputies.

Legislative seats under the *Frente* are divided equally between the two major parties. In 1966, there were 190 deputies and 106 senators elected, 95 and 53 respectively from each party. The allocation of seats for each department and district are in multiples of two, so that Liberals and Conservatives always obtain an equal number. Normally the size of the legislature is a function of the total population. Each department is allowed one senator for each 190,000 inhabitants and each remaining fraction over 95 thousand within a maximum and minimum set by law. Each representative in the lower house represents 90 thousand persons or remaining fraction over 45 thousand in each department. No department now has fewer than two representatives. There are presently 19 departments represented in the Senate, 20 in the House. Voting is staggered; legislative elections being held a month or so before the presidential election.

Where political competition emerges is in the submission of candidate lists for the party seats. Even under the *Frente,* Colombia adheres to a system of proportional representation that employs the closed list ballot. The four major party factions and ANAPO submit lists of their candidates under the label Conservative or Liberal. The victorious faction of any district election may be one of six principal lists: Conservative-*Ospinista,* Conservative-*Alvarista,* Conservative-ANAPO, Liberal-*Llerista,* Liberal-MRL, or Liberal-ANAPO.[20] The voter selects from party workers whichever ballot corresponds to his preference, then deposits the party-printed ballot when voting. Although representation of Liberals and Conservatives is not controlled by the popular vote, ballots are tabulated for party and party faction to give an accurate reflection of their relative strength, as well as determine factional composition of the party quota. The factional representation is determined by a proportional representation formula applied to the party's allotment for a district.

Voting is open to all persons over 21 who hold a *cédula* (identification card) from the *municipalidad* in which they live. Literacy is not required. Women were given the right to vote in 1954 under the Rojas regime. Suffrage for the 1966 elections was estimated by the government to be 7,128,073. One problem for voters is the necessity of voting in their registered *municipalidad*. With rapid urban migration, especially to Bogotá, and suburban decentralization, many persons find it nearly impossible to return to their original *municipalidad* to vote. A substantial number of potential voters are thereby effectively disenfranchised. It is possible to vote in another area if one re-registers and votes at specifically determined *mesas* or polling stations. Few bother to do this. In Bogotá alone the government reported that no more than 45 thousand persons out of an estimated 850 thousand eligible reregistered.[21]

Voting in cities is at specifically designed voting stations. In Bogotá these are centered around the heart of the city into which voters pour during election day. The specific *mesa* or table where one votes is ascertained by locating the number of one's *cédula* on long lists posted around the city, and locating the polling table appropriate for that number. No attempt is made to keep voting on a "neighborhood" basis. Women vote separately from men, as in many Latin nations. In 1966, 4,183 communities in Colombia established voting facilities, utilizing approximately 22 thousand *mesas de votación*.[22]

To vote, one appears at the correct *mesa*, shows his *cédula*, has his name officially recorded, and deposits his party-distributed and printed ballot in the official urn. This technique encourages straight party (that is, faction) voting, although the voter can rearrange his ballot. Voting is supervised at each *mesa* by an electoral committee comprised of two representatives from each of the two parties, requiring a total of 88 thousand persons for the task. Voting tabulation at the *mesas* is reported to the municipal registrar in each area who in turn forwards results to the national registrar office in Bogotá. Partiality and fraud can influence the process of reporting at various points, especially in small *municipalidades*. The surprisingly high voter participation in some of the more remote areas may indicate a kind of ballot box fraud. There is a hierarchy of electoral courts, headed by the national electoral commission, which adjudicates contested results.

4. CAMPAIGNING AND ELECTIONS: A CASE STUDY OF 1966

The dynamics of Colombian party politics can be clearly seen by a look at the 1966 national elections for municipal, legislative, and presidential offices.[23] By any standard, the 1966 elections were a crucial and difficult undertaking for the nation. The viability of the FTN was at stake, and traditional party factions were challenged by the emergence of ANAPO. The continuation of civilian government was itself open to question should ANAPO succeed in winning a congressional or presidential victory. The military, which strongly supported an effectvie FTN, was opposed to any direct or indirect return of Rojas, since its elite had played a significant part in eliminating him from power. The possibility of a Rojas victory seemed remote, but a reduced margin for the FTN could cripple the program of reform and development many Colombian leaders considered the only safeguard against renewed anarchy.

The issues of the campaign preceding the legislative elections of March 20, 1966 and the issues of the presidential campaign were not significantly different, merely sharpened in the latter three month campaign. The issues can best be dichotomized as public and private. The public issues centered largely about economic questions: inflation caused by the 1964 peso devaluation and the rising living costs, the deteriorating plight of urban proletariates, and the development of rural projects including land distribution. Also crucial were the political issues implied in the *Frente* itself. Its leaders were convinced, probably correctly, of the need to revitalize the image of the FTN after the disastrous abstentionism of 1964 and in light of the ANAPO challenge.

The private issues were of two types: those that affected the political party elites, and those that affected the voters. Voters by and large were torn between very strong, traditional party and *patrón* loyalties, and distaste for the deteriorating standard of living. A conserative would vote for the Conservative party, a liberal for the Liberal party, since in either camp one's vote could be affirmative, dissident, or protest. Political hostility had been profound between Colombia's political party elites, but no longer was between the Conservative leadership of Ospina and the Liberal leadership of Lleras. These two leaders recognized their contemporary mutual interest. The MRL was largely an instrument for López whose campaign slogan was "change." Álvaro Gómez, because of personal hostility to Lleras Restrepo dating from his father's presidency the past decade, and partly from his own ambitions, refused to support Lleras and tried to prevent his nomination.

The campaign for both elections was national in scope, although more consistently so for the *Frente* forces. The FTN candidates had more intense and favorable exposure through newspapers. The MRL had little direct access to newspapers. The *Alvaristas* had access in Bogotá to the newspaper *El Siglo,* which had been established by Laureno Gómez in 1935. The Rojas forces started their own newspaper for the campaign, but it was a poor effort, irregularly printed and badly written. The *Frente's* clearest statement came from *El Tiempo* and *El Espectador* in Bogotá, both highly partisan to the *Frente.*[24]

A second factor limiting the effectiveness of the anti-*Frente* forces was inherent in the centralized Colombian governmental system that appointed local government and administration. While this process had been "nonpartisan" since 1957, both parties having had representation, only those factions and leaders favorable to the *Frente* were appointed. In many rural areas local bosses were the FTN campaign "organization," and repression of anti-*Frente* forces was not uncommon. In the presidential campaign, Lleras traveled to each department and its capital, and to all other significant cities. With more limited resources, initiative, and time, Rojas' supporters relied on local organizations of an impromptu nature. Patronage and money were critical in providing cohesion and motivation for both FTN and ANAPO organizational workers.

Although the presidential campaign was largely a parade of familiar faces and leaders, a new personality emerged as ANAPO's presidential candidate, José Jaramillo Giraldo. To participate seriously in the presidential contest, Rojas (a Conservative, and technically denied all political rights after his trial by the Colombian Senate) needed a Liberal party candidate. He first tried to persuade former Liberal mayor of Bogotá, Fernando Mazuera, to run, but he refused. So, too, did others. After a long search culminating only 38 days before the election, Rojas finally decided on Jaramillo. He hardly could have selected a more colorless or servile candidate. Jaramillo's two assets were his proved loyalty to Rojas and his registration as a Liberal party member. His principal defect was that he was an unknown and ineffective candidate.

Far more useful to ANAPO was Rojas' daughter, who had been elected Senator from the Cundinamarca department in March. His daughter, María Eugenia Rojas de Moreno, was an articulate, aggressive, effective spokesman who possessed a popular appeal disturbingly reminiscent in her own way of Eva Perón.[25] She spoke often and emphatically of her father's "accomplishments" (several public works programs) and about the "decline in Colombian life" since 1957. Jaramillo seemed anticlimactic. He all but admitted that a vote for him was a vote for Rojas, and embraced Rojas as the "best president (*sic.*) Colombia ever had . . ." Rojas himself made a dramatic appearance in Bolívar Plaza, April 22, 1966, extending his support to Jaramillo.[26] ANAPO followers, particularly students, staged demonstrations in Bogotá between the elections, many of which deteriorated into riots. Special target was *El Tiempo*, symbol of the establishment. Communist youth did the same with predictable results, but Bogotanians were generally indifferent to both groups.[27]

In urban areas like Bogotá, Medellín, and Cali, the campaign was enlivened by separate radio and television appearances by the presidential candidates. These "debates" were not significant politically since they reached a small percent of Colombians whose attitudes were already formed.

As the period between the two elections drew to a close and the presidential voting approached, the central issue in the campaign became clear: the viability of the *Frente*. Lleras, speaking in a literate, refined, rather pedantic manner, stressed the importance of "meeting Colombia's problems" directly. He urged motification of the two-thirds voting rule in the legislature to permit action by a simple majority on administration programs. Generally his design was to increase enthusiasm and elicit a large turnout which *Frente* leaders were convinced would serve to increase their proportion of the vote. ANAPO's campaign stressed dissatisfaction, rejection of the *Frente*, and somewhat ironically condemnation of the "oligarchy" which ruled Colombia. The ANAPO campaign clearly identified its candidate as the "candidate of the opposition."

The election became a barometer of public attitudes toward Colombian government and politics, allowing political attitudes to be channeled into political action by voting affirmation, dissent, or protest, or alternatively to register alienation by abstaining from voting altogether.

5. VOTING BEHAVIOR: THE 1966 EXAMPLE

National participation of 41 percent in the March, 1966 legislative elections was similar to that in the 1962 elections, and higher than the 1964 low of 26 percent.[28] Participation fell to 37 percent in the May presidential election, the four percent decline representing the poorest participation in a Presidential election since 1958.

The special district of Bogotá was the only electoral unit in Colombia to experience a rise in voter participation between the two elections: nearly 7 percent higher participation in the presidential election. An explanation for the increase in Bogotá cannot be ascertained solely on the basis of electoral data, but several hypotheses seem reasonable. Voter awareness and politicization is probably higher in Bogotá than elsewhere, and the intensity of the campaigning of both *Frente* and ANAPO was higher in the capital area. The level of participation may also have reflected a heavy protest vote in Bogotá, for ANAPO's portion of the presidential vote rose by 10 percent from one election to the next while the *Frente's* vote rose only 3 percent.

The remainder of the country experienced a decline in voter participation from the legislative to the presidential election. The extent of the decline, and its considerable variation, is shown by department in Table 4-2. Generally the more populous departments experienced less of a decline in participation in the presidential election than smaller departments did, which could be as much a comment on their civic cultures as on their political dispositions.[29] To more sparsely settled, less nationally integrated and less politically aware departments, involvement in the national presidential campaign was less relevant.

The presidential returns appeared to give an emphatic victory to the *Frente* and its participating *Llerista* and *Ospinista* factions. In the presidential race, Lleras captured approximately 1,850,000 of the 2,600,000 votes. The *Frente* did less well in urban voting than in rural voting. If one considers the returns from the capital cities in the departments, which include the major cities of the nation, Lleras captured 66 percent of the total vote, the remaining 34 percent of the urban vote going to Jaramillo. This is particularly noteworthy since the FTN polled more strongly in urban than rural areas during the legislative elections. In both urban and national voting, ANAPO's presidential vote increased 9 percent. The FTN increased its share of the national vote 14 percent, but its share of the urban vote only 7 percent. This indicates either a higher percentage of urban voters who had voted in the legislative election for the MRL or *Alvaristas* switched to ANAPO, or that those who

TABLE 4-2. DECLINE IN VOTER PARTICIPATION FROM LEGISLATIVE TO PRESIDENTIAL ELECTION (IN PERCENT)

0–5 Percent	5–10 Percent	10–15 Percent	15–20 Percent	20 Percent +
Antioquia	Atlántico	Caquetá	Huila	Chocó
Boyacá	Bolívar	Córdoba		Guajira
Caldas	Cundinamarca	Santander		Magdelena
Cauca	No. Santander			Meta
Nariño	Valle			Tolima

TABLE 4-3. National and Urban Party Faction Vote in 1966
Legislative and Presidential Elections

PARTY/ FACTION	LEGISLATIVE		PRESIDENTIAL			
	Percent nat. vote	Percent urban vote	Percent nat. vote	Percent urban vote	Nat.	Urban
FRENTE	57	59	71	66	+14	+7
Llerista	39	47				
Ospinista	18	12				
ALVARISTA	12	7				
MRL	12	10				
ANAPO	19	24	28	33	+ 9	+9

did not vote in the presidential election were mostly previous supporters of the *Frente*. The latter interpretation seems more likely,
although in Bogotá where total participation increased 7 percent,
ANAPO's share increased 10 percent against an increase of only
3 percent for the FTN. The distribution of party vote in the legislative and presidential elections nationally and in urban areas is
shown in Table 4-3.[30]

Several conclusions are reasonable based upon this information.
ANAPO's vote was disproportionately urban, as revealed by the
5 percent differential in the May presidential voting. ANAPO increased its vote by the same percentage in urban and rural areas.
The FTN realized a large (14 percent) shift in voting in the national presidential election, either or both (1) a gain from the non-
participating MRL or *Alvarista* factions (probably the former),
and (2) less decline in the presidential voting than among followers
of the MRL and *Alvaristas*. The MRL, once considered the most
"liberal" of all the factions, did not actually do as well in urban
voting as it did nationally in rural areas, presenting a traditionalistic, regional voting pattern instead of a proletarian, urban one. The
strongest single vote in urban areas was for the *Llerista* faction
of the FTN. The *Ospinistas* only received 12 percent of the national
urban vote in the capitals against 18 percent for the nation at large.
The *Lleristas* received 47 percent of the legislative urban vote
against 39 percent for them nationally. The competitiveness of the
Ospinista, Alvarista, MRL, and ANAPO factions in national voting
should be underscored: less than 7 percentage points (12–19 percent) of the total national vote separated the three factions. The
Lleristas by contrast received over twice as many votes as any
other political faction in Colombia in legislative voting.

In presidential voting ANAPO increased its vote by 9 percent.

It is impossible to say just where these came from, but two interpretations seem most reasonable. Since the ANAPO candidate in the presidential election offered no real contest for the FTN's, the motivation for voting ANAPO may have been largely protest which was less affected by falloff. Many of the *Alvaristas* voters probably shifted to Conservative ballot ANAPO rather than FTN. Indeed the large ANAPO vote in the city of Neiva was clearly the result of a local *Alvarista* leader, Senator Felio Andrade, endorsing the ANAPO ticket. The shift from MRL to FTN would seem at least rationally if not empirically easier than a shift from MRL to ANAPO. However, the shift to ANAPO was not always so rational. In the strongly Liberal Department of *Valle del Cauca*, the local MRL supporters lent their influence to ANAPO's candidate. Formal or informal endorsement very often by local *Alvarista* or MRL leaders made the difference, along with local issues, in swinging an area's votes to ANAPO or the FTN.

A different kind of interpretation must be made of the two elections. In the legislative election, with higher voter participation, real issues were at stake: the most crucial being who would represent a department's party delegation—regulars (*Lleristas* or *Ospinistas*), dissidents (*Alvaristas* or MRL) or the ANAPO candidates. In the presidential election, which Lleras was clearly destined to win, the motivation of many voters was more internalized: either abstain, endorse the FTN and support Lleras, or protest by voting for Jaramillo. The strong showing of ANAPO particularly in Bogotá, can be interpreted only as a protest vote.

The representation of the party factions in the legislature can be seen in Table 4-4. The seating gave the FTN a total of 106

TABLE 4-4. PARTY/FACTION REPRESENTATION IN COLOMBIAN LEGISLATURE FOLLOWING ELECTIONS OF MARCH 20, 1966

PARTY/ FACTION	LOWER HOUSE (*190 seats*)		UPPER HOUSE (*106 seats*)	
	No.	Percent	No.	Percent
CONSERVATIVE	95	50	53	50
Ospinista	35	18.5	21	20
Alvarista	26	14.0	17	16
ANAPO	33	17.0	15	14
Other	1		0	0
LIBERAL	95	50	53	50
Llerista	71	37.5	46	43
MRL	21	11.0	7	7
ANAPO	3	1.5	0	0

TABLE 4-5. DISTRIBUTION BY FACTION OF NEWCOMERS
ELECTED TO LEGISLATURE

PARTY/FACTION	LOWER HOUSE		UPPER HOUSE	
	No.	Percent of delegation	No.	Percent of delegation
FTN: Llerista	30	42	10	22
FTN: Ospinista	20	57	6	28
ALVARISTA	13	50	2	13
MRL	11	49	0	0
ANAPO	30	83	7	43
TOTAL	104	(55)	25	(23)

seats in the lower house and 68 in the Senate. Both totals were short of the two-thirds minimum required for passage of major legislative measures (127 in the lower house, 71 in the Senate). This representation, anticipated by Lleras in his request to modify the two-thirds rule, was of less significance than it would appear since both dissident and protest factions were rarely able to unite. Shortly after the opening of the Congress, the rule was changed by government supporters.

Of the 296 members elected to the Colombian legislature, 129 or about 40 percent of these were first-term. This considerably strengthened the administration's leadership position by opening new channels for bargaining and patronage. Of the 129, 25 were senators and 104 deputies. The distribution of newcomers by party faction is shown in the chart, Table 4-5.

Three senators of the previous legislature were elected to the lower house in 1966, and more conventionally 40 members of the previous lower house were elevated by election to the Senate. By departments the representation of parties and factions in 1966 is shown in the chart, Table 4-6.

One conclusion is inevitable from the representation of party factions in the legislative chambers: the party factions, while dominated by the *Llerista* Liberals, are remarkably competitive throughout most of Colombia's departments. Rather than view Colombia as a two-party system it might be as reasonable to view it as a multi-party system with alliances. It is entirely possible that the system will gravitate toward such a concentration of party activity following the termination of the FTN and its constitutional props.

A common observation made of Colombia is its regionalism. Four large cities dominate the rest of the country: Bogotá, Cali, Medellín, and Barranquilla.[31] These in turn reflect separate regions:

the highlands around Bogotá, the Cauca Valley, Antioquia and the Magdalena Valley, and the coastal lowlands. Colombia is divided by mountain ranges (*cordilleras*) that run roughly north and south. Travel by land is often difficult, and distinct cultures have developed in these and other clusters of population. When the performance of the FTN and ANAPO is compared by departments where each did proportionately best in popular vote, a regional separation of the two alliances' popularity can be seen. The FTN polled heavily in the western departments of Chocó, Cauca, Quindío, Valle, and the northern departments of Bolívar, Córdoba, and Antioquia. ANAPO obtained more of its vote in the eastern departments of Boyacá, Meta, Norte de Santander, and Cundinamarca. Several of the departments where ANAPO did proportionately best had experienced recent guerrilla disturbances. There was no correlation between the size of the departments and their propensity to support the FTN or ANAPO, although ANAPO obtained more of its votes in smaller departments and urban areas.

Both the MRL and the *Alvaristas* suffered in the legislative elections of 1966. In the 1962 elections the *Alvaristas* achieved 16 percent of the popular vote and 36 seats in the lower house, 16 in the Senate. In 1966, they received approximately 12 percent of the popular vote with 26 representatives and 17 senators. Both houses increased in size in 1966: the lower by six seats, the upper

TABLE 4-6. REPRESENTATION OF PARTY FACTIONS IN LEGISLATURE, 1966

DEPARTMENT	LOWER HOUSE							UPPER HOUSE					
						ANAPO							
	Ller.	Osp.	MRL	Alv.	Lib.	Con.	Total	Ller.	Osp.	MRL	Alv.	ANAPO	Total
Antioquia	7	7	3	1	1	3	22	3	3	2		2	10
Atlántico	4	2		2			8	2			2		4
Bolívar	4	1	1	3		1	10	2			2		4
Boyacá	5	2	2	1		2	16	3	2	1	1	1	8
Caldas	6	4	2	2		2	16	3	2	1	1	1	8
Cauca	2	2	1			1	6	2	2				4
Córdoba	2	1	1	1		1	6	2	2				4
Cundinamarca	8	3	2	3	2	6	24	5	1	1	1	4	12
Chocó	2	2					4	2	2				4
Guajira	2			2			4	2	2				4
Huila	2	1	1	1		1	6	2			2		4
Magdalena	2	1	1	1		1	6	2			2		4
Meta	2					2	4	2				2	4
Nariño	3	1	1	2		1	8	2	1		1		4
No. de Santan.	3	2				1	6	2	2				4
Quindío	2			2			4	2			2		4
Santander	4	2	1	2		1	10	2	1	1	1	1	6
Tolima*	3	1	2	1		2	10	2	1	1	1	1	6
Valle	8	3	2	2		5	20	4	1	1	1	3	10
Caquetá			1			1	2						
TOTALS	71	35	21	26	3	33	190	46	21	7	17	15	106

* In Tolima's 5th district, an independent was elected.

by eight. The MRL in 1962 received 20 percent of the popular vote with 33 representatives and 7 senators. The loss in 1966 for the MRL was enormous, and after the election Lòpez indicated his willingness to resign leadership of the movement, a gesture that was rejected. In addition to its failure to win the urban vote, the MRL may have experienced a temporary acceleration in its 1962 vote by regular liberals whose intransigence prevented them from voting for the FTN under Conservative party leadership. The MRL offered a Liberal alternative no longer needed with the nomination of Lleras Restrepo in 1966 and the return of the FTN leadership to the *Lleristas*.

As frequently occurs, there was a higher turnout of male voters than female. In Bogotá, male voters supported ANAPO's candidate Jaramillo by more than 3–2 over female voters, while slightly more female voters supported Lleras than male. The trend, reflecting a conservative, less hostile voting disposition among women, was not surprising and probably held for most of the country. Despite his conscious appeals to women during the campaign, Rojas would have fared better had he not enfranchised them in 1954.

Biannual congressional elections were held in March, 1968, for renewal of the Chamber of Deputies. The results, shown in Table 4-7, indicated a strengthening of the ANAPO delegation, as well as a strengthening of the *Llerista* sector of the Liberal party and *Ospinista* sector of the Conservative party.[32] The greatest loss was for the MRL; however, the *Alvaristas* lost nearly half their delegation. So complete was López Michelsen's defeat that he formally renounced his opposition to the FTN, and joined President Lleras' cabinet in 1968 as foreign minister. ANAPO's 20 percent of the national vote remained essentially the same. The results of

TABLE 4-7. RESULTS OF LEGISLATIVE VOTING, MARCH, 1968

Party/Faction	Seats in lower house		Percent national vote		Change from 1966
CONSERVATIVE	102		46.5		
Ospinista		50		24.5	+ 6.5
Alvarista		15		7.5	− 4.5
ANAPO		36		14.0	
Other		1		.5	
LIBERAL	102		51.0		
Llerista		93		47.0	+ 8.0
MRL		3		.5	−11.5
ANAPO		6		3.5	

the election gave the FTN a two-thirds majority in the lower house, enough to pass significant FTN legislation if discipline could be maintained. Participation, however, fell to an unprecedented low of only 23 percent of those eligible, a serious blow to the prestige of the FTN regardless of the nominal victory it won among those who did vote. In view of the relative consistency of the ANAPO vote, one can only speculate that abstention must have come heavily from the MRL and *Alvarista* ranks, voters who may be in the market for a new expression of their hostility.

Presidential elections were held in 1970, the final exercise provided under the FTN. Conservatives divided over selecting a candidate. The party's dominant leader, Ospina, imposed his choice on a rebellious convention. The candidate was Misael Pastrana, formerly ambassador to the United States, whose disputed nomination was later "ratified" by the now united Liberal party. Two Conservatives, formerly supporters of the FTN, opposed Pastrana in the presidential election: Belisario Betancour, the younger and more dissident of the two, was once minister of labor and drew support from professional and urban middle classes of Bogotá; Evaristo Sourdis, a vigorous party leader, had strong support in the northern coastal region. The fourth candidate was Rojas Pinilla, who personally ran for ANAPO as a "Conservative." In an intensely bitter campaign, centrifugal political forces successfully lured away FTN support. Pastrana won by less than 66 thousand votes, while ANAPO's congressional representation increased substantially. Congressional supporters of Sourdis and Betancour became a critical variable in continued FTN control in the legislature. The 1970 results are summarized below in Table 4-8.

Several inferences can be made from the electoral analysis of recent campaigns. There is a high level of alienation and protest to the FTN regime that is part of a larger trend visible since the

TABLE 4-8. RESULTS OF 1970 NATIONAL ELECTIONS

	PRESIDENTIAL		CONGRESSIONAL	
	Total vote	Percent	Deputies(210)	Senators(118)
Pastrana (FTN)	1,612,467	40	87	57
Rojas (ANAPO)	1,546,449	40	73	35
Betancour	446,211	12	24	12
Sourdis	323,093	8	20	11
Other			6	3

SOURCE: Unofficial results from the Registraduria Nacional del Estado Civil and *El Tiempo*.

inception of the FTN in late 1957. The voting interpretation rests on several observations:

(1) There has been a consistent decline in voter participation in presidential elections, and a general pattern of decline in legislative elections. Abstention has risen to the level where 77 percent of the eligible voters in 1968 preferred not to vote. Voting for the FTN steadily declined until 1968, when the intensity of voting reached so low a level that the increase in the FTN percent may be more apparent than real.

(2) Increases in ANAPO's vote were most conspicuous in the urban areas, especially Bogotá, where voting for ANAPO in the 1966 presidential elections became a positive expression of protest, a more hostile act than the alienation expressed by abstention.

(3) There was a shift in national voting away from *Alvarismo* and the MRL toward a more radical protest represented by ANAPO.

(4) The *Lleristas* emerged as the strongest force in the contemporary political struggle, absorbing their own principal internal party opposition (MRL), and receiving nearly a majority of the vote in the 1968 election.

(5) The urban protest vote may be more "conservative" than radical, reflecting what has been called a "lower-class authoritarianism."[33] The success of former dictator Rojas rather than the MRL or Marxist groups indicates perhaps a reminiscence of the past, when economic conditions had deteriorated less. If there is any remaining ideological difference between the two party configurations in Colombia, and it is doubtful that there is today, then it is perhaps indicative that the majority of ANAPO's votes were cast through the Conservative party label even though in Bogotá it has traditionally been the weaker party.

6. Conclusion

The emergence of ANAPO may be less electorally significant than culturally indicative. It reflects, along with the increasing tide of voter alienation expressed through decreasing participation, a deterioration of public confidence in the FTN, its programs, accomplishments, and leadership. Although since 1958 a two-party system has been enforced, subsidized by the electoral and representational systems, it is equally certain that allegiance and identification with the *idea* of two major parties and their historical rivalry persists, even when the reality of two competing parties is questionable.

Violence has greatly subsided in the nation over the past decade. What remains is mostly uncontrollable banditry. But violence and personal survival is also identified in Colombia with the two-party conflict, and party animosities among the masses do not appear to have lessened perceptibly. The reality of a competitive, two-party system hovers over Colombian politics, but its reality is found in the legal and cultural institutions rather than political behavior or natural divisions in the political system.

III. URUGUAY: A COMPETITIVE, TWO-PARTY SYSTEM

Of the three nations with two-party systems, only Uruguay has achieved both a competitive electoral context and sustained political stability.

One of the smaller nations in Latin America, Uruguay has an area of 72 thousand square miles, about the size of North Dakota, with a population of 2.7 million. The nation lacked an indigenous population when immigration began from Europe. Today Uruguay has a homogeneous citizenry and a very low population growth rate. The nation is essentially middle-class in living standards and aspirations, with high educational and health standards. The economy is pastoral and agricultural, being a principal supplier to Europe of beef and high quality wool.[34] Plagued by perpetual import deficits, Uruguay unwisely attempted a rapid industrialization following World War II, which because of limited markets, scarce capital, and high production costs, has placed additional burdens on the economy.

The capital, Montevideo, contains better than 50 percent (1.4 million) of the population. Only two other cities have reached a population in excess of 60 thousand, Paysandú and Salto. Both are port cities on the Uruguay River, built for trading with Argentina. Uruguayans are self-consciously proud of their heritage of stable government and impartial elections, and take an unusual interest in political parties and national campaigns. Uruguay had two bloodless *coups* (1930, 1942) but their influence was transient. National politics, like many other Latin American nations, is flamboyant, volatile, personalistic, noisy, and often extravagant. What distinguishes Uruguay is not so much the style of its politics as the strength of the cultural consensus which supports the electoral, party, and governmental institutions.[35]

The most significant influences on Uruguayan politics in the nineteenth century were its size and location. A buffer state between the always rivalrous Brazil and Argentina, Uruguay was subjected to the meddling and competition of its two large neighbors. Its compactness and developed communications made national integration relatively easy.

Two political parties compete in national politics. The dominant force is the *Partido Colorado* (PC) (Red Party), historically strongest in the metropolitan capital area. The opposition is the *Partido Nacional* (PN) (National Party), generally known as the *Blancos* or Whites. Despite the vast cultural and physical differences between Colombia and Uruguay, their contemporary party systems evolved under somewhat similar conditions. Like Colombia, Uruguay was torn by party inspired civil war that erupted for much of the nineteenth century. Confronted with fewer inherent obstacles to political integration than Colombia, and benefiting from exceptional leadership in the early twentieth century, Uruguay unlike Colombia found a way out of the morass of civil war. Uruguay's party system, however, like Colombia's owes its maintenance as much to electoral and legal factors as it does to inherent political forces.

1. EVOLUTION OF MODERN URUGUAYAN PARTIES

Uruguay's contemporary parties date from independence in 1830. The Colorados, identified principally with urban Montevideo, attracted European immigrants during the late nineteenth century. The Blancos found their strength in provincial areas. During the turbulent nineteenth century the Colorados received aid for their civil war from Brazilians and certain European powers. The Blancos, who controlled much of the rural areas where Argentine investment was heavy, received support from Argentina. Nineteenth-century Uruguay, like many other Latin American nations and our own frontier areas, was held together by guns and force. The country was divided among political bosses, both Blanco and Colorado, and effective national power had yet to be consolidated.

Modern Uruguayan politics begins with the emergence of the great Colorado leader, José Batlle y Ordóñez.[36] Strongly nationalistic, anticlerical, and committed to the concept of stable, representative government, Batlle founded one of the most influential newspapers in South America, *El Día*, that still publishes under his banner. Batlle developed sophisticated ideas about economic welfare and nationalization, inspired more by his quest for political stability than by utopian economics. Batlle served as president twice (1903–1907, 1911–1915), continuing to refine his ideas and exerting a tremendous influence on his nation's politics and government until his death in 1929. Today, Batlle's heritage is probably the strongest single force in contemporary Uruguayan politics.

Following his election in 1903, Batlle and the Colorados won a decisive victory in the still raging civil war with the Blancos, and finally ended the national violence. He initiated economic reforms during his first administration, and formulated many others. After a brief stay in Europe where he observed and admired the Swiss system of collegial government, Batlle returned for a second term as president. During this administration he pursued a policy of economic nationalism, advanced social welfare, and strengthened the system of public education. Batlle's motivation was political: he was trying to prevent a return to national violence by removing some of the social and economic inequities that he believed promoted it, as well as searching for an institutional arrangement that could minimize the chances for authoritarian government.[37]

His controversial scheme to abolish the presidency and initiate a Swiss-styled collegiate executive was slow to win support. He fought unsuccessfully to gain approval for the reform in a 1916 referendum. Two years later he reached a compromise with the rival Nationalist leadership that retained the presidency, but reduced sharply its powers and instituted a National Council with the opposition guaranteed a minimum of one-third of the seats. The Colorados continued to dominate national elections, but rarely achieved decisive control of both the legislature and the National Council. Institutional stalemate often occurred, with results ranging from inactivity to chaos. The 1930 world depression hit Uruguay hard, and gave opportunistic Gabriel Terra, a former follower of Batlle, an excuse to blame the nation's economic plight on the constitution. With the assistance of Blanco leader Luis Alberto de Herrera, Terra staged a *coup* in 1930 and annulled the constitution. In 1934, a national referendum approved a third constitution, which abolished the collegial executive, maintained the weakened presidency, and gave extensive powers to the legislature and a legislative cabinet. Complicated as the new constitution was, it was designed to maintain the Terra-Herrera alliance, keep national power in the hands of the legislative parties, and divide national administrative offices between their personal adherents. Herrera's presence became increasingly embarrassing for Uruguay during the late thirties and early forties, because of his outspoken support for the Axis powers in Europe.[38]

A second *coup* occurred in 1942, after which a new (fourth) constitution reinstated the strong presidency and abolished the cabinet system. With the encouragement and support of Batlle's nephew and heir, President Luis Batlle (1947–1951), another constitutional referendum in 1952 established the full collegiate executive system. A nine-member National Council was created with the chairmanship rotating among members of the majority party.[39] Three seats were guaranteed to the opposition party, and Uruguayan electoral law was changed to provide direct representation of factions according to their popular vote.

From 1953 to 1956 the economy suffered from inflation and rising costs of living, induced by a declining market for beef and wool exports, strains from an abortive attempt at industrialization, and a growing burden from the vast welfare system. The first by-product of this economic crisis was a resounding victory in 1958 for the Nationalist party, the first time in the twentieth century that it had succeeded in winning a national parliamentary election and control of the executive branch, in this case the National Council.[40]

By the late fifties both parties, encouraged by the electoral system, were seriously factionalized. The Blancos found it difficult to establish any consistent national policy in the council to counteract the economic decline. The 1962 election was won by the Nationalists, a slim margin returning them to power for a second four-year term. By the 1966 election, economic problems were being translated into political ones in the form of strikes, demonstrations, and leftist political movements. Under consideration was another constitutional revision, the sixth, to abolish Batlle's unworkable National Council plan in favor of a strong presidency. The Nationalists had enjoyed power only eight years in the twentieth century, but the party was strongly competitive throughout most of the period, as revealed in Table 4-9.[41]

Although they are never able to challenge the two major parties, minor parties abound in the Uruguayan culture. Many endure no more than one or two elections. Historically these "third" parties have exerted sufficient electoral influence to prevent a major party from receiving a clear majority in a number of elections, specifically those of 1925, 1926, 1928, 1931, 1946, and from 1958 to the present.

One of the small parties is the Christian Democratic party. The PDC resembles its counterparts elsewhere in Latin America, and like them suffers from several chronic political ills: insufficient funds, divisive doctrinal divisions, and conservative Catholic social

TABLE 4-9. COMPARISON OF URUGUAYAN
PARTY VOTING, 1919–1966 (IN PERCENT)

Election	Colorado	National	Other
1919	53	43	4
1920	53	47	—
1922	50	48	2
1925	50*	49	1
1925	49*	48*	3
1926	49	49	2
1928	49	48	3
1930	52	47	1
1931	50*	45*	5
1932	67	26	7
1933	53*	41	6
1934	54*	38	8
1938	61	32	7
1942	57	23	20
1946	48	31	21
1950	53	31	16
1954	51	35	14
1958	38	50	12
1962	44	47	9
1966	50	40	10

SOURCE: *Camara de Senadores, Elecciones Uruguayas* (1968).
* Total party percent for all factions given.

elites unsympathetic to more liberal policies of the party. The PDC has had a particularly difficult experience in Uruguay. Founded originally in 1872 as *Unión Cívica,* the party was the first Latin American Christian Democratic party, and has existed for nearly a century with fairly liberal political views. In 1962, it changed its name to the more modern PDC, consistent with movements in other Latin American nations. The electoral system works against it; the nation generally and the Colorado party specifically is already committed to a broad scale welfare system and economic reform; and the political culture tends to be somewhat anticlerical. The PDC experienced mild but consistent growth from 1958 to 1965, building support among students but never receiving more than 4 percent of the national vote. The anticipated "great leap forward" in 1966 failed to materialize, despite a well-financed, thoroughly organized campaign, and the party received fewer votes in 1966 than in 1962. The defeat was humbling, and suggests that a quick rise in the party's fortunes parallel to the situation in Chile seems unlikely.[42]

Stronger than the PDC is FIDEL, or the *Frente Izquierda de Libertad*. FIDEL, as its apt name implies, is a coalition of leftist-Marxist groups including the Communist party. The Communist party has generally been free to participate in elections, but has never polled more than 1–3 percent of the total vote, except for 1946 when it received 5 percent. In that election, however, all minor parties polled heavily, receiving a combined 21 percent of the vote. Led by the old Communist party hierarchy, FIDEL combines a militant, university-based communist youth movement and several sympathetic labor unions. It wages vigorous campaigns, stages demonstrations and year-round protests against the traditional parties and the regime.[43]

There is a Socialist party, split into two major factions. One faction known as List 3000 is led by aging socialist Emilio Frugoni, whose place in Uruguayan politics resembles that of Norman Thomas in the United States. A more vigorous and radical List 90 receives more votes than its rival faction, although the amount is still less than one percent. All minor parties in Uruguay operate under severe handicaps imposed by the electoral laws and representation system.

The discussion of Uruguayan parties so far has proceeded under the assumption that there is a two-party system. Actually the parties are so factionalized, with each of the factions enjoying both a legal and political existence independent from the larger party, that one could also argue that Uruguay is a multi-party system in disguise. Before continuing with a closer look at the *sublemas*, it might be useful to pause and consider the distinctive electoral system under which the parties compete, and which insures a degree of autonomy to the factions.

2. ELECTORAL SYSTEM AND PARTY ORGANIZATION

Of all the institutional influences on the parties, none is more profound than the electoral laws and practices that control participation of the parties, campaigning, and voting.[44] Uruguay employs a variation on proportional representation built around the d'Hondt distributive formula and a closed-list ballot. Representation in the lower house is responsive to population in the 19 departments of the nation. The Chamber of Deputies contains 99 members. The 30-member Senate is elected at large from the nation. Under the

1966 constitution, the vice-president of the republic is also a member of the Senate. The unique feature of the system is the formalization of party factions known as *sub-lemas* within the major parties (*lemas*). Voting is by party and *sub-lema* lists, which are printed and distributed by *sub-lemas* following a government prescribed form.

Sub-lemas are distinguished for campaigning and balloting as numbered lists, with descriptive titles identified with a leading personality or cause. For any election hundreds of different lists exist, since separate numbers are used for each *sub-lema* in each district. The *sub-lemas*, after receiving legal recognition, are permitted to print and distribute lists (ballots), often requesting a campaign contribution from the voter in return for a ballot. After voting, each *sub-lema's* votes are totaled separately, then all votes for a *lema* are totaled to determine the number of party seats awarded. Under this arrangement, a *sub-lema* benefits or suffers from the general fortunes of the *lema*, sharing proportionately to its specific vote in the election.

Following the basic d'Hondt formula for allocating seats, a *sub-lema's* total vote in a department (in the case of the Senate, the entire nation) is divided by consecutive divisors (1, 2, 3, 4, etc.), and each *sub-lema's* quotients arranged in descending order. Seats are awarded successively according to the highest remaining quotient until all seats won by the party (*lema*) based on its percentage of the total vote are distributed. Any *sub-lema* adds votes to the *lema*, and is rewarded by sharing its proportion of the total representation. Under the former collegial system, the *lema* that won control of the legislature received two-thirds of the seats on the National Council, the opposition receiving the remaining one-third. The majority *sub-lema* of the majority *lema* gained control of the two-thirds majority.[45]

Almost any group can register with the national electoral commission, and print a list following the official format. Use of the *lema* symbol and name, however, is controlled by the *lema* itself. A product of the system is the dismaying number of electoral alliances and crossalliances made during elections. Candidates may adopt a specific *sub-lema* for their district, but substitute their own names at the top of the list and thereby create a new list and new number. A *sub-lema* list in a given district may involve no more than the addition or substitution of a name or names in the printed hierarchy of another list. A small *sub-lema* benefits from the publicity and popularity of a major *sub-lema*, while pursuing its own personalistic ends. In a sense the system integrates a primary within a general election, except that the system goes further by permitting factional representation in the national legislature. What maintains and supports the system is that both the *lema* and the *sub-lemas* ultimately benefit from the process; the only groups that are significantly hurt are third "parties" (*lemas*) that must legally and electorally compete with the two major parties, but are more politically equivalent to *sub-lemas* in size and scope. By custom there is a surprising degree of party unity and cooperation in the legislature after elections.[46]

Uruguayan businessmen like businessmen universally find it appropriate to contribute to both political parties prior to the campaign. Many legislative candidates have sufficient personal wealth to contribute to their *sub-lema*, where much of the spending occurs. The largest single campaign contributor is the state, which helps defray campaign costs for parties receiving a minimum vote. The subsidy is allocated on a "per vote" basis, and redistributed to *sub-lemas*.

Party structures are extensive and highly institutionalized in Uruguay. Illustrative is a vast network of political clubs, particularly in urban areas, that affiliate with *sub-lemas*. The club movement is so intense in the Montevideo area that it resembles the system once found in large United States cities like New York, except in Uruguay several parties have clubs. Each neighborhood has its clubs, identified by long, colorful names and brightly painted headquarters. The neighborhood clubs organize workers, collect campaign funds, do campaign work, distribute propaganda, and, most of all, secure votes by direct, interpersonal exchanges. The cement that holds the club system together is the patronage and welfare available at the national level. Uruguay's limited size and extensive welfare and patronage systems allow nearly everyone to tap this source, and most Uruguayans do. It is estimated conservatively that three-quarters of a million persons receive government payments through pensions, welfare, or direct employment. Almost every family in the nation is touched one way or another by the system of direct payments. The somewhat inefficient and diffuse civil service creates gigantic problems in administration of the welfare programs, problems that generate requests for favors and special concessions. The task of resolving administrative dilemmas is facilitated in large measure by the club organizations. Candidates are indebted to clubs for campaign work and loyalty, and club members are indebted to elected representatives for special assistance. Not all of the activity of the clubs is political. They are also social units within the neighborhoods and communities they serve. An appreciation of the "grass-roots" basis of Uruguayan politics, and the continuing dialogue between the governed and the governing, begins at the level of the clubs.[47]

Leadership is recruited partly through the clubs and partly through more conventional party channels not unlike those in the United States. Major political leaders in positions of party or government power generate constellations of subordinates who rise through the maze of party hierarchy according to proven ability and/or loyalty. The process of recruitment is normally a difficult and slow one, but being related to a "political family" can speed the process considerably. The personalistic nature of Uruguayan party politics makes recruitment as illogical as it sometimes is in the United States. Position, family, and wealth are good credentials for a political career. Minor parties, which can never offer the reward of political power, must rely on ideological and psychological motivation to recruit leaders.

Sub-lemas shift from one election to another. There are several major ones, however, in each party that have remained significant over a fairly long period of time. The Colorados were historically divided between pro and anti-*Batllista* elements. A serious division occurred in the fifties during the Presidency of Luis Batlle within the *Batllista* movement itself. One faction, known as List 15, was led by Luis Batlle, and commanded the majority of the movement's followers. List 15 was popularly based, and oriented to the labor movement. Luis Batlle's cousin and a son of José Batlle y Ordóñez, César Batlle, led an opposition List 14 that was a more conservative, orthodox expression of *Batllismo*. The difference was personal, however, not ideological. Following Luis Batlle's death in 1964, the leadership of List 15 fell to his son, Jorge Batlle. A major reshuffling of *sub-lemas* followed, partly stimulated by Luis Batlle's death and partly by an emerging constitutional crisis, with the proponents of the collegial executive being challenged by the advocates of a reformed, strong presidential system. The dominant position in the party went to a new coalition headed by the successful, 1966 presidential candidate, Oscar Gestido. Jorge Batlle gathered together the forces of List 15 who approved of the constitutional reform, and became the second strongest *sub-lema*. More traditional elements supported Amílcar Vasconcellos and other leaders who organized a third-ranking *sub-lema,* opposed to the constitutional reform. A fourth group, known as List 99, was led by Zelmar

Michelini. This organization was the most "liberal" of the factions, and the weakest. Other *sub-lemas* existed within the Colorado party, but the principal ones drew about 95 percent of the 1966 vote for the party.[48]

The major *sub-lema* of the National party is headed by Martín R. Echegoyen, who has inherited the strong movement of Luis Herrera, and combined with it another group formerly headed by Benito Nardone known as the *Ruralistas.* Nardone, who died in 1964, led a potent combination of rebellious farmers and rural peasants. The Echegoyen *sub-lema* also includes a small faction known as the *Movimiento Popular Nacionalista* (MPN), and uses the rather complex *sub-lema* title, *"Herrerismo-Ruralismo-Movimiento Popular Nacionalista."* A more moderate wing of the party, known as *Reforma y Desarrollo* (Reform and Development) is led by Senators Washington Beltrán and Felipe Gil. Known as List 400, it occupies the second place in the National party. A third *sub-lema,* also avowedly following the Herrera tradition, is known as *sub-lema "Dr. Luis Alberto de Herrera,"* and is led by Zorrilla de San Martín and Alberto Heber Usher.[49] In addition to Echegoyen and Heber, the 1966 presidential candidates included Alberto Gallinal, a political novice supported by List 400 and other splinter factions and coalitions. Gallinal's position in the party is still unclear.

As differentiated and autonomous as these factions are for the purpose of campaigning, they are not as rigidly separate, inflexible, or hostile as factions normally are in Colombian parties. Their autonomy is guaranteed by the electoral system, and supported by the personalism of Uruguayan politics. But the *sub-lemas* are more united in fact than they may appear superficially, with considerable opportunity for parliamentary compromise and negotiation.

3. CAMPAIGNING AND VOTING: A CASE STUDY OF THE 1966 ELECTIONS

The 1966 campaign evolved in a critical period of Uruguayan history. Three factors contributed to the political crisis: rapidly worsening economic conditions, a constitutional crisis promoted by administrative and policy stalemate in the National Council, and a rigorous ideological offensive mounted by the Christian Democrats on the one side and the Marxist FIDEL on the other, a challenge to the very basis of the two-party system.

Economic conditions had steadily declined in Uruguay for more than 15 years, although the rate of decline accelerated rapidly in the previous 5 years. A few comparative indexes will illustrate how profound the dilemma was. The Uruguayan *peso* in 1955 sold at the rate of 2.06 to the dollar; in 1966 the rate was about 75 to the dollar; by 1968 it had reached 250 to the dollar. The internal cost of living doubled in 12 years from 1943 to 1955; in 4 years, 1956–1959; in 3 years, 1960–1963; in 2 years, 1963–1964; and in 1 year, 1965. The first six months of 1966 saw a 40 percent rise in the cost of living despite vigorous efforts to slow it down prior to the election. Average per capita income in Uruguay declined 14 percent in a period of little over a decade. Livestock, the basis of national wealth and export, actually were fewer in 1966 than half a century ago, although national population had doubled during the same period. The rate of industrial growth, designed to make Uruguay less dependent on costly imports, declined from a high of 8.5 percent for a period from 1945–1954, to a low of 3.8 percent in 1966, which was below the Latin American average. Unemployment had risen since 1961 by 100 percent, although government employees actually rose 25 percent in the past decade. These statistics were translated for voters into chronic economic hardships and a deteriorating standard of living. In fairness it should be underscored that even in its state of decline, the Uruguayan standard of living was both higher and more equalized than in almost any other Latin American nation.[50]

The National party government was unable to resolve the growing labor problems which plagued the nation. Several general strikes were called in 1966, causing havoc in the nation's finance, transportation, port facilities, and other important segments of the economy. Land use remained inefficient, production of grains at a disastrously low level, and for a meat-exporting nation, there was the paradox of "meatless days" in Montevideo.

The most controversial political issue was constitutional reform. After months of bickering and disagreement, the major *sub-lemas* of each party agreed on a compromise reform to be submitted in referendum during the 1966 elections. The compromise was reached only a few weeks before the November election, which greatly complicated the already complex campaigning. The reform measure required in effect that two separate sets of elections be held simultaneously: one based on the assumption that the reform would fail and the collegial system be retained, the other based on the assumption that the reform would pass and a presidential system be adopted. Local and departmental elections were also scheduled. The reform issue not only complicated the voting, but had significant effects on the composition of electoral alliances and the nature of political affiliations.[51]

To illustrate the complexity of campaigning and voting, an example can be used of a 1966 sub-lema and its different lists from the National party. Since the presidential context was paramount, the voter would probably make his first decision on the choice for the presidency. Past affiliations and a more limited field of candidates facilitated this choice. Assuming the voter came from the National party, the choice was essentially limited to Alberto Gallinal, Martín Echegoyen, and Alberto Heber. If the voter selected Echegoyen, he could vote for him both for president on one list, and as "leading candidate" for the National Council on the separate list submitted for that purpose. If the voter lived in Montevideo, he then had 22 different lists from which to select, all of them carrying the name of Echegoyen and his running-mate for vice president or the National Council, Esc. Dardo Ortíz. On each of the 22 lists were the names of candidates for the two houses of the legislature, each list substituting or rearranging the order in which that party's sub-lema candidates would be elected. One of the 22 sub-lema lists was known as Tradición y Lealtad Nacionalista (Tradition and Nationalist Loyalty) and carried the numbers 65 and 165 for the collegial and presidential alternatives respectively. This sub-lema was also known as "Sala Tallería," the name of the candidate for deputy that distinguished it from the sub-lema's other 21 lists for Montevideo. The two lists, 65 and 165, were distributed on street corners to the prospective voter in an envelope, which also contained a third list (numbered 265) giving the sub-lema's candidates for municipal offices. A grey sheet marked "SI" ("Yes") was also included, intended to indicate the voter's approval of the referendum. The 22 lists for Montevideo that supported Echegoyen, Ortíz, the constitutional reform, Ing. Isidoro Vejo Rodríguez (the candidate for mayor) and the group of municipal and special election council members, was known collectively as sub-lema "Herrera-Ruralistas." This sub-lema, remember, was also affiliated to another sub-lema in the National party, the Movimiento Popular Nacionalista, which also supported Echegoyen and Ortíz, but endorsed a candidate named Peñades for the Senate instead of Echegoyen, whose name also appeared on the other sub-lema's senatorial list. The MPN's lists also gave different municipal and other local candidates. In total, the "Herrera-Ruralista-MPN" sub-lema coalition submitted about 250 lists in about 65 different envelopes throughout the nation. Of course, no specific voter had to choose from all these or their competitors in Montevideo, for included in the total were many for other local areas. But he did have scores of possible choices to make. In this election, while the voter could not rearrange the names on the lists, he could vote one list for the presidency, an entirely different one—perhaps even different party—for the collegial alternative, and one of several referendum plans that had been submitted. Hundreds of possible combinations faced the Montevideo voter, most of whom relied on prepared packets of lists acquired from familiar faces from familiar *sub-lemas* standing on familiar street corners.

Perhaps out of necessity to simplify the process, campaigning in Uruguay is very personalistic. In 1966, several significant substantive issues existed, but personalism dominated the campaign. The most frequently invoked personalities were José Batlle, Luis Batlle, Luis de Herrera, and Benito Nardone—all of them dead. Even FIDEL, which lacked revered traditions or personalities of the major parties, joined in the personalistic campaigning by invoking the banner of Artigas, the great nineteenth-century Uruguayan liberator-statesman, whose connections with the *Fidelista* movement was remote at best.

The presidential campaign originally gravitated to three personalities: Batlle, Gestido, and Echegoyen. Late in the campaign Alberto Gallinal complicated the alternatives by entering as a presidential candidate. Batlle's campaign appeal, apart from his famous name and respected father, was dependent on his youthful, vigorous, campaign style. Gestido, a respected, retired air force general, presented a lower-keyed, common sense approach to politics. Echegoyen, carrying the *Herrerista* banner, was a veteran campaigner, but handicapped by his advanced age and somewhat out-of-date campaign style. Gallinal, an attractive candidate, had held office only as *Intendente* for the department of Florida. A very wealthy landowner, he was known as a gregarious, energetic, generous aristocrat who personally built and equipped public schools and highways in his department from his own personal wealth. Echegoyen's candidacy was professionally organized and planned, Gallinal's inexpertly devised. The PDC waged an expensive, ideological campaign, presenting the image of a major, national party, which was not the case. FIDEL also waged an elaborate, well-organized campaign, but centered it primarily on the city of Montevideo.

Every conceivable campaign device is used: handbills, posters, billboards, rallies, mailings, public speeches, radio and television, newspaper advertising, and an endless cacophony of blaring sound-trucks which restlessly rove the nation's streets day and night. Campaigning is limited in time by electoral codes, but the protracted period is intensely active. Newspaper coverage is partisan, since most of the newspapers have definite *sub-lema* and party affiliations. Voting is simple, requiring only the presentation of the *cédula* of registration at a neighborhood precinct station, and depositing the envelope containing the several ballots in an official urn. No arrests are made on election day except for serious crimes. Illegal, but tolerated activities such as gambling, encourage a carnival atmosphere.

Voting participation is normally very high in Uruguay. Of the 1.7 million voters eligible in 1966, 1.2 million or about 74 percent participated. Participation is evenly high throughout the nation; the rate for Montevideo is no higher than elsewhere, an unusual situation for Latin America where participation normally falls off rapidly outside the capital.[52]

The constitutional reform required a minimum of one-third of all eligible voters, or 50 percent plus 1 of all those who voted—whichever was greater. The measure passed securely with about 61 percent of the vote. The passage of the reform automatically invalidated the ballots cast for the collegial system.

Gestido won the presidential race, with Echegoyen, Batlle, and Gallinal following in that order. The 1966 presidential vote is indicated in Table 4-10.[53]

The Colorados captured approximately half the popular vote, the National party just under 40 percent, FIDEL under 6 percent, the PDC under 3 percent, with the remainder going to several small parties. In Montevideo, the Colorado party did better than it did nationally, with about 51 percent of the popular vote against

TABLE 4-10. 1966 PRESIDENTIAL VOTING IN URUGUAY

COLORADO PARTY		607,633
Gestido	262,040	
Batlle	215,642	
Vasconcellos	77,476	
Michelini	48,022	
Arechaga	4,064	
NATIONAL PARTY		496,910
Echegoyen	228,309	
Gallinal	171,618	
Heber	96,772	
TOTAL		1,104,543

32 percent for the National party. FIDEL received most of its vote from the capital, about 11 percent of the total. The PDC received under 4 percent of the vote in Montevideo. The Colorado party carried 11 of the 19 departments in 1966, against only 6 in 1962 and 1 in 1958. Of the departments carried by the Colorado party in the presidential race, Gestido carried 5 against Batlle's 6; however, the normally Nationalist-controlled departments went for Gestido rather than Batlle, suggesting the more partisan response elicited by the latter's name. The slim margin held by the National party was replaced by an equally slim majority for the Colorados. Party and *sub-lema* vote and representation are presented in Table 4-11.[54]

The Gestido *sub-lema* captured a plurality in both houses, followed closely by Batlle's List 15 group and Echegoyen's sector of the National party. The election was a definite victory for the Colorado party, and temporarily gave President Gestido a strong mandate for change. Although the PDC lost only one seat, their lone senator, it was a harsh and perhaps final defeat for the party that had expected to increase its vote. FIDEL came out of the election stronger than when it entered.

President Gestido took office in March, 1967, only two months following the revelation of a secret, urban guerrilla movement known as the *Tupamaros*.[55] Terrorism and mass protest increased over

TABLE 4-11. PARTY AND SUB-LEMA AND REPRESENTATION

LEMA/SUB-LEMA	CHAMBER OF DEPUTIES 1962	CHAMBER OF DEPUTIES 1966	SENATE 1962	SENATE 1966	1966 POPULAR VOTE
COLORADO PARTY	*45*	*50*	*14*	*16*	*607,633*
Desarollo y Justicia (Gestido, Legnani, Segovia)		21		7	261,977
List 15 (Batlle, Abdala)		18		6	210,947
Batllismo (Vasconcellos, Lopez-Toledo)		7		2	77,476
List 99 (Michelini)		4		1	48,022
Others		0		0	9,211
NATIONAL PARTY	*46*	*41*	*15*	*13*	*496,910*
Herrerismo-Ruralismo (Echegoyen)		20		6	230,897
Reforma y Desarrollo (Gallinal)		13		5	170,904
Herrera-Haedo (Haedo, Heber)		8		2	94,920
FIDEL	*3*	*5*	*1*	*1*	*69,750*
CHRISTIAN DEMOCRATIC PARTY	*3*	*3*	*1*	*0*	*37,219*
Other parties	*2*	*0*	*0*	*0*	*20,250*

the next few months, while economic conditions continued to deteriorate. In December, 1967, President Gestido suffered a fatal heart attack, and the vice-president, Jorge Pacheco Areco, assumed the responsibilities of the office. A program of economic austerity and martial law gradually seemed to return the nation to a condition of economic order, although fundamental political divisions remained and guerrilla activity increased.

4. CONCLUSION

Uruguay has achieved an unequaled record for twentieth-century Latin America by maintaining its representative government, impartial elections, and vigorous, free political parties. Institutionalization in the government and party system is impressively high. The traditional two parties are strong, competitive, and apparently durable even in the face of minority party challenges and extreme economic provocations. The dominance of the Colorados for all but eight years of the twentieth century has not apparently weakened the resolve of the National party leaders to respect electoral outcomes.

The persistence of the two-party competitive system is a credit to the well-informed, responsible electorate, and to the adaptability of the parties. Encased within the two-party framework is a series of factions, each possessing political autonomy and electoral identity, with considerable mobility for entry and exit from the factional system. Factions permit expression of the strongly personalistic streak in the Uruguayan political culture, without overwhelming the institutions themselves. After elections, the parties unite for legislative cooperation to a remarkable degree. Although parties have regional foci of electoral strength, these divisions have not been a highly devisive influence in the nation. Party hierarchies and recruitment tend to be elitist, but a continuing dialogue is maintained between leaders and constituencies through an intricate network of political clubs. These clubs encourage communication between constituents and their representatives, provide campaign organizations, and resolve persistent snags in the administrative and bureaucratic processes of the state. The most remarkable fact is that historically Uruguayans have come to set violence outside the cultural parameters of legitimacy, and placed high value on the mechanisms, structures, and processes of electoral competition and political parties. The tenacity of the political system to withstand the political pressures from recent economic stresses without military interference is a significant achievement. Multiple factions, their organizational structures and political clubs, the high level of political awareness and sophistication, and the compactness of the national electorate have combined to provide a continuing link between the governed and the governing in Uruguay in a way unknown in Honduras, Colombia, or the majority of Latin American nations. This crucial link provides an outlet for hostility, a response to social and economic strains, and a sense of involvement and commitment from the majority of Uruguayans. The fact that the political culture and representational processes exist within the framework of a two-party system is more or less a historical and legal coincidence, although the institutional framework has provided strength of its own in the process of national integration.

IV. CONCLUSIONS

The three examples of two-party systems provide strong contrasts in Latin America. Each exists in a differently styled political system, ranging from "authoritarian-traditional" to "modern-representative." Each system has processes similar to the others. Entry and exit of parties into the system is limited and difficult. In Honduras, the MNR tried unsuccessfully to break the two-party system in the mid-50s; in Uruguay, several parties, particularly the Christian Democrats and the Marxist groups, have met failure in trying to displace the traditional parties; in Colombia, even the most radical challenge of the traditional party elites, ANAPO, has worked within the legal framework of the two parties. Uruguayan and Colombian electoral laws and voting regulations support the two-party system, penalizing outside groups through recognition and representation. In all three cultures, the two parties find strong support from the century of political socialization that has transmitted their symbols from one generation to the next. It is probably true that in each nation the parties could be more easily changed than challenged. In Colombia where party symbols and loyalties are strong, the two parties have generated political violence with profound social consequences. Except for the culture imposed by the two-party system, one would not expect political socialization to be as intense in Colombia as it is.

Party factions play a role in leadership recruitment in Uruguay and Colombia by providing a national platform for highly motivated and skillful leaders, even when natural hierarchical, oligarchical, and elitist tendencies would otherwise restrict the channels of recruitment. In both Uruguay and Colombia there is a close correlation between specific families and party organizations.

Although the evidence for Honduras is limited, party awareness seems to be less dispersed and less intense throughout the country than it is in Uruguay and Colombia. The Uruguayan Colorados and Colombian Liberals historically have been strongest in the capital cities, the Nationalists and Conservatives in the rural areas. But in neither nation is the trend unchallenged. The Colorados have significant strength in rural departments in Uruguay, and the Nationalists have carried Montevideo electorally. The Liberals have strength in some regional departments of Colombia, and the Conservatives control some regional cities. Party socialization has been substantial in both political cultures as a result of the two-party competition.

In all three cases, the two-party systems organize elections around "ins" versus "outs." Interestingly enough, in each country the "outs" have been the same party over a long period of years: the PL in Honduras, the PC in Colombia, and the National party in Uruguay. Each party occupies a traditional minority position in its country, rarely if ever winning a national presidential election or legislative plurality. Yet each of these parties has continued to maintain itself in the face of electoral failure. The National party in Uruguay, having won office only twice in the twentieth century, is still a vigorous, well-organized, well-financed political party. This is particularly revealing since the competitiveness of Uruguayan politics, were it not so thoroughly a two-party system, would long ago have provided signals for the entry of another opposition party. The profound opposition that may come from a clear "confrontation" of parties in a two-party system, on the other hand, is revealed by the violence and stalemates that have occurred in recent decades in Honduras and Colombia. Uruguay during the nineteenth century experienced extensive party warfare from much the same cause. The conclusion that must be reached is that two-party competitive systems in Latin America may not only be no more intrinsically stable than other forms of party competition, but in fact may be less stable, may provoke more violence and on a wider scale than either multi-party or single-party systems.

In each of the three cases modern party politics has had direct roots in the nineteenth-century Liberal and Conservative competition. Even these names have been retained in Honduras and Colombia. Other nations periodically generate a two-party competitive system, but in no instance has this form of party competition occurred in Latin America over any period of time when the two parties were products of the twentieth century.

As often happens in Latin American politics, institutional similarities bridge tremendously broad gulfs in behavioral and environmental qualities. The traditional preoccupation with interpreting two-party experience in the Anglo-American tradition has often ignored the operation of such systems elsewhere in the world, particularly in Latin America. Some of the apparent contradictions between the Latin American and North American experiences cast shadows on many of the traditional interpretations made in the United States concerning the stability and representativeness of two-party competition.

NOTES

[1] Implications of a two-party system are discussed by V. O. Key, Jr., *Politics, Parties, and Pressure Groups*, 4th ed. (New York: Crowell, 1958), pp. 225–49; also by Maurice Duverger, *Political Parties* (New York: Wiley, 1963), pp. 208–28. Key is surprisingly naive regarding two-party systems, as illustrated by his comment that "The maintenance of a two-party competition—a winner take all system—must, over the long run, rest on a mutual recognition of equal loyalty to the political order," (*Politics, Parties, and Pressure Groups*, p. 227). Duverger's familiarity with Latin America is not much better. He dismisses further consideration of two-party systems in Latin America ". . . because the frequent and effective interference of the government in both polls and parties denatures the whole system . . . ," (*Political Parties*, p. 220).

[2] The most satisfactory, if wholly out of date survey of Honduran politics, is William S. Stokes, *Honduras: An Area Study in Government* (Madison, Wis.: University of Wisconsin Press, 1950).

[3] Economic background on Honduras is available in Vincent Chechi et al., *Honduras: A Problem in Economic Development* (New York: Twentieth Century Fund, 1959).

[4] Contemporary background is furnished by Charles W. Anderson, "Honduras: Problems of an Apprentice Democracy," in Martin C. Needler, ed., *Political Systems of Latin America* (Princeton, N.J.: Van Nostrand, 1964).

[5] Harry Kantor, *Patterns of Politics & Political Systems in Latin America* (Chicago: Rand McNally, 1969), pp. 139–41.

[6] *Ibid.*, p. 144.

[7] Robert Alexander, *Communism in Latin America* (New Brunswick, N.J.: Rutgers University Press, 1957), pp. 371–77.

[8] For two general references on Colombia, see John D. Martz, *Colombia: A Contemporary Survey* (Chapel Hill: University of North Carolina Press,

1962); and Pat M. Holt, *Colombia Today and Tomorrow* (New York: Praeger, 1964).

[9] See A. Lipman, "Social Backgrounds of the Bogotá entrepreneur," *Journal of Inter-American Studies* 7 (April 1965): 227–35; Alfonso Torres Melo, *? Qúe Es La Oligarquia Colombiana?* (Bogotá; Ediciones del Caribe, 1966); and Benjamin E. Haddox, *Sociedad y Religión en Colombia* (Bogotá: Ediciones Tercer Mundo, 1965).

[10] Eduardo Santa, *Sociologia Politica de Colombia* (Bogotá: Ediciones Tercer Mundo, 1964), pp. 71–83.

[11] Concern with these two events is limited to their influence on contemporary political parties and voting. There are extensive interpretive and descriptive sources on *La Violencia*, two useful ones being Robert C. Williamson, "Toward a theory of political violence: the case of rural Colombia," *Western Political Quarterly* 18, No. 1 (March 1965): 5–44; and Germán Guzman Campos, Orlando Fals Borda, and Eduardo Umann Luna, *La Violencia en Colombia*, Vol. 1 (Bogotá: Ediciones Tercer Mundo, 1963); also R. S. Weinert, "Violence in pre-modern societies: rural Colombia," *American Political Science Review* 60, No. 2 (June 1966): 340–47. Portions of this section are based on material originally published in *Inter-American Economic Affairs* 21, No. 2 (Autumn 1967). Reproduced with permission.

[12] Norman A. Bailey, "La violencia en Colombia," *Journal of Inter-American Studies* 9, No. 4 (October 1967): 561–75. Also see Guillermo Salamanca, *Los Partidos Politicos en Colombia* (Bogotá, 1961); see discussion of Harry Kantor, *Patterns of Politics*, p. 425.

[13] A somewhat benevolent but thorough analysis of Rojas Pinilla is contained in Vernon Fluharty, *Dance of the Millions: Military Rule and the Social Revolution in Colombia, 1930–56* (Pittsburgh: University of Pittsburgh Press, 1957).

[14] By *alienation* I mean withdrawal from politics, a failure to identify personal with national interests, resulting in noninvolvement or nonaction. By *protest* I mean the positive expression of political hostility by action, as in voting. Protest is against something or someone, in Colombia an elite, the *Frente*, deteriorating economic conditions, or the status quo. By *dissent* I mean a milder form of opposition, less disruptive of the constituted political system than protest. A useful introduction to party politics is John D. Martz, "Political parties in Colombia and Venezuela: Contrasts in substance and style," *Western Political Quarterly* 18 (June 1965): 318–33. Often student protestors in Bogotá are clearly too young to have been affected by the cultural heritage of *La Violencia*.

[15] One similarity to U.S. and British parties is what has been called "grassroots organization," most active during periods of campaigning. It has not been an unmixed blessing in Colombia. The topic is discussed by Russell H. Fitzgibbon, "The party potpourri in Latin America," *Western Political Quarterly* 10, No. 1 (March 1957): especially 17. John Martz, "Political parties in Colombia and Venezuela," finds the phenomena less important today in Colombia, a conclusion that parallels my own.

[16] An excellent, straightforward analysis of contemporary party politics is A. Angell, "Cooperation and conflict in Colombia," *Political Studies* 14 (Fall 1966): 53–71.

[17] Kenneth W. Johnson, "Political radicalism in Colombia, 1962–1964," *Journal of Inter-American Studies* 7, No. 2 (January 1965).

218   PARTY SYSTEMS AND ELECTIONS IN LATIN AMERICA

[18] Robert H. Dix, *Colombia: The Political Dimensions of Change* (New Haven: Yale University Press, 1967), pp. 256–90.

[19] A brief and generally accurate description of the electoral and representational systems in Colombia is contained in *Colombia: Election Factbook, March–May, 1966* (Washington, D.C.: Institute for Comparative Study of Political Systems, 1966), pp. 28–36.

[20] Kantor, *Patterns of Politics*, pp. 406–9.

[21] *El Tiempo*, April 24, 1966.

[22] *Ibid.*, April 28, 1966.

[23] Material in this section based on R. McDonald, "Political protest and alienation in voting: The case of Colombia," *Inter-American Economic Affairs* 21, No. 2: 3–22. Reproduced with permission.

[24] *El Tiempo's* coverage of the campaign was so partisan as to attribute much ordinary crime in Bogotá during the campaign to "alleged Rojas' supporters." The paper printed ANAPO news, if at all, in the back pages. Articles were normally very editorial, with the interpretation of news slanted toward the FTN. For the impact of mass media on peasants in Colombia, see S. M. Rogers, "Mass media exposure and modernization among Colombian peasants," *Public Opinion Quarterly* 29 (Winter 1965): 614–55.

[25] María Eugenia is not so fondly remembered for her role in the infamous "bull-ring massacre" of Sunday, February 5, 1956. For a detailed description of the incredible incident, see Fluharty, *Dance of the Millions*, pp. 295–98.

[26] *El Espectador*, April 23, 1966.

[27] An unusual factor was introduced into the 1966 campaign by the death of Camilo Torres Restrepo, a distant relative of the presidential candidate. Torres, a young priest, left the Church in 1965 to devote his efforts to revolutionary activity with the FLN, and was killed by the Colombian military in action around the department of Santander. Torres, from an upper class Colombian family, wrote extensively, his most effective publication being *La Revolución: Imperativo Cristiano* (Bogotá: Ediciones del Caribe, 1965), and was a symbol to many younger Colombians also dissatisfied with the "older" generation leading the nation. Torres was convinced traditional political processes would not produce fundamental change in existing Latin American systems, and urged an alliance between Christians and revolutionary movements. His death and his ideas are increasingly discussed throughout Latin America.

[28] Source: National Registry of the Civil State.

[29] Generally economic conditions in more sparsely settled departments are worse than in urban ones, but the disintegration is less apparent. See Martz, "Political parties in Colombia and Venezuela."

[30] Source: National Registry of the Civil State.

[31] Actually there are many other regions that can be identified or subdivided in Colombia. For the limited analytic purposes here, the present categories are sufficient.

[32] Source: National Registry of the Civil State.

[33] See S. M. Lipset, *The Political Man* (Garden City, N.Y.: Doubleday, 1960), pp. 87–114.

[34] For a further discussion, see Russell H. Brannon, *Agricultural Development of Uruguay* (New York: Praeger, 1968).

[35] A dated but still perceptive portrait of Uruguay is Russell H. Fitzgibbon, *Uruguay: Portrait of a Democracy* (New Brunswick, N.J.: Rutgers University Press, 1954).

[36] The intellectual contributions of Batlle are reported in Antonio M. Grompone, *La Ideología de Batlle* (Montevideo: Ediciones Arca, 1962).

[37] For additional analysis of Batlle, see Phillip B. Taylor, *Government and Politics of Uruguay* (New Orleans: Tulane University, Department of Political Science, 1960).

[38] An Uruguayan's viewpoint on Terra and the referendum is found in Oscar Bruschera, *Los Partidos Tradicionales en el Uruguay* (Montevideo: Ediciones del Rio de la Plata, 1966), pp. 37–42.

[39] See Russell H. Fitzgibbon, "Adoption of a collegiate executive in Uruguay," *Journal of Politics* 14, No. 4 (1952): 616–42; also, Milton I. Vanger, "Uruguay introduces government by committee," *American Political Science Review* 48, No. 2 (June 1954): 500–13.

[40] An excellent analysis of political interests and groups in Uruguay is found in Philip B. Taylor's, "Interests and institutional disfunction in Uruguay," *American Political Science Review* 58, No. 1 (March 1963): 62–74.

[41] Source: Corte Electoral, Sec. Estadistica.

[42] Background on Uruguayan PDC available in Edward J. Williams, *Latin American Christian Democratic Parties* (Knoxville: University of Tennessee Press, 1967), p. 25. An early manifesto is available by Tomas G. Brena, *Democrácia Cristiana en El Uruguay* (Montevideo: Impresora Zorrilla de San Martín, 1946).

[43] Robert J. Alexander, "Communism in Uruguay," in *Communism in Latin America* (New Brunswick, N.J.: Rutgers University Press, 1957), pp. 135–48.

[44] See Phillip B. Taylor, Jr., "The electoral system in Uruguay," *Journal of Politics* 17, No. 1 (1955): 19–42.

[45] Part of this section is based on my article, "Electoral Systems, Party Representation, and Political Change in Latin America," *Western Political Quarterly* 20, No. 3 (September 1967), 694–708. Reproduced with permission.

[46] For discussion of *sub-lema* laws, see *Election Factbook*, pp. 43–49.

[47] The significance of the clubs was noted years ago by Fitzgibbon (*Uruguay: Portrait of a Democracy*), p. 148, but their complex dimensions have yet to be investigated satisfactorily.

[48] Kantor, *Patterns of Politics*, pp. 634–37.

[49] See Taylor, "Interests and institutional disfunction in Uruguay," pp. 65–66, for a discussion of the Herrera forces in Uruguay.

[50] Kantor, *Patterns of Politics*, p. 643. Kantor observes that one of the reasons for the Uruguayan economic dilemma is found in the national budget. No funds have been set aside for national economic investment and development.

[51] For a complete review of the issues, personalities, and participating groups in the 1966 election see *Uruguay: Election Factbook*.

[52] *Ibid.*, pp. 16–17.

[53] Source: Corte Electoral, Sec. Estadistica.

[54] *Ibid.*

[55] *New York Times*, January 23, 1969. See also, *Carta de Montevideo*, March 31, 1969.

CHAPTER 5

Single-Party Dominant Systems:
Nicaragua, Mexico, and El Salvador

By definition a single-party dominant system is one in which a minimum of 60 percent of the seats in legislative chambers are controlled by one political party. The assumption of the definition is that by controlling 60 percent of the seats or more, the dominant party is in a position to make policy virtually without concern for other political parties. Often in such instances legislatures do not represent the center of governmental policy-making, but at most officialize or ratify the executive and party hierarchy decisions. It is also assumed that such a configuration of party power influences the style of party politics, voting, and elections.

Six Latin American countries fall into this general category: Mexico, Nicaragua, El Salvador, Cuba, Haiti, and Paraguay. Of these there are dramatic variations in the style of operation and the power bases of the dominant political parties. Mexico and Haiti can be placed at opposite ends of a spectrum in regard to their dominant party's power base and functional relevance to the general political system. The existence of a political party in Haiti can be asserted only by stretching the concept of party to its outer limits. "President-for-life" Duvalier rules Haiti personally with a cadre of bodyguards and professional "enforcers" in almost a cinematic gangster style. The party is nothing more than a few trusted cronies who possess an honorary status of legislative deputy. A party cannot be said to exist in the sense that it influences policy-making or the national electorate.[1]

On the other end of the spectrum, Mexico's single-party dominant system not only plays a role in policy-making, but in limited respects permits an important, elementary competition within its carefully controlled structures. It would be incorrect to say that

220

the dominant Mexican party makes policy, but the channels of communication provided by the party structure coincide meaningfully with national decision-making in Mexico. The party facilitates decision-making although it does not in the legislative sense participate in national policy-making. The highly organized, affluent party structure incorporates all major political, social, and economic groups within the nation, and their elites generally support the principle of single-party government, although often competing among themselves for their own self-improvement. The situation in Mexico is not unlike the United States where one state party can dominate another. While interparty competition is meaningless, often intraparty bargaining maintains an element of competition. In Mexico, however, the dominant political party is so multifunctional that it is often difficult to separate it from the concept of nation-state.

Most of the remaining four nations fall somewhere in between these poles. Paraguay, somewhat like Haiti, is dominated by a single party controlled by a fairly old-fashioned but less oppressive dictator. While the party is more institutionalized in Paraguay than in Haiti and has roots in previous regimes, it consists of little besides the personal friends of the President. They are carefully screened, usually supported by patronage, and known to be loyal to the regime. The party performs nominal electoral functions although it is essentially guaranteed a fixed legislative representation regardless of election returns. There are some indications that the Paraguayan party system may be expanding, allowing more and varied groups to participate more freely in electoral experiences.[2]

Nicaragua's ruling party is similar to Paraguay's. A more outspoken opposition exists in Nicaragua, although its role is one of perpetual minority critic. Its leaders are often jailed, and it has no chance of gaining power. In Paraguay and Nicaragua party histories are violent. Governments have alternated, usually by civil warfare, between the supporters of one party or the other. Both party systems are historically rarefied, restricted to the economic, political, and family elites of each nation. Neither nation has achieved a tradition of restrained party competition, although in Nicaragua parties may have been more broadly perceived than in Paraguay for focusing national political controversy.

The "official" party in El Salvador has elements of several traditions. It is unquestionably an elitist group maintained by a fragile alliance between powerful military leaders and a handful of traditional families that have historically controlled the wealth, social structure, and politics of their country. The dominant political party even more than in Mexico is a reflection of political power, not a source of it. It performs nominal electoral functions and officializes government policies in the national legislature. Opposition parties are allowed greater legislative representation than in Mexico. At least one significant new political party has recently emerged with substantial mass support. A party of the Christian Democratic tradition, it does not owe allegiance to the official party but is tolerated within limits by the oligarchy. A second, more radical, Marxist opposition party skirts the edges of legality. Other minor parties exist, many of them no more than personalistic splinters from the dominant ruling elite.

Characterizing party politics in Cuba is difficult, partly because of the recent experience of that nation and partly because we have so little information about it.[3] Two controversies immediately emerge in any discussion of contemporary Cuba: one about the personality of Fidel Castro, the other about the influence of the older, Communist party of Cuba. Whatever else can be said, several generalizations seem reasonable. Government policy is not made within the ruling party, but by Castro and a small clique of immediate lieutenants. No opposition is encouraged or tolerated by the regime, particularly political parties. No elections have been held nor are they likely, removing any electoral functions from the party and political system. Because of the constant threat of purges, and the quixotic, enigmatic, impulsive nature of Cuba's leader, the party cannot develop much in the way of institutionalized channels or structures. Cuba's national party is largely an ideological mechanism designed to build support for the regime, disperse limited kinds of patronage to the loyal and committed, and help maintain the political security of the regime.

Other contrasts can be seen among the single-party dominant systems in Latin America. Mexico is an impressively responsive, decentralized, flexible, and, if you like, "democratic" political system when compared with Haiti, Cuba, Nicaragua, or Paraguay. The latter three states are highly centralized, monolithic regimes where personal welfare and liberty are either accidental or politically motivated for short-run gain.[4] Political opposition exists in Mexico and El Salvador in limited ways, not at all in Cuba and Haiti, and in irregular, often violent ways in Paraguay and Nicaragua. Parties have firm historical traditions in Mexico, Nicaragua, and Paraguay, but not in the other countries. The structures for institutionalization exist in Cuba and El Salvador, but traditions and symbols are still relatively weak.

Is it possible to view single-party dominant systems as early stages of national institutionalization?[5] Or, alternatively, to construct any developmental concepts designed to explain the evolution of single-party dominant systems? The answer to both questions is probably no. Mexico's characteristic single-party "controlled democracy" has evolved slowly over a period of more than forty years. While the political system has broadened its bases of support and become more institutionalized and internally competitive, the changes have been slow and perhaps not very profound. The chances of a second competitive party emerging in Mexico are slim, and rest primarily on the disposition of the majority party to allow such an eventuality. El Salvador may be moving toward a more competitive party system, but since this change began in 1962 it is premature to draw any definite conclusions. Cuba and Haiti presently do not seem to be changing very much if at all. In Nicaragua and Paraguay where more traditional dictators rule, it is likely that change in the party systems must await a change in the regimes; that is, a revolution or *coup*. Such a change seems unlikely in Paraguay and improbable in Nicaragua, although the latter is the more fragile political balance of the two. Some guerrillas are active in Nicaragua, and there are signs of growing dissatisfaction with the Somoza regime. But countervailing forces of economic prosperity, a well-paid, professional military, and a stubbornly committed leader combine to make any significant changes in Nicaragua in the near future difficult and unlikely.

If preconceived ideological perspectives are set aside, it is difficult to be categorical about the single-party dominant systems in Latin America. They have produced relatively open, competitive, stable political systems sensitive to personal liberty, individual integrity and welfare (as in Mexico) while simultaneously being used for narrowly based authoritarian ends. They can be maintained by terror or by consensus, or a combination of the two. There are even signs in El Salvador that they are capable of reconstituting themselves. Mexico and Paraguay are encouraging limited opposition by additional political parties, while considerable opposition, often violent, exists in Nicaragua. For lack of information, Cuba has been excluded from further consideration, as has Haiti for lack of relevance. Paraguay is mentioned elsewhere in this survey. A closer examination of the party systems, voting, and elections in the remaining systems of Mexico, Nicaragua, and El Salvador reveals more subtle traits for comparison.

I. NICARAGUA: AN AUTHORITARIAN SINGLE-PARTY DOMINANT SYSTEM

Nicaragua, with the largest territory in Central America, has a population of no more than 1¾ million, most of it centered in the humid lowland regions of the great lakes of Nicaragua and Managua. The major cities—Managua, León, Masaya, and Granada—lie in this area. The population is largely *mestizo*, with a small group of whites, Negroes, and Indians. The country is dominated by Lake Nicaragua, which is 100 miles long and 45 miles wide. The economy is largely agricultural, well diversified between corn, beans, coffee, cotton, rice, sugar cane, and cattle. Industrialization is limited largely to cotton and sugar processing and recently meat packing. Constitutionally Nicaragua is a unitary republic divided administratively into 16 departments and a national district.

There are six major regions in Nicaragua. The northern Pacific lowlands, dominated by the city of León, is dependent upon tropical crops like tobacco, cotton, and coffee. The area has always been a center of Liberal party support, identified since 1935 with the Somoza dynasty. The national district (essentially the city of Managua) contains more than 20 percent of the national population and almost all of its business activity. The greatest diversity of political activity occurs in Managua, which has never been identified with either traditional party. The western Lake region is dominated by the city of Granada and dependent mostly on beef production. Its population is heavily urban, being contained in several moderate sized cities. This urbanization has attracted the emergent Christian Democratic party. The northern mountains, a cooler, wetter region, is politically variable. The major city of Matagalpa is dominated by agriculture with some mining. The largely rural eastern lake region is entirely agricultural, with poor transportation it tends to be somewhat isolated from the remaining sectors of the country. The sixth region—the Atlantic—contains 47 percent of the national territory but only 6 percent of the population. Its hot, humid climate and dense vegetation has made its resources rather inaccessible. Its major city, Bluefields, contains English-speaking Indians who immigrated from the Caribbean.[6]

1. BACKGROUND TO CONTEMPORARY POLITICAL PARTIES

Nicaragua had an extraordinary experience with the United States during the nineteenth and early twentieth century. The small country became the object of competing North American banking and financial interests when its lakes provided a successful land-water route from the Caribbean to the Pacific before the construction of the Panama Canal. Political interference became a chronic fallout of this interest, and the United States invaded the country several times. North American interference was also encouraged by Nicaragua's persistent, chaotic political instability. The country like many Latin American nations in the nineteenth century experienced two-party competition and warfare that often degenerated into anarchy and revolution. The two parties, typically called Liberals and Conservatives, regularly waged war on each other from independence until U.S. occupation in the early twentieth century.[7]

Nicaragua gained independence on September 15, 1821 as an outpost of the Mexican Empire, and joined its sister nations in the United Provinces of Central America until 1838 when it seceded to become independent. Internal politics consisted largely of the Conservatives based in Granada fighting the Liberals in León for national supremacy. Political counterparts to these parties in other Central American nations furnished aid and assistance to the Nicaraguan parties in the hopes that their side would be victorious. To reduce the violence the capital was relocated from León to Managua, a city located about half-way between the feuding cities. Increasing international rivalries between England and the United States for rights to a cross-isthmian route complicated domestic Nicaraguan politics. Cornelius Vanderbilt formed a company to establish service through the San Juan River and Lake Nicaragua.

In 1854 the Liberals, outraged by a new constitution imposed on them by the Conservatives, enlisted the aid of a North American, William Walker. The exploits of adventurer and opportunist William Walker remain even today stranger than fiction. Originally supported by money from the Vanderbilt interests and wealthy southern racists who sought a refuge for their ideas in the closing days of the Civil War, Walker easily defeated the Conservative forces at Granada. But instead of installing the Liberals in power and bowing to the Vanderbilt interests, Walker himself assumed power and became the "president" of Nicaragua. His rule lasted only a few years, as the alienated Vanderbilt interests subsequently aided the Conservative cause and enlisted the Costa Rican army to invade Nicaragua and "liberate" it from Walker. It is perhaps ironic that the successful campaign by Costa Rica in Nicaragua is still considered today one of the high points in Costa Rican history, an event carefully noted in Costa Rican schoolbooks. Walker's eclipse was followed by a period of relative calm while the Conservatives enforced stability and ruled until 1893.

In 1893 chaos returned. The Liberal army led by José Santos Zelaya successfully overthrew the Conservative regime, and began a rule of international opportunism and domestic chaos. The United States sympathetically aided Zelaya's domestic political enemies, and by 1910 forced him out of power. At the "request" of the new Conservative government, United States' advisors were sent to Nicaragua along with economic assistance in the form of loans from New York banks. An attempted anti-U.S., Liberal-inspired revolt in 1912 brought 100 North American Marine Guards to the U.S. legation in Managua, followed by an escalation of military occupation to 3,000 Marines who remained in the country until the beginning of Franklin Roosevelt's presidency. The alleged reason for the occupation was to insure stability, and incidently to guarantee repayment of the bank loans. Looking forward to an eventual withdrawal from Nicaragua, the Marines built a domestic "national guard" to maintain political order afterward. When they ultimately withdrew the Marines installed as leader of this "professional force" Colonel Anastasio Somoza García.[8]

For more than 35 years the Somoza regime has been the most durable dictatorship this century in Latin America. Anastasio died at the hands of an assassin prior to the 1956 presidential election, and was succeeded by the eldest son, Luis, who served as president from 1957 to 1963. His brother Tachito (from his father's nickname, Tacho) took over the powerful National Guard. Luis' relatively enlightened regime was popular, and he would doubtless have won even an honest election. Educated in the United States and imbued with a more liberal philosophy than either his father or brother, Luis' untimely death in 1965 brought an end to this ameliorating influence. René Schick was hand-picked by the Somozas to succeed Luis as President in 1963. Even under the Somoza's constant shadow, Schick gained respect for his personal fairness and impartiality. Schick died in 1966 only months before the 1967 presidential campaign was to begin. All power gravitated to Tachito, who ran himself in 1967 for the presidency. Tachito's exhibitionism and military manner do not make him particularly popular among Nicaraguans. Stories are told of how Tachito, when visiting provincial cities, traveled across the countryside in his tank, followed by the roar of more tanks filled with his loyal national guard. Rumors of discontent and guerrilla activity are increasingly common in Nicaragua, but the odds against a possible revolt are enormous despite growing discontent.[9]

2. REPRESENTATION AND VOTING IN NICARAGUA

In Central America only Nicaragua adheres to a two-chamber legislature. The lower house, Chamber of Deputies, contains 54 elected members serving five-year terms. The Senate contains 16 elected members plus positions for ex-presidents and the defeated minority party presidential candidate. Deputies are elected from special districts, senators from the nation at large. Women were first enfranchised in 1957 under Luis Somoza's regime. Voting is obligatory, but the sanctions are not enforced. All voting is by party; no votes can be cast for individual candidates.

Theoretically the electoral system is proportional representation. However, the reality of two-party activity and the built-in stipulation that the minority receive a minimum one-third of the legislative seats produces in fact a majority-type system. The majority party, always the Somoza dominated Liberal party, receives the remaining two-thirds of the seats.[10] Election returns are certified by the Supreme Election Tribunal, which is also dominated by the Liberal party.

Party-list voting is useful to the Somoza regime in perpetuating its control. It minimizes the effectiveness of *personalismo* for opposition candidates, since they must rally support for the party rather than a single candidate. It also rewards the Liberal party machinery with patronage and influence, which in turn promotes a "spontaneously" high vote for the party candidates. Since all candidates for the Liberal party are nominated and elected only with party approval, there is thereby a minimum chance for an opportunist to challenge the party from within. Guaranteeing one-third of the legislative seats to the opposition is also a calculated policy of the Liberals to maintain their dominance. The two-thirds legislative majority fully protects the party from any unforeseen problems while still maintaining the myth of an opposition. Completely crushing the opposition could strengthen it by casting the spell of martyrdom upon it, while the one-third maximum destroys incentive for the opposition to "work harder" during a campaign. Opposition party representation also challenges international critics who label Nicaragua a dictatorship. While Nicaragua is indeed the most rigidly controlled political system discussed in this chapter, almost all others are technically more dominated in legislative representation by the dominant party. Nicaragua's guarantee to the opposition is not unique in Latin America. Paraguay's President Stroessner employs the same technique for essentially the same reasons.

3. CONTEMPORARY POLITICAL PARTIES IN NICARAGUA

The dominant *Partido Liberal Nacionalista* (PLN) existed long before Somoza came to power. Somoza had been an active member of the party for more than 14 years before he took control of it with the help of the National Guard.

The experience of the Liberal party in Nicaragua is a good illustration of how even in an otherwise effectively controlled authoritarian regime a political party can be a useful instrument for governing. Although Anastasio Somoza's regime was personalistic and did not actually depend upon the Liberal party for support, the Liberal party became an exclusive club for trusted lieutenants and supporters. Government employees and landowners often owe their economic and even personal security to the regime. Party faithful provide financial support for the party, and receive in return profitable concessions such as jobs, licenses, import monopolies, access to the bureaucracy, and the more intangible symbols of status and prestige. The titles of deputy and senator, even when devoid of power, are as highly valued in Nicaraguan society as elsewhere. While the Somoza family has benefited disproportionately from the regime, it has cleverly and selectively allowed others to benefit also. The party built a strong organization that has carried the message of the Somoza regime to all parts of the country. It is indisputable that the effectiveness of the Liberal party as an organization, maintained not by some vague theoretical or doctrinal cohesion but by tangible, politicoeconomic bonds, has contributed measurably to the success of the Somozas in perpetuating their regime for more than 3 decades.

Under the Somozas the Liberal party has experienced periodic purges, not uncommon in single-party dominant systems. The most significant of these brought Tacho to formal power in 1936. The commander of the National Guard, Juan B. Sacasa, was a Liberal who became president in the 1932 election. Although related to Tacho by marriage, Sacasa ultimately was deposed by Somoza in 1936. Since then the Somoza family has maintained hegemony over all aspects of Nicaraguan life. Today party cohesion is maintained by a multiplicity of techniques, and purges are by and large unnecessary. The intertwining of governmental, economic, and party elites is so complete that other mechanisms of control—like violence or terror—have become largely unnecessary. Since the basis of Liberal party control is familial, opposition when and as it arises in Nicaragua is also familial. Challenges to the Somozas normally come from other wealthy Nicaraguan families. The family nature of national politics is not uncommon in Latin America, particularly in nations as small as Nicaragua.

Somoza's purge of Sacasa produced a division in the Liberal party. Many of its members were shocked by Somoza's bold action. A portion of the party remained loyal to Sacasa but was disunited and dissipated. For more than 10 years efforts to unite anti-Somoza elements proved futile until 1944 when the *Partido Liberal Independiente* (PLI) was formed. The PLI tried in both 1947 and 1959 to reach an agreement with the Conservative party to achieve a united front against the Somozas, but strong personal jealousies in both parties prevented cooperation. The PLI supported President René Schick from 1963 to 1966 with the hope that their support might pry the president away from the Somozas.

The traditional opposition in Nicaragua has been the *Partido Conservador Tradicionalista* (PCT). The PCT, an offshoot of the original Conservative party, was formed in the 1940s over the question of cooperation with the Somozas. Originally directed by General Emiliano Chamorro, the PCT broke with the so-called Civilists under Carlos Cuadra Pasos who called for cooperation. The Chamorro group was numerically stronger than the Civilists, but underwent a turbulent period during the past two decades. In 1950 General Chamorro signed a so-called General's Agreement with Tacho to guarantee the opposition certain privileges (including the one-third guaranteed representation) in return for explicit loyalty to the regime. The agreement lasted 4 years until Chamorro and the PCT attempted an armed revolt against the Somoza regime that was quickly crushed. The party reorganized for the 1956 campaign but was vigorously repressed following the assassination of Tacho during the campaign. Again in 1959, PCT leaders attempted a revolt, this time organized in exile from Costa Rica. The expected result was virtual annihilation of the party organization in Nicaragua.

The PCT recently reorganized again under Dr. Fernando Agüero, a distinguished Nicaraguan ophthalmologist. Calling for widespread governmental reforms, Agüero tried to recruit younger blood into the organization. Agüero's leadership was often arbitrary, and encouraged considerable internal dissention. The Somozas were able to promote additional dissention within the PCT. From a weakening position Agüero sought a United Front in 1966 against the candidacy of Tachito Somoza.

The remaining opposition in Nicaragua comes largely from the new *Partido Social Cristiano*. The PSC affiliates in spirit to the broader Latin American Christian Democratic movement, although in fact is more conservative than many of those parties. It emerged first in 1949 as the *Unión Nacional de Alianzas Populares* (UNAP) or National Union of Popular Alliances. It functioned until 1955 as a loose alliance without the status of a party. In September, 1957, the PSC was formally constituted by leaders of the UNAP and some disaffected followers of Agüero's PCT. The PSC is comprised largely of white-collar workers (excluding government workers who must belong to the Liberal party) and a few intellectuals. It has had limited electoral success in Managua and Granada, but has yet to demonstrate that it can become the principal antagonist to the PLN.

Several other minor parties exist on the border of legality. One is the Nicaraguan Conservative party, *Partido Conservador Nicaragüese* (PCN), which was formally organized in 1956, but had its origins in the Civilist movement of the 1940s. The PCN was prompted by a request from Luis Somoza for an opposition party to run against him in the 1956 campaign, since otherwise none would participate following the boycott of the PCT. In return for providing token opposition, the PCN obtained the usual one-third of the legislative seats despite an almost total lack of members, organization, and votes (it received less than 10 percent in 1963). Because of the defection of the PCT, the PCN legally became the nation's second party. It tried to join with the PCT in the United Front in 1967, but failed to reach agreement and nominated its own candidate, Alejandro Abaunza Marenco.

The far left has not been effective or even visible in Nicaragua since the late 1940s, when it enjoyed a brief period of relative success infiltrating unions and middle-class organizations. The Communist party was declared illegal in 1947, and has remained underground. Several pro-Castro organizations, such as the *Mobilizatión Republicana* (MR), have appeared clandestinely but have little following or influence. The *Partido Acción Revolucionaria* (PAR) is a remnant of the so-called third force in Nicaragua originally known between 1953–1962 as the National Renovation party,

Partido de Renovación Nacional (PRN). PAR campaigned against President Schick in 1963, with no success, and supported the United Front in 1967.

Despite a heritage of two-party rivalry, warfare, and competition, and despite what on the surface appears to be vocal opposition, the Nicaraguan political system is dominated by a single party. Elections find the party with, at best, weak or token opposition, and often with none. Never under the Somozas has there been any possibility that the power of the PLN would be peacefully transferred to another group. After 1947, when Tacho dismissed Leonardo Argüello as president for "not following orders" the impossibility of anyone ruling without Somoza support was clear. There have been elections which the Somozas could have won easily, even with open competition, for their regime has not been entirely unpopular. Compared with, say, Trujillo in the Dominican Republic, Pérez Jiménez in Venezuela, Rojas Pinilla in Colombia, Somoza rule has not been notably harsh, oppressive, or incompetent. The regime has induced impressive economic growth that has raised most living standards if not always as rapidly as the Somozas'. The rising and broadening economic expectations may ultimately combine with the decline of the Somoza dynasty to reverse slowly the political fortunes of the family.

4. VOTING AND CAMPAIGNING IN NICARAGUA

Since the regime controls electoral returns, voting data for Nicaragua is not very reliable. Total registration of voters is rather vague, but about 570 thousand persons were presumably eligible to vote in 1963, according to the Nicaraguan government. Of those, 451 thousand, or about 79 percent participated. Based on the total population of Nicaragua (estimated in 1963, at 1,535,588) these figures seem reasonable.[11]

Participation in the 15 departments and the national district of Managua range from a high of 58 percent of the total population in the small department of Río San Juan to a low of 20 percent in the medium-size department of Boaca. Only 26 percent of the population voted in Managua.

The case of Río San Juan department is a good illustration of how tenuous the election data may be. In other nations we have noted that smaller and/or more remote departments tend to experience generally lower voter turnout. Río San Juan would appear a major exception, since with only 1 percent of the national popula-

TABLE 5-1. VOTING IN 1963 ELECTION BY DEPARTMENT

Department	1963 population	Votes cast	Percent Of nat. population	Percent of population voting
Boaca	71,615	14,337	5	20
Carazo	65,888	19,684	4	30
Chinandega	128,624	38,205	8	30
Chontales	75,575	19,218	5	57
Estelí	69,257	20,615	5	30
Granada	65,643	21,706	4	33
Jinotega	76,935	20,170	5	26
León	150,051	52,587	10	35
Madriz	50,229	14,456	3	29
Managua	318,826	83,276	21	26
Masaya	76,580	21,781	5	28
Matagalpa	171,465	40,520	11	24
Nueva Segovia	45,900	12,675	3	28
Río San Juan	15,676	9,007	1	58
Rivas	64,361	16,694	4	26
Zelaya	88,963	45,863	6	52

SOURCE: Supreme Tribunal of Elections.

tion 58 percent of the department's population voted. But Nicaragua also reports that only about 42 percent of the population nationally is over 20, and voting is restricted to those over 21. It therefore seems unlikely that Río San Juan could find 58 percent of its population over 21 even if everyone voted, since that would be 16 percent higher than the national average over 20 years of age. A comparison of 1963 voting is contained in Table 5-1.[12]

The largest number of votes came from the more populous departments of Managua, León, Masaya, and Granada, all of which were close to the median level of voting participation for the nation as a whole.

Campaigning is varied and unpredictable in Nicaragua. One of the few constants is that the dominant party spends the greatest effort and most money, and that the opposition is likely to shout fraud whenever the opportunity arises.

No elections were held from 1936 when Tacho seized power until 1947. In 1947, the Conservative party refused to participate charging that the government would never allow free elections. The small PLI nominated Enoc Aguado, who for technical reasons ran on the PC label. Many Nicaraguans still argue that Aguado probably won the election, although his opponent, Somoza-endorsed Leonardo Argüello, received officially 50 percent more of the total vote. The results are academic, since Tacho removed Argüello a few months after he took office, and installed his elderly uncle (Víctor Román y Reyes) in office.

The 1951 "general's agreement" between Tacho and Chamorro made all electoral results a foregone conclusion, and guaranteed the opposition the one-third fixed representation. In an election characterized by abstention Tacho won by a wide margin.

Martial law was declared for the 1957 election following the assassination of Tacho. Luis Somoza persuaded Eduardo Amador Pineda to run against him under the hastily formed PCN banner in return for the one-third legislative representation. Ravaged by arrests and harassment following Tacho's death, the PCT abstained.

The PCT reentered the electoral arena in 1963 to challenge the PLN candidate, René Schick. The PCT candidate Fernando Agüero demanded O.A.S. supervision of the elections, a move calculated to embarrass the Somozas who rejected it. Impulsively, Agüero threatened to "stage a revolt" if the Somozas refused to allow the O.A.S. to supervise the election. From a superior position of power, Tachito called Agüero's bluff. The next move was Agüero's, who tried to save face by "storming" the national palace with his followers, pistol in hand, shouting profanities against the regime. Agüero was placed under house arrest for the remainder of the campaign, and the PCT promptly withdrew from the election. Schick won the election by better than 10–1 margin over the PCN candidate, Diego Manuel Chamorro.[13]

Tachito wanted, like his father, to control both the National Guard and the presidency, but Luis Somoza, until his death, remained steadfastly opposed to the idea for strategic reasons. With Luis' death all opposition to Tachito evaporated, and familiar faces reemerged for the 1967 campaign. The PCT again nominated Fernando Agüero, who ran with the more or less united support of the *Unión Nacional Opositoria* (UNO) comprised of the PCT, PLI, and PSC. The PCN supported Alejandro Abaunza Marenco. Also active in the campaign against Tachito was Pedro Joaquín Chamorro Cardenal, editor of the antigovernment newspaper *La Prensa*, who had himself been jailed often by the Somozas in the preceding decade. Although not a friend of Agüero, Chamorro supported him to achieve a unified opposition.

The 1967 campaign was a violent, bitter one. Agüero felt no restraint in attacking Somoza. Once he harangued 30 thousand followers in downtown Managua in a bitter anti-Somoza speech, urging the army to rise against the regime and follow the UNO, and moved his listeners nearly to violence.[14] Government troops moved into the area, and Agüero took refuge with about a thousand of his followers and only a limited number of weapons in the Gran Hotel of Managua. There they made captives of about 100 hotel guests, mostly North Americans, and shot it out with government troops for about 24 hours. Four guardsmen and 60 of Agüero's followers were killed. Agüero was finally captured, but stubbornly refused to withdraw from the election which he lost by about 2 to 1. The PCN candidate received only a handful of votes. The UNO received the customary one-third of the congressional seats (6 Senate and 18 deputies), which were divided among the participating parties. By losing the presidency, Agüero became a senator. Pedro Chamorro became the scapegoat for the Managua riots, and was jailed. Both the OAS Human Rights Commission and the Inter-American Press Society criticized Chamorro's imprisonment.

5. CONCLUSION

It would be misleading to say that Nicaragua's political parties do not perform functions in the national political system. The dominant PLN performs electoral, communications, and patronage functions. The PLI, PCT, and new PSC participate during elections, and seek to broaden their popular base at the expense of the Somozas. Although the UNO is an unstable, proto-liberation movement with little prospects for endurance, it has permitted several smaller parties to gain entrance to the national congress in spite of the two-thirds/one-third rule governing the allocation of seats. Elections are held, even if the results are not in doubt, the voting often fraudulent, and the circumstances surrounding the campaigns often violent and irresponsible. Since 1947 the Somoza's, whose control over Nicaragua has been as total as that in any country, have viewed elections as an important instrument for consolidating their control, and perhaps as a dangerous ritual to suppress. Elections stimulate parties to persist despite their lack of electoral success, legislative influence, or political power. The constrained parties may provide a source of opposition and political institutions that can eventually survive the regime itself.

While it is more difficult to be categorical about the Somozas than about other dictatorships, certain facts are unchallengeable. Their rule has been dynastic, authoritarian, dictatorial, and often strong-armed. All welfare springs from the Somozas, who have benefited enormously from their position amassing a fantastic personal wealth. By and large their rule has not been harsh, and the country has experienced steady economic growth in the past decade. Most of the prosperity has not filtered down to the lower classes, but some has. The Somozas are more than a regime in Nicaragua, they are a way of life. The irresponsibility of the traditional opposition has as much as anything reinforced their rule, since the alternatives to the Somozas seem chaotic. While dissatisfaction seems to be increasing, the regime is maintained by a powerful, professional National Guard, and the prospects for mass uprisings are dim. Nicaragua's party politics may not be worthy of emulation, but it is nonetheless relevant in evaluating the overall national political processes.

II. MEXICO: A COMPETITIVE SINGLE-PARTY DOMINANT SYSTEM

Mexico's one-party system is highly developed organizationally. It permits representational competition within the party's structures, and allows extensive personal liberties within the broader political system. One political party—the *Partido Revolucionario Institucional* (PRI), Institutional Revolutionary party—totally dominates national political life although other parties are permitted to organize and compete electorally. Governmental decision-making hierarchies are rather isolated from popular sanctions with the elites tending to be self-perpetuating. There is an element of arbitrariness in public policy and legal processes which is characteristically Mexican, yet the system has worked for more than forty years and provided rewarding economic, social, and cultural results. More than in any other single-party dominant system, Mexican politics and government is highly institutionalized, and consensus for it is broadly based within the national political culture. The system warrants close scrutiny, for it tends to challenge and refute many common cliches of one-party rule, and may, in fact, provide a useful model for other developing nations.

1. BACKGROUND TO CONTEMPORARY POLITICAL PARTIES

Mexico's contemporary political history begins with its profoundly revolutionary period 1910 to 1920. During this decade Mexican politics was far from the institutionalized force it is today.

Stability was achieved only momentarily through the imposition of superior force. The only cohesive force within the country was "The Revolution," which was a powerful myth and in reality capable of justifying anything done in its name. The Mexican Revolution was truly national, not merely a change in political regimes. It had profound social, economic, class, political, and even religious themes, and provided a national catharsis as Mexico looked inward to the task of finding itself as a nation. The Indian gained an identity within the national culture, as did the *mestizo*. Land, the principal access to personal wealth and security, gained ideological status. The concept of popular if not representative or democratic government was an impetus for new political-governmental forms. Mexico is one of the few nations in the world to have experienced a full, modern revolution. It must be remembered that the Mexican Revolution preceded the Bolshevik Revolution by almost a decade, and in some respects was as comprehensive as the latter if not as well conceived or ideologically articulated.[15]

It is relevant to compare the one-party politics that emerged in Mexico following its revolution with the context of one-party politics in many of the recently independent African and Asian nations. By 1910, Mexico had been an independent nation for the better part of a century, and had succeeded in throwing out the Spanish and the French, and fighting a gallant, if unsuccessful, war against the United States. The 1910 Revolution was an internal social revolution, not directed against a colonial power or a different race. In Mexico there was no group of well-educated, foreign-trained leaders united by a common hatred of the colonial oppressors. The Revolution by and large was not in the hands of cosmopolitan, sophisticated leaders or a group that could form an "independence" party following the violence. Mexico's revolution was led by outlaws, army bosses, opportunists, and regional *caudillos* whose primary purpose was to crush the opposition and establish their own power. As the basis of the revolution expanded, a few more sophisticated, altruistic leaders emerged, but their intellectual veneer was mostly extraneous to the hard tasks of consolidation. Power during the revolutionary period resided in the hands of those who could seize and retain it, and it is out of this real politique that a new regime had to be forged. The fact that the events of the revolution persisted for nearly a decade is indicative of the vengeance, brutality, and power struggle involved in the process. Unlike the more recently independent countries, then, there were neither structures nor functions for political parties in the context of the

Mexican Revolution. It is not surprising that political parties were not a significant factor during the Mexican revolutionary period.

The evolution of the present PRI in its complex, sophisticated, institutional structure was slow and arduous.[16] The period from 1920 to 1928 was one of gradual consolidation of the primary political forces in Mexico, followed in 1929 by the establishment of the first major dominant political party, the *Partido Nacional Revolucionario* (PNR), which was a percursor to the PRI. The PNR was replaced in 1937 by the *Partido de la Revolución Mexicana* (PRM), which lasted until 1945. In 1945 the present PRI was established. In each phase of political institutionalization the processes were largely peaceful. Increasingly the parties aimed toward institutionalizing the successes of the Revolution. A brief summary of the evolution of the PRI reveals this process of consolidation and institutionalization very clearly.

By 1920 three strong political leaders had emerged from the revolutionary struggle. These men—Adolfo de la Huerta, Alvaro Obregón, and Plutarco Elías Calles—rose after the regime of Venustiano Carranza who in 1917 had become the effective head of state. Carranza was maintained in office by his control over the military *jefes*, without whose support his regime could not survive. During this formative period in Mexican politics, civilian groups sometimes known as parties began to emerge. Although some of the groups had loose affiliations with labor or agrarian leaders, most derived their following purely from the charisma of the leader around whom the group emerged. While power clearly rested in the military, some military leaders increasingly saw the advantage a civilian veneer lent their rule. Robert Scott explains the emergence of embryonic party structures on two grounds: parties provided a useful means of establishing civilian support and increasing the respectability of military regimes, while on the other hand the groups could play a limited role in balancing power between competing military elites.[17] The dominant characteristic of these nascent groups was the marginality of their political relevance.

Carranza had the fortune to preside over the visionary Constitutional Convention of 1917 in Querétaro, and formed a Constitutionalist party to expand his control beyond military support. He also enriched himself at the expense of the national treasury, and was ultimately overthrown by Obregón, Calles, and de la Huerta who became known as the "Triumvirate of Agua Prieta. De la Huerta as acting "president" declared the Carranza party illegal, and controlled the 1920 elections so as to permit Obregón's Liberal

Constitutionalist party to win. After taking office, Obregón withdrew support from the party and it collapsed. Two new parties emerged to take its place: the *Partido Nacional Laborista* (PNL), National Labor party, and *Partido Nacional Cooperatista* (PNC), National Cooperatist party, based on the agricultural cooperative movement. Both "parties" courted Obregón's favor since he was the basis of power, not vice-versa. For a while it appeared that the PNC was gaining dominance when Obregón refused to let the PNL participate in a local election in Mexico City. However, the PNC made the error of supporting de la Huerta in an abortive attempt to overthrow Obregón, and afterwards lost favor with Obregón. After breaking the de la Huerta revolt, Obregón named his successor—Calles—in the 1924 elections. The PNL was the only legal party at that time, but Obregón became increasingly concerned about the consolidation of power by its leader (Morones) in the latter months of his presidency. He thereupon turned toward another group, the *Partido Nacional Agrista* (PNA), Agrarian National party, that had supported him against de la Huerta. When Calles assumed power he continued to favor the PNA as had Obregón, but soon broadened his base by reinstating the PNL and making Morones a cabinet minister in a gesture calculated to diminish Obregón's continuing influence. Calles recognized that he could never rely on agrarian support for it was firmly controlled by his predecessor, and an arrangement with labor proved mutually advantageous.

Obregón remained influential, and an impending clash over the 1928 presidential election threatened to reinstate the revolutionary violence or force one of the two men to withdraw. Fate provided a strange twist to the conflict. Calles bowed to Obregón, and proposed a constitutional amendment to permit Obregón a second presidential election. The revolutionary cry of "no-re-election" made Obregón's action unpopular. Morones particularly was disinclined to see Obregón return, but reluctantly supported his re-election. Before assuming office, Obregón was assassinated by a religious fanatic, leaving Calles with only a short period in office in which to resolve the crisis.

Calles could not bring himself to impose arbitrarily his own rule on the nation for a second term without an election.[18] The constitutional amendment passed for Obregón had required one full term between elections. Calles persuaded the military and local bosses to accept a provisional president, a puppet whom he could manipulate. His choice, a civilian political boss from the state of

Tamaulipas named Emilio Portes Gil, was approved by the National Congress as provisional president. To avoid future problems Calles took steps to consolidate his control over the regime by calling, in his last congressional message, for the formation of a "revolutionary" party encompassing all the dissident elements in the nation. In 1929 at the historic city of Querétaro the new party, the PNR, was officially proclaimed.

The PNR was a loose affiliation of local bosses and machines, various agrarian, labor, and other interest groups, and the ever present military including still powerful *caudillos* from such states as Sonora, Michoacán, San Luis Potosí, Puebla, Veracruz, and other prominent areas of Mexico. The military viewed the formation of the PNR as an instrumentally prudent strategy to consolidate national control rather than as a challenge to their de facto power. Calles cajoled and bribed interest groups to join, including the previously hostile Agrarian Party. Even by 1929 the Mexicans had demonstrated their instinctive capacity to organize and multiply their organizations. Only Morones and his Labor party remained outside the PNR. In the long-run the decision proved to be an almost fatal error, for other labor groups flocked to the PNR and received favorable governmental treatment.

Calles' strategies worked well. He continued to dominate national politics through the PNR, sanctioning the selection of state governors and formulating national policy. The party prospered from its strong position and dispensed patronage. Government workers and aspiring businessmen contributed regularly and generously to the party. Financial security strengthened party institutions, making them less dependent on governmental concessions. By 1932 what had been established as a loose confederation of national interests was increasingly consolidated and centralized into an elaborate network of party structures and affiliated organizations. Calles reinvoked the "no-re-election" provision of the constitution, for he had found an effective way to perpetuate his own influence. Through three puppet presidents from 1928 to 1934 Calles maintained his influence despite a growing relationship between the presidency, the bureaucracy, and the party hierarchy. Increasingly as Calles aged and prospered he grew more conservative. Reform programs virtually ceased outside the area of education. Against a backdrop of growing popular unrest the PNR met in 1934 to select a new presidential candidate. The candidate was Lázaro Cárdenas, personally approved by Calles. The convention also adopted a six-year plan as a sop to popular unrest, an idea rather self-consciously modeled after the Soviet practice. Cárdenas was highly regarded as a competent civil servant and former army officer.

Cárdenas' presidency from 1934 to 1940 had lasting effects on Mexico and its party politics. Cárdenas was by any standard a self-made man, having risen from very humble origins. He promptly challenged the Calles interests as he closed their profitable casinos, dismissed most of Calles' ministers, and eventually decided to reconstitute the PNR itself. Cárdenas systematically removed *Callista* supporters from the party hierarchy by intimidation and bribes. Former president Portes Gil, who had headed the party, "retired" to private life. Cárdenas eventually challenged Calles himself and won. Calles was hustled by plane to southern California where he lived until the conclusion of Cárdenas' term. Cárdenas had quickly, decisively consolidated his power and influence over Mexican governmental and political institutions.

Without debating the accomplishments of the Cárdenas regime, it is a fact that substantial change occurred. Cárdenas promoted land reform, expanded educational opportunities, nationalized the petroleum and railway interests, established a vast system of social security, encouraged the growth of labor unions, and designed programs to promote national economic growth. He incurred the wrath of many conservative Mexicans and North American observers who resented the nationalization. He broadened the membership of the PNR to include union members and *campesinos*. By 1936 more than 1 million Mexicans were considered active members in the PNR.

One segment of Mexican society on which Cárdenas hoped to build his support was labor.[19] He encouraged a leftist intellectual, Lombardo Toledano, formerly a leader in the Morones labor organization who had defected upon the latter's fall from favor, to form the *Confederación General de Obreros y Campesinos Mexicanos* (CGOCM), the Mexican Peasant and Worker's General Confederation. Encouraged by Cárdenas' support and favorable national legislation, Lombardo Toledano used the CGOCM as a nucleus for an even broader organization, the *Confederación de Trabajadores Mexicanos* (CTM), Mexican Labor Confederation, which included all kinds of workers. With official favor the CTM flourished from its inception and soon became the largest and strongest Mexican labor organization. To offset Toledano's growing influence, Cárdenas created within the PNR statewide peasant leagues coordinated by the minister of education and loosely united into the *Confederación Nacional de Campesinos* (CNC), Farmers National

Confederation. Political divisions reflecting European conflicts of the late 1930s alienated many Mexican Labor leaders from communist supporters, and created severe conflicts within the PNR over the issue of cooperation with communist groups. After a brief and probably insincere attempt at a popular front, which could never have succeeded because of military opposition, Cárdenas in late 1937 called for the dissolution of the PNR and the creation of a new "revolutionary" party.

The new organization was the PRM, a streamlined structure reflecting the basic areas of support for the Cárdenas regime: agriculture, labor, the military, and a popular sector. Nominations became a function of state and local party organizations. Each sector received a number of nominees roughly equal to its strength in the district. By officially including the military as a sector of the party, Cárdenas attempted to minimize the possibility of military intervention. Previously established interest groups formed the nuclei for each of the four sectors of the party. Besides the military, the CNC provided a focus for agrarian interests while Lombardo Toledano's CTM gave focus to the labor sector. A new popular sector was created as a catch-all to absorb federal employee unions and other groups that did not affiliate to existing farm and labor sectors. The popular sector gave a direct outlet to the emerging middle sectors, whose leaders were becoming disproportionately influential because of their superior resources and concentration in the capital. The military sector was unpopular, and with the agreement of most military leaders was dissolved three years later in 1940. Its participants fell into the popular sector, and continued to exert both direct and latent influence on the government and party. Cárdenas wisely avoided any direct conflict with the military, facilitating the retirement of Generals as affluent members of Mexican society.

The PRM consolidated and centralized political control in Mexico, although governmental decision-making remained essentially a presidential perrogative. Party hierarchy helped control and balance the remaining power of local political chiefs who periodically circumvented established institutions in favor of more direct action. The party prospered with contributions flowing freely from its expanded base of government workers, labor union members, and other sources. While the new party structure gradually absorbed the organizational bases of local power from the bosses, the government increasingly limited their sources of revenue and taxation. The PRM was so effective in centralizing political power that pressures for relaxation of national control engendered a reform movement in the 1940s. In 1946 these pressures were expressed in a third renovation of the national party structure and name, this time producing the current PRI.

The PRI structure retained the three basic party sectors but placed all electoral and political activities in the hands of central party organs. The nomination process was revised, allowing free nominations for all but the presidency through direct primaries instead of the sector allocations. The presidential candidate was theoretically selected by the convention, but actually it continued to be an informal process organized by the existing president, past presidents, and party hierarchies. Lombardo Toledano feared reform would weaken his position specifically, and the position of labor generally. Labor was concentrated geographically and could not compete effectively in primaries. He resigned from the PRI and attempted to form his own political party.

Local selection of candidates still did not encourage local control or competitive selection, since the process was tightly controlled by the local party machinery and, when necessary, by the central party. Recently the PRI has allowed greater participation in the nomination processes by permitting local groups to select alternate slates of candidates to the national party councils. The national party reduces the alternatives to two, which are finally contested in local conventions. This practice was started in Baja California in 1959, and quickly spread to other areas incurring strong opposition from some national leaders.

Today the PRI is a vast network of political communication, patronage, and recruitment, so closely linked with government that they are inseparable. It is true that all sectors in the party do not find the cohabitation comfortable, but there are strong incentives—electoral, legal, and political—for remaining inside the establishment. From weak, disorganized beginnings, the Mexicans have developed a party system within a party, a grand coalitional institution reinforced by patronage, controlled by the tremendous power, prestige, and bureaucracy of the presidency, yet sensitive to popular dissatisfactions and flexible to permit considerable mobility within the hierarchy of the party. For these reasons Mexico's party system is both effective and politically developed.

2. ELECTORAL SYSTEM AND PARTY ARENA

Like Venezuela, Brazil, and Argentina, Mexico is a federal republic. Like its sister republics, Mexico's federalism is a carefully limited and controlled one.[20] The states enjoy little fiscal and financial autonomy. There are 29 states, two territories, and a federal district (the city of Mexico). Each state has two senators, and the two territories one senator each. In 1958 there were 162 districts represented in the lower House that are divided by population. Mexico is the only nation in Latin America to employ an electoral system similar to the United States: single-member districts, majority type.

In 1964 Mexico adopted several amendments to Article 54 of the Constitution to establish a skew in the representational system. This skew was designed to give added representation to minority parties in the national parliament. A legally recognized party is entitled to up to 20 additional seats in the legislature, including those won by conventional means, if it receives more than 2.5 percent of the popular vote. Five seats are awarded for the first 2.5 percent of the vote, and an additional seat for each .5 percent received. Under this plan the lower chamber must vary in size according to minor party voting. In 1958 before the skew was enacted there were 162 members of the lower House. In 1961 there were 172, in 1964, 175, and in 1967, 212 members. Although the skew modifies the basic system, its actual effects are slight, as seen in Table 5-2. It is designed to accomplish two goals: to subdue the image of one party dominance which the PRI finds increasingly embarrassing to defend both internally and externally, and to admit minor parties into the congressional arena without endangering the PRI's control. The party wishes to silence critics while avoiding martyrs. Since a maximum of 20 additional seats are possible for any single party, no party is likely to extend its influence at the expense of the PRI. By requiring a minimum of 2.5 percent for eligibility, the Mexicans have excluded the smallest parties whose

TABLE 5-2. COMPARISON OF PARTY REPRESENTATION IN
MEXICAN CONGRESS, 1958–1970

	DEPUTIES					SENATE				
	1958	1961	1964	1967	1970	1958	1961	1964	1967	1970
PRI	153	172	175	177	178	60	60	60	60	60
PAN	6*	5	20	20†	20	0	0	0	0	0
PPS	1	1	10	10	10	0	0	0	0	0
PARM	1	0	5	5	5	0	0	0	0	0
PNM	1	0	0	0	0	0	0	0	0	0

* Only 4 took their seats.
† One seat unopposed by PRI, "given" to PAN.

presence would only encourage coalitions and be a nuisance to the regime.

There is a lesson about electoral systems in the Mexican experience: they are useful to control party representation not only in competitive systems but when there is a clear party monopoly.[21] Were Mexico to adopt proportional representation, given present voting patterns, the PRI would still receive the same overwhelming number of seats. Under the present system it is almost futile to try to generate support for a new party since significant congressional representation under the Mexican electoral laws is all but impossible. The financial burden assumed by a potential party would be enormous. In Mexico as in one-party state systems in the United States, meaningful political dialogue occurs with the nomination rather than the election. Without popular primaries basic political decisions are removed in Mexico from the customary electoral context.

3. POLITICAL PARTIES IN CONTEMPORARY MEXICO

Besides the PRI there are a number of relatively inconsequential political parties in Mexico whose political functions do not duplicate those of the PRI except for limited periods during national elections. The most significant of the minor parties include: *Partido de Acción Nacional* (PAN), National Action party, *Partido Popular Socialista* (PPS), Socialist Popular party, *Partido Auténtico de la Revolución Mexicana* (PARM), Authentic Party of the Mexican Revolution, and the *Partido Nacionalista Mexicana* (PNM), Mexican Nationalist party.

Mexican statutes define political parties as "associations for electoral purposes and political orientation by law made up only of Mexican citizens in full exercise of their civil rights . . . ." The secretary of *Gobernación* has considerable latitude in administrating the regulatory statutes, including the power of recognition. To gain recognition a party must recruit 75,000 members nationally, with a minimum of 2,500 in each of no less than two-thirds of the states. Parties are also required to hold state conventions to select delegates for a national convention. A program of principles, an official name, and a party symbol must be notarized and registered.

While the regulations are nominal, they work against labor or proletarian based parties whose following is geographically concentrated. The Mexican Communist party has been unable to receive recognition despite its sizeable following, on the technicality of distribution. In contrast, the PARM, an instrument for disenchanted revolutionaries within the PRI, obtained recognition and maintained it under questionable conditions. An unregistered party's candidates may receive write-in votes, but less than 10 thousand out of 7.5 million were cast in 1958.

4. CONTEMPORARY MEXICAN POLITICAL PARTIES

Partido Revolucionario Institucional. The PRI is often described as a functional party; that is, one whose organs are conceived on economic-occupational bases. In some respects the PRI is a network of interest groups bound together by an elaborate system of administrative structures, electoral and patronage systems, and mutual ideological-value perspectives.[22] Although the PRI is an impressively centralized organization, there are elements of diversity within it. Certain of its component sectors enjoy a degree of autonomy and coexistence which the party elite can influence but not destroy.

The point has been made that political functions in more "developed" societies tend to be performed by more specialized structures and processes, while political structures in "developing" societies are characteristically multi-functional, less specialized. If one accepts this proposition, then Mexico must be considered a developing society for its party structure is multi-functional. The party organizes elections, recruits leaders into national elites, helps administer governmental programs by short-circuiting the bureaucracy, ameliorates potential and existing interest group conflicts through behind-the-scenes processes, and provides and communicates basic symbols for national identification and mobilization. The PRI also lubricates the legal system by providing useful Mexicans (defined by fairly objective economic standards) with more direct access to courts and favorable administrative decisions. Contained within the PRI is an elaborate system of political communication which is flexible, pragmatic, and successful in meeting political demands placed upon the system. Apart from the ambiguous concept of democracy, it is possible to see the PRI as a competitive system within a party since major interests are articulated and aggregated internally. There are interests outside the party, but they are of relatively little national importance.

Entrance into the PRI for most Mexicans is through the component sectors. The most powerful and largest sector is the CNOP, or National Confederation of Popular Organizations. With its ten branches it supplies a remarkable percentage of contemporary Mexican leaders. The second sector in size is the farm sector, the CNC, while the CTM or Mexican Workers Confederation is third in size.

With the multiplicity of party organizations, many PRI leaders simultaneously hold party, public, and organization offices at local, state, and federal levels. The overlapping of leadership roles, where an individual wears several "hats," has a cohesive influence on otherwise competitive elites. This overlapping of individual roles helps promote multiple identifications by elite members, and encourages them to seek upward mobility to greater national power. The system thereby builds, in conformity, incentives that tend to overcome particularism in favor of national identifications.

An exhaustive review of PRI organizational structure is beyond the scope of our analysis.[23] While oversimplified, it is essentially true that the three sectors participate in selecting the regional executive committees for the geographical subdivisions (states, territories, and the federal district) which in turn select the municipal and district committees. Delegates to the national convention theoretically select the grand commission comprised of 30 members, 10 from each sector, and the president and secretary-general of the central executive committee. Additional members of the central executive committee are selected by the national sector organizations. The executive committee is the most politically significant organ of the PRI because of its superior leadership resources and formal powers. It represents a de facto group of powerful Mexican leaders from major segments of national life who have broad group bases for their political influence. The executive committee is the primary party decision-making body, and a potent adjunct to presidential power. It responds to political communication from the geographic, national, and functional groupings in the nation, as well as directing the daily activities such as patronage, discipline, and recruitment of members and leaders. It controls nominations, and dispenses rewards for party loyalty. The actual decision-making processes of the executive committee are veiled from outside scrutiny. The executive committee, like the PRI generally, is an accurate reflection of real power in Mexico, if not the ultimate source of it.

Perhaps the most elusive aspect of PRI politics is the presidential nominating process. Nomination is tantamount to election. Basically the choice is made under the leadership of the current president, who consults with other party and governmental leaders. These usually include past presidents, who have strong followings within the PRI, and leaders from the party sectors and local communities. Just how many or who is involved varies from one instance to another as does the influence of specific individuals. The president reaches the zenith of his personal influence and power toward the end of his term, having had most of six years to consolidate his control and disperse patronage. He initiates the nomination process by sounding out relevant leaders on possible choices. By the time the nomination is near the number of "realistic possibilities," it is narrowed by a natural process of recruitment whereby some individuals simply are more conspicuous than others. Some traditions govern the process. Presumably an effort is made to alternate between a liberal and moderate candidate. After the very liberal Cárdenas, the more conservative Camacho was selected. Conservative Cortines was subsequently followed by liberal López Mateos and then the more moderate Gustavo Díaz Ordaz. Presumably, if the tradition holds, the new Mexican president, Luis Echeverría (1970–1976), will be more liberal. Another tradition is to try to reach a consensus among the top leaders on the nominee. He must be somehow acceptable to most of the elite; not an easy prerequisite in any national political system. It is not uncommon for the nominee to have held cabinet level appointment under the outgoing presidency, often as the minister of *Gobernación* since its responsibilities are more politically oriented than most ministeries.[24] The selection process since 1936 has produced by and large an able group of presidents. However constrained the nomination process may have been, it is difficult to imagine a more impressive list of presidential nominees.

We have suggested that the PRI's organizational structure has been a significant instrument to political and governmental stability in Mexico, and that it has emerged spontaneously as a consequence of trying to solve problems of national integration. It is often asked whether this "natural organism" is sufficiently flexible and adaptive to meet the challenges of the rapid change in Mexico, or whether its component sectors are likely to break apart and become the nuclei for a proliferated party system. We have already identified strong legal, political, and financial controls on the system which tend to argue against a factionalization of the PRI. It should also be underscored that the PRI leadership has proved very willing to heal party ruptures and readmit dissident elements when they break away. Moreover, at least two of the sectors are so closely tied to the fate of the PRI that disaffection seems unlikely. The CNOP or popular sector is wholly a creation of the PRI, while the CNC has traditionally been close to the leadership of PRI. The problems of maintaining patronage and supporting an organization of dissident peasants are so overwhelming as to virtually preclude the possibility. Only the labor sector seems capable of secession. But the possibility is at least as obvious to PRI officials as it is to us, and unquestionably they take all necessary precautions to prevent a split. The unfruitful attempt by Toledo Lombardo to break away from PRI to form his own party is a grim reminder to potential labor dissidents. Based on the most complete evidence available, it would seem that any prediction of a split in the PRI would be premature at best, and probably inaccurate for the foreseeable future.

Partido de Acción Nacional. PAN is as close to being an opposition party as exists in Mexico. Yet neither its popular vote nor its congressional representation have reached more than the token stage.

PAN emerged in 1939 as a conservative group of Mexican businessmen united in their hatred of Cárdenas and his programs and committed to the leadership of Manual Gómez Morín, an outspoken antagonist of Cárdenas. PAN's early efforts failed to attract a sizeable following or unify conservative elements in Mexico. It supported other party candidates in the presidential elections of 1940 and 1946. In 1952 it ran its own candidate, Efraín Gonzáles Luna, and in 1958 made a rather unfortunate choice, Luis H. Alvárez. Neither man waged what could be described as a competent campaign against the PRI.

PAN has generally been regarded in Mexico as a refuge for the "outs"; that is, those relatively few interests who were not absorbed in the PRI establishment.[25] These included ecclesiastical interests and certain business and professional leaders who failed for personal, religious, or political reasons to identify with PRI. PAN tried to broaden its political base by affiliating with the proto-Fascist *sinarquista* group in the 1950s but with little success. It sought affiliations of dissident labor unions scattered in provincial areas (particularly Monterrey), but most unions of importance were eventually won back to PRI. By 1958 the anti-intellectual *sinarquistas* disaffected, leaving PAN at the mercy of the flamboyant tactics of its presidential candidate, Luis Alvárez. In 1959 the party selected Lic. José Gonzales Torres as the leader to eventually run against Díaz Ordaz in the 1964 election. Gonzales had obvious connections with Catholic organizations, and appeared to be return-ing PAN to the rarefied opposition position it had occupied prior to 1952. In spite of colorless leadership, PAN fared reasonably well in 1964, and encouraged once again tried to broaden its popular base by appealing to an alienated type middle-class voter who might be won away from PRI. Off-year Congressional elections in 1967 indicated this might be a fruitful policy as PAN increased its vote in the federal district and won two mayoralities. In 1970 PAN won 14 percent of the vote.

The strategic and tactical problems facing PAN are enormous. The most obvious is the single-member district majority electoral system, which requires PAN to win a clear majority of votes before receiving any representation. Political realities being what they are in Mexico, this is extremely difficult for PAN to do. The cost of national campaigns is high and burdensome for the handful of wealthy supporters. It is not very rational to contribute to PAN *instead* of PRI if one must rely on government for business or tax concessions. It is an open secret in Mexico that PAN receives contri-butions from sources prompted by official PRI leadership, which indicates a rather open-minded attitude thus far by PRI toward its "competitor."[26] PRI would rather have PAN continue in its present condition than exterminate it, for it provides both a useful foil and harmless competition to enhance the "democratic" appear-ance of the system. It siphons off a harmless minority of voters while providing a generally unattractive alternative to PRI. Perhaps the greatest obstacle for PAN has been finding an issue on which to attack the PRI. Clericalism in Mexico is a dead issue since the revolution, as it is in many other Latin American nations today. Culturally schizophrenic, Mexico is at the same time both a highly religious and anticlerical nation. The most promising avenue for electoral success for PAN would seem to be capturing the alienated lower-middle sector Mexican whose position is eroded by inflation or increasing well-being of the traditional lower classes, and who fails to see a PRI sector as an avenue for solving his socioeconomic dilemma.

Partido Nacionalista de Mexico. The PNM is no longer legally a party since it failed in 1964 to receive the minimum vote neces-sary to maintain its status. In 1952 and 1958 it supported official PRI presidential candidates. Technically Mexico's oldest existing party, the PNM espoused conservative, pro-clerical ideas from its inception in 1927. However, it never opposed the revolution or the government, and was not only tolerated by the regime but allegedly subsidized by it. Today the party is discredited, without a following, and in a state of advanced decay.

Partido Auténtico de la Revolución Mexicana. PARM is also dissolving but for reasons different than those in the case of PNM. PARM was instituted under the Alemán regime (1946–1952) by older members of the 1910 revolutionary generation. Alemán's regime was plagued by indiscretions, corruption, and scandals. Many of his supporters became wealthy at the public expense. PARM sought a return to "true revolutionary aims," and enlisted popular leaders including Senator Jacinto Treviño, and General Juan Barragán. The subsequent administrations of Cortines and López Mateos remedied the abuses of Alemán's presidency, and the justification of PARM evaporated. Senator Treviño was appointed governor of the state of Coahuila, and Raul Madero received a high administrative appointment in the government. PARM barely received the minimum vote in 1967's election and is likely to dissolve within the near future.

Partido Popular Socialista. The PPS was formed by labor leader Vicente Lombardo Toledano following his dispute with President Alemán in 1947 over the formation of the PRI to replace the PRM. The PPS has steadily declined in importance since its inception. Basic support for the PPS has come from Lombardo's labor movement, alienated unions, intellectuals and academics of liberal or Marxist persuasion, artists, some Communists and other segments of the discontented Mexican left-wing.[27] Two major unions—the Rail and Petroleum Workers—affiliated with the PPS but later returned to the PRI. The issue of establishing a relationship with Mexican Communists has constantly plagued the party's leadership and divided the party. Lombardo attempted unsuccessfully to return the PPS to the PRI in 1954. The PRI refused because of opposition by some PRI leaders to alleged Communist influences in the PPS. Many PRI leaders feared Lombardo's capacity to rebuild his following and perhaps challenge the party's leadership. Lombardo's own leadership in the PPS has periodically been challenged, further weakening the fragile party organization. In 1958 and 1964 the PPS openly endorsed the PRI presidential candidate to avoid the financial burden of a hopeless campaign. The PPS has received party delegates under the PR skew and retains its legal status but with diminishing electoral returns or encouragement from the PRI.

Several other small parties exist without legal recognition. The Mexican Communist party is the most significant. It has not been legally recognized due to failure in meeting the minimum registration requirements. It is factionalized on personal, ideological, and organizational fronts, and has a problem in trying to appear more revolutionary than the PRI. It has external financial support from abroad for its extensive publications.

Mexico's minor political parties are little more than a footnote to the reality of PRI's dominant position. Although a refuge for discontents, purged, and amateur politicians, the minor parties provide no serious electoral challenge or convincing alternative to the PRI regime. They periodically permit a weak glow of electoral competition, and are protected by the government for this purpose.

5. Coalitions: The Case of the Movimiento de Liberación Nacional

Coalitions are uncharacteristic of single-party dominant political systems, but occasionally they occur. To promote more effective propaganda, the opposition parties in Nicaragua formed the U.N.O. and challenged the Somozas. Several minor political parties in Mexico have entered into "working arrangements" with the PRI to briefly enhance their financial or representational advantages. A genuine opposition coalition had been unknown until the recent evolution of the MLN.[28] The MLN emerged in 1961 as a result of pro-Castro excitement in Mexico, and held a "National Assembly for National Sovereignty, Economic Emancipation, and Peace." Its membership came from the Communist party, the Popular Socialist party, the small *Partido de Obreros y Campesinos Mexicanos* (POCM), Mexican Farmers and Workers Party, and other small groups. Only the PPS was officially recognized as a party. The MLN drew encouragement from former president Lázaro Cárdenas, although his role in the organization was unclear. The MLN called for "full implementation of the Mexican Constitution," which meant broader land distribution and nationalization, and "international solidarity for peace against U.S. imperialism." Lombardo soon withdrew the PPS as a result of personal quarrels with MLN leaders, which further split PPS elites. Cárdenas rapidly cooled to the MLN, withdrawing active support from the movement. From the coalition a political party was formed, *Frente Electoral del Peublo* (FEP), but it failed to obtain official registration. Lombardo's PPS supported PRI's Díaz Ordaz in the 1964 election and won enough votes under the new PR skew to receive ten seats in the legislature. It is alleged that the government "gave" Lombardo the necessary votes to receive 10 seats in exchange for his support of the PRI candidate and withdrawal from the MLN. Whatever the reason, the PPS gained a momentary advantage, while the MLN again demonstrated the difficulty of challenging the PRI from a left-of-center position.

6. VOTING AND CAMPAIGNS

Voting trends in Mexico generally fail to reveal major political variables in the country. The voting is heavily for the PRI, participation outside the capital is often extremely low, and electoral data is unreliable and often fraudulent. The latter is surprising, for the PRI with its political, organizational, financial, and legal-institutional advantages could win and honestly report the voting. Yet the regime still views voting as a currency for bargaining and frequently tampers with the results. With so many other aspects of its regime firmly institutionalized, it is surprising to find Mexico's leaders using fraudulent and unsophisticated means to further the ends of the government.

Voting is compulsory, but typically not enforced. Women were given the right to vote in 1952. National participation trends in recent presidential elections are given in Table 5-3.[29] The apparent decline in registration and increase in participation in 1958 are due to two factors. The eligible electorate expanded from 1952 to 1958 as women were enfranchised, but many were not registered by 1958. The increased voting in 1958 probably reflected the unusual popularity of the candidate, López Mateos.[30]

The Mexican presidential campaign is fervent, conducted by the PRI as though it were possible to lose. The PAN candidate is considered the opposition candidate since most minor parties have endorsed the PRI candidate. There are strong ritualistic functions to the performance of Mexican electoral rites. Affirmation and identification are prime reasons for voting.

Use of mass media is one of several ways in which the 1964 Mexican campaign resembled a North American one. In 1964 Gus-

TABLE 5-3. SUMMARY OF NATIONAL REGISTRATION AND PARTICIPATION IN RECENT PRESIDENTIAL ELECTIONS

Election	Percent eligible registered	Percent registered voting
1952	85	61
1958	67	84
1964	80	65
1970	88	64

tavo Díaz Ordaz campaigned intensively, shaking thousands of hands, enduring scores of Rotary banquets, and attending rallies, receptions, and conferences organized by the PRI's three sectors. His speeches tenuously outlined the general direction for Mexican policy in the next six-year administration. More importantly the campaign gave the president-elect an opportunity to renew personal political bonds that tie together the complex party machinery. For the electorate a presidential campaign is a kind of nationalistic communion in which the Mexicans renew their allegiance to the community and the PRI. It is an opportunity to view the new president, and him the varied electorate. Party structures are strengthened through this communal exercise and calcified organizations revitalized. Newly recruited and upwardly mobile leaders in the PRI are given an opportunity to demonstrate their political skills, and are appraised by the party elite for possible absorption into the "establishment." During the electoral period the Mexican party system gives the illusion of a representational process, and perhaps moves closer toward the reality.

The one-sidedness of presidential voting is revealed in Table 5-4. In all elections except 1952, the PRI candidate was endorsed by the PPS and PARM. The "dip" in Cortines' vote in 1952 is probably due to the loss of faith the PRI suffered following the Alemán administration. The relatively high vote for Camacho in 1940 is, likewise, a reflection of the relatively high popularity of President Cárdenas.

The PPS, PARM, and PNM are disinclined to oppose the PRI in a presidential race because of the enormous expense, difficulty, and futility of the task. By endorsing the PRI candidate they can remain within the mainstream of Mexican politics, and use the endorsement to barter with the regime for favors. More opposition would be a nuisance to the PRI, since a minor party candidate would receive attention beyond that justified by the number of

TABLE 5-4. SUMMARY OF PRESIDENTIAL BALLOTING IN MEXICO, 1940–1970

Election	Winner	PRI VOTE		PAN VOTE	
		No.	Percent	No.	Percent
1940	Camacho	2,176,600	93	151,100	6.5
1946	Alemán	1,786,900	80	443,400	18.7
1952	Ruiz Cortines	2,713,419	76	285,555	8.1
1958	López Mateos	6,769,754	90	705,303	9.5
1964	Díaz Ordaz	8,368,446	89	1,034,337	10.5
1970	Echeverría	11,850,000	85	1,950,000	14.1

TABLE 5-5. REGIONAL DIFFERENTIATION IN MEXICO

Core Area	West	North	South
Aguascalientes	Colima	Baja California	Campeche
Guanajuato	Jalisco	Chihuahua	Chiapas
Hidalgo	Nayarit	Coahuila	Guerrero
México	Zacatecas	Durango	Oaxaca
Michoacán		Nuevo León	Quintana Roo
Morelos		Sinaloa	Tabasco
Puebla		Tamaulipas	Yucatán
Querétaro			
San Luis Potosí			
Tlaxcala			
Veracruz			

votes he received. PAN's candidate receives disproportionate attention by the press and the PRI, but this is a calculated gesture to make PAN "the opposition."

Mexico is divided into four geographic regions plus the federal district that is somewhat larger than the capital city. Mexico City, with its 7½ million residents, is decidedly the political center of Mexico. The basic regions and the states that comprise them are identified in Table 5-5.[31] There are no significant regional voting patterns, largely because of the preponderance of the PRI in all regions. PAN often has polled more votes in the north than elsewhere, but its primary strength is not in the provincial regions but the federal district itself. Strong tendencies for affirmative voting outside the capital are reinforced by the organizational incapacity of PAN to challenge the PRI outside the D.F. To encourage PRI voting in regional areas the PRI does not hesitate to use all the resources of the government and the somewhat indentured business community. Outside the D.F. there is PAN support in the two secondary cities (Guadalajara and Monterrey), and to a limited extent in the states of Michoacán, Yucatán and the rapidly developing northern states. There is no correlation between centers of PAN voting and population density, location, or economic factors. The two most impressive national characteristics of PAN voting are its relatively even distribution among the states and its strength in the federal district.

The federal district is divided into 24 congressional districts of approximately equal size—100 thousand voters each. An analysis of the 1967 congressional elections indicates the uniform strength of the PAN vote in the capital. The government reported that

2,373,993 persons were registered in the federal district in 1967, and 71.4 percent of those eligible voted.[32] This is an unusually high participation for the off-year elections. Elsewhere in our survey of Latin American voting we have suggested that, in the capital city, the strongest political party tends to do the least well. This characteristic is also true for Mexico: PRI obtained only 64.7 percent of the D.F. vote, with 28.3 going to PAN, 4.6 to the PPS, and 2.4 to PARM. Nonetheless, PRI carried all the single-member districts except District 9 which it allowed PAN to win. Table 5–6 clearly indicates that competition in congressional races of each federal district was limited to PRI and PAN. In no district did the more liberal PPS become the challenging party. The vote for PAN remained surprisingly constant throughout all districts despite significant variations in the economic, educational, and class base

TABLE 5-6. Congressional Voting in Mexico, D.F., 1967

ELECTORAL DISTRICT	VOTING (in 10,000)		
	Registration	PRI	PAN	PPS
1	97	48	17	2
2	109	46	20	4
3	88	42	14	4
4	85	40	13	3
5	82	37	11	2
6	100	46	15	3
7	101	44	18	4
8	95	38	19	2
9	95	*	37	3
10	119	54	21	7
11	82	32	21	3
12	100	45	17	3
13	118	47	24	4
14	127	56	21	4
15	107	46	15	3
16	101	40	20	3
17	94	37	19	3
18	105	45	17	3
19	118	49	23	3
20	152	71	23	3
21	151	66	24	3
22	122	54	23	3
23	106	39	22	2
24	101	37	15	2

SOURCE: *Comision Local Electoral*, Mexico D. F.
* District 9 uncontested by PRI.

of the urban districts. With few exceptions, PAN and PRI vote fluctuated only on the basis of overall size of the total vote in each district. The PPS vote, small in total size, was also more evenly distributed throughout the districts than would be expected from its class-oriented appeals. In view of the even distribution of the 36 percent opposition vote in the D.F., one might conclude that the districts are drawn to dissipate minority party strength.

The relatively poor showing of PRI in the D.F. raises some interesting thoughts. It is significant that the more conservative PAN draws votes in the capital from PRI rather than the avowedly radical PPS that one might expect to capitalize on urban unrest, unemployment, slums, inflation, and poverty. Obviously this phenomena is encouraged by the PRI, which prefers an opposition party on the right rather than the left. However the even distribution of PAN voting gives PAN a claim to being a reasonably competitive party. The D.F. is the center for an emerging Mexican middle class whose real economic interests and ideological/cultural interests are not always consistent with those of the PRI. This emerging middle class tends to be more church and family oriented than the nation as a whole, while at the same time most seriously pressed by both inflation and the challenge of a mobile lower class. The commitment of the PRI to state-sanctioned entrepreneurship and mobility for the poor, are of little importance to the urban, middle-class voter whose higher education and economic well-being make him more politically aware and inclined to vote. As the general currents of change that he inevitably identifies with the PRI regime challenge his economic and cultural values, his only recourse is PAN. If this interpretation is correct, PAN's vote in D.F. should increase in coming elections as inflation, and the general size and level of prosperity of the middle class expand.

Participation in the interim congressional elections of 1967 was high. Nationally, 65 percent of the registered voted, while in the capital 71.4 percent voted. All contested seats in the lower chamber and the seven governorships were handily won by the PRI. PAN won one seat, and received the maximum of 19 additional seats under the PR skew. Ten seats were awarded to the PPS, and 5 to PARM. The latter continued to decline so that its minimum 75,000 registrants is now open to question. Table 5-7 reveals an almost perfect inverse correlation between PRI and PAN voting in the states. The states, arranged by population, indicate no ten-

TABLE 5-7. Congressional Vote by
Party in Mexico, 1967 (in percent)

	PRI	PAN
México, D. F.	65	28
Veracruz	94	3
Jalisco	83	14
México	85	11
Puebla	86	9
Guanajuato	80	14
Michoacán	79	16
Oaxaca	92	4
Guerrero	95	3
Chiapas	96	1
Hidalgo	97	3
Nueva León	80	17
Chihuahua	76	23
San Luis Potosí	93	6
Tamaulipas	92	5
Coahuila	92	7
Zacatecas	90	8
Yucatán	86	10
Baja California	76	22
Durango	87	11
Sinaloa	87	5
Tabasco	99	1
Sonora	78	21
Querétaro	92	6
Tlaxcala	96	3
Morelos	77	17
Campeche	99	1
Aguascalientes	84	15
Nayarit	90	4
Colima	90	9

SOURCE: Cómisión Electoral
NOTE: Arranged by states in descending
size.

dency by size for party voting. The range of votes for PAN was narrow (6 percent to 24 percent), with relatively few strong centers. Since PAN is clearly beyond the possibility of power, voting for this party would appear largely to be protest that functionally differs from the bulk of PRI voting. Its votes appear to be an amalgum of discontented or alienated voters from the small, wealthy, land-owning class, the militant church supporters, some small businessmen who fail to benefit from PRI affiliation, and provincial

as well as urban middle class who fear a challenge to their class
security.

6. THE PAN CHALLENGE IN SONORA: A CASE STUDY

The one unexpected outcome of the 1967 elections occurred
in the state of Sonora in the extreme northwest of the country.
Sonora borders the state of Arizona, and much of its population
looks north toward the United States rather than south toward
the D.F. PAN came very close to winning the gubernatorial election
in Sonora, and forced the PRI regime to take unprecedented measures to prevent PAN from taking control of the state. While the
causes for the PAN advance may be more local than national in
implications, the possibility that PAN could secure statewide power
raises critical questions for the Mexican political system as a whole.

PAN benefited in Sonora from a protest vote of massive proportions due to internal political conflicts within the PRI organizational
structure. The struggle produced normally unknown student protests and violence, and stimulated a voter turnout of almost 50
percent of the registered voters (350,000) instead of the normal
10 percent. The controversy arose from the imposition by the national PRI headquarters of an unpopular local leader—Faustino
Felix Serna—as candidate for governor. Serna, a wealthy rancher
and oligarch, was selected over several other PRI leaders of clearly
greater popular support. Normally the national party arranges
necessary local concessions to avoid such a conflict, but it failed
to do so in this case. At one point the demonstrations in the state
capital of Hermosillo and the cities of Santa Ana and Magdalena
were serious enough for federal troops' intervention.[33]

The PAN candidate, Gilberto Suárez Arvizu, quickly moved
to capture the local discontent by appealing to local sympathies
and criticizing "federal control." In a tense election atmosphere
the balloting appeared to be giving the gubernatorial election to
PAN. In Hermosillo the PAN candidate led by a comfortable margin. So did the PAN mayorality candidate in Hermosillo, and his
counterparts in Santa Ana and Magdalena. However, when the
final results were revealed, the PRI had "won" the gubernatorial
race with about 55 percent of the vote. Reports on voting indicate
that PAN polled heavily in the urban areas, where it also had ample
observers to check on the balloting, but very poorly in rural areas
where it had inadequate observers. The rural voting patterns may
have been affirmative; they also may have been fraudulent. In the

agricultural, coastal town of Hutabampo, the PRI received 14,193 votes out of a total of 15,127, with PAN receiving only 38 votes. PAN had no observers in Hutabampo. PAN alleged that voters in the small village of Imuris were summoned by the local bosses at gunpoint to vote. The results were 1,539 out of 2,125 votes for the PRI and only 280 for PAN. Voting returns were announced very slowly, and the events of Sonora that were publicized nationally resulted in considerable embarrassment for the regime.

Since it is likely that PRI could have survived the loss of the governorship of Sonora, it is important to speculate why it chose to retain the post at such a high political cost. Originally the problem might be traced to the bureaucracy and isolation of the national party hierarchy. However, a more fundamental problem was also involved. While the PRI permits opposition, and has even been known to encourage it in limited ways, the idea of an opposition party taking power was alien to most of the PRI elite. The danger of the precedent it might set, and the encouragement it might give to future opposition groups was the real threat. While there is more to Mexican representational government than party competition or alternation of power, the latter ideas have not yet gained acceptance within the ruling elite in either principle or practice.[34]

7. SUMMARY

Nowhere in Latin America and rarely in the world has a political party achieved and maintained the sophisticated integration of organizations, financial resources, leadership skill, ideological fervor, regularized channels for communication and recruitment, and overall political stability of the PRI in Mexico. The general calibre of leaders recruited to top echelons is remarkable, and their flexible pragmatism would be a lesson for other Latin American leaders. The nation has benefited from its political stability as has the PRI. The party is responsive to a large sector of Mexican interests despite its hierarchical centralization. Although party competition is minimal, the PAN has made limited progress toward mobilizing discontent and unrest as it arises. Perhaps the greatest barrier to the development of PAN is the capacity of the PRI to benefit from its errors, to bury grudges, and to find a correlation between party welfare and national development. Despite the lack of interparty competition, intraparty competition does occur and organizationally and representationally is formalized. Communication appears to move both upward and downward in the party structure, and the channels for self-advancement are relatively open. Perhaps the keystone of PRI success is its commitment to improving the welfare of a majority of Mexicans, and providing the nation with a tangible hope for an improving future. The party system like the nation itself is the product of a great deal of realistic thought, calculation, trial and error. Whatever limitations the party system may have for other cultures, it has demonstrated its relevancy to the Mexican experience.

III. EL SALVADOR: THE PROCESS OF POLITICAL DEVELOPMENT AND MODERNIZATION

Nicaragua's one-party system has been described as an extension of personal rule and Mexico's as an institutionalization of many national political interests. Salvador's one-party system is more newly developed than the other two, and perhaps best conceived as an amelioration of revolutionary pressures for change and an intransigent oligarchy that has historically enjoyed a monopoly on social, political, and economic power.

The smallest of the Latin American republics, Salvador is about the size of New Jersey with a population of 3.4 million. For all its compactness the nation is a microcosm of Latin American culture. Its population growth (3.6 percent annual increase) is high and places pressures on its economy. 56 percent of the citizens are under 19 years of age. Illiteracy is high by North American standards (about 50 percent) yet median for Latin America. Historically the nation has been dependent on the economic vagaries of a single crop—coffee. The Spanish concept of extended family characterizes the small oligarchy that administers the country much as a large estate. Eight percent of the people of Salvador derive 50 percent of the national income. Salvadoreans are a homogeneous *mestizo* race, urbanized (40 percent) despite the agrarian economic base. Communications are rather highly developed. No place in the nation is more than a day's travel away, and the nation is united by mass media and served by adequate sea, highway, and air connections with other nations.

Since 1950, Salvador has enjoyed economic and industrial growth and diversification. External capital has been attracted by its favorable tax policies, its ample supply of urban labor, its strategic location for distribution to the Central American Common

Market countries, and its good communications. Although coffee still dominates agriculture, diversification toward cotton, grains, dairying, and other activities has occurred.

1. SALVADOREAN POLITICS IN PERSPECTIVE

Salvador offers a good illustration of the concept of political development.[35] The process has been occurring since 1948, although a quickening of the pace can be detected in the past five years. The process has been interrupted by two successive governmental *coups,* which redirected rather than stopped the change. There is no certainty that the process will yield a competitive political party system, but there are indications that the ultimate style will be more competitive than the present one. What is significant is that the process of political development is reorienting and resocializing the political culture of Salvador, affecting both political behavior and decision-making of the national government. From the specific experience of Salvador some more general observations about political development can be made.

Concrete indicators from voting behavior illustrate the process of development. Voting data is not the only source of such indicators, nor even necessarily the most significant, but it does clearly establish certain trends that can be conclusively identified. Patterns of voting registration serve as an index of political *awareness.*[36] Registration in Salvador involves a rigid set of legal procedures in which all voters must participate. The right to vote is almost universal to all over 18 who inscribe at the registery of electors provided by the central council of elections. Registration normally is supervised by local municipal agents. The voter is issued a registration card within 60 days of an election that must be presented prior to voting. National voting lists are compiled from the registration roles. Registration is a primary, but crucial political act necessitating sufficient awareness by the individual of the electoral procedures and their significance to motivate his action. As an indicator of political *involvement* it is possible to view voting participation patterns in three recent elections, assuming that additional motivation beyond registration is required to vote.[37] For motivation a voter must somehow identify his own personal goals and perspectives with those of the government (should he vote for the government's *officialista* party) or the opposition (should he vote for one of the minor opposition parties). Neither registration nor voting in Salvador can be expected to reach as high an intensity as in a more politically developed nation, but the trends are the more important factor. Growth of minor political parties (there are 3 or 4 of significance) indicates *subsystem autonomy*, since each can be identified with a broadly based set of groups and distinctive types of leadership elites not previously encompassed within the national political community.[38] As an institutionalization of the development process one can perceive changes in the electoral machinery, the emergence of more permissive electoral laws, the growth of electoral impartiality, and the extension of party organizations on a permanent rather than an ad hoc basis. Also important is the more ambiguous but critical change of elite perceptions toward relief, reform, and an extension of the political community even at the risk of encouraging mass-supported political parties.[39]

Within the past two decades El Salvador has begun a fitful emergence from a traditionalistic, authoritarian regime toward a more politically developed, culturally differentiated political system with emerging subsystem autonomy. In the process changes have occurred within the elites, the party system, and political behavior. The development pattern has been conditioned by factors often characteristic of Latin American politics: local and regional differentiations, governmental centralization, and political dominance by the capital city where political socialization, communication, and integration are more intense. In El Salvador the stimulus for political development radiates with descending intensity from the capital of San Salvador to the provincial and rural areas.

2. Background to Contemporary Political Parties

Factors historically relevant to Salvadorean politics condition the development processes. One factor is the army, which dominates the government and the majority party, the *Partido de Conciliación Nacional* (PCN).[40] By no means unanimous in its outlook, the Salvadorean army maintains a distinctively professional interpretation of its role in national politics, including an obligation to maintain the security and integrity of the state. Another traditional factor is the "oligarchy," a small group of interrelated families that for generations have controlled nearly all the land, resources, and wealth of the country. They vie with each other and the military for control of governmental institutions. Salvador's geography is a continuing influence on its political development. The smallest of the Latin American nations, Salvador's compactness, high population density, developed transportation and communication systems, and racial homogeneity have combined to produce a well-knit political culture despite modest indexes of literacy, health, per capita income, and other factors of national welfare.

Imposed on these traditional characteristics are two new influences that accelerate the development trend. One is the increasing prosperity of the area. Salvador has benefited disproportionately from the efforts for economic integration in the Central American Common Market, and from increasing foreign investment, economic diversification, and industrialization.[41] Economic growth has permitted a gradual increase in living standards for urbanized, middle sectors of Salvador, as well as a steady rise in inflation to challenge their new economic achievements. With economic development there are increased profits for the oligarchic and military establishment. Economic development has produced an apparent change in the political perspectives of elites corresponding to what Almond and Powell define as "cultural secularization."[42] This change, reflected in numerous policy and institutional reforms, has made military and oligarchic leaders more responsive to national unrest, and encouraged them to try to perpetuate a healthy economic growth with broadly based dividends. A powerful segment of the ruling elite views political stability as a practical necessity for perpetuating their own economic welfare. Mass support for the regime becomes a means of minimizing political unrest and a pragmatic goal to be pursued. The regressive effects of political instability upon elite economic welfare has been illustrated for many Salvadorean leaders by the example of neighboring Guatemala.

Historically Salvador has had little experience in self-government, mass parties, elections, or even a system for stable political change. The first consequential elections were not held until 1931, and these were followed by an extended period of imposed government. Throughout the nineteenth century Salvador was ravaged by violent party warfare between "liberals" and "conservatives." This kind of elite feuding between the families and with the military produced alternating reigns of terror organized by the two "parties." Eventual stability occurred under the Liberal party at the end of the nineteenth century. Between 1913 and 1927 the oligarchy had coalesced sufficiently to permit two of the dominant families (Meléndez and Quinónez) to alternate in power. Following the competitive but inclusive elections of 1931 the current minister of war, General Hernández Martínez, staged a *coup* and imposed a ruthless regime until his overthrow in 1944. He maintained power by manipulating the oligarchy, the military, puppet presidents, and the masses, one against the other.

In 1948 moderate elements of the military assumed power and embarked on a program of "controlled reform." One of the instruments they created was the *Partido Revolucionario de Unificación Democrática* (PRUD), a political party designed to consolidate the regime and build an element mass support for its policies. Although considerable reform followed in education, public health, housing, social security, unionization, and economic development, the regime carefully avoided the explosive question of land reform, important to members of the oligarchy which supported PRUD. The *junta* elected Major Oscar Osorio president in 1950 by a 3–2 popular margin over another military candidate. Osorio was followed by Lieutenant Colonel José María Lemus, who was elected under questionable conditions in 1956. Lemus soon embarked on a program of repression against "left-wing" tendencies within the country, inspired by the abortive attempt of Arbenz to establish a protocommunist regime in neighboring Guatemala. Osorio felt Lemus had gone too far, and in 1959, with the growing support of the oligarchy and military, he formed a new political party to oppose Lemus. Osorio and his followers interpreted the 1948 revolution as an attempt to raise the lowest segments of society without destroying the system itself. For them reform was an instrument of stability if not an ideological crusade. Lemus' growing enemies eventually consolidated their position and expelled him in the bloodless *coup* of October 26, 1960. His increasing reliance upon violence and suppression threatened to return the system to the old pattern of strong-arm politics.

The new military and civilian *junta* promptly ended Lemus' policies and allowed several left-wing parties and groups to reform. Only a few months later, in January 25, 1961, a second *coup* occurred following a reshuffling of military alignments. The second civilian-military *junta* in 12 weeks expressed its disapproval of the alleged leftist inclinations in the preceding regime and placed new restrictions on the recently emancipated political organizations. The *junta* reaffirmed its allegiance to the principle of "controlled reform" of the 1948 revolution, and called immediate elections for a constituent assembly to revise the 1950 constitution. The *junta* firmly controlled the election for the 1961 constituent assembly, which drafted a new constitution and named Colonel Julio A. Rivera provisional president. In 1962 Rivera was officially elected to a full presidential term. The constitutional assembly converted itself into a regular Congress, and was subsequently renewed along with municipal offices in 1964, 1966, 1968, and 1970. Presidential elections were held in February, 1967.[43]

3. THE PARTY ARENA IN EL SALVADOR

The development of Salvadorean parties during the post 1948 period is a revealing footnote to the power struggles within the military and oligarchy. Traditional Salvadorean parties had been elite based with little connection to broader based interests in the nation. The oldest of the contemporary parties is the *Partido de Acción Renovadora* (PAR), Renovating Action party, created in 1944 following the overthrow of dictator Hernández Martínez. For the first six years of its history the PAR was an instrument for its founder, Colonel José Asencio Menéndez, and assumed a passive opposition role following the 1948 revolution.

The 1948 revolutionary government organized PRUD, which in the following decade helped rally support for the regime's reformist policies. PRUD became known as the *officialista* party, and won all ensuing elections by controlling the electoral procedures. Minor parties were not encouraged to participate with the overwhelming odds favoring the government party. The PAR continued in opposition, but more significant criticism was offered in the 1956 presidential election by Robert Canessa and his party, *Partido de Acción Nacional* (PAN). PAN drew support from younger military groups and part of the oligarchy, but disappeared shortly following the election. Another party, *Partido Institucional Democrático* (PID), emerged as a regionally based party in the city of Santa Ana in 1955, but failed to maintain itself.

Not until 1960 did a more permanent party, the *Partido Demócrata Cristiano* (PDC) emerge to challenge PRUD. In 1964, it became the first opposition party in more than 33 years to gain representation in the National Assembly. A second potentially mass party was founded in 1961 just prior to the second military coup. During the short-lived liberalization, a *Fidelista* party emerged under the name, *Partido Revolucionario Abril y Mayo* (PRAM), only to be outlawed by the new *junta*. It was followed by the *Partido Reformador Nacional* (PRN) comprised largely of the same elements, and also declared illegal for alleged communist affiliations. Other parties continued to emerge, but only the PCN, PDC, and PAR maintained the myth and pursued the reality of mass parties.

The 1964 national election was a disaster for the PAR; it was replaced by the PDC as the nation's second largest political party. An internal upheaval in PAR followed the defeat, producing a new leadership avowedly radical and sympathetic to Marxist ideology. The new group had taken over the PAR by enrolling new members from the PRN, and forcing out the old leadership after the 1964 defeat. The old PAR leadership reassembled with some dissident PCN leaders to form the new *Partido Popular Salvadoreño* (PPS), which showed some electoral strength in 1966 and 1967. The PPS was more conservative and personalistic than the other parties, and its electoral success uneven throughout the country.

By 1968 only the PCN, PDC, and PAR could be considered national political parties. The newly aligned PAR, the growing PDC, and the dominant PCN gave Salvadoreans three strong parties seeking a mass following from a left-of-center position, despite the disparate elites that direct them. The PCN retained its oligarchic-military leadership and support, the PDC mobilized a more bourgeois leadership and following, and the PAR recruited lively student participation as well as traditional leftist support. The more permissive proportional representation system adopted in 1964 further encouraged minor party activity by rewarding it with national legislative representation. The PCN, like PRUD before it, tried to create a reform-oriented, centralized party structure modeled after the PRI in Mexico. The PDC derived encouragement from the international Christian Democratic movement as it sought precedent for a reform ideology. The PAR, which suddenly became a proto-Marxist instrument, employed the most bellicose appeals to build support among voters in the capital department of San Salvador. Although Salvadoreans were able to expect more competitive elections, no one doubted the determination of PCN leadership to avoid its own demise. Reform of the political system once started was difficult to reverse, so the major dilemma for the PCN was to control and turn it to the benefit of the regime.

The growth of party institutions over the past decade can be seen graphically in Table 5-8. As the table indicates, PRUD monopolized all representation in the National Assembly from 1950 to 1960, when it was replaced by the PCN. In 1964 the new electoral system permitted three parties to be represented in the assembly. In 1966, the number was increased to five.[44]

Although PRUD and PCN totally dominated national elections, opposition parties were more successful in municipal elections. The PAR managed to win six of the 261 mayoralities in 1958.

TABLE 5-8. Party Representation in Salvadorean National Assembly

	1950	1952	1954	1956	1958	1960	1961	1964	1966	1968	1970
PARTY:											
PRUD	54	54	54	54	54	54					
PCN							54	32	31	27	34
PDC								14	15	19	16
PAR								6	4		
PPS									1	4	
PREN*									1		
MNR†										2	1
UDN‡											1
TOTAL	54	54	54	54	54	54	54	52	52	52	52

* *Partido Republicano de Evolución Nacional*, a personalistic instrument of Colonel Luis Roberto Flores.

† *Movimiento Nacional Revolucionario*, a leftist successor to the PAR, outlawed in 1968.

‡ *Union Democrática Nacionalista*, created for 1970 election.

In the 1960 election, PAR scored increasing victories in municipal elections, capturing the capital city of San Salvador, the second largest city, Santa Ana, as well as Santa Tecla, La Libertad, and many other small but important urban areas. During its first election in 1961, the PCN swept most of the mayorality elections as well as the national constituent assembly. In 1964 the PDC was able to challenge the PCN at the municipal level as PAR had challenged PRUD previously. The PDC acquired 37 of the 261 mayoralities in 1964, including the important contest in the capital, San Salvador. The latter contest brought to power one of the PDC's most popular and effective leaders, Ing. José Napoleón Duarte, whose reformist administration was returned in 1966 with a landslide vote, and a mayorality victory for the PDC in one-third of the cities.

With increasing party activity and competition Salvador experienced a growth of impartial electoral institutions. Indicative of the trend was the electoral reform law of 1964 which created a central council of elections to organize and supervise elections. With the reform the government gave its assurance that there would be no tampering with the election procedures or results. Recent experience confirms the government's statement; by and large the machinery of elections has been impartially controlled.

Historically, elections had been variable in Salvador. During the earlier years under the PRUD, charges of electoral fraud were common, and considerable evidence suggests the accusations were often true. The government found it relatively easy to coerce or cajole uneducated rural peasants into voting for the regime. Fraud has always been more difficult in San Salvador where dense population, party activity, and greater political awareness made fraudulent practices more obvious. The implications of fraud prior to 1964 were somewhat academic, since the electoral system was so regressive that there was little chance of a second party winning seats away from PRUD or PCN.[45]

It is impossible to trace all the factionalization within the major political parties. The shift of the PAR toward a more militant, younger, Marxist elite in 1964 has been mentioned. The PCN also has been factionalized. It has been divided between military and oligarchy, and by divisions within each group. Sometimes the divisions were personalistic, but there is a significant policy-ideological division within the PCN over the policy of liberalization and reform. The struggle between the traditionalistic "hard-liners" and the reform-oriented "soft-liners" was evident during the 1966 presidential nominating convention of the PCN. Salvador has not satisfactorily resolved the problem of deciding presidential succession. Three contenders for the nomination emerged prior to the convention: Colonel Maurício Rivas, identified with the soft-line advocates and probably the most popular candidate; Lieutenant Colonel Mario Guerrero, identified with the hard-line faction; and Colonel Fidel Sánchez Hernández, minister of the interior under President Rivera. Although less popular than his opponents, Sánchez was endorsed by President Rivera who made an impassioned appeal to the convention for his nomination. Although the convention did nominate Sánchez, its 49 delegate votes were divided 26 for Sánchez—a bare majority—13 for Rivas, 9 for Guerrero, and 1 for a civilian candidate. While Rivera was able to impose his successor on the party, the PCN convention was clearly more than a ratifying assembly, giving almost half of the votes to other candidates.[46]

Increasing national party activity, competition, and organization, initiation of a permissive and impartial electoral system, and restraint by the regime in dealing with new party activity, all indicate a changing political culture in Salvador during the past few years. Individual voting behavior also reflects this trend.

4. VOTING BEHAVIOR: AN ANALYSIS

Several conclusions based on voting behavior in 1964, 1966, 1967, and 1970 national elections illustrate the trend of political development in Salvador. These conclusions are drawn from national and regional patterns of registration, participation, and party voting.

National registration, participation, and voting are summarized in Table 5-9.[47] Several important trends are immediately discernable. There is a steady increase in both registration and participation, and the rate of increase for participation exceeds that of registration. The most remarkable increase in participation was in 1966, when the national increase was 6.5 percent against a registration increase of 1.2 percent. Since the percentages are compensated for population growth and the participation figures for increased registration, the total rate of increase in participation is impressive. The significant increase in participation for 1967 especially underscores the expanding political involvement, since the outcome of the election was a foregone conclusion.

The 1964–1968 decline in PCN voting is attributable to the growing institutional strength of PDC opposition, while the strong 1970 PCN vote may be explained partly as a patriotic response to the 1969 Honduran-Salvadorean "war." Opposition parties trade votes among themselves for the 35–45 percent that the PCN does not win. Consistently strong PCN voting perhaps expresses a sanguine and stable consensus about the regime. The PCN vote is not impressively high when compared to Mexico's one-party dominant system. In Mexico the PRI normally receives better than 75 percent of the national vote. Salvador's new system of proportional representation, while more favorable to minor parties than the previous system, still gives the dominant party an edge in winning legislative seats. The PCN normally receives about 60 percent of the legislative seats, with less than 55 percent of the total popular votes. The smaller parties in turn lose seats proportionately faster than they lose votes. The PDC in 1966 received 32 percent of the popular vote, but received less than 27 percent of the legislative seats. Nevertheless, the PCN had conceded almost 40 percent of the national legislative seats to the opposition through propor-

TABLE 5-9. NATIONAL REGISTRATION, PARTICIPATION, AND PARTY VOTING IN EL SALVADOR, 1964–1970 (IN PERCENT)

	Regis-tration	Partici-pation	PCN	PDC	PAR	PPS	Other
1964	36.0	28.6	58.6	26.1	15.3		
1966	39.5	32.1	53.4	31.4	6.8	2.4	6.0
1967	40.7	38.6	54.4	21.6	14.4	9.6	
1968	41.2	33.4	47.1	43.1		6.0	3.8
1970	44.2	32.4	65.7	31.7			2.6

tional representation. Proportionate to the popular vote this is far more than the PRI has allowed its opposition parties to receive in Mexico.

Increased national registration trends hold for the fourteen departments as shown in Table 5-10. The only exceptions were the departments of Santa Ana and Cuscatlán, which did not increase their total registration proportional to the population increase in 1967.

The largest mean increase in registration for the period 1964–1967 occurred in the more populous departments: Salvador, Santa Ana, La Libertad, and San Miguel. The absolute level of registration in each department relative to the total possible, was directly affected by geographical proximity to the capital department of San Salvador, although there are exceptions to this tendency. The central (or core) area is not consistently the most populous area. The capital department contains nearly 19 percent of the total national population, but the remaining departments in this region contain from 4 to 10 percent each; those adjoining the capital department fall on the low side of the population distribution index. Despite a lower population, departments near the capital experienced high increases in registration, confirming the relevance of proximity to the capital. San Salvador and its environs

TABLE 5-10. DEPARTMENTAL REGISTRATION IN SALVADOR FOR ELECTIONS OF 1964, 1966, AND 1967 (BY PERCENTAGE ELIGIBLE)*

Department	1964	1966	Percent increase	1967	Percent increase
San Salvador	47	51	+4	54	+4
Santa Ana	39	42	+3	42	+0
La Libertad	36	38	+2	39	+1
San Miguel	31	36	+1	37	+1
Usulután	32	36	+4	37	+1
Sonsonate	35	39	+4	40	+1
La Unión	30	34	+4	35	+1
La Paz	35	39	+4	40	+1
Chalatenango	32	34	+2	35	+1
Cuscatlán	41	43	+2	43	+0
Ahuachapán	30	33	+3	34	+1
Morazán	28	31	+3	32	+1
San Vicente	34	36	+2	38	+2
Cabañas	29	31	+2	32	+1

* Percentages indicate relation of actual registration to total legally possible. Table is adjusted for population increases, and arranged by department according to size.

TABLE 5-11. DEPARTMENTAL VOTING PARTICIPATION IN SALVADOR FOR
ELECTIONS OF 1964, 1966, AND 1967 (PERCENTAGE OF REGISTERED
PARTICIPATING)*

Department	1964	1966	Percent increase	1967	Percent increase
San Salvador	30	35.8	+5.8	40.7	+4.9
Santa Ana	25	31	+6	38.5	+7.5
La Libertad	28	30.2	+2.2	36.7	+6.5
San Miguel	28	29.3	+1.3	48.5	+19.2
Usulután	34	32.3	−1.7	34.5	+2.2
Sonsonate	21	27.7	+6.7	31.4	+3.7
La Unión	28	31.9	+3.9	33.8	+1.9
La Paz	25	24.6	− .4	34.1	+9.5
Chalatenango	30	36.5	+6.5	38.6	+1.9
Cuscatlán	31	35.6	+4.6	36.1	+ .5
Ahuachapán	31	32.7	+1.7	39.2	+6.5
Morazán	36	34.9	−1.1	45.7	+10.8
San Vicente	24	30.1	+6.1	36.2	+6.1
Cabañas	31	29	−2	36.5	+7.5

* Increases in participation relative to registration by department adjusted for population increases. Departments listed in descending order according to population.

seem to exert a disproportionate influence on the remainder of the country as political socialization radiates out in decreasing intensity. Except for certain regional foci, political awareness reflected through registration patterns increases with proximity to the central core area.

Voter participation, indicated in Table 5-11, increased steadily throughout the nation during the period analyzed. The only exceptions to this trend were four departments in 1966 (Usulután, La Paz, Morazán, and Cabañas) that experienced a momentary decline of 1.7 percent, .4 percent, 1.1 percent, and 2 percent; all of these except Usulután responded the next year with abnormally high increases in participation, 9.5 percent, 10.8 percent, and 7.5 percent, well above the national average of 6.5 percent. Rapidly increasing participation suggests significantly expanding political involvement in Salvador. The rapidly accelerating voter participation is compared to registration increases in Table 5-11.

As with registration, participation patterns show definite regional growth characteristics. There is a strong development pattern surrounding the capital department of San Salvador, with another isolated, weaker trend about the department of Morazán. The basic regional participation patterns grew in 1966 and 1967 demonstrating the influence of the capital core area and the secondary region that by 1967 included the department of San Miguel adjoining Morazán. Both departments in the secondary pattern increased their vote for the PCN in 1967. It is probable that increased voter participation in this secondary region was stimulated by government and PCN efforts to counterbalance anticipated losses in the core area. PCN's motivation on selecting this particular region for concentrated organizational work in 1967 is not surprising in view of the relatively strong PDC voting in Morazán in 1966. Had the PDC voting continued in this region or spread throughout other eastern departments, the PCN would have experienced a significant national decline. The specific relation between increasing participation and the PCN vote in the eastern departments is suggested in Table 5-12. Registration increased in both departments at a rate below the national average, reaffirming that the increased participation was critical to increased PCN voting.

Departments that experienced significant increases in registration did not necessarily experience simultaneous increases in participation. Probably many newly registered voters were not sufficiently socialized to activate the personal involvement necessary for voting. A general inverse correlation between registration and participation is seen despite the overall upward trend.

Generalizing from the Salvadorean experience, at least two distinct steps seem to be involved in the general process of political socialization toward elections: first the step of awareness, and second the step of involvement.[48] Of the two steps the latter is of greater significance to political parties since it affects their relative national strength. That the rate of participation increase was more rapid than the rate of registration increase is due in part to heightened party activity. Also in a politically developing system each increment in registration (awareness) becomes more difficult as more culturally isolated or unintegrated persons must be brought up to a level of national political awareness.

TABLE 5-12. COMPARISON OF INCREASED PARTICIPATION AND PCN VOTE IN EASTERN REGION (IN PERCENT)

DEPARTMENT	PARTICIPATION			PCN VOTE		
	1966	1967	Percent increase	1966	1967	Percent increase
Morazán	34.9	45.7	+10.8	68.4	81.0	+12.6
San Miguel	29.3	48.5	+19.2	65.0	76.3	+11.3

TABLE 5-13. COMPARISON OF PARTY VOTING TRENDS BY DEPARTMENT, 1964–1970 (IN PERCENT)

DEPARTMENT	PCN					PDC					OTHER				
	64	66	67	68	70	64	66	67	68	70	64	66	67	68	70
Salvador	38	31	41	35	44	39	56	25	57	27	13	13	22	10	29
Santa Ana	54	54	47	44	55	22	25	18	40	31	24	21	35	16	14
La Libertad	65	49	50	44	63	25	36	34	56	29	10	12	16	0	8
San Miguel	66	65	76	57	62	22	16	12	40	32	12	19	12	3	6
Usulután	80	67	54	57	63	9	11	15	28	17	11	22	31	15	20
Sonsonate	74	67	53	50	64	8	17	23	25	15	18	16	22	25	21
La Unión	66	64	69	56	71	21	10	14	44	19	13	26	17	0	10
La Paz	63	53	49	49	67	20	42	32	40	21	17	5	19	11	12
Chalatenango	54	65	51	53	59	35	25	31	40	19	11	10	18	7	22
Cuscatlán	67	65	49	55	68	30	29	38	45	28	3	6	13	0	4
Achuachapán	77	65	72	52	65	18	11	8	15	15	5	24	20	33	20
Morazán	57	68	81	66	57	27	30	14	34	16	16	2	3	0	17
San Vicente	54	66	60	55	65	46	30	28	45	23	0	4	12	0	12
Cabañas	77	73	63	59	65	16	9	7	17	13	7	18	30	24	22
NATIONAL	59	53	54	47	60	26	31	22	43	27	10	16	24	10	13

Although the national and departmental increases in registration for 1964–1966 and 1966–1967 showed a close correlation (Table 5-10) there was no such correlation between national participation increase and departmental participation increases for the same years.

The national participation increased substantially in 1967, but a tremendous variation in increases is found for each department. The explanation for the unevenness probably lies in the close correlation between party activity and socialization toward involvement (participation), while the more even development in registration reflects a more complex, overall process of political socialization toward awareness (registration) executed by government and informal mechanisms.

Party voting patterns and trends confirm the political development trend. Clearly the fortunes of any particular party cannot be correlated to the development process, but patterns of minor party growth and competition, their relation to the PCN as well as previously identified variables, are related to political development. Comparison of voting by party and department is shown in Table 5-13.

Voting for the PCN on a departmental basis varied less than did voting for minor parties. There was a general decline for the

PCN when compared to the pre-1964 levels until 1970. This decline was stimulated by the more permissive electoral system and increased minor party activity. The PCN showed a clear decline in five departments (Usulután, Sonsonate, La Paz, Cuscatlán, and Cabañas) at an accelerating rate in all but La Paz. These departments are small to medium sized, located generally in the central core of the country. Most were the object of considerable PDC organizational work, and show strong PDC voting tendencies. The PDC made significant gains in the departments of Usulután, Sonsonate, and Cuscatlán in 1967, despite a national trend in which the PDC vote declined nearly 10 percent during the same period. The PPS also benefited—if not so dramatically—from the decreased PCN voting in these departments from 1964 to 1968.

The PCN did best in smaller, more isolated departments, not in the central core area. Several factors contributed to PCN strength in these areas: superior financial and organizational facilities, available governmental patronage and communication. Minor parties necessarily limited their appeals to regions with heavier population or those close to the capital. Some of the PCN departments may have exhibited more traditionalistic, less politically developed voting tendencies. That is, they tended to endorse the *officialista* party rather than view voting as a mechanism for expressing alienation or dissent.

Only one party—the PDC—was able to defeat the PCN in a department. The PDC carried the capital department of San Salvador in national voting in 1964, 1966, and 1968, the latter year by a wide margin. Otherwise the PCN easily carried most departments in each election, despite strong challenges by the PDC on several occasions: in 1964, the PDC came within 7 percentage points of the PCN in the department of San Vicente, within 11 points in La Paz in 1966, and within 11 points in Cuscatlán in 1967. All these departments are contiguous in the central area where the PDC experienced its strongest growth.

The PDC failed to maintain its growth pattern in the 1967 presidential election, its total percentage of the national vote falling below that of the 1964 election. The PAR regained its losses of 1966, making strong gains in Santa Ana and Salvador where it polled heavier than the PDC. The PPS candidate received 9.6 percent of the 1967 vote, spread unevenly throughout the nation. PPS voting ranged from a high of just under 30 percent to practically none in several departments, particularly more populous ones. Generally PPS voting patterns must be described as localistic rather than national. The PCN suffered some of its heaviest losses in departments where the PPS did well, suggesting a closer correlation of PPS voting to PCN than to minor party voting. The PPS was also closer to the PCN in campaign appeals; rumors spread prior to the 1967 election that the PPS might withdraw in favor of the government's candidate. No major issues separated them. The PPS' campaign was decidedly personalistic, its organizational structure the weakest of the three largest parties. For all these reasons the PPS is perhaps best viewed as a traditionalistic Salvadorean party largely unrelated to the political development trend in the country.

In the majority of departments voting indicates a closer competition between minor parties than with the PCN. The exception of San Salvador has been discussed. The capital area can be said to be more politically developed than the remainder of the country, although not implicitly the model on which the remainder of the country must develop. The PCN can still win a plurality in San Salvador—as in 1967—but the competition of the PAR and PDC is a critical factor. In the majority of the remaining departments minor parties seem to exchange votes from one election to another within the general national party trends. This fact could be interpreted as a negative indicator of development, since a fairly stable percentage of disenchanted voters, somewhat fickle in their party loyalty, vote for whichever opposition party makes the more persuasive antigovernment campaign appeals. Vote switching may alternatively be viewed as a function of emerging minor party competition, since fluid party affiliations and identifications are characteristic of increasing party activity in areas where there is little historical precedent for it.

There are clear geographic distributions to party voting tendencies throughout Salvador, as indicated in Table 5-13. Both the PDC and the PAR are most effective in contiguous departments. The PDC, stronger of the two, shows the tendency most clearly. Except for the department of Morazán in 1966, the PDC did consistently best in contiguous departments including or surrounding the core area of San Salvador. Registration and participation were also relatively higher in these departments. PAR showed regional strength in Santa Ana and adjoining departments, with a secondary trend around the capital area and, in 1966, the western departments. The PCN showed no clear regional trend until 1967, when perhaps as a consequence of its extra organizational efforts in San Miguel and Morazán, the PCN developed definite foci in the eastern region. Unlike the minor parties, however, the PCN did comparatively well in all departments, making the regional influence less clear and certain.

It is misleading to view Salvadorean voting principally as a popular, decision-making exercise analogous to the context of more politically developed nations. Outside the capital, voting is often unrelated to nominal electoral functions like leadership recruitment or policy decisions. Salvadorean elections are a political "communion" in which the expanding national community increasingly participates.[49] The propensity is strong to support the established order and affirm one's allegiance to it. The heresy of political opposition makes slow, faltering inroads on the established ritual, but where it does, Salvadorean elections functionally shift toward a more politically developed concept of voting and party competition.

5. SUMMARY

Recent electoral evidence suggests a trend of political development in El Salvador producing higher levels of political awareness, political involvement, subsystem autonomy, and institutionalization. Simultaneously broadly based political parties are attempting to extend their popular support through appeals to middle and lower sectors for improved welfare. The process is affected, perhaps governed, by numerous cultural and demographic factors, and seems to be developing with regional growth patterns.

Part of the stimulus for political development is found in the changing, secularizing perspectives within the ruling elites. They have evolved a longer range interpretation of their own welfare induced by economic incentives for political stability. Development is also fostered and protected by more favorable institutional infrastructure found in the recent proportional representation system, the regularizing of electoral procedures and improvement in supervisory impartiality, as well as the growth of essentially nonrevolutionary but opposing party organizations grounded in quasi-autonomous political groups.

The impact of political development on electoral behavior in Salvador has been significant. Participation and registration have risen consistently and impressively throughout the country. Accelerating participation over registration suggests both increased popular involvement and the problems of politically socializing the least integrated segments of a politically developing society. Participation and registration patterns are clearly related to the intensity of political communication, proximity to the capital, intensity of population concentration, and competitiveness of party activity. The extension of political awareness and political participation appear to be two distinct steps in political socialization, separable both as to cause and rate of development.

General consensus for the regime has been maintained by the *officialista* PCN at a reasonably high level, although localized trends both favorable and unfavorable to the PCN can be isolated in voting. The PCN has been most effective in building support in geographically remote and smaller departments, while the minor parties have built strong support in the central core area surrounding San Salvador. The PDC has defeated the PCN in the capital, while it and the PAR have won numerous municipal offices. Both the PCN and minor parties show increasing inclinations for regional growth patterns, despite evenly distributed growth rates.

The overall impact on Salvadorean politics has been a resocialization and intensification of its political culture toward institutionally controlled mechanisms of political articulation, aggregation, and communication. The trend may be self-amplifying in that with each year and each election it becomes increasingly more difficult— and in the long run perhaps less politically stable—to revert to more traditional, authoritarian patterns of governmental control.

Although national Salvadorean parties are not necessarily the cause of political development, they are clearly critical instruments in promoting the process. There is as yet no indication of the style of politics and government that will ultimately emerge; some form of "controlled competition" encompassing fundamental if not subtle divisions within the nation seems plausible. Continuation of the development trend depends largely upon its causal factors: an increasingly secularized leadership elite in the military and oligarchic groups, and a patience from emerging opposition elites to endure a gradual rather than protracted process. Excessive pressure by opposition elites for rapid change, particularly if accompanied by appeals to violence or demagoguery, could shift the critical balance of power within the ruling hierarchy into the hands of more traditionalistic, more militant leaders and produce a reaction to development. The consequence could be a return to traditional methods of enforcing national consensus. Momentary interruptions producing changes in governmental personnel have not destroyed the development process, although they conceivably could. As the Salvadorean political system expands to include previously irrelevant, unaware, or disenfranchised participants, a new center of equilibrium is reached in the political development process. The intriguing question is whether the Salvadorean experience is in itself unique, or pertains to political development elsewhere in the "third world."

IV. SINGLE-PARTY DOMINANT SYSTEMS IN LATIN AMERICA: A CONCLUSION

Although we have looked at only three Latin American single-party dominant systems, several conclusions can be drawn from this limited exercise. From our survey we conclude no direct correlation between the type of electoral system and the resulting party system. Mexico has a majority-type electoral system, El Salvador proportional representation, and Nicaragua a combined majority and proportional representation system that guarantees minimum minority representation. Mexico's experience reveals that single-party dominant systems are not inconsistent with the concepts of interest representation and competition, anymore than they are inconsistent with broader cultural and personal political liberties. Nicaragua by contrast is a dictatorship, and the party is an instrument to reinforce the regime's control. In El Salvador the principal function of the party is to maintain relative calm and order, and ameliorate what are nominally explosive tendencies within the society. Mexico has achieved one of the most stable political systems in Latin America. Nicaragua has been stable under the Somozas but not without violence. El Salvador has been chronically unstable, but more recently has incorporated elite *coups* gracefully in its overall political processes without totally disrupting parameters of national policy or endangering individual welfare. Opposition parties exist in each system. In Mexico and Nicaragua they mobilize latent hostility, but in Salvador they increasingly challenge the dominant party itself. Elections have been a regular process in Mexico for more than half a century, but in Nicaragua and El Salvador for less than two decades. Opposition party voting is proportionally stronger in the capital cities of Mexico and Salvador than elsewhere in the countries. Participation and registration in Mexico has remained relatively constant since the party system stabilized in the 1930s, while in Salvador clear development trends can be isolated historically and geographically. Participation in Nicaragua has been uniformly low. Opposition parties in Mexico have sensed the boundaries beyond which their activity cannot effectively go, and seek a working relationship with the dominant party. Opposition parties in Nicaragua know few strategic or tactical boundaries and are unrestrained in their attacks upon the government and ruling family. El Salvador is searching for a stable party balance between opposition and loyalty. In the long run this search may be the most critical factor in its national politics. Only Salvador's party system appears to be transforming itself systemically into a more competitive type.

The major similarity in the three systems is the tendency for the dominant party to become identified with the government itself. Mexico's PRI is almost the national decision-making process. Nicaragua's Liberal party is an extension of Somoza rule. The PCN in Salvador is the government party and commonly known as *officialista* by Salvadorean voters. There is an undeniable political and financial advantage to a party in such a position. On the other hand the party and government are more vulnerable to direct attacks since political and governmental opposition become synonymous. PAN has attempted (often with the help of the PRI) to become known as the opposition. Conservatives in Nicaragua have clearly so identified themselves, and the PDC and PAR in Salvador are competing for the position.

Dominant party voting in Mexico is functionally mixed: affirmative, identifying, and ritualistic. In Nicaragua and Salvador voting tends to be largely affirmative, although there is a developing trend of protest voting in the latter. Elections are indifferently reported in each country. Fraud seems least necessary but most feasible in Nicaragua, and of decreasing importance in Salvador. With so many more subtle and effective controls available, it is surprising how little restraint Mexico's PRI has shown in tampering with election returns.

Whatever else one may conclude from a comparison of single-party dominant systems in Latin America, it is obvious that diversity outweighs similarity on the basis of empirical evidence. Single-party systems are varied in the structure of their institutions, the functions they perform, and particularly their impact on the more broadly defined governmental processes and national political culture.

NOTES

[1] Political analyses of Haiti are scarce. A useful if brief introduction is Rayford W. Logan and Martin C. Needler, "Haiti," in M. C. Needler, ed., *Political Systems of Latin America* (Princeton, N.J.: Van Nostrand, 1964), pp. 149–62. Also, Selden Rodman, *Haiti: The Black Republic* (New York: Devin-Adair, 1954).

[2] In addition to Leo B. Lott's chapter on Paraguay in the Needler collection, *Political Systems of Latin America*, pp. 381–402, the best materials are Paul H. Lewis, "Leadership and Conflict Within the *Febrerista* Party of Paraguay," *Inter-American Studies* 9 (April 1967): 283–95; Frederick Hicks, "Politics Power, and the Role of the Village Priest in Paraguay," *Inter-American Studies* 9 (April 1967): 273–83; and the more general book by George Pendle, *Paraguay: A Riverside Nation* (London: Royal Institute of International Affairs, 1954).

[3] There is no shortage of publications on Cuba under Castro. Reasonable introductions are found in T. Draper, *Castro's Revolution* (London, 1962) and Dudley Seers et al., *Cuba: The Economic and Social Revolution* (Chapel Hill: University of North Carolina Press, 1964). A useful comment on pre-Castro party politics is William S. Stokes, "The Cuban Parliamentary System in Action, 1940–1947," *Journal of Politics* 2 (May 1949): 335–64.

[4] These states are not "totalitarian" in the sense that Franz Neumann and others have used the term, simply because none can so effectively control their populations.

[5] There is a growing consensus that one-party systems are appropriate to stimulate national integration in the "third world." Whatever the relevance elsewhere, the experience in Latin America with the possible exception of Mexico would not substantiate this position. For a statement of the concept, see Claude Ake, *A Theory of Political Integration* (Homewood, Ill.: The Dorsey Press, 1967), pp. 82–95. The application of this development concept to Africa is found in James Coleman and Carl Rosberg. *Political Parties and National Integration in Tropical Africa* (Berkeley: University of California Press, 1966).

[6] A correlation of geographic-environmental factors and Nicaraguan politics is found in James L. Busey, "Foundations of Political Contrast: Costa Rica and Nicaragua," *Western Political Quarterly* 11 (September 1958): 627–59.

[7] José Gomez, *História de Nicaragua* (Madrid: Esuela de Artes Gráficas, 1955).

[8] A useful account of the emergence of the Somoza regime is Charles W. Anderson, "Nicaragua: The Somoza Dynasty," in M. C. Needler, *Political Systems in Latin America*, pp. 91–111.

[9] Tachito acknowledged guerrilla activity in the mountains around Matagalpa in a recent interview. *New York Times*, December 8, 1967, p. 32.

[10] For a discussion of the Nicaraguan electoral system in theory see, *Nicaragua: Election Factbook February 5, 1967* (Washington, D.C.: Institute for the Comparative Study of Political Systems, 1967), pp. 35–36.

[11] Eligibility statistics are compiled from several sources, including the Supreme Tribunal of Elections.

[12] Supreme Tribunal of Elections, published in *Novedades,* February 26, 1963.

[13] *El Mercurio* (Santiago, Chile), February 5, 1967.

[14] *El Mercurio* (Santiago, Chile), February 7, 1967.

[15] The history of the Revolution is available in José Vasconcelos, *Breve História de Mexico* (Madrid, 1952); and Alberto Morales Jimenez, *História de la Revolucion Mexicana* (Mexico D.F., 1951).

[16] The emergence of the PRI is well described by Robert E. Scott, *Mexican Government in Transition* (Urbana: University of Illinois, 1964), pp. 115–44.

[17] *Ibid.,* p. 118.

[18] L. Vincent Padgett, *The Mexican Political System* (Boston: Houghton Mifflin Co., 1966), p. 32.

[19] For the development of the Mexican labor movement, see Howard F. Cline, *Mexico: Revolution to Evolution, 1940–1960* (New York: Oxford University Press, 1963), pp. 222–29.

[20] August O. Spain, "Mexican Federalism Revisited," *Western Political Quarterly* 9 (September 1956): pp. 620–32.

[21] Many Mexican intellectuals have been critical of the Government's control of national politics through the electoral system. See Lic. Hector Solis Quiroga, *Los Partidos Politicos en México* (México, D.F.: Editorial Orión, 1961), pp. 26–33.

[22] There are many useful studies of the PRI. A Significant redefinition of the system was made by L. Vincent Padgett, "Mexico's One-Party System: A Re-evaluation," *American Political Science Review* 51 (December 1957): 995–1008; see also his *Popular Participation in Mexico's One Party System* (Doctoral dissertation, Ann Arbor: University Microfilms, 1955). A more general introduction is found in Frank Brandenburg, *The Making of Modern Mexico* (Englewood Cliffs, N.J.: Prentice-Hall, 1964). Perhaps the most perceptive if now slightly dated analysis of the PRI is Scott, *Mexican Government in Transition,* particularly pp. 115–96.

[23] See Scott, *Mexican Government in Transition,* pp. 145–76.

[24] Former Secretaries of *Gobernación* who rose to the Presidency include Miguel Alemán, Adolfo Ruiz Cortines, Gustavo Díaz Ordaz, and Luis Echeverria. López Mateos was secretary of labor under Ruiz Cortines.

[25] An excellent survey research project on right-wing alienation, including PAN supporters, is Kenneth F. Johnson, "Ideological Correlates of Right-Wing Political Alienation in Mexico," *American Political Science Review* 59 (September 1965): 656–54.

[26] Johnson goes only so far as to suggest an arrangement between PRI and PAN whereby PAN recognizes election results in exchange for being the "official opposition" and receives a guaranteed parliamentary representation. Johnson reports that fraud was "unnecessary" in the 1964 elections, but PRI intended to honor its commitment to PAN irregardless. *Ibid.,* p. 660.

[27] Scott, *Mexican Government in Transition,* pp. 188–92.

[28] The evolution of the MLN is traced by David T. Graza, "Factionalism in the Mexican Left: Frustration of the MLN," *Western Political Quarterly* 17 (September 1964): 447–60.

[29] Like most Latin American nations, voting statistics are variable in Mexico. Those used in this chapter are distilled from many sources, including those released by the government. It is indicative that those used by Scott

(*Mexican Government in Transition*), Cline (*Mexico*), and Padgett (*The Mexican Political System*) do not always agree. Another source is Pablo Gonzales Casanova, *La Democrácia en Mexico* (Mexico, D.F.: Ediciones E.R.A., 1965). The tables presented here are intended to be suggestive, not necessarily definitive.

[30] A rather pessimistic account of the 1958 election is Phillip B. Taylor, "Mexican Election of 1958: Affirmation of Authoritarianism?" *Western Political Quarterly* 13 (Spring 1960): 722–44.

[31] Cline, *Mexico*, pp. 334–35.

[32] Official statistics released by the PRI in July, 1967.

[33] Election in Sonora reported by Rubén Salazar, *Los Angeles Times*, July 4–9, 1967.

[34] Another blow to the PRI was the loss of the city of Mérida in the Yucatán. The PAN candidate, Víctor M. Correa Racho, won over the PRI candidate, Nícolas López Rivas (a high official in the state government) by a margin of better than 3–1. The issues and election were similar to the case of Sonora, where local antagonisms with the central government alienated the electorate. These two losses produced a significant reorganization at the state and national party levels. See Henry Giniger, *New York Times*, February 25, 1968, p. 8.

[35] The concept of *political development* is used here as an analytic tool. There is no prescriptive assumption that development is "desirable" or even "inevitable." The concept is used to suggest certain causal factors producing a shift in the kind of equilibrium characteristic of the Salvadorean political system, and to specify and interpret recent electoral phenomena in light of this overall trend. For further background on this general orientation to "development," see H. Eulau, "Harold D. Lasswell's Developmental Analysis," *Western Political Quarterly* 11 (June 1958): 229–42.

Contemporary political analysis of El Salvador is scarce. See Charles W. Anderson, "El Salvador: The Army as Reformer," in Martin Needler, *Political Systems*, pp. 53–72. Portions of this section are based on material originally published in *Journal of Politics* 31, No. 2 (May 1969). Reproduced with permission.

[36] This characteristic of development is somewhat similar to what Almond and Verba discuss as *political cognition*. See G. Almond and S. Verba, *The Civic Culture* (Princeton, N.J.: Princeton University Press, 1963), pp. 79–100.

[37] This characteristic is similar to what A.F.K. Organski terms the "politics of industrialization" in his, *The Stages of Political Development* (New York: Knopf, 1965), pp. 9–12.

[38] The notion of "subsystem autonomy" is elaborated by Robert A. Dahl, *Modern Political Analysis* (Englewood Cliffs, N.J.: Prentice-Hall, 1963), p. 25ff. Almond and Powell also view political parties as indicators of developing political infrastructure or subsystems. G. Almond and G. B. Powell, *Comparative Politics: A Developmental Approach* (Boston: Little, Brown, 1966), pp. 46–57. The minor parties seem particularly relevant since they possess both greater role differentiation and autonomy from the regime than the PCN, both qualities indicative of the development process.

[39] The critical task of institutionalizing aggregative functions in developing and modernizing authoritarian systems is discussed in Almond and Powell (*Comparative Politics*, pp. 112–14). The general terminology for this section

SINGLE-PARTY DOMINANT SYSTEMS   283

unless otherwise noted is from G. Almond and J. S. Coleman, *Politics of Developing Areas* (Princeton, N.J.: Princeton University Press. 1960), pp. 17–52. The problem of changing elite perception is empirical but elusive. While the problem may perhaps one day be resolved by survey research techniques, such a task is beyond the scope of this study. The change indicated was perceived on the basis of extensive field interviewing with Salvadorean leaders in 1966 and 1967.

[40] It is not inconsequential in light of the conclusions of this analysis concerning the effectiveness of the PCN in smaller, more remote areas of the country to call attention to the report that current military leaders in Salvador have been largely recruited from villages rather than the central core area of the country, and therefore often are beholden to plantation owners. See John J. Johnson, *The Military and Society in Latin America* (Stanford, Calif.: Stanford University Press, 1964), p. 107.

[41] This relatively dominant position occupied by El Salvador in the Central American Common Market is reported by Joseph S. Nye, Jr., "Central American Regional Integration," *International Conciliation* No. 562 (March 1967): p. 41.

[42] "Secularization is the process whereby men become increasingly rational, analytical, and empirical in their political action. . . . The secularization of culture is the processes whereby traditional orientations and attitudes give way to more dynamic decision-making processes involving the gathering of information, the evaluation of information, the laying out of alternative courses of action, the selection of a course of action from among these possible courses, and the means whereby one tests whether or not a given course of action is producing consequences which were intended. ." Clearly the process is only beginning in El Salvador. See Almond and Powell, *Comparative Politics*, pp. 24–25.

[43] Useful electoral background information is contained in *El Salvador Election Factbook: March 5, 1967* (Washington, D.C.: Institute for the Comparative Study of Political Systems, 1967).

[44] For an analysis of the 1966 congressional and municipal elections, see the present author's "Stable Political Change in Central America: Three Recent Examples," *Atenea* 3 (December 1966): 21–33.

[45] A more complete analysis of the implications of the more restrictive, majority system electoral plan used in Salvador is contained in R. McDonald "Electoral Systems, Party Representation, and Political Change in Latin America," *Western Political Quarterly* 20 (September 1967): 694–708.

[46] Reported by the *El Salvador Election Factbook,* pp. 16–17.

[47] Electoral data included in this analysis has been gathered from official government releases. The data has also been checked against newspaper and party reports, and adjustments made as necessary to resolve discrepancies in governmental reports. In all instances actual voting has been translated into percentages to facilitate comparison and minimize the effects of errors in absolute totals. Registration figures have also been adjusted for population increases each year 1964–1967 on a departmental level using known increase factors. The data nonetheless is used to suggest general trends and party relationships; it is not offered as definitive or subtle profiles of voting in Salvador.

[48] Almond and Powell suggest two kinds of involvement: one favorable

to the regime (in the Salvadorean experience promoted by the PCN) and the other unfavorable to it (in Salvador the minor parties). The distinction is a blunt one, similar in mood to Karl Mannheim's notion of *Ideology and Utopia*. See Almond and Powell, *Comparative Politics*, pp. 121–27.

[49] This interpretation of Salvadorean election rituals is similar to the distinguished Mexican poet Octavio Paz' description of Mexican culture in *Labyrinth of Solitude* (New York: Grove Press, 1961), p. 24ff.

CHAPTER 6

Concluding Propositions on Voting and Party Politics in Latin America

The preceding chapters have reviewed basic notions of party politics in the contemporary Latin American context. Characteristic environmental factors that control party activity are implicit in this identification. What factors stabilize or maintain party competition, and what factors induce change? Recognizing the nearly universal ritual of elections in a region of varied governmental styles, what are the political functions of electoral procedures, campaigns, and voting? What meanings can be assigned to electoral participation and voting in Latin America? What voting patterns are characteristic of the region and individual nations?

I. POLITICAL ENVIRONMENT AND PARTY POLITICS

Parties in Latin America have legal and behavioral qualities that regularly are expressed in electoral contexts. What these qualities are has been our principal concern.

The legal expression subjects parties to manipulation, by regimes, for limited political purposes. This in turn affects competition and the utility of parties for channeling political demands. The behavioral expression of parties comes from environmental political factors that create demands upon the political system, and upon political leaders, who view parties as instruments for personal power. The behavioral expression is frustrated when legal systems, either from insensitivity or design, fail to respond to new realities within a culture. The legal expression is frustrated when support for recognized parties fails, either because of resistance to imposed or irrelevant parties, or because of intense political opposition.

One theme that shapes the evolution of party structures is

the historical expansion of the political system or community, to integrate persons or regions previously irrelevant.[1] This expansion controls national political systems by establishing parameters for competition.[2] Latin American political parties have variably facilitated and obstructed national integration.[3] Pressures for integration are diverse, some coming spontaneously with economic development, population growth, and urbanization; pressures are also calculatedly induced by governments and opposition elites.

It stands to reason that when integration is weak or proceeding slowly, the reality is political disunity.[4] This reality is expressed as regionalism and class hostility for areas and groups outside the threshold of relevance. A survey of parties and elections reveals the importance of regionalism as an indicator of integration and integrative conflict. Similarly, group and class integration is indicated by participation, registration, voting dispositions, and the number and relative strength of political parties expressing integrative pressures. From this viewpoint, party activity and elections are a principal indicator of national politics and a barometer of fundamental social change.

Observers of Latin America have made serious errors in generalizing regional, cultural, and environmental qualities to "explain" crossnational political realities. The dilemma is the assumption that overwhelming environmental similarities in Latin America produce general political traits. Nearly a century and a half of isolated, national, cultural evolution should perhaps more appropriately suggest *diversity* rather than homogeneity as the principal tendency among Latin American nations. Without rejecting the idea that similarities can exist, this study has tried to suggest that, as in other regions of the world, these similarities must be regarded as the exception rather than the rule. They appear, not because of universal regional factors, but because of distinctive combinations nationally derived.

We offered categories of environmental factors not to predict or explain regional political similarities, but to describe how variations on a general theme have produced distinctive national political cultures. Beyond conventional social, economic, cultural, and historical factors, demographic and legal-institutional factors have been identified as particularly important to party activity in Latin America. The principal concepts drawn from these factors to describe party politics are personalism, hierarchy, familialism, status and professionalism, urbanization, secularization, demography, and electoral institutions.

Personalism, the reliance on individual personality or charisma, is a universal quality of party leadership, although it seems more characteristic of some nations and periods than of others.[5] In Latin America, personalism has been a primary characteristic of party politics, particularly functional in pre-institutional and transitional societies to cement diverse political forces. Personal loyalties develop easier than institutional ones, even if they also disappear more easily. The specific personal qualities that succeed vary with cultures, as do the balances between personalism and institutionalization.[6] It is easy to see personalistic pressures in Panama or Ecuador, but similar pressures are also present, though less conspicuously, in institutionalized systems like Uruguay and Costa Rica, where a more even balance is struck between personalism and institutionalization. Personalism is no more common in Latin American politics than elsewhere, but is merely more conspicuous in the absence of institutional restraints.

Like personalism, social hierarchies are a factor that affects party politics.[7] One expression is class systems, which vary so much between nations that generalizations are deceptive.[8] When a society is controlled by a small, influential group, insulated from the remainder of society, the hierarchy is oligarchical. Oligarchy is, however, an imprecise concept, for there are as many kinds of oligarchy in Latin America as there are instances.[9] Most party decision-making is oligarchical, but these oligarchies vary in the sources of their power (land, wealth, business, military, etc.) and the competitiveness of their sub-elites. Oligarchy is a characteristic of fundamental cultural realities, reinforced by distinctive economic institutions and historical traditions. It expresses a reality as much as creating one. What is often significant about Latin American oligarchies is their competitiveness, and restlessness with existing power distributions.[10] Established power groups may be insulated and self-perpetuating, but there are still conflicts within the oligarchies over questions of power. The "rules of the game" for oligarchic politics vary from one nation to another. Some nations restrict competition to the group itself, others draw upon mass unrest to reinforce leverage over opposition elites.

The notion of hierarchy in Latin American politics raises very fundamental questions about the nature of party competition. One of the "development" standards, often applied to Latin American politics by outside observers, is the model of "pluralistic" competition.[11] Pluralism is an ideological assumption that interests and groups within a community retain an element of autonomy, the "right" to compete for strategic advantage, and an obligation to accept defeat as well as victory.[12] Pluralism seems particularly consonant with North American politics, and with the cultural values that support it.[13] This "group base of politics," which has been influential and useful for analyses of North American politics, is sometimes applied to judge the relative level of development (that is, complexity) of Latin American societies, assuming that as industrialization or integration occurs, societies become more pluralistic.[14] Conceptually, hierarchy in a pluralistic model is strategic rather than organic (inherent) to the nature of society itself.

Is the pluralistic model relevant for Latin America to explain existing hierarchical qualities? Has complexity in Latin American societies induced pluralistic values or pluralistic competition? I am inclined to answer these questions negatively, and propose that this response has significant implications for the study of party politics in Latin America. Ideological values in Latin America often seem to recognize an organic hierarchy in society, not a pluralistic or strategic one.[15] Groups compete with the assumption that their right to supremacy is inherent in the constituted order, consistent with the very nature of the community itself. This holds not only for established interests, traditional families or military organizations, but also for bourgeois and radical movements that seek not a pluralistic society, but a restructured organic one.

Mexico illustrates the notion of an organic state. Its party system is preoccupied with defining local, regional, and national hierarchies for participating groups and interests. Competition exists within the Mexican political community, but it is localized between states or regions, where the dominance of an interest or group is normally an empirical fact. National politics is a fragile, hierarchical composite of society in which competition is controlled.[16] Meaningful public competition in Mexican national politics is almost anomalous to the idea of a well-structured, organic state. The possible irrelevance of pluralistic models, even for essentially complex Latin American societies, demands further consideration, not only for Mexico but for such organic regimes as the Christian Democrats in Chile, the *Fidelistas* in Cuba, and other broadly based as well as authoritarian regimes. Where the organic model is more valid than the pluralistic one, different notions of party formation, leadership, and competition must be implicit.

Studies of party followers in the United States suggest the importance of familial influences in forming attitudes and controlling behavior.[17] The likelihood of familial influences in more traditional societies is strong, particularly when elite family units are cohesive amid a differentiated society. Familial cohesion establishes channels for participation, communication, and recruitment to party elites. While familial influences on behavior of the general public are unknown, their presence can be assumed.

The political relevance of familialism is particularly consonant with the notion of an organic state. Colombian politics becomes more meaningful when the idea of familialism is applied. Representation in the Colombian legislature, a rough index to national power elites, reveals not only regional and party bases, but also familial bases for representation. The same is true in the more modern political system of Uruguay, where familial influence is strong but within an essentially party-oriented, representative mold. On a more routine basis, access to party elites is greatly facilitated if not controlled by family connections. Families are not necessarily monolithic or internally hierarchical; rivalries and feuds between familial branches can find expression in party politics.[18]

One way in which class hierarchy is reinforced is through education and occupation. Recruitment to party elites is also affected by status and occupational characteristics of the participants. Parties encourage recruitment by rewarding adherents with access to critical economic elites within the community. Some professions besides law seem particularly useful for political advancement in Latin America because of their inherent social status. Medicine is one such profession, providing an unusually large number of successful political leaders. Other professions, because of their controls over the environment (particularly military and business elites), provide effective channels for recruitment. Education, partially expressed by status and profession, also directly governs recruitment, participation, and influence, by sensitizing the individual to political means for increasing personal power and achieving sociopolitical mobility. In a legal as well as sociological sense, education to literacy determines the parameters of the actual political system by controlling who is included and excluded from party organizations and electoral processes. Education also generates internal pressures for change by fixing status, occupation, and economic expectations. As pressures for inclusion are met, the political system expands through the society; when they are not met or translated into public debate, educationally induced pressures create conflicts in national politics. These pressures are particularly critical when, after achieving literacy, socialized demands and expectations rise faster than the capacity of the economy to satisfy them, or the responsiveness of the political system to acknowledge them. "Sanguineness" is a critical balance in Latin American politics between cognition of one's condition and expectations for its improvement. Factors that promote it are as important an output of the political system as increased material benefits.[19]

Geography influences party activity. Political integration and party competition cannot help but be influenced by physical integration and communications realities. Demographic variables are also important, particularly racial characteristics of the population and settlement patterns that influence group relationships and party activity. *Mestizo* classes, a mixture of European and Indian races, polarized rather than integrated populations. Racial differentiation created barriers to integrating the Indian into Latin American political systems, although perhaps the barriers were no more formidable than those for minorities in the United States.

The core area concept identifies an unusual political relevance for the capital region. Original settlement patterns created isolated pockets of civilization instead of an expanding frontier that in the United States equalized and integrated political movements. Conflicts between Latin American urban areas have been as politically significant as conflicts between rural and urban areas. Provincialism, as in Argentina and Colombia, has produced conflicts between different rural/urban conglomerates. Urbanization, an important trend in many nations, has created new pressures and new opportunities for parties. Intense organization, efficient financing, sources of leadership, and political awareness are factors that give special importance to urban party activity in Latin America.[20]

Economic factors affect party evolution in traditional ways. Classes based on wealth control national integration and participation in ways similar to the United States: by providing capital, leisure, skills, resources, and access to pursue power. Poverty increases the costs of participation by destroying leisure and making survival the principal preoccupation.

Secularization—the separation of political from other societal concerns—helps define a trend in national integration that affects party politics.[21] The apparent secularization pressures in El Salvador reveal a greater tendency for the elites to define domestic policy empirically, and to consider empirically the costs of internal political conflict and ways to minimize it.

Electoral systems and legal-institutional frameworks are critical for party evolution and nearly all aspects of party-related activity. Access to legislatures and formal registration of party organizations control a group's ability to participate in the system, and create pressures through frustration for defying the system. Besides party registration, electoral systems selectively regulate enfranchisement, party competition, and representation through allocation of party seats. These controls normally involve relatively low political costs, for they are subtle, seemingly neutral factors. The common residence requirement, (for example, that a citizen vote in the district where his *cédula* was issued), discourages participation from migrant sectors of the population who are also politically alienated from the regime. Such controls can to an extent determine the range of outcomes possible in an election and party competition.

Coalitional formation, normally regarded as politically inspired, is influenced and often controlled by electoral and legal devices. Colombia's FTN, a coalition of dominant elites in "competing" parties, was induced by a constitutional referendum. Complex intraparty coalitions form in Uruguay during elections as a result of electoral laws that not only permit, but guarantee factions a semiautonomous position. Brazil, with substantial coalitional activity, protected party coalitions at the state level during elections. By contrast, Chile outlawed formal coalitions, prompting informal arrangements and "gentlemen's agreements" like those recently used by FRAP.

These environmental realities control party growth and activity, and often predetermine their relevancies to national decisionmaking. Economic realities place most of Latin America in the "third world" of developing countries, which has implications for defining political tasks and setting priorities. There is much in Latin America that is "Western" or "developed" in style, as well as much that is indigenous to the region and individual nations.

II. MAINTENANCE AND CHANGE IN PARTY SYSTEMS

The party systems schema, used to organize our national analyses, rests upon the realities of party representation in Latin American legislatures, because that seems to be the most universal and tangible outcome of party activity, however variable its implications for policy-making. The classification defines party systems in terms of dominance or party balances: the extent that alternatives within a system are coalesced into organized party structures. The model implies that certain qualities are shared by those systems that conform to the same dominance mode, and that as differences occur within a mode, external factors in the political system or culture mitigate the tendencies of the party system. Movement from one mode or party system to another raises the most fundamental questions of party politics. The concern with Latin American party systems has been: 1) how party systems are maintained by institutionalizing or subsidizing them, and 2) how party systems are transformed from one type to another through institutionalization or subsidization.

The terms are somewhat extraneous to this analysis, but the notions of "political development" and "political decay" in party systems illustrate the idea of party system change.[22] Change reflects "development" if it strengthens party structures or expands the boundaries of party systems to include sectors previously outside. Change reflects "decay" if it weakens party institutions or contravenes a previously relevant party system in deference to force, terror, or insulated elitism. The terms identify directions of change within a party system, not fixed stages in a continuing, predetermined process. Responding to political realities, a party system may alternatingly develop and decay. The processes must be viewed within specific historical and cultural perspectives appropriate to each national system.[23] Most indicators of change cannot be quantified, and are at best suggestive. No comparison between the relative development of one system and another seems reasonable. Increasing dominance, reflected by changing party balances within the system, does not necessarily indicate political development. The critical distinction is whether the increasing dominance is based on institutional growth generated in the culture, which is consistent with development, or is based upon "regime subsidization," which is not necessarily consistent with development.

Maintenance of party systems rests on institutionalization and subsidization. Institutional supports come spontaneously from extended party socialization, and indicate that party organizations are rooted and functioning well enough within the national culture to resist challenge. Subsidization comes from either overt coercion by the regime, or more covert, subtle controls—legal, cultural, social, political, or charismatic. Subsidization is a manipulative process, rationally designed and implemented by regimes. Most party systems are maintained by a mixture of institutional and subsidizing supports, the combination of which is an empirical question in studies of party systems.

When systems are unable to maintain themselves either by institutions or subsidies and vacillate periodically from one kind to another, they are transitional or pre-institutional. They lack the nominal controls necessary to define the context and boundaries of political party competition. Even when party systems cannot maintain themselves, however, stability can still exist in the overall political system from supports induced elsewhere. Our concern is limited to party systems and party politics.

Single-party dominant systems reveal how a high level of dominance is maintained by a combination of subsidy and institutional supports. Of the three examples cited, Mexico is closest to an institutionally dominant system, although party system maintenance has been largely induced by the regime. Subsidization followed the effective concentration of police and military power in the central government, a concentration won at great expense and duration in the context of the revolution, and also by skillful maneuvering in the decade preceding formation of an official party. Overtly coercive power still supports the Mexican party system, but less politically costly devices, including a regressive electoral system, ample party patronage, and ideological zeal, help cement the dominant PRI so that over the years the process has become partially self-amplifying.

The dominant Nicaraguan party is maintained largely by the regime's police and military power, but more recently economic incentives have been skillfully extended by the ruling family for conformity. Through a coincidence of history, cultural institutionalization of the national parties provides a vehicle for the regime's power that disguises the more overt means of support.

El Salvador is experiencing a process of political development in its party politics, producing institutions with greater mass relevance. The stage of development is primitive, and must rely upon considerable subsidization by the regime. Yet it is possible to see a gradual development of institutional infrastructure, greater involvement, secularization, and institutionalization in the party system. The incentive for development appears to come from the military and economic oligarchy's desire to lower the political costs of stability (and by implication the economic costs) through greater reliance upon institutional rather than coercive supports.

Two-party systems are also maintained by institutionalization and subsidies. Honduras' political parties persist as a vestige of a not too relevant past. Their limited and weak functions underscore their virtual irrelevance to national decision-making. Limited national integration is an obstacle to institutionalization, so that the regime must rely on coercive supports outside the party system to maintain stability and resolve conflicts in the political system. However historically based in national culture the parties are, their base is shallow and excludes the majority of Hondurans.

Colombia's two-party system is based in the history and social fabric of the nation. Parties politicize masses to support the interests of elite factions that control the organizations. Politicization is an effective lever for one elite's intimidation of another, producing a freewheeling, often unstable game that has erupted into violence and, during a recent decade, approached anarchy. Elite collusion, epitomized by the 1957 Sitges Agreement, has produced a moratorium on interparty competition, and by a "gentlemen's agreement" limited competition to intraparty elites. Subsidization takes the form of national election laws, the National Transformation Front, as well as more overtly coercive supports. Because national parties are culturally based and broadly perceived if not broadly relevant, the party system is potentially significant to national decision-making however constrained the contemporary experience.

Uruguay's two-party system is partially subsidized by the national election laws, but it rests heavily upon the historical relevance and durability of the two-party organizations. An important cultural trait has permitted these factions (*sublemas*), with few exceptions, to maintain a working relationship following elections. Institutionalization, participation, involvement, and relevance for most national sectors has produced a politically vigorous party system.

Like their more dominant counterparts, multi-party systems are also subsidized and institutionalized. The most common subsidization is the electoral system. Movement from multi-party loose to multi-party dominant competition is easier, and more common than between the other system types. Changing dominance in multi-party competition is more directly related to subtle but significant institutional pressures for growth and decay.

Argentina, in many ways an advanced nation, failed historically to integrate critical portions of the national community into the party system, causing a decline in the system's relevance to national decision-making and a challenge to its institutional basis. Military dictatorships and a decade of *Peronista* demogogery substituted coercive dominance for decaying institutional dominance.[24] The division in the Radical party over questions of leadership symbolizes the decay in the party system, while the substitution of a permissive proportional representation electoral system for the old Sáenz Peña electoral law removed an important support from the system. Chile, largely through institutional growth, has consolidated its party system, reducing the number of parties gaining representation and increasing the dominance of those remaining. Costa Rican parties have achieved a reasonably high level of institutional dominance, thanks to the effectiveness of the PLN and the inclusion of a broad sector of the community in the party system.

Venezuela and Brazil failed to achieve much dominance in their multi-party systems. Extreme regionalism in Brazil complicated the institutionalization of parties, encouraging their personalization, as did the relatively late period historically when modern parties emerged. Venezuela, also late in evolving modern parties, achieved considerable party dominance only to be frustrated by the failure of AD party leaders to maintain their organization's unity and vitality. Whether the Christian Democrats alone or in conjunction with the AD can consolidate the party system is problematical.

Panama and Ecuador, weak multi-party systems, have failed to make party organizations relevant to national decision-making. In both cases personalistic movements have overwhelmed weak party organizations. Similarly, the transitional systems, where strong parties sometimes exist, have failed to maintain their party systems by any means, producing fluctuating, volatile national politics.

Cultural and environmental factors inhibit institutional dominance, and sometimes challenge the effectiveness of coercive supports. These factors include: 1) pronounced regionalism and localism caused by historical isolation of communities within the national territory or by limited population; 2) reliance on personalism as a substitute for institutions over an extended period; 3) failure or unwillingness of political leaders and elites to renovate old party organizations or initiate new ones, consonant with cultural changes and demands, that would expand the system to include more diverse elements; 4) reliance on military or dictatorial coercion for so long that cultural perspectives fail to define conflicts in terms of parties, or perceive parties as relevant for solving grievances and acquiring equity.

Party systems influence party organizational growth, interparty competition, and electoral processes. The principal effect of the party system on organizations is controlling entry and exit of parties into the national political arena. With increasing dominance entry becomes more difficult for new organizations, particularly to the stage of obtaining legislative representation. This stage, however tentatively achieved, is a critical juncture for new parties since it provides them a public platform and confirms their ability and their "right" to participate.

Dominance controls entry and exit several ways. If the dominance is subsidized by coercion, regimes can willfully restrain additional parties from participating. Willful exclusion normally takes one of three courses: 1) the party is declared illegal or revolutionary, and denied participation; 2) the electoral system is weighted against small or new parties, or laws regulating party registration are made severe to deny entry to new organizations; 3) election results are fraudulently manipulated by the regime to prevent legislative recognition of party strength. One or a combination of these strategies is chosen rationally by the regime according to the nature, origin, and strength of potential opposition.

Most Latin American governments occasionally declare party organizations illegal for basically political reasons. This has been a characteristic experience of Marxist and communist organizations, but parties like AD in Venezuela, APRA in Peru, and the *Febreristas* in Paraguay have also been affected. Single-party dominant systems have a special disposition to declare parties illegal, although this is rarely the principal means by which single-party systems are maintained. Mexico has resorted to this strategy infrequently in recent years, and El Salvador has employed it occasionally. Nicaragua uses the power of recognition to influence opposition intraparty elites, and thus solicit the "least hostile" leadership. Two-party systems also have relied on electoral exclusion to control entry into the system. Honduras, where the regime is most based on coercion, is the clearest example. Colombia's electoral system under the Sitges Agreement automatically excludes new parties by denying them representation. However, ANAPO's tactic of working within the traditional party context as an alliance, has partially circumvented the plan. Argentina's multi-party system once controlled dominance by denying entry to parties through a distributive formula (the Sáenz Peña law) which gave the plurality party two-thirds of the legislative seats for a district and the second party the remainder. Fraud tends to be politically risky and costly, and is used most in instances where dominance can only be maintained by coercion.

Institutional dominance restricts entry and exit by requiring premium resources for organizations trying to challenge established parties. Contextural factors discussed above make party socialization difficult for new organizations, particularly geographic isolation, poor communications, illiteracy, and transitionalism which creates a cultural lag in party politics.

III. ELECTIONS, VOTING, AND PARTY POLITICS

Even a casual observer can see how varied the implications and processes of Latin American elections are. Yet universally, all governments, whether of democratic or authoritarian persuasion, feel obliged to go through a ritual of periodic elections. Elections are obviously central to democratic and representative processes, but they are also central to more authoritarian governmental processes. Even in authoritarian contexts elections can be traumatic, unstable, violent experiences. There seems to be a nearly universal expectation of elections with both domestic and international implications for any regime that ignores it. The purest representative objective is to observe electoral results, while the purest authoritarian objective is to control electoral results. Most Latin American elections fall somewhere in between these alternatives.

1. FUNCTIONS OF ELECTIONS

The meaning of elections, that is, the functions they perform in a political system, is relative to the system and to its historical context.[25] We have tentatively proposed a series of electoral functions, a mixture of which normally characterizes most specific cases. As elsewhere, Latin American elections provide channels for leadership recruitment, and sometimes furnish broad outlines for public policy. Elections also perform more characteristic Latin American functions. One such function is the legalization of regimes, a common dilemma for regimes that come to power by force. A popular way to legitimize regimes is to hold a controlled referendum or elect a constituent assembly, that can legalize a regime by providing it a new constitution. The constitutional obsession in Latin America and frequency with which some nations draft new constitutions must be viewed in a political rather than legal perspective. The most rational way of legitimizing a regime is to recognize that the community's political system has been literally "reconstituted." Constitutions are less important than the symbolic act of drafting them.

Another common function in Latin American elections is advancing political integration and unification of the national community. Elections are a concentrated, intense, political experience that can stimulate national awareness and commitment to a regime. Mexican elections are meaningful when viewed in this light, as are elections in other nations preoccupied with the objectives of political integration. To disregard such elections because they may be largely manipulated and governmentally meaningless is to ignore their political function: to promote cognition of the state and regime, encourage nationalism, and provide a strong statement of community aspirations.

Where integration is weak, Latin American elections also serve ritualistic functions with more cultural than political significance. Drawing notions of obligation, allegiance, faith, and celebration from the cultural context can help interpret political behavior during national elections. The importance of this function is variable between and within Latin American nations, reflecting "traditionalistic" rather than modernizing or modern cultural elements.[26]

These functions, and conceivably others, are ideal-types, useful to interpret tendencies in Latin American elections, but realistically never existing in pure form. Elections combine these and other functional tendencies, and are normally multi-functional in their consequences. These electoral functions may be performed elsewhere in a political system, and their specific consequences may vary from one system to another. Electoral recruitment in Uruguay, for example, has principally legislative implications. To the extent that Mexican elections perform recruitment functions, the implications of the recruitment are largely restricted to the party bureaucracy. Mexican elections provide an opportunity for the PRI to discover new talent, and for aspiring talent to demonstrate its organizational and political skills.

What significance do elections have for party and voting analysis? They define the purpose of party activity, and the relation of individual leaders to party structures. They interpret campaign strategies, tactics, and competition. They even raise questions about financing party activity generally and elections specifically. Legitimizing elections, for example, often produce an imbalance in campaign sources for the dominant group that controls state revenues. Private contributions to regime parties are politically prudent, involving no political costs to the donor when the electoral outcome is not in question. Under such circumstances, financial burdens of the opposition are profound.

2. FACTORS INFLUENCING ELECTIONS

Besides environmental, legal, and institutional factors that set parameters for electoral outcomes, a political factor—fraud—must be considered. The possibility of fraud challenges the meaningfulness of electoral data and analyses based on it. Fraud has been conceived two ways by this study for Latin American elections: 1) as a cultural expression, where moral and-political implications are relative to the environment in which it occurs; 2) and as a direct, less subtle control over electoral outcomes with normally higher political risks and costs.[27]

Often it is assumed that when there is no fraud, electoral outcomes are "democratic" or "representative"; when there is fraud, outcomes are disregarded as "authoritarian" or "inaccurate." Although there is some justification in these viewpoints, it is more realistic to view fraud as another control on electoral outcomes, more direct but similar to institutional and environmental ones found in even democratic processes. Authoritarian regimes use fraud only when they lack the skills required for more subtle electoral controls, or hold aspirations so inconsistent with the general will that no electoral experience can be sufficiently controlled in advance to support the regime. The notion of fraud is most useful when limited to clandestine activities designed to control outcomes.

Pre-electoral fraud is common in Latin America, and consists of buying votes, transporting voters in public or military vehicles to the polls, repressing potential opposition voters, discriminating against voter registration, unfair districting, and voting procedures that reward some socioeconomic groups and penalize others. Instances of these have been discussed in the preceding chapters. Post-electoral fraud includes stuffing ballot boxes, falsely reporting actual voting, providing quotas for local bosses to fill, disqualifying opposition ballots on technicalities, and conspiring to allocate legislative seats regardless of the vote. Pre-electoral fraud is more common than post-electoral fraud, for the simple reason that it is less conspicuous and generally less risky, particularly in urban areas.

Documenting fraud is difficult, yet important to voting analyses. The nations whose elections are consistently or profoundly fraudulent are few, and urban areas seem less inclined to be fraudulent. The kind of fraud and its pervasiveness varies with electoral functions. Legitimizing and ritualistic functions encourage fraudulent practices since overwhelmingly favorable support is required for a regime. The principal danger to voting analyses from fraud is that it reduces their accuracy and reliability, and requires strong trends or high correlations before conclusions are justified. Fortunately so much can be learned, for the present, with even relatively broad margins of error that the dilemma is not severe. Conceptualizing the electoral experience to a particular environment, and providing a necessary basis for interpreting voting data are more critical. Possibly a statistical check on the probability of fraud within the data can be developed to reinforce documented and intuitive reports, and minimize the impact of fraud on voting analyses.

Accepting a cultural definition of elections raises problems for crossnational voting comparisons. Premature crossnational comparisons perpetuate conceptual errors by glossing over essential local qualities and using too highly aggregated data.[28] For example, it is absurd to compare national participation in Ecuador, where the majority is ineligible by law to participate, with participation in Venezuela, where most are eligible. Voting analyses seem most promising within nations at increasingly more local rather than national levels of comparisons, or between similar local units in nations where legal-institutional and cultural contexts are not too varied. One possibility for crossnational comparison is urban or "core area" voting in national elections. Crossnational comparisons will eventually emerge as substantiated interpretations are made for national systems.

3. CHARACTERISTICS OF VOTER PARTICIPATION

Recognizing the limitations and tentativeness of the preceding analyses, can any propositions be raised about possible Latin American voting behavior characteristics? Voting is significant in Latin America in ways uncharacteristic of North American cultures. For those who are allowed to vote, registration seems to imply an elementary but critical level of political awareness at which the participant perceives a relationship to the broader political community. What is normally assumed a minimal involvement in more integrated cultures is, in many Latin American communities, a significant expression of awareness. Voting participation implies an additional step toward integrating the individual into the community. Voting requires motivation beyond the awareness implied in registration. The participant must view the political system as relevant to his own condition and situation. Participation indicates not only an individual's perception but also his identification with the state and its political processes. Political perception and identification, conditioned by environmental factors, vary with groups and regions and are expressed in national registration and participation patterns.[29] Not surprisingly, perception and identification generally drop sharply outside the core areas, despite regional centers of high awareness and participation. Participation patterns are useful indicators of fundamental expansion and contraction in the relevant political system. Environmental factors that condition awareness and participation include literacy, proximity to the core area, economic well-being, race, urbanization, party activity, and regime policies. Political manipulation and leadership generate greater participation and awareness; subtrends in provincial El Salvador illustrate this process. Normally awareness and participation develop through political socialization carried on by political parties. Recognizing the realities of national integration in Latin America, the symbolic act of voting may contain far more implications in this region than elsewhere.[30]

As voting occurs, certain phenomena have general applicability according to the preceding national analyses. Some of the generalities are regional, others perhaps more universal.

Regionalism. Most nations exhibit regional voting patterns. The bases of regional voting are found in settlement and population patterns, and in the relative weakness of national integration. Regionalism affects voter registration and participation, and often party disposition. Parties are highly regional in a few nations, particularly Brazil and Ecuador, and to a lesser extent in Venezuela, Colombia, Argentina, and Uruguay. Chile, whose profound geographic and cultural regionalism might be expected to find political expression, is remarkably nonregional in party voting dispositions, and suggests a high level of compensating political integration. Given the problems of communication it is perhaps significant that the influence of regionalism in Latin America is no greater than it is. Most parties have traditional local strengths, but a large number are essentially national in scope.

Lower-Class Authoritarianism. The characteristic process which S. M. Lipset identifies as "lower-class authoritarianism" appears to be present in Latin American voting.[31] The substantial electoral support for former dictators in highly urban areas (Perón in Buenos Aires, Rojas Pinilla in Bogotá, and more recently Pérez Jiménez in Caracas) indicates a possible expression of the phenomenon. These men and their counterparts elsewhere provide simple answers to complex socioeconomic problems, and rally to their cause economically vulnerable lower classes, who are constantly challenged, even in growing economies, by inflation and lack of economic mobility.

Alienation. Alienation trends are revealed by participation patterns and by blank votes in national elections. Some nations have experienced widespread voter apathy and alienation. The clearest example is Colombia, where recent elections have mobilized less than 25 percent of the eligible voters. Trend analyses reveal increasing alienation in Colombia over the past decade from more politically aware sectors of the population. Recent Argentine elections also have revealed considerable voter alienation. Alienation patterns vary within nations, normally being more pronounced in provincial and rural areas. Weaker socialization and communication during electoral periods are also responsible for lower turnout in these areas.

Core Area Phenomena.   There are core area phenomena that give extraordinary importance to political activity in Latin American capitals and their environs. Core area political activity is more intense and more diverse than elsewhere in the nations. There is a strong voting tendency for dominant parties, regardless of their ideology or the type of system in which they operate, to experience substantial falloff in their core area vote. Table 6-1 demonstrates this tendency.[32] The core area opposition tendency affects liberal, reform regimes as often as conservative, traditional ones. The pattern suggests rather high levels of discontent in core area electorates, perhaps induced by economic factors, expressed as opposition party activity. Urban voting is a distinctive and important quality of Latin American politics that deserves far more attention. Traditional definitions of urban/rural political conflict are insufficient. Voting reveals significant conflicts between urban areas, and between provincial areas comprised of rural and urban components, which are critical to understanding national politics.

Transient Opposition Voting.   There is evidence to suggest that opposition voting in many Latin American nations is more

TABLE 6.1 COMPARISON OF URBAN VOTING IN LATIN AMERICA
(IN PERCENT)

Nation	Election	Dominant party	Party's national vote	Core area vote	Remaining national vote	Urban loss
Venezuela	1963	AD	32.8	13.7	38.9	−25.2
Mexico	1967	PRI	83.0	65.0	87.0	−22.0
El Salvador	1967	PCN	54.4	41.0	61.0	−20.0
Colombia	1966	FTN	57.5	54.0	61.0	− 7.0
Nicaragua	1963	PLN	90.0	85.0	92.0	− 7.0
Costa Rica	1966	PLN	49.5	45.5	53.0	− 6.5
Bolivia	1956	MNR	82.2	80.0	84.2	− 4.2
Panama	1968	PP	55.0	54.0	56.0	− 2.0
Argentina	1963	UCRP	24.9	24.5	25.7	− 1.2

unstable and transient than elsewhere. Voters switch party identifications rather freely from one election to another, depending on which party is best able to organize a strong antigovernment campaign. Voting for dominant parties is more stable, reflecting established identifications with the regime.

There are other patterns that have some generality in Latin America. The concept of *ins* versus *outs* has been largely uncharacteristic of Latin American party politics. Differences between *we* and *they* have been more common and enduring. The difference may be found in the absence of a pluralistic ethic that the *outs* accept defeat and wait patiently for another attempt to defeat the *ins*. The *outs* normally do precisely that in Latin America, but often with the assumption that *we* cannot endure as long as *they* are in control; that is, until the political order is fundamentally reconstituted.

There are cultural lags in voting, particularly in rural areas, which permit parties and personalities to endure long beyond any reasonable capacity to reach power. Chronically weak party institutions often rely upon perception of personalities and party symbols rather than organization as a basis for voter motivation, and these perceptions endure beyond when an organization would collapse.

So much emphasis has been given in the United States to revolutionary forces in Latin America that critical evolutionary forces may have been slighted. As prophets of doom, we have understressed the fixed points in a changing order, and failed to appreciate the cultural distinctiveness and diversity of Latin American politics. When governmental institutions change rapidly as they do in some Latin American nations, and rely on factors external to our own notion of politics, it is natural to view Latin American politics as mercurial. The study of political parties and elections identifies a fixed point in Latin American politics, which can help reveal both the dynamics of change and the points of stability.

NOTES

[1] The idea of geographic and social integration is also developed by Gino Germani in "The City As An Integrating Mechanism," in Glenn H. Beyer, ed., *The Urban Explosion in Latin America* (Ithaca, N.Y.: Cornell University Press, 1967), pp. 175–76.

[2] An attempt to specify some "empirical" indicators of political integration is found in Claude Ake, *A Theory of Political Integration* (Homewood, Illinois: Dorsey Press, 1967), pp. 8–11.

[3] The function of parties in political development is surveyed by Joseph La Palombara and Myron Weiner, eds., *Political Parties and Political Development* (Princeton, N.J.: Princeton University Press, 1966).

[4] See Marion Levy, Jr., *Modernization and the Structure of Societies* (Princeton, N.J.: Princeton University Press, 1966).

[5] Values of personalism for the middle class in Latin America are discussed by John P. Gillin, "Middle Segments and Their Values," in Robert Tomasek, ed., *Latin American Politics* (Garden City, N.Y.: Doubleday Anchor, 1966), pp. 23–40.

[6] See René de Visme Williamson, *Culture and Policy: The United States and the Hispanic World* (Knoxville: University of Tennessee Press, 1949).

[7] Gillin, "Middle Segments and Their Values," pp. 29–32.

[8] One of the early recognitions of class and party connections is Max Weber, "Class, Status, Party," in H. H. Gerth and C. Wright Mills, eds., *Max Weber: Essays in Sociology* (New York: Oxford University Press, 1946), pp. 180–95.

[9] A general consideration of the elite basis of Latin American politics is contained in S. M. Lipset and Aldo Solari, eds., *Elites in Latin America* (New York: Oxford University Press, 1967), especially pp. 94–231.

[10] See Robert E. Scott, "Political Elites and Political Modernization: The Crisis of Transition," in Lipset and Solari, *Elites in Latin America*, pp. 117–45.

[11] The ethnocentricism of "modernization" theories is observed by Karl von Vorys, "Use and Misuse of Development Theory," in James C. Charlesworth, ed., *Contemporary Political Analysis* (New York: Free Press, 1967), pp. 350–63.

[12] Ideological implications of pluralism were considered by Morris Ginsberg, *The Psychology of Society* (London: Methuen, 1921), especially p. 135.

[13] The classic application to the U.S. is David B. Truman, *The Governmental Process* (New York: Knopf, 1951). See also Robert A. Dahl, "Hierarchy, Democracy, and Bargaining in Politics and Economics," in Bailey, Simon, Dahl et al., *Research Frontiers in Politics and Government* (Washington, D.C.: Brookings Institution, 1955), pp. 45–69.

[14] This viewpoint is essentially adopted by Martin C. Needler, *Political Development in Latin America: Instability, Violence, and Evolutionary Change* (New York: Random House, 1968), pp. 9–14.

[15] A similar conception of Latin America as "organic" rather than pluralistic or dualistic was made by Rodolfo Stavenhagen, "Seven Erroneous Theses About Latin America," in Horowitz, de Castro, and Gerassi, eds., *Latin American Radicalism* (New York: Random House, 1969), pp. 102–6.

[16] Essentially the same operation in the Mexican system is noted by Bo

Anderson and James D. Cockcroft, "Control and Cooptation in Mexican Politics," in Horowitz et al., *Latin American Radicalism*, pp. 366–89.

[17] For one example see Campbell, Converse, Miller, and Stokes, *The American Voter* (New York: Wiley, 1960), pp. 146–47.

[18] A brief analysis of kinship organization of Argentine *criollos* illustrates the same conclusion; see Arnold Strickon, "Class and Kinship in Argentina," in Heath and Adams, eds., *Contemporary Cultures and Societies of Latin America* (New York: Random House, 1965), pp. 324–41.

[19] Politicization, particularly in reference to personalism and urbanization, is discussed by Daniel Goldrich, "Toward the Comparative Study of Politicization in Latin America," in Heath and Adams, *Contemporary Cultures*, pp. 361–78.

[20] See Philip M. Hauser, ed., *Urbanization in Latin America* (New York: International Documents Service, Columbia University Press, 1961), for an excellent collection of articles on the sociopolitical effects of urbanization; also see Beyer, *The Urban Explosion*, pp. 189–214 for a discussion of the same.

[21] For definition of "secularization" see G. A. Almond and G. B. Powell, Jr., *Comparative Politics: A Developmental Approach* (Boston: Little, Brown, 1966), pp. 24–25.

[22] The ideas of "development and decay" are based on those developed by Samuel P. Huntington, "Political Development and Political Decay," *World Politics* 17, No. 3 (April 1965): 386–430, although his emphasis was the total political system.

[23] Needler makes the same point in *Political Development*, pp. 27–42.

[24] A compelling documentation of the Argentine dilemma is Gino Germani, "The Transition to a Mass Democracy in Argentina," in Heath and Adams, *Contemporary Cultures*, pp. 454–72.

[25] An excellent statement on electoral functions, some of which parallel those presented here for Latin America, is contained in Richard Rose and Harve Mossawir, "Voting and Elections: A Functional Analysis," *Political Studies* 15, No. 2 (June 1967): 173–201. Rose and Mossawir are concerned particularly with the British experience, but they make a strong case by way of introduction about functional specification of electoral behavior.

[26] A comprehensive discussion of functional changes in "modernizing" societies is found in Marion J. Levy, Jr., *Modernization and the Structure of Societies* (Princeton, N.J.: Princeton University Press, 1966).

[27] A more theoretical view of the "benefits" and "costs" of corruption in terms of political development is contained in J. S. Nye, "Corruption and Political Development: A Cost-Benefit Analysis," *American Political Science Review* 61, No. 2 (June 1967): 417–28. Nye is concerned with far more than electoral fraud or Latin America, but the arguments he makes are essentially valid to the more restricted subject.

[28] One rather sane collection of crossnational voting studies that does not try to make premature analogies is S. M. Lipset and S. Rokkan, *Party Systems and Voter Alignments: Cross-National Perspectives* (New York: Free Press, 1967). Particularly useful is Glaucio Ary Dillon Soares, "The Politics of Uneven Development: The Case of Brazil."

[29] Registration patterns are not available for all nations, since registration is not always required. The basic concepts of "awareness" and "participation" are still valid, however, as steps in the integrative process.

[30] V. O. Key observed years ago that ". . . the significance of variations in the nature and extent of participation probably can be grasped only by extensive crossnational analyses . . . the nature of the political order may affect patterns of participation as well as the reverse." *Politics, Parties, and Pressure Groups,* 4th ed. (New York: Crowell, 1958), pp. 638–39.

[31] S. M. Lipset, *Political Man: The Social Bases of Politics* (New York: Doubleday, 1960), pp. 87–126; also see his discussion of *Peronismo,* pp. 173–76.

[32] Taken from R. McDonald, "National Urban Voting Behavior: The Politics of Dissent in Latin America," *Inter-American Economic Affairs* 23, No. 1 (Summer 1969): 3–20. Reproduced with permission.

National Elections
in Latin America, 1946–1970

Nation	Date	Presidential (P) Congressional (C) State/Province (S) Municipal (M)
ARGENTINA	February 1946	P-C-S-M
	March 1948	C-M
	November 1951	P-C-S-M
	April 1954	C-M
	July 1957	Constitutent Assembly
	February 1958	P-C-S-M
	March 1960	C-M
	March 1961	C-M
	March 1962	C-M
	July 1963	P-C-S-M
	March 1965	C-M
BOLIVIA	January 1947	P-C-M
	May 1951	P-C-M
	June 1956	P-C-M
	July 1958	C-M
	June 1960	P-C-M
	June 1962	C-M
	May 1964	P-C-M
	July 1966	P-C-M
BRAZIL	January 1947	C-S-M
	October 1950	P-C-S-M
	October 1954	C-S-M
	October 1955	P
	October 1958	C-S-M
	October 1960	P
	October 1962	C-S-M
	January 1963	Plebiscite
	April 1964	P (in Congress)
	October 1966	P (in Congress)
	November 1966	C-S-M
CHILE	April 1947	M
	March 1949	C
	April 1950	M
	September 1952	P

Nation	Date	Presidential (P) Congressional (C) State/Province (S) Municipal (M)
	March 1953	C-M
	April 1956	M
	March 1957	C
	September 1958	P
	April 1960	M
	March 1961	C
	April 1963	M
	September 1964	P
	March 1965	C
	April 1966	M
	March 1969	C
	September 1970	P
COLOMBIA	May 1946	P
	March 1947	C-M
	June 1949	C-M
	November 1949	P
	September 1951	C-M
	March 1953	C-M
	August 1954	P (in Congress)
	December 1957	Plebiscite
	March 1958	C-M
	May 1958	P
	March 1960	C-M
	March 1962	C-M
	May 1962	P
	March 1964	C-M
	March 1966	C-M
	May 1966	P
	March 1968	C-M
	April 1970	P-C-M
COSTA RICA	February 1946	C
	February 1948	P-C-M
	December 1948	Constituent Assembly
	October 1949	C-M
	July 1953	P C-M
	February 1958	
	February 1962	P-C-M
	February 1966	P-C-M
	February 1970	P-C-M
CUBA	June 1946	C-M
	June 1948	P-C-M
	June 1950	C-M

Nation	Date	Presidential (P) Congressional (C) State/Province (S) Municipal (M)
	November 1954	P-C-M
	November 1958	C-M
DOMINICAN REPUBLIC	May 1947	P-C-M
	May 1952	P-C-M
	May 1957	P-C-M
	December 1962	P-C-M
	June 1966	P-C-M
	May 1970	P-C-M
ECUADOR	May 1946	Constituent Assembly
	September 1947	P (in Congress)
	June 1948	P-C
	June 1952	P-C-M
	June 1854	C
	June 1956	P-C
	November 1956	M
	June 1958	C
	June 1960	P-C-M
	June 1962	C-M
	October 1966	Constituent Assembly
	November 1966	P (in Congress)
	June 1968	P-C-M
EL SALVADOR	March 1950	P-C-M
	March 1952	C-M
	March 1954	C-M
	March 1956	P
	May 1956	C
	July 1956	M
	March 1958	C
	April 1958	M
	April 1960	C-M
	April 1962	P-M
	March 1964	C-M
	March 1966	C-M
	March 1967	P
	March 1968	C-M
	March 1970	C-M
GUATEMALA	December 1947	M
	December 1948	C
	November 1950	C
	December 1950	P
	December 1951	M

National	Date	Presidential (P) Congressional (C) State/Province (S) Municipal (M)
	January 1953	C
	October 1954	P-C
	December 1955	C-M
	October 1957	P-C-M
	January 1958	P-C-M
	December 1959	M
	December 1961	C
	May 1964	Constitutent Assembly
	March 1966	P-C-M
	March 1970	P-C-M
HAITI	May 1946	C
	August 1946	C
	October 1950	P-C
	September 1957	P-C
	April 1961	P-C
	June 1964	Presidential Referendum
HONDURAS	October 1948	P-C
	October 1954	C
	October 1956	Constituent Assembly
	September 1957	Constituent Assembly
	November 1957	P
	February 1965	Constituent Assembly
	March 1965	P
	March 1968	M
MEXICO	July 1946	P-C-S-M
	July 1949	C-S-M
	July 1952	P-C-S-M
	July 1955	C-S-M
	July 1958	P-C-S-M
	July 1961	C-S-M
	July 1964	P-C-S-M
	July 1967	C-S-M
	July 1970	P-C-S-M
NICARACUA	August 1947	Constituent Assembly
	August 1947	P (in Congress)
	June 1948	C
	May 1950	P-C
	February 1957	P-C
	February 1963	P-C-M
	February 1967	P-C-M

National	Date	Presidential (P) / Congressional (C) / State/Province (S) / Municipal (M)
PANAMA	May 1948	P-C-M
	May 1952	P-C-M
	May 1956	P-C-M
	May 1960	P-C-M
	May 1964	P-C-M
	May 1968	P-C-M
PARAGUAY	April 1949	P-C
	July 1950	C
	February 1953	P
	July 1954	P
	February 1958	P-C
	March 1960	C
	February 1963	P-C
	October 1965	M
	February 1968	P-C
PERU	July 1950	P-C
	June 1956	P-C
	June 1962	P-C
	June 1963	P-C
	December 1963	M
VENEZUELA	October 1946	Constituent Assembly
	December 1947	P-C-M
	November 1952	Constituent Assembly-M
	April 1953	P (in Congress)
	December 1957	P-C-M
	December 1958	P-C-M
	December 1963	P-C-M
	December 1968	P-C-M
URUGUAY	November 1946	P-C-M
	November 1950	P-C-M
	November 1954	Council-C-M
	November 1958	Council-C-M
	November 1962	Council-C-M
	November 1966	P-C-M

Index

Abuanza Marenco, Alexjandro, 233
Afonso, Almino, 68
Agüado, Enoc, 232
Agüero, Fernando, 229, 233, 234
Ake, Claude, 280n, 304n
Alemán, Miguel, 250, 253
Alende, Oscar, 106, 109, 114
Alesandri, Jorge, 121, 124, 133, 134, 139
Alesandri Palma, Arturo, 120
Alexander, Robert J., 90n, 216n, 219n
Allende, Salvador, 121, 125, 135
Alliance for Progress, 88, 176
Almond, Gabriel A., 29n, 30n, 282n, 283n, 284n, 305n
Alvárez, Luis, 248
de Alvear, Marcelo, 106
Amador Pineda, Eduardo, 233
Amunategui, Gabriel, 169n
Anderson, Bo, 305n
Anderson, Charles W., 216n, 280n, 282n
Andrade, Felio, 192
Angell, A., 217n
Aprista, 8, 10, 44, 152, 154, 296
Apter, David, 30n
Aramburu, General Pedro E., 100, 108–9, 114
Arana, D.B., 168n
Argentina
  demography, 97
  election of 1963, 113–15
  participation, 109–10
  Peronismo, 99–100, 164, 180
  political culture and context, 96–98
  political differentiation, 98
  political parties, coalitions, and groups
    Confederación General de Trabajadores (CGT), 14, 105, 108
    Federación de los Partidos del Centro (FPC), 108, 112
    federalists, 104
    Frente Nacional y Popular (FNP), 109, 114
    Movimiento de Integración y Desarrollo (MID), 106
    National Construction Federation, 108
    Partido Comunista Argentino (PCA), 106, 108, 116
    Partido Conservador Popular (PCP), 109

Partido Demócrata Cristiano (PDC), 107, 112, 114
Partido Demócrata Progresista (PDP), 108, 109, 114
Partido Laborista (PL), 113
Partido Peronista (PP), 8, 12, 14–15, 26, 100–1, 104–16, 164, 294
Partido Socialista (PS), 104, 111
Partido Socialista Argentino (PSA), 107
Partido Socialista Democrático (PSD), 107
Partido Socialista Vanguardia (PSV), 107
Partido Único de la Revolución (PUR), 105
Tres Bandera, 113
Unión Cívica (UC), 105
Unión Cívica Radical (UCR), 99, 101, 105–6, 111
Unión Cívica Radical Intransigente (UCRI), 105–7, 109–11, 114–15
Unión Cívica Radical del Pueblo (UCRP), 106–7, 109–12, 114–15
Unión Popular (UP), 109–10, 113–14
Unión del Pueblo Argentino (UDELPA), 108–9, 114
  unitarians, 104
  political party evolution, 98–109
  registration, 109
  representation, 101–4
  voting trends, 110–13
Argüello, Leonardo, 231–32
Arias, Arnulfo, 11, 82–83, 89
Arias Espinosa, Ricardo, 11
Arosomena, Carlos Julio, 88
Artigas, José, 210

Bailey, Norman S., 217n
Balbín, Ricardo, 106, 114
Balmaceda, José Manuel, 119
Barrios, Gonzalo, 52
deBarros, Adhemar, 65
Batlle, César, 206
Batlle, Jorge, 206, 210, 211, 212
Batlle, Luis, 201, 206, 210
Batlle y Ordoñez, José, 11, 199–200, 201, 206, 210
Belaúnde-Terry, Fernando, 11

313